CONFLICT IN LAOS

The Politics of Neutralization

CONFLICT IN LAOS

The Politics of Neutralization

Arthur J. Dommen

FREDERICK A. PRAEGER, *Publishers*
New York · Washington · London

To my schoolmate,
ROBERT CAMPBELL JAMES

FREDERICK A. PRAEGER, *Publishers*
111 Fourth Avenue, New York, N.Y. 10003, U.S.A.
77–79 Charlotte Street, London W.1, England

Published in the United States of America in 1964
by Frederick A. Praeger, Inc., Publishers

Third printing, 1967

© 1964 by Frederick A. Praeger, Inc.

Library of Congress Catalog Card Number: 64-21661

Printed in the United States of America

Preface

Americans, I fear, have a tendency to become alarmed by developments in foreign affairs that run contrary to their own interests and, once alarmed, they lose sight of the causes of these developments. The conflict in Laos has been one of these entanglements, of which the world is full, wherein the threat has come to be mistaken for the cause: We have ended by believing that all our troubles stem from an inherently aggressive enemy, forgetting that among the enemy are those who were once our friends and that much of his success has been the result of the repetition of our own mistaken actions.

Recent history has shown once again that a surrender to the pat formulas of ideology leads to the abdication of common sense. It is in the hope of preventing still another instance of this pattern that I have attempted to gather the salient facts of the conflict. It has not been an easy task. Laos has been the subject of diplomatic consultations in such diverse places as Geneva, London, Paris, Washington, Moscow, Vienna, central Siberia, and Key West. Events in Laos have more than once brought a sense of impending crisis to capitals of far larger countries. Meanwhile, the inhabitants of Laos have for the most part been only vaguely aware that their future was being discussed in such grave terms.

My researches raised more questions than they answered. It is obvious that many of these cannot be answered until the publication of diplomatic correspondence and personal memoirs by the principals. For instance, an analysis of the arguments advanced by the Russians in Phnom Penh when Prince Souvanna Phouma flew there in December, 1960, will be possible only when the Prince himself has retired from public life and takes up his pen. Likewise, General Phoumi Nosavan's decision to oppose the Prince's regime by force of arms will be fully explained only when we have access to still-locked diplomatic files.

I owe a debt of gratitude to Jerry A. Rose, a working journalist like myself, who took the time to read the first draft of this book, and to Guy Searls, who lent me the use of his private library and study overlooking Hong Kong harbor.

I also wish to express my thanks to Mrs. Beth Blake, of Washington, D.C., who assisted me in locating materials in the Library of Congress and from whose intimate familiarity with the peoples, countryside, and customs of Laos I have benefited.

Acknowledgment is also hereby made to Donald Wasson of the Council on Foreign Relations, New York, for assistance enabling me to make full use of the archive materials in the library of the Council; also to Professor A. Doak Barnett of Columbia University for kind permission to peruse his files of Communist source material at the East Asian Institute; to Joseph Buttinger for permission to work in his library, which contains one of the best collections of published materials on Indochina; and to the Library of Hong Kong University.

Above all, my thanks go to the countless persons—Lao, Vietnamese, American, French, and of every nationality—who have in some way been connected with developments in Laos and whom I have interviewed over the past five years.

Finally, this book would not have been possible without the keen eyes and sound sense of Phyllis Freeman of Frederick A. Praeger, Inc., and Shirley Zimmerman, who assisted me in the preparation of the manuscript. I also received logistical support from Lorna Brennan of the Council on Foreign Relations in the typing of the final draft.

A. J. D.

New York City
September, 1964

Contents

MAPS

TABLES

Introduction

The present conflict in Laos is in one sense the prolongation of a centuries-old process whereby the feudal principalities of the left bank of the Mekong were bound by ties of vassalage and forced alliances to their more powerful neighbors to the southwest and over the Annamite Mountains. In another very real sense, however, this conflict is marked by entirely new forces of attraction and subjugation, with far-reaching implications for a world in which the confrontation between the nuclear powers has reached stalemate and the gap between the have peoples and the have-not peoples is wider than it has ever been.

In 1954, when the French were fighting against defeat at the hands of the Viet Minh, the principal issue was whether the colonial power would succeed, by force of arms, in retaining its hold. For the United States, the question then was whether to lend its support to those patriots fighting for the independence of their country, as U.S. observers on the scene, both diplomatic and nondiplomatic, urged. As a result of considerations that had little to do with the justness of the harsh struggle waged by the nationalists, support was thrown instead to France.

Even then, the United States coveted no material possessions in Laos and the other countries of Indochina. It was conceivable that it might assume a new role once the colonial war ended. Americans went to Laos to establish technical-assistance missions. But the fighting did not stop. Cynically encouraged by the Vietnamese Communists across an ill-defined border, a minority faction of the nationalist movement that had been alienated by the West sought to widen its influence in Laos, using guerrilla warfare to achieve this goal.

The innocent inhabitants of Laos who came in contact with the roving agents of this guerrilla movement were told that the emphasis of the American aid program was on military armaments and training, and that the people in the villages were deriving little or no advantage from the American presence, which they had accepted on the premise that the United States promised to defend them against the aggression they feared. This aggression, furthermore, did not take place. Instead, the armed minority of the Pathet Lao arrogated to themselves the banner of nationalism and proceeded to exploit the shortcomings of a central government grown indolent and corrupt.

These developments gradually turned the balance against the United States in a situation where an open resort to American military superiority was excluded time and again because, as the State Department reminded the world, the United States was not a colonial power like France. As the exclusion of Western influence from Laos became more and more of a real possibility, the future of American policy toward other countries of Southeast Asia where, unlike Laos, the United States had committed itself by treaty to defense against aggression, was placed in jeopardy.

The Vietnamese Communists, having consolidated their authority at home, were now bringing Leninist organization and ruthless discipline to a movement "to liberate Laos from neocolonialism." Their appeals in a country of sparse population and little exploitable wealth were unorthodox: There were in Laos no groups consigned to lives of misery, as in Java; no tradition of agrarian revolt, as in China; no industrial proletariat, as in Tonkin. The political awareness of even the townspeople was far lower than in Vietnam, making it difficult to arouse potential recruits to revolutionary consciousness.

But the Vietnamese Communists made considerable progress, especially since their own regime had none of the material resources, the food surpluses, the jet-aircraft factories, or the vast fleet at sea possessed by the United States. Their agents, indoctrinated with a sense of inevitable victory, allowed themselves to be transformed into the servants of a higher political necessity; their dour, expressionless faces were their hallmark. Their subsistence was rice, a few vegetables, and an indoctrination lecture every day —nothing else.

There were many unexpected turnabouts in all this. Because a withdrawal of American aid implied an almost automatic Communist takeover, United States protection became a virtual necessity for people who had fought to rid their country of foreign entanglements. A decade after independence, a visitor to Laos could not but feel that the prestige of France, a colonial power defeated in a liberation war that took a heavy cost in French lives and honor, was actually higher than that of the United States, the champion of the self-determination of peoples. In subordinating its native belief in the liberty of peoples to what appeared to be a temporary necessity, the United States had forfeited the powerful appeal of this ideal and thereby undermined its long-range goal of assisting the construction of a politically stable society willing and able to resist the Communist "wave of the future." In contrast, the Vietnamese Communists, because they were willing to sacrifice themselves for their principles, made those principles respectable in the eyes of other Southeast Asians in the same predicament.

The conflict was bound to have repercussions in neighboring states. Infiltration and subversion by North Vietnamese agents in Laos constituted a threat to Thailand and South Vietnam. American actions in Laos harbored a threat to North Vietnam. Both the Communist powers and the non-Communist powers disregarded the spirit of the cease-fire agreements signed in Geneva in 1954, although they continued to pay lip service to the provisions of these agreements.

All this while, there existed considerations for international consent to the withdrawal of Laos from the eddies of Cold War politics. No account of foreign intervention in Laos would be complete without an analysis of the very real vectors toward neutralization.

The attempt to renegotiate a neutralization agreement came at a very late date. By then, the conflict had involved the Russians, who were caught in a dilemma of allies not exactly to their liking— most importantly, the Chinese. The confrontation between the United States and North Vietnam had produced unprecedented tensions in Laos and the other Indochinese countries. If these tensions drew in the Communist Chinese, as the rivalries of the feudal princes of centuries ago had drawn in the armies from the north, the outcome would be the imposition on a happy and carefree people of an imperialism far more pervading than any they had ever known.

The implications of the Laos conflict are clear. Given the close identity of views between the men responsible for North Vietnam's successes in Laos and the men in Peking, one may well consider whether the "inevitability of victory" in which the Communists place such faith is on the side of the guerrilla movements in Asia, Africa, and Latin America. It is these continents that have been pronounced by Peking to be the decisive battleground of the future between "imperialism" and "socialism."

The United States is accustomed to thinking of itself in the forefront of progress. Yet, in many ways its experience in Laos showed it to be unable to translate its ideals into current reality. It bound itself all too readily to the most feudal elements in a country whose need is to shake off feudalism and emerge into the twentieth century. The United States Congress has been reluctant to appropriate funds for economic development abroad, yet it is ready to spend millions to support a war without victory against Communist-directed insurgents in Laos and South Vietnam—countries where the sympathy of the population may already be irrevocably lost.

The Lao leaders themselves have warned on several occasions of the perniciousness of foreign ideologies intruding into their land. Their warnings should be heeded. France's war in Indochina became mired in ideological ambiguities, as John Foster Dulles himself recognized. The American role in that war was hardly the result of a clear thinking through of the issues involved.

I have concluded my analysis of events past with certain suggestions for an effective neutralization of Laos such as was not provided by the unenforced neutralization agreement of 1962. The United States and the Soviet Union recognized that neither had any interest in allowing itself to become embroiled in a war over Laos. Given the military power available to the great powers, and the divergences among Communist leaders that reveal themselves more clearly today than ever before, an effective neutralization of Laos is not beyond the realm of possibility.

The prerequisites of such an outcome lie in the proper orchestration of military power with adroit diplomacy. This is not an easy task. But if we admit that the mistakes of the past can serve as lessons for the future, the study of the events of the past decade in Laos will yield ample reward.

1.

The Kingdom of the Million Elephants

When the sun set on France's Indochina empire in 1954, the largest entity left by the cease-fire agreement, with an area of approximately 91,000 square miles, was the Kingdom of Laos. Of no recognizable shape, the kingdom is a sparsely inhabited, landlocked territory lying in the heart of Southeast Asia. Each of its sixteen provinces borders a more populous foreign country, as if to affirm the paramount fact that throughout its history Laos has suffered the consequences of an intimate and at times destructive involvement with powerful neighbors.

In understanding the reasons for this unhappy circumstance, however, a geophysical map will be of more use than a political one. Aside from the valley of the Mekong and its left-bank tributaries, the country's relief is one of complex mountain and plateau forms. The mountain slopes are covered by dense vegetation and are so steep, and the valley bottoms so confined, that little space remains for cultivation. Only here and there, in tiny upland clearings, men have managed to burn away the forest and establish their thatched-roof villages in a wild domain of torrents, precipices, and mist-shrouded peaks.

The Annamite Mountains stretch from southern China down to the Gulf of Siam, where they fade into vestigial hillocks in the alluvial plain of the Mekong in southernmost Vietnam. The crest of these mountains forms the eastern border of present-day Laos. From the east, the general slope of the mountains is downward to the valley of the Mekong. This crest of the Annamite chain also marks the dividing line between the two great cultures of Asia—the Indian and the Chinese. The Lao are a Hinduized people; the Vietnamese, a Sinicized people.

Except for small areas of Sam Neua Province and the extreme eastern end of Xieng Khouang Province, the entire area of Laos is drained by rivers flowing westward and southward from these mountains. Outside of these two areas and the valley in which Dien Bien Phu is located, not a single river of any size crosses the border between Laos and Vietnam in its 800 miles of twisting through this rugged landscape.

Four natural passes cut through the Annamite chain. These are, from north to south: the valley of the Mo River, in eastern Xieng Khouang Province; the pass at Nape and the Mu Gia Pass, both in Khammouane Province; and the saddle in Savannakhet Province at Lao Bao. Under the French Protectorate, dirt roads were constructed through the passes in Xieng Khouang and Savannakhet, opening them to vehicular traffic. These roads, called Routes Coloniales 7 and 9, were the most direct means of access to the sea from northern and southern Laos, respectively.

Except for these passes, footpaths until recently afforded the only passage across the Annamite Mountains. There is now a road from Sam Neua to North Vietnam, but only a rough pony trail connects Sam Neua with the main body of Laos.

Laos lies in the path of the southwesterly monsoon. For six months of the year, mist and cloud hang low over these mountains, and drenching rains turn footpaths into soggy, muddy rivulets.

At the center of northern Laos lies the Plain of Jars, a high, rolling plain of bright-green grasslands interspersed with clumps of trees on the hilltops. This plain, resembling the dairy land of southern Wisconsin, has an average elevation of 3,600 feet above sea level. It is ringed with mountains; one of these, to the immediate south, has a 9,240-foot summit, the highest in Indochina south of Hanoi. The plain takes its name from the more than 100 ancient stone jars found strewn through the meadows near its center. The jars, large enough to hold a small man in squatting position, are thought by some scholars to be funeral urns. Tests have placed their age at about 2,000 years, indicating that they were fashioned long before the Lao people entered the area. Because marks on the inside of the urns appear to have been made by iron chisels and because the only known iron-workers in this part of the world 2,000 years ago were the Chinese, some scholars believe that the jars are Chinese relics.

In southern Laos is another lofty plateau, the Bolovens, said by agronomists to contain the country's richest agricultural potential. The great Mekong, which rises in Tibet and courses south through the gorges of China's Yünnan Province, enters Laos a few miles north of Muong Sing village, and then forms Laos' western border, first with Burma, then with Thailand. In April, just before the first monsoon storms, the Mekong is a narrow stream hiding among outcroppings of gray and black rock, its exposed bed presenting no barrier to the foot traveler. In September, the river is at its rain-swollen maximum; in the south, it is a mile-wide, thirty-foot-deep, chocolate-colored stream carrying a heavy load of mud, tree trunks, and lesser debris on a long voyage to the sea.

Most of Laos is covered by a tropical rain forest. Dark green the year round, it forms a canopy of lofty treetops. Branchless tree trunks rise straight up from the sunless forest floor, their tops festooned by giant lianas, often a foot in diameter. Scattered in the crowns are orchids, ferns, and wild figs.

Occasionally the rain forest gives way abruptly to less dense groves of smaller softwoods, their foliage not so profuse, which are mixed with a heavy undergrowth of ferns, grass, wild ginger, tropical rhododendron, and bamboo thickets. Often there is a secondary cover of wild bananas and coconut and areca palms. These are overgrown clearings, where the virgin forest was burned off long ago, either by a natural fire or by a wandering tribal family needing enough bare ground to plant a year's crop of maize or hill rice before moving on to the next valley.

These vast forests are the home of tiger, panther, and herds of wild elephant and deer. When these forests provide the hideouts of armed guerrilla bands, news dispatches most often refer to them as jungles.

The People

The peoples of Laos are distributed about their country in a distinctive pattern in which altitude is the indicator. The aboriginal inhabitants of Laos were the Kha, a dark-skinned race of Indonesian origin. (According to a Lao legend, the Kha came from a giant gourd that, when pierced with a red-hot iron by the King of Heaven, emitted a stream of people, naturally dark from the charred meat of the gourd.) Today, the Kha live on the middle slopes of the mountains, where they hunt and practice a shifting cultivation of rice, maize, tobacco, and cotton. They are found in all mountainous regions of Laos, but are especially numerous in the south and particularly on the Bolovens Plateau. They live several families to

CHINA

NORTH VIETNAM

BURMA

+ 6512
+ 10312
Red River
+ 7149
Black River
6043 +
6500 +
Ma River
+ 6181
+ 7100
7300 +
Hou River
Seng River
+ 7405
6821 +
+ 6500
Nam Tha
5774 +
Mekong
7257 +
Plain of Jars
+ 3445
+ 8175
+ 6939
Lik River
8054 +
Ngum River
8894 +
Song Ca
GULF OF TONKIN
+ 9242
6300 +
5463 +
Sane River
Ca Dinh River
Phou Khao Khouei
577 +
Mekong
7498 +
Annamite Mountains
+ 5320

THAILAND

Korat Plateau

Bang Fai River
Bang Hieng
River

0   25   50   75   100   125   150   175
miles

Altitudes in feet

Annamite Mountains

Bolovens
5584 +
Plateau

+ 7060

Kong River

SOUTH VIETNAM

+ 83

River
Menam

Mekong
+ 4603

GULF
OF
SIAM

290

CAMBODIA

Map 1.   Physical Features of Laos

a "long house," which is set on thick wooden piles, its interior partitionless and smoke-blackened.

The Lao, who constitute less than one-half the total population today, live in the broad, fertile valley bottoms. They are descendants of a great migration of Thai peoples from southern China that occurred between the sixth and thirteenth centuries. Like the inhabitants of Thailand, they are Theravada Buddhists, and the languages of the two peoples are closely related.

Another group from the same migration—the Black Thai, White Thai, and Red Thai tribes—very early settled in the upper valleys in the mountainous areas around Muong Sing and Dien Bien Phu, between the Red River and the Mekong. They remain distinct from the lowland Lao; like them, they are rice cultivators, but unlike them, they are not Buddhists.

Subsequent arrivals were the Yao, who settled on the lower mountain slopes, followed by the Meo, who occupied the highest crests and ridges. They came from southern China in the last major migration, in the middle of the nineteenth century, which was almost as important as the earlier Thai migrations. The Meo, whose villages are not normally found in Laos anywhere below 3,500 feet, cover wide areas of Xieng Khouang Province, and in smaller numbers live in Luang Prabang, Sam Neua, Phong Saly, and Nam Tha provinces. They total between 300,000 and 500,000.

The Meo, fiercely independent and hardier than all the other tribes, are the warrior race of Laos, comparable to the Gurkhas of Nepal. They build their houses on the ground, usually not more than a dozen to a village. Indefatigable walkers and horsemen, they range the upper mountain slopes for days, hunting with their long, homemade flintlock rifles the game that keeps them alive and provides the medicinal potions that they believe bring health and long life: skin of gaur (a wild buffalo), deer's soft horn, marrow of tiger bone, gall of bear and python. The staple diet of the Meo village consists of ground fried corn, Chinese cabbage, eggplant, onions, and pork or fowl.

Two other minorities complete this picture of diverse peoples. These are the Vietnamese and the Chinese, communities of about 30,000 each, living mainly in the towns.

The Emergence of a Strong Lao State

The man who gave the territories of what is now Laos their first shape as a unified state was a fourteenth-century Thai prince named Fa Ngoun, a convert to Buddhism who had spent his youth as an exile at Angkor. He established his court at Muong Swa, on the Upper Mekong, and invited to it bonzes (Buddhist monks), scholars, and craftsmen. He acquired a 500-year-old Buddha called the Prabang, which later gave Muong Swa the name of Luang Prabang (Town of the Golden Buddha).

During this era, the rulers of the surrounding states on the east, south, and west—Annam, Champa, Angkor, Sukhothai, Ayuthia, Chieng Mai, and those of the Shans and the Burmese—were busily intriguing against one another; meanwhile, Annam was at war with China. By playing off these petty princes against one another, Fa Ngoun extended his rule to all the principalities along the Mekong, and captured Vientiane. His domain, when consolidated in 1353 under the name Lan Xang (Kingdom of the Million Elephants), reached from the crest of the Annamite Mountains on the east to the watershed division between the Mekong and the Menam, and from China in the north almost as far as Angkor Wat in the south. It included Chieng Mai and much of the Korat Plateau in what is today Thailand, and portions of present-day northern Cambodia.

Fa Ngoun was succeeded in 1373 by his son, Sam Sen Thai. In an age of warring feudal lords, his reign was one of peace, marked by the building of many *wats* (pagodas), and by the creation of a novel system of local government. Under Sam Sen Thai's system, local governors were selected by the King or by a council of notables, usually from the family of the previous incumbent. Any qualified person had the possibility of assuming a high office in the state.

The two successive kings, father and son, ruled over a group of vassal princes and exacted recognition from neighboring emperors and potentates. Their source of power was a centralized standing army of 150,000 men, divided into infantry, cavalry, and elephant corps, supported by a supply corps of 20,000 coolies. In practice, each of the local governors exerted considerable control over the soldiers recruited from his district, who also served as the local police force. With this machinery of state, the two kings preserved the independence of Lan Xang from enemies without and from dissolution within.

However, after the death of Sam Sen Thai, in 1416, the divisive forces in this early Lao kingdom proved stronger than the cohesive. The fact that the Mekong, with its alternating shallow rapids and flood-spreading crests, could not be used as an avenue of communication favored provincial autonomy rather than centralized authority. Under Sam Sen Thai's successors, his territories became prey for his more powerful neighbors.

An invasion from Annam threatened Lan Xang with extinction in 1478, when Vietnamese troops captured Luang Prabang and drove out the King, Sai Tiakaphat. However, the King's son, Prince Theng Kham, rallied his subjects and pushed the Vietnamese out of the kingdom. The father then vacated the throne in favor of his son, who began his reign under the name Souvanna Palang.

The first records of Europeans arriving in Lan Xang date from the reign of Souligna Vongsa (1637–94). They were traders and missionaries, who found the Lao a happy and carefree people but saw little prospects of either economic advantage or Christian converts. A Dutch merchant, Gerrit van Wuysthoff, arrived in 1641 and left soon thereafter. A Jesuit, Father Giovanni-Maria Leria, stayed on five years before despairing of success in his missionary work.

An interesting sidelight is provided by one notable accomplishment of Souligna Vongsa's generally peaceful reign: a boundary agreement with the empire of the Trinh in the Red River Delta. Since it was the Lao custom to build houses on stilts six to nine feet high, while the Vietnamese built their houses on the ground, a clear-cut division of territory was agreed upon: houses on stilts went to the Lao side, houses on the ground to the Vietnamese.

Souligna Vongsa died in 1694, leaving no living sons. The throne was seized by Tian Thala, the highest-ranking mandarin of the Royal Palace. Six years later he was overthrown and put to death by a provincial governor named Nantharath. Upon this, Souligna Vongsa's minor grandsons, Kitsarat and Inthasom, fled from Vientiane to Luang Prabang.

The news of this coup reached Sai Ong Hue, the son of Souligna Vongsa's brother, who had been living in exile in Annam. That same year, 1700, Sai Ong Hue marched on Vientiane at the head of an army of Vietnamese soldiers. He captured the town, had Nantharath put to death, and proclaimed himself King. He sent his half brother, Thao Long, to take possession of Luang Prabang in his name, and Kitsarat and Inthasom, once more fearing for their lives, fled northeastward to a principality ruled by a princely cousin named Khamone Noi.

In 1707, with an army of 6,000 raised by Khamone Noi, the two grandsons marched on Luang Prabang and captured it. Kitsarat was proclaimed King and sent an ultimatum to Sai Ong Hue in Vientiane that he should consider the provinces north of the Nam

Thuong, or Thuong River, as a kingdom outside his sovereignty. Sai Ong Hue's kingdom was further reduced in 1713 by the secession of a number of territories to the south along both banks of the Mekong, which grouped themselves into the Kingdom of Champassak. The old Kingdom of Lan Xang was now split up into three separate kingdoms: Vientiane, Luang Prabang, and Champassak.

Constant warfare among rival princes racked the countryside in the eighteenth and nineteenth centuries, opening it to forays by the more powerful Siam, Annam, and Burma. A Siamese army captured and sacked Vientiane in 1827, after its ruler, King Anourouth, had unsuccessfully attempted to march on Bangkok. The victorious army forcibly resettled thousands of Lao on the Korat Plateau on the right bank of the Mekong in the hope that they would cause less trouble there.

Anourouth fled across the Annamite Mountains to Hué, where the Emperor Minh Mang offered to help him reconquer his kingdom. In 1828, at the head of an expedition of Vietnamese troops, Anourouth marched back to Vientiane. However, most of the troops deserted en route, and as soon as he arrived in his ruined capital he was again chased out by the Siamese. This time he fled to the Kingdom of Xieng Khouang, a small principality centered in the Plain of Jars, which had managed to survive by paying tribute to both Lan Xang (and its successors) and Annam.

Chao Noi, King of Xieng Khouang, confronted a difficult choice, whether to offend Siam or Annam. He decided on the latter, and handed Anourouth over to the Siamese, who carried him away to Bangkok, where he died in 1835. Chao Noi's action predictably angered Minh Mang, who demanded that he come to Hué to explain his action. Instead, Chao Noi sent an envoy with rich presents, hoping to lessen the Emperor's displeasure. His gesture failed, however, and Minh Mang sent a Vietnamese force to seize him and had him publicly executed in Hué. His little kingdom then became a prefecture of the Empire of Annam, in 1832.

Annam's rule over the annexed territory of Xieng Khouang was harsh in the extreme. Its people were even compelled to wear Vietnamese dress. The outcome was a revolt, during which the Vietnamese governor was killed. After restoring order, the Vietnamese won over Chao Pho, the eldest son of Chao Noi, and in 1855 gave him the lofty title of "imperial mandatory prince" and control over the administration of Xieng Khouang. The little principality continued to pay tribute to both Annam and Luang Prabang, but after 1855 the tight grip of the Vietnamese beyond the Annamite Mountains relaxed somewhat as the emperor at Hué increasingly had to cope with the French.

The Advent of the French

In the middle of the nineteenth century, European powers were landing traders on the China coast in eager hopes of exploiting that vast, mysterious country. The traders were followed by the military, who were sent to consolidate the concessions wrested from a decadent empire. France, led by a small minority of activists envisioning control of the easiest route to the fabled wealth of Yünnan, dispatched military forces to the Red River Delta in 1872. French land and naval expeditions defeated Vietnamese troops and Chinese mercenaries and imposed a Treaty of Protectorate over the court of Hué. In 1884, France won the right to place its Residents over the mandarin administrators of Annam and Tonkin and to install a Resident-General in the citadel of Hué. French military outposts were established at Lai Chau, Son La, and Van Bu in the mountains of northwest Tonkin.

Siam, fearing that the court of Hué would invoke the Protectorate to compel the French military to reassert Annam's claims beyond the Annamite Mountains, launched its own large-scale military expedition into northern Laos in 1885. The pretext used by the Siamese was that they were protecting the inhabitants from further incursions from southern China. Indeed, for some fifteen years, Laos had been invaded by armed bands plundering and killing, and these had inflicted great suffering on the population, which called them the Ho, or Chinese.

The Siamese occupied the Plain of Jars and then dispatched two of their *commissaires* to the capital of Luang Prabang to supervise the Kingdom's affairs. Thereupon, the Quai d'Orsay sent a note to Bangkok warning that Hué claimed sovereignty over both Xieng Khouang and Luang Prabang and asking Siam to agree that a joint commission examine the boundaries of Luang Prabang on the spot. Subsequently, on May 7, 1886, Siam granted France the right to post a vice-consul to Luang Prabang. Creation of this post seemingly indicated French recognition of Siam's sovereignty over Luang Prabang, since consulates function only in foreign territories. But the matter was to end badly for the Siamese, for the Frenchman appointed to this post, Auguste Pavie, was fully alert to its prospects.

Pavie was an official of the Cochinchinese Postal and Telegraph Services who had shown considerable imagination in dealing with the peoples of southern Indochina. He departed from Bangkok with eight Cambodian bodyguards and two servants at the end of the year, and on February 11, 1887, he disembarked from his pirogue at Luang Prabang town. There the Siamese *commissaires* accorded him a polite but suspicious welcome, somewhat similar to that accorded Americans in later days by the French. The *commissaires* proceeded to frustrate his initial attempts to arrange an audience with the aged King, Oun Kham.

Four months after his arrival, at the onset of the rainy season, the Siamese troops who were the protectors of the Kingdom withdrew to Bangkok. They took along as hostages the four brothers of Deo Van Tri, a powerful White Thai chieftain at Lai Chau. In revenge, Deo Van Tri's army, composed largely of Chinese troops, descended on the undefended capital and burned it to the ground. Many of its terrified inhabitants were killed, but Pavie, acting with shrewd foresight, spirited away the septuagenarian Oun Kham to safety downstream, saving his life and preventing him from falling into hostile hands.

Thereupon Pavie persuaded the King to give up the Siamese protectorate, which had proved utterly worthless, in favor of a French protectorate. That was the beginning of French colonial rule in Laos. There is little evidence that it was the product of a grandiose and premeditated scheme. Rather, it appears to have been the accidental creation of one extraordinarily able and imaginative man.

Pavie months later returned the hostages to Deo Van Tri in perfect health, and so earned the gratitude and friendship of the Thai tribes of the Tonkin border region. And by a combination of force and skillful diplomacy, he also freed the country of the worst of the Ho marauders.

Pavie was a doer, forever clambering into his pirogue for a quick trip upstream to look into some local situation. He traveled from Luang Prabang to Hanoi, to Bangkok, to Saigon, and to most of the river junctions and outposts in between. He would sit down with his small retinue in a village headman's house and exchange tales over a jug of stiff *choum,* or rice wine, sucked through long straws, and the next day he would be off on the trail again, over mountain passes and through steaming valleys. In this way he won over the tribal leaders and could show the French tricolor in regions two weeks' march from any sizable town.[1]

---

[1] Pavie's journal, which reads like an adventure story, was later published: *Mission Pavie en Indochine, 1879–1895* (10 vols.; Paris, 1898–1919).

In 1888, at a large gathering in the Dien Bien Phu valley, he personally received Siam's renunciation of its claim to the Douze Cantons (in Thai, Sipsong Chuthai), an extensive almond-shaped territory lying along a perpendicular drawn midway along the Luang Prabang–Hanoi axis.

Incidents between Siamese and French officials in Khammouane disturbed Pavie, and in February, 1889, he traveled there to warn the Siamese representatives to avoid any hostile moves. By now, the official French position was that this territory, which had once paid tribute to Annam, was French-protected by virtue of the Treaty of Protectorate with Annam. (This application of European legal concepts to the feuds among the principalities of Indochina has been a basic concept for later apologists for French colonization.)

After further incidents, the French dispatched a naval contingent to Bangkok. Under this pressure, Siam signed a treaty on October 3, 1893, renouncing all claims on the left bank of the Mekong, both north and south. Subsequent Franco-Siamese conventions in 1902, 1904, and 1907 attached certain right-bank territories to Luang Prabang and Champassak.

One of Pavie's last achievements before leaving Laos was the organization of the northernmost provinces, including the careful mapping of the border with Vietnam (apportioning part of the Douze Cantons to the latter and part to Luang Prabang) and joint surveys with British and Chinese commissions to establish the borders with Burma and China. The former was fixed at the Mekong by an Anglo-French declaration of January 15, 1896, and the latter by an agreement with China during 1896–97.

With these adjustments, Laos assumed its present external boundaries. Before the advent of the French, Laos had never been surveyed, and the drawing up of maps of the country was an important administrative accomplishment of French rule.

In 1889, the town of Vientiane was made the administrative capital of French Laos. From Vientiane, the Senior Resident exercised indirect control over the protected Kingdom of Luang Prabang and direct control, through Residents, over the remaining provinces.

By 1905, Laos comprised the following entities:

1. The Kingdom of Luang Prabang, which included the present provinces of Luang Prabang, Sayaboury, Sam Neua, and the two southern districts of Phong Saly. The monarch retained his royal title and prerogatives under French protection, but in all important

respects its administration was controlled by French officials.

2. The defunct Kingdom of Vientiane, which had not had a monarch since its plunder by a Siamese army in 1827.

3. The defunct Kingdom of Xieng Khouang, which had been annexed by the Vietnamese in 1832.

4. The defunct Kingdom of Champassak, whose royal family lost their prerogatives in 1900. (A portion of the kingdom lying on the right bank of the Mekong remained under Siamese suzerainty.)

5. The northern territories of Nam Tha and Phong Saly.

The French administration gave these territories a common front against outsiders, putting an end to the piecemeal depredations of Siam, Annam, and Burma. Internally, however, the French had to play a balancing game of shifting loyalties among the diverse tribes. At times the latent conflicts came to the surface, and in one twenty-year period the colonial administration spent ten years putting down three internal threats of armed conflict. The first occurred in 1901, when a number of Kha chiefs and sorcerers in southern Laos, apparently angered by French interference in their slave trade, whipped their people into a rebellion that was not fully quashed until 1907. In 1914, the Thai tribes in Phong Saly Province flared up in a revolt that was to occupy French colonial troops for a full two years. In the last of the three risings, the Meo in 1919 started raiding and looting the Lao, Kha, and other peoples, and were only halted two years later when the French reduced the affected area by cutting off its rice supply.

In addition to warring tribes, the thinly spread French security forces had to cope with pirate bands. In November, 1914, thirty Chinese pirates captured the town of Sam Neua and murdered the French *commissaire*.

The Lao benefited generally under the mild regime of French colonial rule, whose functionaries followed a live-and-let-live policy rather than enforcing any absolute code of behavior. In 1940, there were fewer than 600 French residents in Laos to govern slightly more than 1 million natives.

The official French *présence* manifested itself principally in fiscal control, education, and judicial organization. The tax collector became an accepted feature of French protection, but although taxation was supposedly universal, it never reached into the more inaccessible mountain villages.

French was the accepted language among civil-service workers, from governor down to post-office clerk. In the villages, bonzes controlled education, but in Vientiane and the other major towns,

French teachers taught French curriculums and prepared their students to take university degrees in France. Almost the entire elite of Laos studied in France.

The Buddhist Lao had accepted the French with an open-mindedness sharply in contrast to the suspicion and hostility shown by the Confucian mandarins of Annam. Conversely, the French colonials in Laos were receptive to the natives' serene approach to life. Indeed, some Frenchmen formed a deep emotional attachment to the gentle Lao. One *fonctionnaire,* stationed in a remote outpost of southern Laos, lived there in blissful isolation with his Lao mistress and household. Annually, upon learning that the French colonial inspector was approaching, he would close up his house and take to the jungle until word came that the official presence had left. His excuse, that he was out hunting, was unfailingly accepted by his undeceived superior. France simply did not care so long as the administration ran smoothly.

The French soon learned to depend heavily on existing systems of local government and to avoid upsetting custom and tradition whenever possible. They usually appointed the district officer, called *chao muong* (after the Lao equivalent of the district, the *muong,* and the traditional term for prince or leader, *chao*). But the official one rung below, the *tasseng,* was elected by a council of headmen from the six to ten villages under his authority. The headman, called *nai ban* (after the Lao equivalent of the village, the *ban,* and *nai,* meaning elder), continued to be elected by the village inhabitants under the Protectorate as he had been under the feudal prince. The election procedure was simple: The candidates stood by the village *wat,* or temple, and each villager queued up behind the man he wanted; the candidate who acquired the longest line was elected headman.

In France, public opinion strongly opposed expansion of French responsibility in this strange and faraway land, especially since it appeared to offer little in short-term economic return. As early as 1866, a French survey determined that the Mekong was valueless for commercial navigation. No gold or silver deposits had been uncovered; there appeared to be not even an iron mine worth developing (more recent surveys have revealed some low-grade deposits). Despite French efforts to exploit a tin mine in Khammouane Province and to plant coffee on the Bolovens Plateau, Laos never accounted for more than 1 per cent of the total French export trade from Indochina.

French engineers built beautiful and durable roads in Vietnam and Cambodia, but almost ignored Laos. They did construct an arterial road linking the larger towns along the Mekong—Luang Prabang, Vientiane, Thakhek, Savannakhet, and Pakse. This road was officially called Route Coloniale 13, but the section linking Vientiane and Luang Prabang, the country's two capitals, has long been termed the Royal Road. It was not completed until April, 1943.

The Royal Road stretches straight as an arrow for 20 miles across the dusty plain of Vientiane, bordered by paddy fields and thickets of trees for as far as the eye can see. In the dry season, from September to May, its entire length is open to heavy vehicles.

Farther north, the Royal Road rises slightly as it travels through sparse secondary forest growth. It then enters rugged country, becoming a narrow single track, almost completely obscured by thick foliage.

The road curves generally eastward in a broad arc, circling a final hillock before entering the village of Ban Namone. In the dirt underneath the stilted houses, pigs and flocks of chickens are rooting. In the doorways to the houses squat somnolent men and toothless women. In the valley bottoms are their fields of rice, yielding just enough to feed their families, no more.

After Ban Namone, the Royal Road comes upon a broad, spectacularly beautiful valley at the foot of a 3,000-foot-high limestone wall. This is the valley of Vang Vieng, 65 miles north of Vientiane. A few miles farther, the road begins to climb in earnest, up a series of slopes that mark the halfway point between Vientiane and Luang Prabang.

A series of villages succeed each other: Ban Pha Tang, Ban Thieng, Muong Kassy. Up, up climbs the road, making sharp bends, often with a cliff on one side and a precipice on the other. At Sala Phou Khoun, the road to the Plain of Jars branches off to the right, and the road to Luang Prabang dips down to the left.

Route Coloniale 13, together with Routes Coloniales 7 and 9 through the Annamite chain, constituted virtually the entire network for a territory almost half the size of France. Even these roads were impassable during much of the rainy season, and the journey from Vientiane to Saigon by road was an endurance test even during the dry season. Plans for a railway linking the Mekong Valley and the sea coast never materialized.

Some historians, particularly British historians, see France's colonization of Laos as the result of a single-minded French determination to occupy as much territory as possible before the British could get to it, or to set up a solid bulwark against the British in Burma. But this explanation misses the most noteworthy fact about France's involvement in Laos: It had no positive aim. Instead, it had the negative purpose of restraining Siamese influence on the left bank of the Mekong, which the French felt jeopardized their more valuable holdings in Vietnam.

The French might well have achieved this purpose in other ways. They could have ceded to Siam formal vassalage of the Kingdom of Luang Prabang and the other principalities between the Mekong and the Annamite Mountains. The French could have used their superior military power to extract from the Siamese, intent on preserving their prestige among the Thai-speaking chieftains beyond the Mekong, assurances that no Siamese troops would be quartered in this territory in return for a French guarantee of the security of these tribes, as well as the Kingdom of Luang Prabang, from attack by Annam.

The idea of obtaining Siamese agreement to the assertion of nominal Siamese sovereignty only over the territories on the left bank appears to have been entertained by the French Minister in Bangkok; he communicated his views to the Quai d'Orsay in a telegram on December 22, 1886.[2]

At the death of King Zakarine in 1904, the French Senior Resident, Georges Mahé, took advantage of the practice of selecting a successor from the royal princes regardless of seniority and recommended a younger son, Sisavang Vong.[3] The council of notables took Mahé's recommendation, and Sisavang Vong became King of Luang Prabang.

Laos Today

Despite the decades of French influence, the land and the people basically are still what they were when Pavie arrived in the town of Luang Prabang. Laos is still a land half of Buddhism, half of animism. For the mountain tribesmen, and even for many Lao today, the jungle is peopled with powerful spirits, called *phi,* which must be propitiated with sacrifices, exorcised by complicated rites, and never wantonly abused or angered. There are *phi* in the trees,

[2] *Thailand: How Thailand Lost Her Territories to France* (Bangkok: Department of Publicity, 1940), p. 30.

[3] In Cambodia, the French followed a similar practice, and in 1941 accounted for the selection of Prince Norodom Sihanouk to succeed King Sisowath Monivong, in preference to the sovereign's eldest son, Prince Monireth.

mountains, and rivers, and in animals and in every human being. Some *phi* jealously guard wild or unknown places; others cause disease or misfortune in the village. A particular *phi* is consulted before the planting of rice, to discover the most propitious starting day and the most suitable area. Sometimes a person contains many *phi,* each guarding a particular vital organ. The *phi* of those who died violent deaths roam the earth tormenting people. Certain living persons contain malevolent *phi* and must be kept away from the village.

Visitors to a village, ignorant of local custom, are liable to anger *phi* by stepping in the wrong places, failing to make proper obeisance, or speaking forbidden words. The French grew familiar with these superstitions during their Protectorate. A French officer was leading a patrol of mountain tribesmen through the forest in pursuit of the Viet Minh, when a black goat crossed the line of march. The soldiers, judging this a bad omen, demanded that they return to their camp at once. Such incidents were not infrequent.

In the villages, a happy people cultivate just enough rice for their families, live without paper money or newspapers, and nurture little ambition beyond achieving the satisfactions of a peaceable life. In the towns, a small elite has gone to school and has learned the language and manner of thinking of a faraway country. The French military men brought with them the airplane, which revolutionized transportation; few villages can boast a vehicular road, but many have a cleared landing strip, which means that their inhabitants are in contact—tenuous but real—with the world beyond their bamboo houses. Because the people still measure distances in terms of days of walking on the trail, they can have little concept of what a country like America is, since visitors cannot explain how many days it takes to walk there.

Around the villages of the Meo, a special crop is harvested—the opium poppy. It is odd that it is the sale of this crop that has brought the Meo more into the money economy than the other tribesmen of Laos. The result is visible in the heavy necklaces of silver they wear over their gaily colored tunics.

A field of poppies in full bloom in the Meo country is an unforgettable sight—white, rose-colored, blue, or mauve flowers rippling in the breeze. The poppies are planted in October, and harvested in February or March, when the plants are about a yard high. The village women go to the fields early in the morning before the dew lifts or in the evening, and carefully scarify the pale-green stem from top to bottom with a small copper grater bearing three triangular points. They leave the sap to dry, and then collect it and wrap it in banana leaves. Then the raw blocks of brownish dried sap are sold.

The manufacture of opium, a lucrative monopoly under the French, bringing the Indochina Government General one-seventh of its total budgetary receipts,[4] is still the country's most valuable unofficial export. A recent estimate of production was between 50 and 100 tons annually, stated to be worth "200 francs the kilo in Xieng Khouang, or 5,000 francs in Saigon." Gross annual revenue to the Meo producers was estimated at "15 million francs, and 350 million francs to about a hundred traffickers."[5] An American anthropologist who visited Xieng Khouang Province shortly before the end of the French administration was told by an official that an estimated 60 per cent of the men of the province were addicted to the drug.[6]

Laos is less a nation state than a conglomeration of tribes and languages (eighteen major dialects are spoken in Phong Saly Province alone), less a unified society than a multiplicity of feudal societies. The family clan is all-important.

Life is punctuated by numerous festivals. A Buddhist celebration at the village *wat* means the decking of the temple and its courtyard with multicolored flags, the gathering of a large number of shaven-headed bonzes, their bright saffron robes gay in the sunshine, and ballad singers with chalked faces spinning tales of legendary heroes and divinities in songs, or *molams*. Some feast days are observed by shooting off crude rockets from wooden launching stands, others by throwing bucketfuls of water to the accompaniment of much laughter and joking. Fertility rites are performed annually in many villages of the far north, in the steep valleys of Nam Tha along the China border, in Sam Neua along the Vietnam border, and in the south.

A common ceremony honors a guest in a Lao home by tying a series of white strings around his wrists like bracelets, as a mark of friendship. Like many of the simple things of which Laos is made and which its peoples treasure, it is moving in its simple beauty.

[4] Extracted from figures in *Rapports au Grand Conseil des Interêts économiques et financiers et au Conseil du Gouvernement, 1938* (Hanoi: Taupin), p. 30.

[5] Georges Penchenier, "La Difficulté d'Etre Neutre," *Le Monde* (Paris), June 18–24, 1964 (weekly edition).

[6] George L. Barney, *The Meo of Xieng Khouang Province* (Los Angeles: University of California, Department of Anthropology and Sociology, Laos Project Paper No. 13, 1961), p. 27.

2.

Lao Issara

The beginning of the end of French control over Indochina came in 1940, when France fell to Germany.

After the French defeat, Japan obtained the right to station troops in Indochina and the right to use airfields there, and promised in return to leave intact the French civil service and security forces loyal to Vichy.

President Roosevelt tried unsuccessfully to effect the withdrawal of Japanese forces by means of a plan to make Indochina a "neutralized area." On July 24, 1941, he approached the Japanese Ambassador in Washington with this proposal: If Japan would make a commitment to regard Indochina as a "neutralized area" with the understanding that "the powers concerned would not undertake any military act of aggression against Indochina and would not exercise any military control within or over Indochina," he would do "everything within his power" to obtain from the Allies the same commitment.[1]

During these diplomatic interchanges, troops of the Bangkok government, which had failed in its efforts to obtain an Allied guarantee against Japanese aggression, occupied the portions of Luang Prabang and Champassak yielded by Siam under the conventions of 1902, 1904, and 1907. With Japanese mediation, Bangkok obtained from France the cession of this territory, which amounted to more than 21,000 square miles.

To compensate King Sisavang Vong for his territorial losses, which included the best of the royal teak forests in what is today Sayaboury Province, the Vichy Government agreed to formalize

[1] Department of State, *Peace and War: United States Foreign Policy, 1931–41* (Washington: Government Printing Office, 1943), p. 125.

the Protectorate over the Kingdom of Luang Prabang. Heretofore it had existed legally only in the cumulative provisions contained in declarations by Pavie, in Franco-Siamese agreements regarding sovereign rights over various pieces of territory, and in a number of Franco-Lao conventions, some of which had not even been ratified by the French Government. On August 29, 1941, the signatures of Marshal Henri Pétain and King Sisavang Vong put into force a solemn treaty defining the Protectorate. Under its terms, the territories of Vientiane, Xieng Khouang, and Nam Tha were included under the sovereignty of the Kingdom of Luang Prabang.

The End of the Protectorate

On March 9, 1945, the Japanese forces in Indochina ruptured their agreement with Vichy and staged a *coup de main* against the French, imprisoning all French civil servants and soldiers. A handful escaped into the mountains, managed to make their way northward over rough trails to China, and declared themselves for the Free French. The Japanese proclaimed an end to the colonial regimes in Vietnam, Laos, and Cambodia.

In Laos, King Sisavang Vong and his eldest son, Crown Prince Savang Vatthana, were served with a Japanese demand that they issue a proclamation of independence from the French. Instead, Savang Vatthana decreed a mass uprising of his people against the Japanese. The latter, determined to put down this royal truculence, which they had encountered nowhere in Indochina, sent a detachment of troops on a sixteen-day forced march from Vinh to Luang Prabang, which they occupied on April 5. They promptly packed the Crown Prince off to Saigon, and on April 8, King Sisavang Vong proclaimed the Treaty of Protectorate null and void.

The Japanese removal of the Crown Prince left a free hand to a man much less inclined to favor the French, Prince Phetsarath, the eldest of three remarkable brothers who belonged to the vice-regal branch of the Royal House of Luang Prabang.

In Laos, the title of viceroy, in existence since the establishment of the Kingdom of Lan Xang in the fourteenth century, conferred powers far broader than those associated with the title in the West. The viceroy, or *maha oupahat,* was the highest of the three grades of government officials. He functioned in executive and judicial capacities, and served as the king's most intimate consultant. The viceroy might perform any duties that the king decided on, including negotiating international agreements and leading the king's troops.

Frequently the viceroy convened a council of notables upon the death of the king to choose a successor from among the royal princes.

At various times, the viceroy had been the crown prince, or another of the king's sons, or a collateral relative of royal blood. For the three generations preceding Japan's surrender in World War II, the title had been vested in the family of Oun Keo, a brother of Anourouth, the last king of Vientiane. Oun Keo's son had been killed in the sacking of Luang Prabang in 1887, and Oun Keo's grandson, Boun Khong, had been confirmed as Viceroy by Pavie in 1895.[2] Boun Khong was the father of Phetsarath, who was born in Luang Prabang in 1890.

As was customary for princes of the royal blood under the Protectorate, Phetsarath was enrolled in schools in Hanoi and Saigon, the two seats of learning in Indochina. At the age of fifteen, he was sent to Paris to attend the Colonial College for French administrators. There, he developed an interest in planning the economic development of Laos, as well as a passion for hunting, and he spent one year at Oxford before returning to Luang Prabang in 1918.

Prince Phetsarath had a personal interest in the education of his two brothers, each of them more than ten years younger than he was. They were Souvanna Phouma, born on October 7, 1901, and Souphanouvong, born on July 12, 1912. Phetsarath and Souvanna Phouma were born of Prince Boun Khong's first wife, Princess Thongsy, a member of the reigning branch of the royal house, and Souphanouvong was born of a later wife, a fact that continues to influence his relations with Souvanna Phouma.

Both Souvanna Phouma and Souphanouvong followed in their elder brother's footsteps: secondary education in Indochina, university studies in France, and return to Indochina to enter the civil service under the French.

The young Souvanna Phouma enrolled in the sciences curriculum at the Lycée Albert Sarraut in Hanoi, the best secondary school in Indochina. Souphanouvong followed him there in 1921, and outshone his brother by becoming a formidable goalie on the soccer team and achieving a baccalaureate in both sciences and classics.

Souvanna Phouma went on to the University of Paris, and received a degree in architectural engineering from its Ecole Spéciale des Travaux Publics et du Bâtiment in 1928 and a degree in electrical engineering from the University of Grenoble in 1930. The fol-

[2] Paul Le Boulanger, *Histoire du Laos Français* (Paris: Plon, 1931), p. 202 n.

lowing year he arrived in Vientiane, and entered the bureau of architecture in the Public Works Service at an annual salary equivalent to about $2,300, a highly respectable figure for a Lao in the colonial civil service. With the blessing of the French, he rapidly rose to be chief of the bureau. Among his accomplishments was the restoration of the Wat Phakeo in Vientiane. On August 2, 1933, he married Aline-Claire Allard, a Roman Catholic and the daughter of a French father and a Lao mother.

In 1940, Souvanna Phouma was sent by the French to supervise construction of the Royal Road from Vang Vieng north of Vientiane through the mountains to Sala Phou Khoun, where the Routes Coloniales 7 and 13 would link up. The engineering work earned Souvanna Phouma the title of principal engineer of the first class with the Indochinese Ministry of Public Works.

Meanwhile, Souphanouvong had followed him at the University of Paris. Again he surpassed his older brother, establishing a brilliant record at the Ecole Nationale des Ponts et Chaussées, where he received a degree in civil engineering in 1937. During his summer vacation, Souphanouvong bicycled extensively about the French countryside, and after receiving his degree, he studied irrigation works in North Africa. He also worked on the docks of Le Havre and in the anti-Fascist Popular Front, where he made his first acquaintance with Communists. (How familiar he is with Communist dogma, however, is to this day a mystery. He prefers Greek classics to Marxist-Leninist texts as reading matter.)

Some months later, he again followed in his brother's footsteps, returning to Indochina and taking up a post in the Public Works Service. He was sent to Nha Trang in Vietnam, at a salary of $320 a year, low for Indochina and far below the standard for French engineers with the same qualifications. While in Nha Trang, Souphanouvong married Le Thi Ky Nam, the daughter of a well-to-do local hotel owner. His wife soon revealed a driving ambition and anti-French nationalism. Souphanouvong spent most of the years from 1938 to 1945 building bridges along the excellent road network in central Vietnam, and at the time of the Japanese surrender was in the important communications center of Vinh.

The Lao Issara and the French Reoccupation

The imprisoning of French civil servants and security forces by the Japanese on March 9 was an awakening to Prince Phetsarath and his two brothers. It became clear to them that the French presence in Laos was not necessarily a permanent one, and they acquired the hope, faint at first but encouraged by the democracies' enunciation of lofty war aims, that after the war they might govern their country in independence instead of under foreign domination.

The prestige of France suffered a major blow when it proved incapable of protecting Laos from spoliation by Japan, an Asian power. In Indochina, as in Malaya, Indonesia, and Burma, the Japanese occupation broke the myth of the white man's invincibility.

French power had been shattered by the Japanese *coup de main*. The surrender of Japan and the ending of World War II less than six months later removed at one fell stroke the single remaining cohesive force in Laos and Vietnam.

Phetsarath had held the title of Viceroy since 1941. At the time the Crown Prince was removed from Laos, Phetsarath was also Prime Minister. Clearly, he was the second most powerful political figure in Laos after King Sisavang Vong. When, on August 31, the former French Senior Resident was released from prison in Vientiane, where he had been placed by the Japanese, Phetsarath informed him that, the Vichy Government having gone out of existence, there was no possibility of his resuming his powers. The next day, without informing the King in Luang Prabang, Phetsarath officially reaffirmed the April 8 royal proclamation of independence from France. He followed this up on September 15 with a declaration proclaiming the union of the Kingdom of Luang Prabang and the territory of Champassak in a single, independent Kingdom of Laos.

On September 17, however, he received a telegram signed by a high palace official informing him that the King regarded the Protectorate as still in force. According to one of Phetsarath's supporters, the King was forced to send this telegram by a French agent who had parachuted into Luang Prabang a few days previously.[3] Whatever the case, the telegram proved acutely embarrassing to Phetsarath, and it provoked considerable anger against the King when the people learned of it. A Defense Committee was established. Next, on October 10, a message from Luang Prabang informed Phetsarath that his titles of Viceroy and Prime Minister had been withdrawn. Two days later, on October 12, 1945, the Defense Committee voted a Provisional Constitution, formed a Provisional People's Assembly, and nominated a government, to be known as the Lao Issara (Free Laos), under the premiership of another princely official in Vien-

[3] Thao Katay refers to it as a *"télégramme inspiré par le colonel français Imfeld à Luang Prabang."* (*Le Laos* [Bangkok: Editions Lao Issara, 1948], p. 37.)

tiane, Phaya Khammao, who had been Governor of Vientiane Province. Souvanna Phouma was made Minister of Public Works.

Sisavang Vong steadfastly refused to endorse the Lao Issara, with the result that eight days later the Provisional People's Assembly voted to depose him. In Luang Prabang, a brief popular demonstration broke out in favor of the Lao Issara.

Meanwhile, Prince Souphanouvong, hopeful of an independent regime for Laos after the Japanese defeat and mindful of the support such a regime would require from Vietnam, had made contact with the leaders of the nationalist revolution in the newly proclaimed Vietnamese Republic. The Prince had traveled from Vinh to Hanoi via an airplane flight arranged by General Philip E. Gallagher, the chief of a small group of American military observers in Vietnam, who had been impressed by the efficiency with which the followers of the new Vietnamese President, Ho Chi Minh, had moved in to fill the vacuum left by the Japanese defeat.

Souphanouvong had an interview with Ho, and left bearing a letter signed by the President and introducing him to the Viet Minh Regional Executive Committee of Central Vietnam, the revolutionary apparatus in the region of Vietnam in which Souphanouvong had lived for the past six years. The letter stated that the Prince sought to form a Lao national government, and was to be offered all possible assistance by the Viet Minh regional representatives. When Souphanouvong reached Hué, on his way back to Laos, he was given a guard of fifty armed Viet Minh soldiers to accompany him as he set out for the Lao Bao Pass. This was the first instance of Vietnamese armed support for a Lao nationalist movement. The great importance that Ho attached to the expedition is clearly indicated by his granting the escort permission to carry off 100 of the Central Vietnam committee's stock of 240 rifles.

Souphanouvong, the young aristocrat with a grudge against the French but no experience in guerrilla organization, journeyed with his band of Viet Minh cadres across the Annamite Mountains—pausing at the Laos-Vietnam border to take a solemn oath to continue the struggle until an independent Laos had been won—to Savannakhet on the Mekong.

The first need was for loyal men. Recruits were mustered en route, some at Savannakhet, and many more at Thakhek, where Souphanouvong arrived in October. By November 1, after marching northward along the bank of the Mekong, Souphanouvong and his men arrived at Vientiane, where the Lao Issara government had just been formed. Phaya Khammao, desiring to broaden his political base, appointed Souphanouvong Minister of National Defense and Commander in Chief of the Armed Forces. The Viet Minh stressed the disinterested nature of their support for the Lao Issara, pointing out that although there was military cooperation between the two governments, no Vietnamese held posts in Laos.[4]

The Lao Issara considered the Vichy-signed Treaty of Protectorate no longer binding upon Laos, as is made clear by various messages they sent to the French. Among these was this communication dated November 11, 1945, to the French *commissaire* in Vientiane, who was nervously awaiting the arrival of the French reoccupation force:

> You appear to ignore the facts of the situation in Indochina, as well as the attitude of the governments of the Allies, among whom the Government of France has no place. Your policies are supported only by the imperialistic British Government. You will run head-on into the determination of our people, whom your inhuman and hypocritical colonialism has sought to subjugate. All classes of people in Indochina are familiar with your colonial doctrines and your Protectorate, which is in reality a thinly veiled form of colonization. Only the egotists, traitors to their race, in quest of your gold and false honors, follow you. Your high promises will dissipate like smoke as soon as you have strangled our brave resistance. No, we have decided to live by the immemorial values of our ancestors, values that half a century of French tyranny has suppressed.[5]

Despite this bravado, the Lao Issara realistically saw the wisdom of getting their government accepted by the French, and knew that the chances of this would be greater if it had monarchical rather than republican form. Accordingly, the Lao Issara sent a delegation to Luang Prabang to try to win Sisavang Vong's participation in a constitutional monarchy. Sisavang Vong handed the leader of this delegation a statement affirming (1) that he agreed of his own free will to place himself under the authority of the provisional government, and (2) that from the time of the Japanese surrender to his dethroning, he had concluded no secret diplomatic agreements with any representative of the French Government.

Upon receipt of these assurances, the Lao Issara requested him to assume the throne of a unified Laos under a constitutional monarchy. Sisavang Vong agreed, and amid splendid pomp and circumstance, he was enthroned in Luang Prabang on April 23, 1946. In

---

[4] *Co Doc Lap (The Banner of Independence)* (Hanoi), October 28, 1945.
[5] Quoted in Pierre Gentil, *Remous du Mékong* (Paris: Charles Lavauzelle, 1950), p. 32.

his first royal decree, the King proclaimed legal the October 12 Provisional Constitution and endorsed the government headed by Phaya Khammao.

Meanwhile, French reoccupation forces, after being held up on the lower Mekong awaiting reinforcements that had been diverted to quell an uprising in Cochinchina, were slowly making their way up the Mekong Valley against what resistance the meager Lao Issara army could muster.

The northernmost Lao province, Phong Saly, had already been reoccupied in February by the small Free French detachment that had escaped into China in 1945. The southernmost province, Champassak, with its pro-French governor, Kou Abhay, had been reoccupied without much trouble. But arriving at the town of Thakhek in March, the French forces encountered stiff resistance from the Lao Issara, who were openly assisted by Viet Minh agents. Commander in Chief Souphanouvong took personal charge of the badly outnumbered Lao Issara forces and underwent his baptism of fire from French mortars and machine guns. In the thick of the battle, he was seen walking with his son up and down the lines encouraging his men. He had set up a workshop in the town to manufacture crude grenades, an indication of the rudimentary state of the armament of the Lao Issara forces. On March 21, after bitter street fighting, the French occupied Thakhek, and Souphanouvong fled across the Mekong. In the boat, he was wounded in the left arm by a bullet from a strafing British Spitfire. Heavy fighting continued for several days along the rough track leading from Thakhek to the pass at Nape, which was the primary means of communication with the Viet Minh-controlled areas of Vietnam and so was defended against the French at the cost of many casualties. (British forces under General D. D. Gracey had received the Japanese surrender in southern Indochina.)

The French reoccupation proceeded along lines that soon formed a familiar pattern: The French forces directed their main efforts to securing control of the major towns; the resistance fighters were left free to retire to the countryside, where they embarked on a drawn-out war of attrition at the expense of an apathetic or terrorized peasant population.

The seeds for later French suspicions of American designs on Indochina were sown during these turbulent days. Agents of the Office of Strategic Services (OSS), who were the first Americans to arrive on the scene after the Japanese collapse, accorded a distinctly chilly reception to the French when the latter were liberated from prison camps. Some OSS agents made it quite clear that they opposed the reoccupation. A ten-man OSS mission arrived at Vientiane a month after the war's end and curtly ordered the handful of French personnel there to keep out of the town and to "cease their aggression" against the Lao Issara.[6] But it was principally in Hanoi that early signs of friendliness between the OSS agents and the Viet Minh aroused the French against the Americans.[7]

The French forces entered Vientiane on April 24, 1946, with only minor skirmishes. The Lao Issara government and Phetsarath set fire to a few public buildings and then fled across the Mekong to Siam, apparently intending to reach Luang Prabang. However, French forces assumed complete control of the royal capital on May 13, putting an end to that idea. On September 23, the French tricolor fluttered over Ban Houei Sai, the last provincial capital to be reoccupied.

Forced to remain in Siam, the Lao Issara undertook to harass the French with across-the-river raids into Laos. A strike in early May on the village of Pak Hin Boun, upstream from Thakhek, yielded considerable French arms and ammunition and encouraged the Lao Issara leaders to pursue these tactics. Emboldened by support from the local Siamese population, the Lao Issara attempted a raid on Vientiane. This time, however, French forces pursued them back across the river to the village of Tha Bo, killing a number of raiders and three Siamese. The French High Commissioner in Saigon blamed the deliberate violation of Siamese territory on "the obvious inability of the local Siamese authorities to control the activities of armed bands of Lao and Annamite rebels who have sought protection from these authorities."

Following a Siamese appeal to the United States and Britain to intercede with France to halt such violations, the U.S. Legation in Bangkok dispatched an OSS veteran, Major James Thompson, to make an on-the-spot inspection. At the house of the Governor of Nong Khai, across the river from Vientiane, his host said to Thompson: "Come upstairs. I have a Lao Prince you would find it interesting to meet." Upstairs, the major found a husky, square-shouldered man waiting, his left arm in a bandage, attended by two

---

[6] Peter Kemp, *Alms for Oblivion* (London: Cassell, 1961), p. 46. Kemp, who arrived in Laos in September, 1945, was a member of the British Force 136.

[7] Bernard B. Fall, *Le Viêt-Minh, 1945–1960* (Paris: Armand Colin, 1960), pp. 40–41. Also Fall, *The Two Viet-Nams* (New York: Frederick A. Praeger, 1963), pp. 68–71.

bodyguards. He introduced himself as Prince Souphanouvong. Souphanouvong told the American that his government wanted promises of official United States support for removal of the French from Laos. This meeting proved to be the first in a long series of contacts between the Lao Issara and Americans in territory outside Laos.

With the French reoccupation of their country a *fait accompli,* the Lao Issara leaders settled down to a life of exile in Bangkok, where they were given the tacit protection of the postwar government formed by the Free Thai leader, Pridi Phanomyong. Phetsarath had become the leader of the independence movement after the flight from Vientiane. He had had the foresight to take a fair amount of gold with him, so the Lao Issara had funds for at least a few months of operation as the Lao government in exile.

Souvanna Phouma remained Minister of Public Works, and in addition became Deputy Prime Minister. Souphanouvong still had command of the small Lao Issara forces, a responsibility that kept him in touch with the Viet Minh. (After his interview with Major Thompson at Nong Khai, he had returned in July to Hanoi, where an uneasy watchfulness prevailed between the Viet Minh and the French.) After arriving in Bangkok toward the end of 1946, he had also been made Minister of Foreign Affairs.

Phetsarath and Souphanouvong lived in the southern district of Bangkok in a walled compound containing five or six other houses. Through this compound moved a continual flow of Lao patriots, who came and went on mysterious errands connected with the Lao Issara guerrilla raids, which Souphanouvong and his Viet Minh advisers were beginning to mount in Laos. A Bangkok resident at whose house Souphanouvong's sons Ariya and Anou had been left while their father went off on a foray into Laos, recalls that he came out into his garden one morning and found the two boys eating live beetles from a tree. When he tried to stop them, they replied that this was part of their father's training to enable them to survive in the jungle. Souphanouvong and his Vietnamese wife and expanding brood of children became well-known figures in the Thai[8] capital. (By 1962, Souphanouvong had eight sons and two daughters.)

Souvanna Phouma lived modestly in Bangkok. He had taken a job with the Thai Electric Company, partly to keep himself professionally occupied but principally to provide for his family. While his wife was starting a business in Thai silk, he did the household

[8] In 1939, Siam became known officially as Thailand. In 1945, the country reverted to the name Siam, but since 1949, the official name has been Thailand.

marketing and acquired an interest in domestic affairs that he still retains. His thoughts, however, concentrated mainly on the political and economic future of his country. By May, 1947, he had formulated an ambitious project for the economic development of Laos.

(Phetsarath, a man of great intelligence and courage, was also extremely proud, and was piqued by the refusal of Sisavang Vong, the only figure in the Kingdom who outranked him, to restore his title of Viceroy and to include the position of Viceroy in the Constitution of 1947. After 1949, he voluntarily dropped from sight. He refused to return to Laos until 1957, when his title was finally restored. His death two years later deprived his country of an able and far-sighted statesman. He was also one of the few Lao who had an appreciation of the problems Laos' ethnic minorities presented, and he may have stimulated Souphanouvong's interest in the tribes. Sisavang Vong survived him by only fifteen days.)

The international crossroads that Bangkok had become after World War II enabled the princes to plead their cause with representatives of several nations and private interests. They asked the Americans and the British first for arms, then for money, and finally merely for diplomatic recognition of their government in exile. Souphanouvong, hoping to obtain a sympathetic ear from the Americans at least, tirelessly repeated President Roosevelt's statements that the French should not be allowed to go back to Indochina after the Japanese surrender, that they had done little or nothing for the inhabitants during their colonial administration, and that the backwardness of Indochina bore many resemblances to that of the Philippines at the time the islands were freed from Spanish rule. Later, after the United States had expressed its concern at the Dutch repressive action in Java and had partly cut off Marshall Plan aid to the Dutch, Souphanouvong also argued that since the Dutch had been in power in Java for more than 400 years, the French, who had been in Indochina less than 100 years, merited even less sympathy from the Americans. But for reasons of its European policy, Washington met the pleas of the Lao Issara with silence.

Souvanna Phouma believed that an important value of these contacts was that they compelled the French to take cognizance of the exiled leaders and their sentiments. He gave the French, who were ignoring the promulgation of the Provisional Constitution of October 12, 1945, an opportunity to advance an acceptable compromise.

Meanwhile, in Vientiane, in June, 1946, the French had set up a Franco-Lao joint commission to discuss the future relations between metropolitan France and its Lao Protectorate. This commission produced a document confirming the existence of a unified Laos under the sovereignty of the King of Luang Prabang but retaining all the French political, military, and economic powers over the Kingdom. These went so far as to allow the French to appoint administrators in each province. Laos became a member of the Indochinese Federation, a grouping without real autonomy created by the French in concession to the awakened nationalist aspirations of the peoples of Indochina. Elections were to be held within the year for a Constituent Assembly; in fifty-three years, this provision was the first concrete step by the French toward preparing the Lao for self-rule. The *modus vivendi* was signed by Crown Prince Savang Vatthana on August 27, 1946.

The French position in Vientiane was strengthened by the collaboration of Prince Boun Oum na Champassak, the heir to the throne of the defunct Kingdom of Champassak. Preferring the French as overlords to the Viet Minh and fearing that the latter's influence would grow in an anti-French guerrilla war, Boun Oum had organized anti-Japanese resistance in southern Laos in support of the Free French after the Japanese coup of March 9, 1945. In a protocol to the *modus vivendi,* Boun Oum's title of Chao (Prince) was confirmed and made hereditary, and he was named Inspector General of the Kingdom for life; in return, he renounced his sovereign rights over Champassak.

The French further bolstered their position by restoring to Laos, on January 19, 1947, the territories annexed by Thailand in 1941. France achieved this by taking advantage of the Bangkok government's desire to obtain membership in the United Nations and efface the stain of its collaboration with the Japanese.[9]

The *modus vivendi* of August 27, 1946, was totally unacceptable to the Lao Issara, who made further attempts before the year was out to obtain a French grant of total independence for Laos. Their hopes now rested largely on Baron Patrick Surcouf, an aristocrat who had returned to postwar Indochina as a businessman and who had great sympathy for the Lao. Through the good offices of Major Thompson, a meeting of the Breton baron and the Lao Issara leaders was brought about in November in Bangkok. At its conclusion, Surcouf assured the Lao leaders he would explain their point

[9] A commission composed of representatives of the United States, Britain, Peru, and the two disputant governments later reviewed the legality of territorial claims along the Mekong and found in favor of France on all counts. The text of the commission's report may be found in *Documentation Française* (Paris), No. 811, January 23, 1948.

of view to the French authorities in Saigon and return to see them again ten days later. However, Surcouf met an unsympathetic response in Saigon and was unable to return to Bangkok. Instead, the staff of the French High Commissioner, Vice Admiral Thierry d'Argenlieu, in no mood to deal with the pretenders to leadership of an independence movement in Laos, waited until the following March and then dispatched another man, who, predictably, achieved nothing in the way of reconciling the Lao Issara leaders.

Growth of Viet Minh Influence

Souphanouvong was beginning to pay more serious attention to his post of Commander in Chief of the Lao Issara forces and to the anti-French tribal-resistance organizers allied with the Viet Minh, whose activities showed signs of bearing fruit.

From the feeling of excitement that he generates even today in discussing these early, organized guerrilla activities against the French, it is evident that Souphanouvong threw himself wholeheartedly into the work; he has always preferred the outdoors to the office desk.

Soon he was making monthly trips into Laos to supervise directly the fight against the French. As a result of his efforts to forge them into an effective guerrilla movement, his followers in the field became skilled at ambushing French convoys and attacking French garrisons from mountain hideouts along the Thai border. Although the Lao Issara attacks were never as dangerous as those that the Viet Minh were beginning to mount in the Red River Delta, they proved a source of constant worry and annoyance to the French.

The Lao Issara guerrillas set up their own primitive arms workshops, using scrap metal taken from wrecked cars and trucks. One man working by himself could, if he was dexterous enough, fashion a crude rifle in a month's time. Souphanouvong's "factories" also turned out tools for the peasants. Out of plant material, women in villages controlled by the Lao Issara made paper to be used for propaganda purposes; one girl could produce about 10,000 pages a month. Batteries and tobacco had to be purchased across the Mekong, but except for this, the Lao Issara were virtually self-sufficient.

Their guerrilla activities in the countryside considerably hampered voting for the Constituent Assembly provided for in the *modus vivendi* of August 27, 1946. Nevertheless, forty-four delegates were elected on December 15, 1946. Over the next few months these delegates worked out, under French supervision, a constitution that gave Laos a spurious independence bound up with yet another organization evolved in Paris, the French Union.

The Lao Issara's ability to survive and even grow despite armed repression by the French was due in no small share to the untiring efforts of the anonymous Viet Minh cadres, who held key advisory posts. This Vietnamese contingent was fully aware that by tying down French forces in Laos it was reducing French efforts to put down the rebellion in Vietnam.

The French posed a grave threat for Ho's young republic. It was even conceivable that all-out war could develop between his armed partisans and the returning French forces. The more the French evidenced their determination to reoccupy Indochina, the more Ho felt the necessity of preserving the gains so far made. As a result, he negotiated an accommodation with the French, the *modus vivendi* of March 6, 1946. Under its terms, France recognized the republic as a "Free State having its own government, parliament, army and treasury, and belonging to the Indochinese Federation and to the French Union." In return, the French agreed to debark a certain number of their troops at specified locations in Tonkin to replace the Chinese Nationalist army of occupation (which, under the terms of the Potsdam agreement, had received the Japanese surrender in all Indochina north of the Sixteenth Parallel). But Ho also extracted the pledge that the French troops were to be progressively withdrawn over a five-year period.

Nonetheless, an escalating frequency of incidents between the French and the Viet Minh occurred toward the end of the year. Alarm spread among the official French community in Tonkin, and voices were raised for the adoption of a "hard line" toward the Viet Minh. The irrevocable split came in December, when barricades were thrown up and blood was spilled in the streets of Hanoi and Haiphong. The Viet Minh staged a withdrawal of their forces from the Red River Delta into the mountains.

"Negotiations with Ho Chi Minh are henceforth ruled out," declared Admiral d'Argenlieu, a man who had spent much of the period between world wars as a Carmelite monk and who entertained fixed ideas about the handling of colonial matters.[10] It was to be more than seven years before the French again negotiated with Ho, and by that time he would not trouble to attend the negotiations himself but send subordinates to approve the terms of the French surrender.

[10] *France-Soir* (Paris), January 2, 1947.

The failure of the *modus vivendi* in Vietnam convinced Souphanouvong that nothing could be gained by negotiating with the French. They understood only one language: force of arms.

The Viet Minh assiduously encouraged Souphanouvong in this belief. Through their official representative in Bangkok, Nguyen Duc Quy, who saw Souphanouvong constantly, and through their well-placed advisers within the Lao Issara field organization, they exploited the Prince's isolation from Western sympathy and support.

The growing Viet Minh influence over Souphanouvong was eroding the unity of purpose with which the three princely brothers had begun their campaign of pressure against the French. Souvanna Phouma, dubious of the wisdom of Souphanouvong's leaning on the Viet Minh, was coming to look more favorably upon what the French were doing in Laos.

In Vientiane, the Constitution worked out by the Constituent Assembly was promulgated by King Sisavang Vong on May 11, 1947, the second Constitution he had promulgated in slightly more than a year. Its terms allowed Laos less real independence than the first. The preamble to the 1947 Constitution proclaimed the unity of the Lao provinces in a constitutional monarchy and declared Laos to be an independent state within the French Union. This entity had been created by the French Constitution of 1946 to give a voice to France's overseas territories. In fact, the French Union strongly underrepresented the peoples of the overseas territories in relation to the population of metropolitan France, and never gained any influence over the National Assembly or the French Government.

Laos now comprised twelve provinces: Phong Saly, Nam Tha, Luang Prabang, Sam Neua, Xieng Khouang, Sayaboury, Vientiane, Khammouane, Savannakhet, Saravane, Attopeu, and Champassak. (In the summer of 1963, subdivisions in a number of these provinces resulted in the formation of four additional provinces: Borikhane, Wapikanthong, Sedone, and Sithandone.)

The thirty-three deputies who constituted Laos' first National Assembly gathered in inaugural session on November 26, 1947, and proceeded to invest a government under the new Constitution. Prince Souvannarath, a member of the Constituent Assembly from Luang Prabang, was named by the King to form the first "independent" government. The National Assembly's most important order of business in this parliamentary apprenticeship was to ratify the application of Prince Souvannarath's government for formal entry into the French Union. On the final day of the session, March 25, 1948,

CHINA

Ou Neua
PHONG
• Lai Chau
SALY
Meng
La   • Phong Saly   NORTH VIETNAM
Muong
Sing   Sop Nao   Dien Bien
Phu
Nam Tha   • Son La
BURMA   NAM THA   Muong Sai   Muong Het   Hanoi
Ban Houei   Ban Nam   Xieng Khô   Haiphong
Sai   Bac
LUANG PRABANG   Sam Neua
Pak Hou   SAM NEUA
Luang Prabang   XIENG
Kiu Ka Cham   KHOUANG   GULF OF
Sala Phou   Ban Liang • Ban Ban
Sayaboury   Khoun   Phong   Khang   Nong Het   TONKIN
Muong   Savan   Khay
Kassy   Xieng Khouang   • Cua Rao
Padong
Vang Vieng   Tha
SAYABOURY   Ban   Thom
Ban Hin   Namone   BORIKHANE
Heup   Paksane   Vinh
VIENTIANE   Nape
Pak Lay   Kam Keut
Vientiane   KHAMMOUANE
Nong Khai   Nhommarat
• Udorn   Mahaxay
Thakhek
THAILAND   Muong   Tchepone
Séno   Phalane
Savannakhet   Muong Phine   Hué

0 25 50 75 100 125 150   SAVANNAKHET
miles   SARAVANE
WAPIKHANTHONG • Saravane
• Ubol
SEDONE   ATTOPEU
• Korat   Pakse
CHAMPASSAK   Attopeu
SITHANDONE
• Khong

• Bangkok
GULF
OF   CAMBODIA
SIAM

Map 2.   Political Subdivisions of Laos

the deputies heard a lecture by the French *commissaire,* who paid tribute to their good will but warned them against "a certain tendency to confuse legislative with executive powers."[11]

The French, because of their growing need to maintain a quiet rear area during their military operations against the Viet Minh, granted more substantial independence to Laos in July, 1949. A Franco-Lao General Convention accorded Vientiane greater latitude in foreign affairs, including the right to apply for membership in the United Nations. Laos was to have its own Territorial army, but it was to be pooled with other French Union forces under a French commander in chief. The convention granting this independence, such as it was, was signed in an elaborate ceremony by Sisavang Vong at the Elysée Palace in Paris. For the first time, the royal flag of Laos, a white, three-headed elephant on a red field, was unfurled in the French capital.

The French were by now in serious difficulties, however, because they had failed to quell the Viet Minh rebellion by quick and decisive military counteraction. From all available indications, the rebel organization was growing stronger day by day. Sensing that greater strength lay on the Viet Minh side, Souphanouvong urged his brother not to collaborate with the French.

But Souvanna Phouma found the compromise acceptable and, against the advice of his two brothers, decided to join the King in Paris, where he was welcomed by the French.

Determined to go it alone with his guerrilla organization, and assured of Viet Minh support, Souphanouvong had established as early as February, 1949, a separate political front for the Lao Issara guerrilla army he commanded. He called this the Progressive People's Organization. By May, the split within the Lao Issara had become irrevocable. Souphanouvong was removed from his ministerial and military posts in the Lao Issara government. In Bangkok, on October 24, 1949, the Lao Issara announced its dissolution, and the following month a French transport plane brought Souvanna Phouma and twenty-five of the more moderate Lao Issara leaders back to Vientiane.

By the end of 1949, the only colonial territories remaining in Southeast Asia except for Indochina were Malaya, Singapore, the British Borneo territories, West New Guinea, and Portuguese Timor. The Philippines, Burma, India and Pakistan, and Indonesia had all regained their independence from European rule. The successful Communist revolution in China coincided with the upsurge of the

11 *Bulletin d'Information de la France d'Outre-Mer,* May, 1948.

nationalist revolution in Indochina. The United States correctly saw that French concessions to the Indochinese peoples' aspirations for independence were the only means of defusing the rebellion and preventing its being taken over by the Communists. The State Department welcomed and encouraged the modest French steps toward granting independence to Indochina, although some American officials on the spot were convinced that these steps were too insignificant to be effective.

On January 14, 1950, from his mountain redoubt in Tonkin, Ho Chi Minh appealed to all foreign powers to recognize his republic. The appeal was taken up by the newly installed Communist government in Peking, and a few days later by Moscow. To demonstrate its desire to see self-determination put into effect in the countries of Indochina, the United States on February 7 announced its recognition of the French-sponsored, indigenous governments in Vientiane, Phnom Penh, and Saigon. Word of recognition was transmitted from the American Consul General in Saigon to the Vientiane government, now headed by Prince Boun Oum. But nearly five years were to pass before a resident American Minister, Charles W. Yost, arrived in Laos.

The following month, the United States dispatched a mission to Saigon to explore the possibility of granting economic assistance to the three governments. The mission discovered that the French were reluctant to allow the three supposedly independent governments to negotiate directly with the United States for economic aid and were completely unwilling to allow them to receive arms directly from the United States. A series of defeats by the Viet Minh in northern Tonkin in early 1950 reinforced French determination not to allow moves by the governments they sponsored to interfere with their prosecution of the war against the Viet Minh. And the French assured American observers that the war would be brought to a successful conclusion if only the United States furnished France the wherewithal.

A subsequent American mission was sent to Indochina to negotiate military and economic aid. It found that it was compelled to make serious compromises between aid for the U.S.-recognized governments of Laos, Cambodia, and Vietnam, and aid for the French in their war against the rebels. The mission achieved some bilateral arrangements, involving only the United States and the recipient country, in economic aid; these concerned outright grants of materials, which were not consigned through French intermediaries. However, the use of commercial imports to generate a counterpart fund of local currency, a successful technique of the Marshall Plan, played into France's hands. Payments for goods were critically affected by the exchange rates of the local currencies, and these rates in all three countries were controlled by France, which thus in effect exercised a veto over such aid.

In these negotiations, the exact relationship of the indigenous governments to France under the French Union became of capital importance, because its statutes stipulated that all agreements with foreign powers must be approved by its High Council. But this relationship was uncertain, as the French Union was even then the subject of protracted discussions in France. It became clear that, given the combination of French stalling in Indochina and the rapid succession of unstable ministries in the Fourth Republic, little progress was being made to implement Secretary of State Dean Acheson's statement that "It must be the policy of the United States to support free peoples."[12] The misgivings were made specific by the Far East Program Director of the Economic Cooperation Administration in a briefing he gave Acheson on May 2, in which he urged that the United States make an effort to find out from the French their exact plans for the Indochinese states and the role of the French Union in this: "These conditions have never been defined, and no one knows what the French Union means." And the Pau agreements, signed by France and the Associated States in November, 1950, did little to clarify the exact nature of the independence of the latter.

In Laos, the negotiations for economic aid ended in an agreement signed on September 9, 1951, by the government of Phoui Sananikone, which had succeeded that of Prince Boun Oum, and the American chargé d'affaires ad interim in Vientiane, Paul L. Guest. This agreement was to remain the basis for American aid to Laos for years to come.

The web of French control still extended everywhere, however. The endless discussions in France about the position of the Associated States, as Laos, Cambodia, and Vietnam were called, and about the future of the French Union were painfully slow in arriving at the complicated machinery that would shift administrative responsibility to the indigenous governments, and even more time was required to set it in motion. Gradually, however, the French handed over a number of administrative functions, namely those embracing foreign trade, communications, customs, finance, and immigration. Complicated interstate committees were established, on most of which the French retained an advisory or actual voting role.

[12] Department of State Bulletin, March 23, 1950, pp. 534–35.

Criticism that the American aid program was not fulfilling the policy objective of hastening the development of free and independent governments in the Indochinese states was met by reassurances by American officials that the French were on the verge of gaining the upper hand in the military situation and the United States must do nothing that might possibly undermine the French war effort. Also, it was pointed out, the French had primary responsibility in Indochina and the United States was not involved in the military conflict.

After the Communist attack on South Korea, Washington adopted the French line that the Indochina War was part of a common effort to contain Communist expansion. The anti-Communist emphasis was used periodically to justify to Congress the allocation of millions of dollars in military aid to the French in Indochina.

On the Fourth of July, 1950, Ho Chi Minh made what was to be his last direct appeal to the American people to "condemn the French colonial war waged under the aegis of the American government." There was no response to this appeal, as the United States found itself more and more deeply involved in the French war effort.

Negotiations for American military aid had been concluded in Saigon to the satisfaction of the French, and the first shipments of arms and ammunition began to flow in. On December 23, the United States concluded a quadripartite mutual-defense agreement that allowed deliveries to the governments of Laos, Cambodia, and non-Communist Vietnam but named the Commander in Chief of French forces in the Far East as the controlling authority for all material destined for the French Union forces fighting in Indochina. A clause prohibited the "illegal transport" of American war material out of Indochina; little of it did leave Indochina, but much of it ended up in Viet Minh hands and later became part of the basic arsenal of the Communist state of North Vietnam.

In Laos, Phoui Sananikone was succeeded as head of government in November, 1951, by Prince Souvanna Phouma. Although it was obvious that the continued French stranglehold on Laos was intolerable to the dissident Lao Issara leaders who had not returned to Vientiane, he nevertheless optimistically announced that his most immediate domestic goal was to achieve a "national union." If he could persuade his half brother to join him, the chances of freeing his government from French domination would be greater.

In response to continued pressures in the Associated States for genuine independence, the French Government on July 3, 1953, declared its intention to invite their representatives to another round of negotiations.

In contrast to vague promises, the true nature of the French motives was revealed by an exchange three weeks later at a meeting of the National Defense Committee in Paris presided over by the President of the Republic. At this meeting, Marshal Alphonse Juin proposed that the defense of Laos be entrusted to the Ministry of Foreign Affairs, which should then formally notify other foreign powers of Laos' vulnerability to Viet Minh invasion, and seek to obtain from the United States and Britain a guarantee of the territorial integrity of Laos and a warning to the Soviet Union and Communist China that such an invasion would entail dangerous consequences. Marshal Juin's proposal was not acted upon. The thought of extricating Laos from the web of ministries and subministries responsible "for relations with the Associated States" and making its territorial integrity the responsibility of an international body was repugnant to the French Government. A major share of the cost of the war was already being borne by the United States, in any case.

Fed up with French stalling on the question of independence, Souvanna Phouma on August 24, 1953, formally requested the transfer to his government of all the services that the French still retained control of, most immediately those connected with civil aviation, meteorology, fuel supplies, and border policing. Negotiations began in Paris on October 15, and a week later produced a Treaty of Amity and Association between France and Laos.

The first article proclaimed, "The French Republic recognizes and declares that the Kingdom of Laos is a fully independent and sovereign State." The second affirmed Laos' membership in the French Union, "an association of independent and sovereign peoples, with freedom and equality of rights and duties, in which all the associates place in common their resources in order to guarantee the defense of the Union as a whole." Certainly this can be interpreted to mean that France was obligated to do everything possible to defend Laos in the event of invasion.

Laos was now on the way to nationhood. But next door in Vietnam, the Viet Minh were fighting a war for independence from France. Inevitably, Laos must be caught up in this conflict.

3.

Collective Diplomacy

France did not purposefully embark upon the Indochina War. Instead, with little comprehension of the nationalist forces it sought to subdue, France undertook a police action and found itself helplessly sliding into a disastrous war without front that was to last for eight enormously costly years. The original reasons for fighting the "police action" soon became confused with such causes as the honor of the French Expeditionary Corps and the crusade against Communism. Eventually, the French goal was just to hang on.

The Viet Minh quickly revealed the efficiency of their machine and their ability to exploit issues to arouse popular support. Their organization derived from a congress of Vietnamese nationalist factions held in the south China town of Chingsi in May, 1941. The meeting had been dominated by a bearded revolutionary, Nguyen Ai Quoc, who had spent lengthy periods in Paris and Moscow. At a Comintern congress he had expressed the Leninist viewpoint on the revolutionary potential of the peasantry in underdeveloped countries, and he had been sent by that body to China in 1925. In 1930, he had become a founding member of the Indochinese Communist Party.

Out of the Chingsi congress had emerged a coalition called the League for Vietnamese Independence, or the Viet Nam Doc Lap Dong Minh Hoi, later to be known as the Viet Minh. Nguyen Ai Quoc adopted the pseudonym Ho Chi Minh, "He Who Enlightens," and he and his followers infiltrated back into Tonkin in 1944. There, they joined forces with a young history professor named Vo Nguyen Giap, who had been organizing partisan activities for the Viet Minh since 1942. Giap's guerrillas had already acquired a sizable arsenal of modern weapons, partly through ambushes of

French patrols and partly as rewards from the Japanese for spying and other forms of cooperation.

When the Japanese surrender came, Ho, Giap, and their partisans moved rapidly into Hanoi, and there, on September 2, 1945, from the balcony of the town hall, they proclaimed the republic. In the war that followed the breakdown of the *modus vivendi* between the Viet Minh and the French, the Viet Minh viewed Laos operationally as an extension of their battlefield against the French in Tonkin, Annam, and Cochinchina. A brief review of the engagements of the Indochina War that affected Laos directly is necessary here.

By the winter of 1952–53, the Viet Minh had consolidated their hold on the northern tier of provinces bordering China and were in a position to turn their attention to western Tonkin and to Laos, which was garrisoned by only 12,000 Lao Territorials and 3,000 French troops under command of Colonel Boucher de Crèvecoeur. In preparation for a spring offensive, Viet Minh guerrillas infiltrated into Laos, gathering intelligence and buying up stocks of rice that they cached along the trails leading southwest from the Tonkin border. At the same time, they sounded out tribal chiefs on their loyalties and obtained the allegiance of a small but important group of Lao agents.

The Viet Minh launched their offensive with two prongs. The first prong, comprising fifteen battalions drawn from the 308th, 312th, and 316th divisions, approached Sam Neua town in early April, 1953. The French and Lao defenders, only three battalions strong, received warning of the advancing larger forces and began withdrawing southward toward the Plain of Jars, of strategic military value because of its command of road communications in northern Laos.

Encountering no resistance, the Viet Minh entered the town of Sam Neua. There, assisted by their Lao agents, they conducted a public "trial" before a "people's tribunal" of the acting Governor of the province and the district officer of Xieng Kho, who were charged with treason because they had helped the French organize partisan resistance to the invaders. The two officials were quickly found guilty and summarily executed before a large crowd of spectators.

Meanwhile, the retreating French column, with only a half day's start on its pursuers, was struggling along a pony track through the spiny bamboo thickets, forests of wild banana trees or oaks, and arid plateaus between Sam Neua and the Plain of Jars.

About fifty miles from the Plain of Jars airfield, the Viet Minh caught up with the retreating column and staged an attack that scattered its men. Only 230 of them—one-third of the French effectives—survived the march and managed to reach the Plain. The airfield and surrounding defenses had in the meantime been reinforced by airborne troops and artillery and the pulling in of troops, including many Meo, from dozens of tiny outposts in Xieng Khouang Province.

The smaller prong of the Viet Minh offensive, consisting of five crack battalions, had departed from the region of Dien Bien Phu and were advancing toward Luang Prabang by the valley of the Hou River, a tributary of the Mekong. They captured Ban Nam Bac, and on April 28, when they were some thirty miles from the royal capital, linked up with part of the column that had captured Sam Neua.

Inside the royal capital of Luang Prabang, the French were hastily reinforcing their garrison. A blind bonze, renowned for his ability to predict events, declared that the Viet Minh would not enter Luang Prabang. The bonze's word spread rapidly. The King rejected French recommendations that he and his retinue be flown to Vientiane, and firmly announced he would remain in the Royal Palace. His son, Crown Prince Savang Vatthana, underscored his father's determination to stay by driving slowly around the town in his blue Chrysler for all to see. In expectation of the worst, all the Chinese shopkeepers locked up their establishments, but the Lao went about without sign of panic.[1]

By the first days of May, the Viet Minh had advanced to within striking distance of Luang Prabang by leaving behind their porters with their heavy mortars, ammunition, and food reserves. But then one of their advance companies fell into a French ambush seven and a half miles north of the capital, suffering about thirty casualties. Perhaps influenced by this indication of French preparedness or by the imminence of the annual monsoon season, the Viet Minh suddenly withdrew. Two days later the monsoon broke with a violent thunderstorm, and the torrential rains began, making impossible any large-scale fighting in the mountain country. Luang Prabang was saved—at least for the time being.

The Viet Minh troops in Sam Neua Province were reinforced by the arrival of the 304th Division up the Route Coloniale 7. They briefly occupied Tha Thom in Xieng Khouang Province on the upper Sane River, a Mekong tributary, but made no serious effort

[1] Henri Deydier, *Lokapâla* (Paris: Plon, 1954), pp. 164–65.

to dislodge the French from their fortified complex on the Plain of Jars. The French Foreign Legion had spent the few days before the arrival of the Viet Minh buying up the opium crop, which had just been harvested, to undercut a possible reason for the invasion.

After the monsoon season, at the end of 1953, a second threat to Laos materialized far to the south. A Viet Minh force, consisting of a division and a regiment, crossed the Annamite Mountains and, by a series of forest trails, advanced westward. They reached the Mekong on December 28 and occupied Thakhek. The French flew in reinforcements to the near-by base of Séno, and within a few days the Viet Minh abandoned Thakhek and dispersed into the hills of southern Laos, where they undertook extensive propaganda and indoctrination work among the mountain tribes. Some of them regrouped and crossed into Cambodia.

In November, 1953, the French had reoccupied, by paratroop landings, the flat-bottomed "bowl" of Dien Bien Phu, ten and one half miles long and three miles wide, transforming it into an armed camp. The French were compelled to protect Laos from invasion under the mutual-defense treaty of October 22, 1953, but at the same time the French commander in Indochina, General Henri Navarre, was under instructions not to take any action that would jeopardize the French Expeditionary Corps. Occupation of a position on the traditional Laos invasion route from which sorties could be effected against the Viet Minh seemed to comply with both conditions.

But by January, 1954, the garrison at Dien Bien Phu was all but encircled. With alarming rapidity, thirty-three battalions had occupied all the surrounding high ground, and an intricate maze of trenches had been pushed to within hailing distance of the barbed wire of the French fortifications. At the beginning of February, General Giap had completed the positioning of his batteries of 105-mm. guns, hauled by coolie labor into camouflaged emplacements on the crests overlooking the valley. He then detached the 308th Division on what he later described as a diversionary expedition toward Luang Prabang.[2] Once again, the hard-pressed air transport command of the French Expeditionary Corps flew reinforcements to Luang Prabang, and again the Viet Minh redoubled their tracks up the Hou River.

In all their operations in Laos, the Viet Minh held the initiative, fighting the war on their own terms. Never once did they allow

[2] Jules Roy, *La Bataille de Dien Bien Phu* (Paris: Julliard, 1963), p. 162.

themselves to be engaged in a full-scale confrontation in which French air supremacy or firepower superiority might be brought to bear. If the French had evacuated a town, as in the case of Sam Neua, the Viet Minh occupied it. If the French had prepared a positional stand, as at Luang Prabang on two occasions, the Viet Minh either retreated or rapidly bypassed the entrenched garrison.

The decision by the French to engage the enemy at Dien Bien Phu was systematic military thinking carried to its most pernicious extreme. When French forces in pursuit of the Viet Minh bands left the lowlands of the Red River Delta and ventured into northern and western Tonkin, they rapidly learned that the old plains system of scattered outposts manned by a platoon or less was hopeless in the mountains. These small forts could be easily picked off, one by one, in night guerrilla raids before reinforcements could be dispatched.

Following what seemed to be a logical train of thought, the French High Command decided to retain their "presence" in the Tonkin highlands by fortifying a smaller number of strongly entrenched camps, to be known as *bases aéroterrestres*. Each would be defended by several large units supported by heavy firepower and supplied by aircraft from the Red River Delta. Each would be a "hedgehog," whose bristling defenses would throw back an attacker with great casualties and without gain. That was the theory.

Accordingly, the French in 1953 had devoted considerable effort to setting up highland bases at Na San and Lai Chau. However, the French High Command consistently underestimated the Viet Minh ability to muster combat formations and engage in protracted hostilities in the rugged mountain country. Already, by August, 1953, the growing menace of Viet Minh encirclement had compelled the French to evacuate Na San. A few weeks later, Lai Chau was abandoned. Thus, at Dien Bien Phu, the French Expeditionary Corps had knowingly committed its best troops to defend a fortress hundreds of air miles from their main sources of supply and completely cut off from ground communications, at the very time the evidence pointed to the folly of such tactics.

The Viet Minh never had any doubt about winning the battle of Dien Bien Phu. They fired the first salvo from the slopes overlooking the entrenched camp with the keen awareness that they had caught the French in a deadly trap. When their fighters overran the entrenched camp, pock-marked from months of intensive mortar and artillery bombardment, there was no surprise, only shock that the French High Command had committed such an enormous error.

"People's War"

The Viet Minh victory would not have been possible without the support of the civilian population in the mountains of Tonkin and the thousands of laborers who kept the fighting men fed and supplied despite French harassment. General Giap, in an interview with Franco Calamandrei published in the Italian Communist Party newspaper *Unità* on April 21, 1954, when the trap had already been closed on the French and the chancelleries of Paris, Washington, and London were wringing their hands over the imminent disaster, declared: "We know that the struggle will still be a hard one, but we are not afraid that American air power will provide a decisive factor in this battle. The basic error committed by the imperialists has been, once again, to neglect the effort of which a people fighting for its independence is capable."

In Giap's view, the Viet Minh victory at Dien Bien Phu was the culmination of years of patient preparation. During this time, the enemy's will to resist had been imperceptibly sapped by a never-ending series of pinpricks. Meanwhile, the peasant masses had been rendered harmless to the Viet Minh cause by the constant attentions of the Viet Minh political propagandizers and organizers. Giap contends that if one is opposed by the mass of the people, nothing can be achieved; if one has their sympathy, much can be achieved; and if one attains their active collaboration, that is the best of all.

A Vietnamese who fought with the Viet Minh and later became a high civil servant in Saigon revealed that the political commissars of military units recruited from the local population had specific orders to make the commanders leave behind their wounded in retreat, even though they would certainly be massacred by French gunfire. The reason for this was simple: for each dead Viet Minh recruit, there would be, next day, five new recruits from the same village—the family of the dead man.

The Viet Minh pressed into service thousands of peasants. In groups and columns of a hundred or more, they transported rice over forest trails to feed the Viet Minh army; by moonlight and starlight, they filled in craters dug by French bombs in Viet Minh-controlled roads; finally, they hauled Viet Minh artillery pieces into positions from which they could rain down a hail of devastating fire on the incredulous French. Singly, the peasants poled rafts across rivers to transport Viet Minh matériel after the French bombed out the bridges, or housed couriers during the daylight hours when no one dared move for fear of attracting a strafing plane, or gathered intelligence on enemy operations for the Viet Minh High Command, deep in its jungle fastness. They did not do all this because they were highly paid; they were, in most cases, paid nothing. They did it because they had been persuaded that they were helping to fight for a just cause.

The war waged for eight years against the French began with small operations by a platoon or company and developed into battalion or regimental operations. "It was this process of development," Giap observes, "that enabled our army to move forward steadily on the road to victory."

He writes about a war of long duration and a war that places a premium on mobility. Giap is concerned with the mobility of the single jungle soldier, recruited from the local peasantry, armed with a crude rifle (perhaps even homemade), camouflaged with a Latania palm hat, and observing all the rules of cover and concealment that he has learned by heart, bearing enough rice to tide him over between villages. In concert with other men equally mobile and well trained, the guerrilla might successfully mount a predawn attack on a lonely outpost and capture a handful of modern rifles. Right then and there, the war would have undergone an evolution escalation comparable to that from a soldier armed with a pike to one armed with an English longbow.

"Guerrilla war is the war of the broad masses of an economically backward country standing up against a powerfully equipped and well-trained army of aggression," Giap writes.

"Is the enemy strong? One avoids him. Is he weak? One attacks him. To his modern armament one opposes a boundless heroism to vanquish either by harassing or by annihilating the enemy according to the circumstances, then by combining military operations with political and economic actions; no fixed line of demarcation, the front being wherever the enemy is found."

This analysis of the war where the front is nowhere and yet everywhere was successfully put to the test against the French Expeditionary Corps of 350,000 men, between 1946 and 1954.

Extent of American Involvement

As the Indochina War dragged on, going from bad to worse for the French, the United States found itself paying a greater and greater share of the cost. The amount spent by the United States is variously estimated, but a reliable figure is $954 million.[3] Most of this cost was borne in the closing months of the war; by September, 1953, the United States was estimated to be paying for fully 70 per cent of the cost of the war.[4] A State Department report dated August, 1953, lists the following war matériel supplied the French Union Forces in Indochina: 170 million rounds of small-arms ammunition, 16,000 transport vehicles and trailers, 850 combat vehicles, 350 military planes, 250 naval craft, 10,500 radio sets, and 90,000 small arms.[5] In response to repeated French requests, the United States agreed toward the end of January, 1954, to send 200 ground personnel to Indochina to assist the hard-pressed French in repairing and maintaining aircraft. When the cease-fire was signed in Geneva, in July, American aid worth $25 million was aboard ships bound for Indochina.

When defeat came to the French forces despite this massive support, the United States experienced profound shock. Secretary of State Dulles unjustly received much of the blame for the unhappy juncture in which the Administration found itself. He was blamed, on the one hand, for failing to "do something" to prevent the Communists from acquiring their first satellite since Czechoslovakia in 1948 and, on the other hand, for causing our allies concern that the United States' overwhelming military power might be launched without consultation on a sledgehammer-against-fly mission that would risk plunging the world into a nuclear holocaust.

The truth is not so simple. The Administration of which Dulles was a key figure had been voted into office barely two years before on a foreign-policy platform that condemned the Democratic Party for its handling of the China issue—specifically accusing it of having "denied the military aid that had been authorized by Congress and which was crucially needed if China were to be saved."

Now, if the Administration had denied military aid to the French in Indochina, it would stand accused of letting another Asian country fall, by default, to the Communists. Moreover, there was McCarthyism, with its imputations of "softness" on the issue of the Communist threat to American security. Its favorite target was, of course, the State Department. These imputations served to reduce further the already narrow field of maneuver on which the State Department normally operates in dealing with foreign countries.

[3] Fall, *The Two Viet-Nams,* p. 458n.
[4] *Financial Times* (London), September 11, 1953.
[5] *The New York Times,* August 19, 1953.

The Debate on Intervention

An important section of the military led by Admiral Arthur Radford, the Chairman of the Joint Chiefs of Staff, increasingly identified the Indochina War with centralized Communist planning in Moscow and Peking. The French, in this view, were fighting to defend the free world, to hold back the yellow hordes of Communist-indoctrinated peasant guerrillas bent on conquering all of Asia —first China, then Vietnam, and which country next? The analogy of a line of falling dominoes was used to illustrate the danger confronting the American defense system based on a chain of islands from Japan to Formosa and the Philippines. It was argued that intervention to meet the threat, either alone or in concert, was preferable to a negotiated surrender. As *The New York Times* put it in a dispatch printed on May 2, the Radford school argued that there should be "no agreement to cease firing or to an armistice or to any settlement that will permit the Communist Viet Minh to build up their strength and resume fighting more effectively later." The article concluded that "In essence, any solution in Indochina short of outright military defeat of the Viet Minh rebels is opposed by the men responsible for the military security of the United States."

In a speech to the Overseas Press Club in New York on March 29, Dulles himself suggested that unspecified forceful measures might be necessitated by the fighting in Indochina:

> Under the conditions of today, the imposition on Southeast Asia of the political system of Communist Russia and its Chinese Communist ally, by whatever means, must be a grave threat to the whole free community. The United States feels that that possibility should not be passively accepted but should be met by united action. This might involve serious risks. But these risks are far less than those that will face us a few years from now if we dare not be resolute today.[6]

Four days later, Dulles and Radford met with a bipartisan group of Congressional leaders and apparently put to them the idea of United States intervention in Indochina. There was no official report on that meeting, but the most likely speculation is that Dulles and Radford proposed that Congress adopt a joint resolution to permit the President to use American forces in Indochina. John W. McCormack, the minority whip in the House of Representatives, was present, and several weeks later said that there had been talk of a mass air attack on the besiegers of Dien

[6] Department of State Bulletin, April 12, 1954, p. 540.

Bien Phu[7] and a proposal that the leaders in the Congress "commit ourselves in Indochina without any assistance from any other country."[8]

At any rate, Dulles immediately set about building at top speed a coalition for intervention. He proposed to President Eisenhower that Britain be persuaded to join the United States, France, and friendly Asian nations in committing ground troops to fight the Communist forces in Indochina; if this intervention triggered the dispatch of troops by the Chinese in support of the Viet Minh, American air power would retaliate by destroying staging bases in south China. Eisenhower approved Dulles' proposal and cabled it to British Prime Minister Winston Churchill and Foreign Secretary Anthony Eden.

But there was an opposing school of thought. It held that the French were not defending the free world, but were attempting to preserve their own interests in Indochina, and that the Viet Minh were not a foreign army fighting a war of conquest but a Vietnamese army fighting for their country's independence. In this view, American intervention on the side of the French, with all the attendant risks, was not warranted.

In April, 1954, a Senate debate showed a large majority reluctant to support intervention if it meant commitment of ground troops. Senator Edwin C. Johnson summed up majority opinion in the Democratic Party by saying that he was "against sending American GI's into the mud and muck of Indochina on a bloodletting spree to perpetuate colonialism and white man's exploitation in Asia."[9] Senator John F. Kennedy quoted a report he himself had made in November, 1951: "In Indochina we have allied ourselves to the desperate effort of a French regime to hang on to the remnants of empire." He then proceeded to cite the difficulties of winning a war without popular support, and drew attention to the fact that not since the Mexican War had the United States intervened against a native population.[10]

Only a minority of Senators unequivocally endorsed intervention. William F. Knowland, the most vocal proponent of the "China Lobby," declared in an interview in early May that Indochina was vital to American security and that he was prepared to lead the Senate fight to send American forces there.[11]

[7] *The New York Times,* January 23, 1956.
[8] *Congressional Record,* February 22, 1955, p. 1655.
[9] *Ibid.,* April 19, 1954, p. 5281.
[10] *Ibid.,* April 6, 1954, pp. 4672–81.
[11] *Evening Standard* (London), May 4, 1954.

The Republicans upon coming into office had ended the Korean War. Clearly, sending American men to fight in Indochina almost immediately afterward would not be a popular step. Indeed, a Gallup poll in March, 1953, had reported 85 per cent of Americans opposed to U.S. involvement in Indochina, and Congressional mail reflected the same attitude.[12]

Within the Joint Chiefs of Staff, there was dissent from Admiral Radford's views. The Army Chief of Staff, General Matthew B. Ridgway, believed that intervention in Indochina could not succeed without committing ground troops, and that this was ruled out because the Army's overseas commitments were too much for the reduced manpower decreed by Eisenhower's "New Look" defense policy. Moreover, the malarial swamps of Indochina were an even more difficult battlefield than the hills and valleys of Korea, particularly since in Indochina it was difficult to tell friend from foe, while in South Korea the populace had been friendly. In an article published in the *Saturday Evening Post* in January, 1956, General Ridgway credited the Army's analysis of the hazards in Indochina with a considerable part in the decision against the project.

The Pentagon reportedly decided that the minimum ground force necessary would be about ten divisions, more than required in Korea. This was about half the total standing strength of the U.S. Army, six divisions of which were already committed in Europe. To support a force of this size would require a major remobilization.

Furthermore, this calculation presumed a limited and local war, on the Korean model. However, majority opinion in the Pentagon was reported to hold that such a limited intervention would be ineffectual, and that it would be essential to cut off the Viet Minh from China, their source of supply. This would probably necessitate a blockade of the China coast and destruction of the Chinese supply line. Thus, the military saw the appalling prospect that the United States would either become bogged down in a jungle war that had little prospect of decisively affecting world Communist power, or be plunged into a full-scale war involving Red China.

Secretary of the Treasury George M. Humphrey announced on May 25 that it was his hope to cut another $5 billion from expenditures during the forthcoming fiscal year. Defense Secretary Charles E. Wilson, also budget-minded, leaned in the direction of General Ridgway.

All this resulted in considerable confusion both at home and abroad. Representative McCormack, who had been privy to the debate within the Administration from the start, urged the Admin-

[12] *U.S. News & World Report,* May 7, 1954, pp. 25–26.

istration to give "to Congress and to our people some idea as to what its policy is in relation to Southeast Asia."

> The American people are confused, and I cannot blame them. When members of Congress are confused, it is only natural that our people should be. This lack of knowledge, creating uncertainty and confusion, is not confined to Democratic members alone. I have had a number of Republican members tell me they do not know where we are or where we are going.[13]

In London, the confusion in the British Government was even greater, as *The New York Times* reported on May 23:

> "You cannot ask us to agree when Cabinet ministers, senators and military leaders have not yet made up their minds about what we are to agree upon," an influential [British] official said.
>
> Ignorance of exactly what the United States wishes to do in terms of the international frontiers in Southeast Asia and its own contribution to their defense has become the principal problem facing the [British] Government.

The British, uncertain over which view had the upper hand in the councils of American policy-making, were fearful of unilateral American action in Indochina without prior consultation. But the firm British view that any action at such a late date was hopeless, and would only serve as a reckless provocation, minimized chances of any British cooperation.

Dulles has been criticized for publicly proposing united action to block aggression in Indochina before seeking French and British support. He has been accused of weakening the Western position at Geneva by going to London and Paris on the eve of the Conference to press for adoption of this policy. His efforts met with a public refusal by the British, and with a French request for immediate United States air intervention in the war, a request refused by Washington, hardly a demonstration of unity. Dulles' peculiar technique of diplomacy, which depended heavily on forceful public statements, compounded the confusion. As one account put it, "Much of what was said and done can be interpreted either as stage thunder or as a real storm brewing, and it should be borne in mind that, given Dulles' belief that loud and clear warnings may sometimes obviate the need for action, these categories are not necessarily mutually exclusive."[14]

[13] *The New York Times*, June 9, 1954.
[14] Coral Bell (ed.), *Survey of International Affairs, 1954* (London: Oxford University Press, for Royal Institute of International Affairs, 1957), pp. 25–26.

But the basic fact is that the conflicting pressures at home and abroad left Dulles, at Geneva, in a most difficult position.

At home, the Radford school talked forcefully in an effort to impress the Communists and bolster the Western bargaining position at Geneva. But the bolder this talk became, the more open were the British in their reluctance to go along with intervention and in their willingness to wait and see what developed at the Conference. And the more difficulty Dulles encountered in his efforts to secure British cooperation in "united action," the less chance he had of getting Congressional authorization to send American forces in support of the defenders of Dien Bien Phu, who were at grips with the Communists. It was a vicious circle.

Once Dien Bien Phu had fallen, the steam was let out of the great debate. Some news dispatches from Washington, obviously inspired by the State Department, even hinted that a trap had been avoided. Suspicion had been growing in Administration circles, it was reported, that Moscow or Peking would like nothing better than to get GI's committed to Indochina.

The 1954 Geneva Conference

The collapse of Dien Bien Phu was the collapse of the French effort to restore the pre-World War II *status quo* in Indochina by force. It could not be done with the resources at France's disposal, and the Americans, after lengthy and heated debate on the subject, were not going to help the French do it, after all. In May, 1954, therefore, delegates assembled in the gleaming white Palais des Nations in Geneva to fashion an acceptable peace.

Represented were France, the Communist-recognized state of Vietnam (the Democratic Republic of Vietnam, with Ho Chi Minh as its President), the non-Communist Associated State of Vietnam (the Republic of Vietnam, of former Emperor Bao Dai, resurrected by the French), Laos, Cambodia, the United States, Britain, Communist China, and the Soviet Union.

The Lao delegation was capably led by Phoui Sananikone, the scion of Vientiane's leading family, a civil servant since 1923, a leading member of the anti-Japanese resistance in northern Laos during World War II, and a minister in the first Lao Government to be formed in Vientiane.

Phoui was immediately confronted with the crucial necessity of defending the sovereignty of the Vientiane government against claims by Ho's representatives that a "resistance government" existed in Laos in the mountains of the northeastern provinces. Apparently in preparation for the seating of a separate Lao rebel delegation, the Viet Minh representatives had brought with them a handsome young Lao with angular features named Nouhak Phoumsavan, who was traveling on a Vietnamese passport.

Drawing attention to the rival Lao and Cambodians, the chief Viet Minh representative proposed that the Conference adopt a resolution declaring that "in the interests of the thorough and objective examination of the question of the cessation of hostilities and re-establishment of peace in Indochina, the Conference recognizes the necessity to invite the representatives of the governments of resistance of Khmer and Pathet Lao to take part in the work of the Conference in regard to the question of the re-establishment of peace in Indochina."[15]

In reply, Phoui declared that the "resistance government" in Laos represented "absolutely nothing." Recognizing such a body, he said, would mean that "all local leaders and party leaders and leaders of movements in all countries would consider they had the right to form governments and represent states."[16] For the Communists, of course, this was precisely the value of such "resistance governments."

Phoui successfully countered these claims, thanks to the stanch support of his efforts by the Western powers and to the halfhearted backing of Ho's gambit by Moscow and Peking. It was easier to set up a band of rebels in the jungle and proclaim them to be a resistance government than to gain recognition for them at an international conference. Recognition came with military victory, and the French still retained the upper hand in Laos. Pham Van Dong, leader of Ho's delegation, did not miss the point of the lesson.

The presence of Vietnamese soldiers in Laos and Cambodia posed a more serious problem for the Conference delegates. Early in the proceedings, the French Foreign Minister introduced the principle of regrouping foreign belligerent forces. Pham Van Dong subsequently took the position that there were no such forces in either Laos or Cambodia. However, the Chinese Foreign Minister, Chou En-lai, hinted privately to fellow delegates that the withdrawal of the Vietnamese from Laos and Cambodia should prove no insurmountable obstacle to agreement.

[15] Cmd. 9186, p. 113. For complete identification of official documents published by HMSO, London, see Bibliography.
[16] *Ibid.*, p. 116.

In the meantime, the French Government had fallen and Pierre Mendès-France, in an attempt to form a new one, had asked the National Assembly to give him until July 20 to negotiate a settlement of the Indochina War. Under this deadline, the Geneva delegates had produced by dawn on July 21 a series of agreements calling for a cease-fire in Vietnam, Laos, and Cambodia and a regrouping of belligerent forces in each country.

The agreement on Laos was signed by a French general on behalf of the commander of the French Union forces and by the Vice Minister of National Defense of the Democratic Republic of Vietnam, Ho Chi Minh's government, acting for the commander of the Viet Minh and for the commander of the army of the Lao "resistance government."

Unlike Vietnam, which was temporarily partitioned at the Seventeenth Parallel, with Ho's government in control of all territory to the north, Laos was reaffirmed as a unitary, independent state with a single government in Vientiane. The members of the forces of the Lao "resistance government" were to regroup in the two northern provinces of Sam Neua and Phong Saly pending integration into the Lao army or demobilization. The cease-fire agreement stipulated August 6 at 8 A.M. local time as the moment for hostilities to end.

From then on, introduction of fresh troops and armaments into Laos was prohibited. Within 120 days, all "Vietnamese People's Volunteers" were to be out of the country. All foreign powers except France were prohibited from establishing or maintaining bases on Lao soil. France was permitted to retain bases at Séno and at Vientiane, with a maximum effective total of 3,500 men. The French military were entrusted with training the Lao national army, and for this purpose were allowed to maintain a training mission of 1,500 officers and noncoms in Laos.

The Conference took note of two unilateral declarations by Phoui's delegation.[17] The first pledged that Laos "will never join in any agreement with other states if this agreement includes the obligation for the Royal Government of Laos to participate in a military alliance not in conformity with the principles of the Charter of the United Nations or with the principles of the agreement on the cessation of hostilities." It further stated: "During the period between the cessation of hostilities in Vietnam and the final settlement of that country's political problems, the Royal Government . . . will not request foreign aid, whether in war material, in personnel or in instructors, except for the purpose of its effective territorial de-

[17] For the texts of these declarations, see Appendix III.

fense and to the extent defined by the agreement on the cessation of hostilities."

In the second declaration, Phoui said his government "resolved to take the necessary measures to integrate all citizens, without discrimination, into the national community." Furthermore, the Royal Government would "promulgate measures to provide for special representation in the Royal Administration of the provinces of Phong Saly and Sam Neua during the interval between the cessation of hostilities and the general elections of the interests of nationals of Laos who did not support the Royal forces during hostilities."

The omission from the bilateral agreement of any details concerning how the dissidents were to be reintegrated and how the two northern provinces were to be turned back to the effective authority of the Royal Government was an advantage which the Viet Minh and their Lao agents were able to exploit in months to come.

On the other hand, the agreement left intact two important series of agreements, into which Laos had entered, with the United States and France, respectively, and which were to have considerable significance for Laos' alignment in world affairs after 1954.

The cease-fire agreement did not affect the agreements for economic and military aid negotiated by the United States and the Royal Lao Government in 1950. These agreements remained the basis of American support for the continued independence and integrity of the Vientiane government. Nor did the Geneva cease-fire abrogate the terms of the Treaty of Amity and Association between France and Laos, which obligated France to defend Laos from foreign aggression.

At the final session of the Conference, a Draft Declaration by the Conference was circulated, and the Co-Chairman, British Foreign Secretary Eden, requested the various delegates to express their views thereon. The Draft Declaration expressed the satisfaction of the participants at the conclusion of cease-fire agreements between the various belligerents, and took note of the unilateral declarations made by the Royal Government of Laos. It also stated: "In their relations with Cambodia, Laos and Vietnam, each member of the Geneva Conference undertakes to respect the sovereignty, the independence, the unity and the territorial integrity of the above-mentioned States, and to refrain from any interference in their internal affairs."[18]

[18] Text in Appendix III.

All participants except the United States and non-Communist Vietnam gave their assent to this wording. American diplomacy was torn between the need to prevent further Communist territorial gains and the need to do everything possible to avoid the commitment of American ground forces to another war on the Asian mainland. As a result of this dilemma, Secretary of State John Foster Dulles had agreed to associate the United States in an armistice agreement in Indochina only under certain conditions.

As the cease-fire agreements worked out at Geneva, particularly the provisions with respect to the political future of Vietnam, reflected the strong position the Vietnamese Communists had gained for themselves, Dulles was reluctant to associate the United States with these agreements. The agreements in effect ratified Communist control over North Vietnam, at least until general elections could be held throughout Vietnam, in July, 1956, and Dulles feared that the Viet Minh with their efficacious political network would ensure that these elections would result in the extension of Communist control to the South as well.

In response to Eden's proposed draft at the final session, after Dulles had returned to the United States, the acting chief American delegate, Undersecretary of State Walter Bedell Smith, explained that his government was "not prepared to join in a Declaration by the Conference such as is submitted," and he thereupon read a declaration of the American position. The United States took note of the various cease-fire agreements and all but the final paragraph of the Draft Declaration (which provided for future consultation among the nations represented at Geneva in case of need to ensure that the cease-fire agreements were respected); also, the United States would "refrain from the threat or the use of force to disturb" the agreements arrived at in the Conference.[19]

The chief delegate from non-Communist Vietnam expressed certain reservations about the wording of the Draft Declaration and sought to have an amendment incorporated in it. To this request, Eden replied, "We cannot now amend our final act, which is a statement of the Conference as a whole, but the declaration of the representative of the State of Vietnam will be taken note of."[20]

Mendès-France has since explained privately that a principal reason that this final document of the Conference took the form of an unsigned Declaration bearing the heading of all participating nations was precisely to avoid the issue of who would sign and who

[19] Cmd. 9239, pp. 6–7.
[20] *Ibid.*, p. 9.

wouldn't. He foresaw that if signatures were required, the United States might well not sign, and then the Chinese also would not sign.

Dulles stated, two days after the final session of the Conference, that "since the United States itself was neither a belligerent in Indochina nor subject to compulsions which applied to others, we did not become a party to the Conference results."[21] It is difficult to reconcile this statement with the declaration of the American delegate that the United States would not upset the agreements reached. Furthermore, while American spokesmen continued to hint that they did not consider the United States bound by the agreements (the Chinese never claimed they were not bound by them), the Indian Government, as Chairman of the International Control Commission set up to supervise their implementation, adopted the position that the United States, as a participant in the Conference, was bound by the agreements reached.

However, given Dulles' suspicions regarding negotiations with the Communists, it is not surprising that he sought to avoid limitations on future U.S. actions in Southeast Asia. The actions he envisaged would become more apparent in the months following the Geneva Conference.

No agreement hard-won through negotiations, such as the Geneva agreements, can be absolutely foolproof. The terms can be circumvented when it comes time to apply them. While the 1954 Geneva agreements ending the fighting in Indochina were in no sense a settlement, they nevertheless provided a mutually acceptable basis for disengaging from armed conflict. The recurrence of such conflict cannot be ascribed solely to the loopholes in the cease-fire agreements. There are also the intentions of one's antagonist, the degree to which he sees it in his interest to adhere to agreements made, and, above all perhaps, the degree to which he believes *both* sides will respect the terms.

Once Dulles had accepted the fact that intervention by American forces could not possibly retrieve the position of the West in the Indochina War, he had specified for Eden the conditions he attached to American acceptance of a negotiated settlement. On June 29, Dulles stated the willingness of the United States to adhere to an agreement that:

1. Preserves the integrity and independence of Laos and Cambodia and assures the withdrawal of Viet Minh forces therefrom.
2. Preserves at least the southern half of Vietnam. . . .

[21] Department of State Press Release No. 400, July 23, 1954.

3. Does not impose on Laos, Cambodia, or retained Vietnam any restrictions materially impairing their capacity to maintain stable non-Communist regimes; and especially restrictions impairing their right to maintain adequate forces for internal security, to import arms and to employ foreign advisers.

4. Does not contain political provisions which would risk loss of the retained area to Communist control.

5. Does not exclude the possibility of the ultimate reunification of Vietnam by peaceful means.

6. Provides for the peaceful and humane transfer of those people desiring to be moved from one zone to another of Vietnam.

7. Provides effective machinery for international supervision of the agreement.[22]

The final agreements reached at the conclusion of the Conference provided for all these conditions. Not the least of these bright spots was the fact that the integrity and independence of Laos were reaffirmed and the Vientiane government was enabled to preserve its non-Communist character and to maintain forces adequate for its internal security.

No agreement, no matter how airtight, can of itself guarantee that its signatories, in Dulles' words, do not "risk loss of the retained area to Communist control." The Geneva agreements of 1954 did not consign Laos to inevitable Communist conquest. Its preservation from such conquest depended on the judicious application of strength and conciliation—in short, on the diplomacy of the Western powers.

[22] *The Memoirs of Anthony Eden: Full Circle* (Boston: Houghton Mifflin, 1960), p. 149.

4.

Collective Defense

The withdrawal of the French military presence from Indochina in the wake of the Geneva cease-fire threatened to create something feared by statesmen—a power vacuum on the rim of a major, expansionist state. For Secretary of State John Foster Dulles, collective security was the solution; after July 20, 1954, he devoted his energies to forging an alliance of anti-Communist governments in Southeast Asia and to extending to their territories the "umbrella" of American nuclear strategic deterrence.

The idea of an alliance of European powers and the United States to protect the small states of Southeast Asia from Communist expansion had first been suggested by the French statesman Robert Schuman in June, 1952. It had figured prominently in discussions concerning "united action" in Indochina prior to Dien Bien Phu, and had subsequently been set down on paper in draft form.

The second component in Dulles' strategy to prevent the Communists from filling the power vacuum was the principle of "massive and instant retaliation."[1] This concept was formalized in a speech delivered by Dulles before the Council on Foreign Relations in New York on January 12, 1954.

The Southeast Asian countries were to be defended not by American troops permanently garrisoned within their borders, but by a guarantee to all of swift and decisive American intervention in the event of invasion by a foreign power. The binding of the United States in a treaty with Britain and France and with the Southeast Asian countries would provide the constitutional basis in the United States for such intervention and would avoid a last-minute con-

[1] Department of State Bulletin, January 25, 1954, pp. 107–108.

frontation between the Administration and Congress when intervention by American forces was judged necessary.

The non-Communist governments of Laos, Cambodia, Vietnam, Thailand, and the Philippines shared a desire for a firm, binding arrangement with the major non-Communist power in the area, the United States. However, because of the agreements reached at the Geneva Conference, in particular the unwritten understandings that the British and French reached with Chou En-lai, it was doubtful whether Laos, Cambodia, and Vietnam could become full members of the planned alliance. On July 23, 1954, Dulles declared that it was "not clear" whether the three Associated States could join the alliance, although they could be included in the area of its protection.[2]

One of Chou's chief objectives at the Conference had been to exclude the United States military presence from Indochina. In the Chinese view, the defense alliance, which was already being talked about openly before the Conference met, would allow the United States to establish new bases on the Asian mainland, station troops there, and dispatch military training missions. During these years, Peking's preoccupation with American bases on its rim colored its entire foreign policy. At Geneva, the Chinese bent all their efforts toward securing guarantees excluding such bases, even allowing they would tolerate the continuance of French troops in the Indochina states provided the Americans were excluded.

The Chinese diplomatic objective was not incompatible with French and British desires to see these states neutralized—that is, with no foreign troops garrisoned on their soil and with no foreign bases. A few days before the Geneva Conference deadline imposed by Pierre Mendès-France, Anthony Eden, Co-Chairman of the Conference and chief representative of a nonbelligerent big power, was using his influence to bring about a cease-fire agreement between the Viet Minh and the French on the one hand, and an accommodation between the extreme demands of the Chinese and the Americans on the other. Toward this end, he held a private meeting with Chou and the French Premier. According to one reliable account,

> Mr. Eden and Mr. Mendès-France reportedly assured Mr. Chou that if an armistice were reached at Geneva that neutralized Vietnam, Laos and Cambodia there could be no question of these states joining the planned Southeast Asia alliance.[3]

[2] *Times* (London), July 24, 1954.
[3] *The New York Times,* July 18, 1954. Also see Eden's account in his memoirs, *op. cit.,* p. 145. Note that whatever Chou's engagement with

Whatever the exact understanding reached, the three Associated States were not included as members of the alliance when it was finally signed the following September in Manila. All three had been favorably disposed as early as May, 1954, toward the conclusion of the alliance, and when Viet Minh elements withdrawing from their attack on Thakhek in the spring of 1954 entered Cambodia, its government had appealed for help to the United States, Thailand, and other friendly powers.

When it became clear after Geneva that these states could not count on near-by American troops to defend them against aggression, they had to seek other alternatives. Laos retained its bilateral mutual-defense treaty with France. Cambodia began exploring the possibility of a viable *rapprochement* with Peking to guarantee its sovereignty. For Thailand, a defense alliance with the United States was the logical way of preventing a repetition of the disaster of 1941, when Bangkok had vainly sought U.S. and British aid in the face of an imminent Japanese move into the country. A close alignment with the United States had become a cornerstone of Premier Pibul Songgram's foreign policy after 1947.

When the representatives of the nations that were to form the projected Southeast Asia Collective Defense Alliance met in Manila on September 6, 1954, Thailand urged the establishment of a joint force under a supreme military commander based in Bangkok. But Dulles explained that the United States opposed earmarking troops for a standing force. In the words of one observer:

> The Americans were unwilling to commit themselves to fight battles on the ground chosen by a prospective aggressor; their right to retain freedom of action indicated less an unwillingness to undertake responsibility or to engage in a necessary fight than a refusal to be compelled to fight a ground war in Thailand or Indochina.[4]

The SEATO Pact

The final treaty was signed by the United States, Britain, France, Thailand, the Philippines, Pakistan, Australia, and New Zealand. The treaty provided:

1. Each of the parties would recognize aggression by means of armed attack in the treaty area against any of the signatories, "or

---

respect to Laos and Cambodia, he did not attempt to establish relations with the non-Communist government in Vietnam, the third Associated State.

[4] George Modelski, *SEATO: Six Studies* (Vancouver: Publications Centre, The University of British Columbia, for the Australian National University, 1962), p. 96.

against any state or territory which the parties by unanimous agreement may hereafter designate," as endangering its own peace and safety, and would act to meet it in accordance with its constitutional processes (Art. 4 [1]).

2. In the case of threats other than by armed attack in the treaty area, the parties would consult immediately on measures for the common defense (Art. 4 [2]). But no action would be taken in any designated territory or state except at the invitation or with the consent of the government concerned (Art. 4 [3]).

3. The parties would establish a council, so organized as to be able to meet at any time, to provide for consultation with regard to military and other planning (Art. 5).

4. The treaty area was designated as "the general area of Southeast Asia" and the general area of the southwest Pacific, as far as 21 degrees 30 minutes north latitude. The parties might amend the designated area by unanimous agreement (Art. 8).

5. The parties undertook to maintain and develop their individual and collective capacity to resist attack and "subversive acts from without," and to cooperate in economic measures including technical assistance (Arts. 2 and 3).

6. The treaty was to remain in force indefinitely. Other states in a position to further the objectives of the treaty might accede by unanimous agreement (Arts. 7 and 10).

To the text was added a protocol designating Laos, Cambodia, and South Vietnam as areas to which the military and economic provisions should be applicable, and an American declaration that the United States' "recognition of the effect of aggression and armed attack and its agreement with reference thereto in Article 4, para. 1, apply only to Communist aggression," although in the case of other aggression or armed attack the United States would consult with the treaty powers.[5]

The treaty made it abundantly clear that the United States would not tolerate any invasion of non-Communist territory in the area on the pattern of the Korean invasion of 1950, initiated either unilaterally by Peking or Hanoi, or in council with Moscow, whose ability to exercise over-all direction of an attack mounted by a vassal state's armed forces had been amply demonstrated in Korea.

Before the Senate Committee on Foreign Relations, Dulles explained the posture of the United States under the treaty:

[5] Text in *Southeast Asia Collective Defense Treaty and Protocol* (Department of State, Treaties and Other International Acts Series, No. 3170 [Washington: Government Printing Office, 1956]).

It is not the policy of the United States to attempt to deter attack in this area by building up a local force capable itself of defense against an all-out attack by the Communists, if it should occur. We do not expect to duplicate in this area the pattern of the North Atlantic Treaty Organization and its significant standing forces. That would require a diversion and commitment of strength which we do not think is either practical or desirable or necessary from the standpoint of the United States.

We believe that our posture in that area should be one of having mobile striking power, and the ability to use that against the sources of aggression if it occurs. We believe that is more effective than if we tried to pin down American forces at the many points around the circumference of the Communist world in that area.

It may be that other countries of the area will want to dedicate particular forces for the protection of the area under this treaty. But we made clear at Manila that it was not the intention of the United States to build up a large local force including, for example, United States ground troops for that area, but that we rely upon the deterrent power of our mobile striking force.[6]

Communist China, with its standing army of 2.5 million men, of course dominated the thoughts of the treaty signatories when they considered the threat of aggression in Southeast Asia. During the Congressional hearings on treaty ratification, Dulles reviewed all the sources of current disturbances in the territories covered by the treaty, and concluded: "All of these facts, and others which I could adduce, indicate that there persists an aggressive intention on the part of the Chinese Communists which belies their protestations of a desire for peace."[7]

The Prospect from Hanoi

Dulles' statements during the Dien Bien Phu crisis had dwelt heavily on Chinese aid to the Viet Minh and on the alleged threat of Chinese intervention in the fighting. Dulles had said less about the character of the Vietnamese Communists, and practically nothing about their methods of warfare.

American policy toward Ho's regime was based on U.S. military capability to deal with overt aggression anywhere in the world. The formal American commitment, under SEATO, to defend the non-

[6] Quoted in *Report of the Committee on Foreign Relations on Executive K*, 83d Cong., 2d sess. (Washington: Government Printing Office, 1955), p. 13.

[7] *Hearings Before the Committee on Foreign Relations, United States Senate on Executive K*, 83d Cong., 2d sess. (Washington: Government Printing Office, 1954), p. 12.

Communist governments of Southeast Asia, including that of South Vietnam, against such aggression was intended to set the men in Hanoi back by bringing the industrial heartland of the Red River Delta under threat of instantaneous destruction.

Against this poised threat, North Vietnam was powerless. Its army of 300,000 men, re-equipped with Soviet-bloc equipment after the 1954 victory, could do nothing against the nuclear weapons of the U.S. Seventh Fleet.

Behind the threat of military sanctions was a U.S. policy intended to isolate Ho's regime diplomatically and economically. It was the same policy that the U.S. had applied to China after Mao Tse-tung's victory in the Chinese civil war. The last American consul departed from North Vietnam, and no official relations were maintained with the regime. In Washington's view, the only legitimate government in Vietnam was the non-Communist government in Saigon.

Britain and France, however, reasoned that the Geneva Conference had established both the Hanoi and Saigon governments as temporary regimes with jurisdiction over separately defined territories pending Vietnam-wide elections, scheduled to take place in July, 1956. In accordance with this view, the two governments maintained consular representatives in Hanoi and ambassadorial representatives in Saigon.

Ho Chi Minh, who had fought to liberate all Indochina from French rule, emerged from Geneva with control over half of Vietnam. French power in Indochina was no more, but American power was rapidly replacing it. The partition had created, in North Vietnam, an entity of 16 million people in a traditionally rice-deficient territory. Its peasantry were exhausted by the long war, and much of its rice-producing land was untilled. The industrial complex of the Red River Delta, an earner of hard currency, had been crippled by warfare, sabotage, and neglect.

It was questionable whether North Vietnam would even be a viable state. The Frenchmen who for years had operated the power plants and communications networks were withdrawing, along with French tanks and troops. The victors pleaded with the vanquished to remain a few days longer in order to train Vietnamese replacements, and the French complied.

After the departure of the French, Ho had only the Communist bloc to turn to for economic assistance. American efforts to isolate North Vietnam and to obtain international diplomatic, financial, and commercial support for South Vietnam were largely successful. Ho welcomed promises of aid from the Soviet Union, Eastern Europe, and Communist China. Too great a reliance on these countries, he knew, would nullify his claim to have broken forever the bond of subservience that had held Vietnam under foreign domination for years past. Another limiting factor was that as time went on, the granting of economic aid within the bloc was based more and more on ideological allegiance and less and less on economic needs.

If the task of economic reconstruction was great, the task of social reconstruction was even greater. The sacrifices taken by the war, not the least of which was the sweeping up of thousands of peasants to battle zones often far from their native villages, left the country-side extremely unsettled. With the beginning of the land-reform program, the disruption of village life was enormous.

The deputies from the south of Vietnam who sat in the National Assembly in Hanoi were a constant reminder to the people of North Vietnam that half their people still remained to be liberated. When this was accomplished, their leaders promised them, once again they would have rice from the south in their bowls instead of rice from China; once again Vietnam would be one and prosperous.

For the men in Hanoi, the status of Laos was inextricably bound up with this unfinished revolution. Laos was strategically vital. Through Laos, agents could be sent into the South, resuming communications cut off by the establishment of the demilitarized zone along both sides of the heavily patrolled Seventeenth Parallel. In this, the control of the northern Laos provinces of Sam Neua and Phong Saly by a favorably disposed "resistance government" was of immense assistance. The existence of this Lao "resistance government" was more than an extension into Laos of North Vietnam's base area for carrying on the struggle for reunification; it was also an important means of putting pressure on the Vientiane government to prevent it from becoming completely amenable to American designs for transforming Laos into an anti-Communist "bastion."

Anyone who has traveled in the region of Laos adjoining North Vietnam can readily appreciate with what ease a determined political movement founded on guerrilla tactics can establish a liaison across these mountains. In all directions, range upon range of lofty mountain crests and saw-toothed ridges succeed one another. From the air, the ground appears matted by a never-ending carpet of green foliage. In the rain-drenched tropical forest of hardwoods laced with vines and creepers, absolutely nothing distinguishes the territory of Laos from that of North Vietnam. The only habitations are tiny hamlets, the only inhabitants are tribesmen walking single file down narrow paths tunneling beneath treetops and winding along stony mountain streams, and the only commerce is the trading of salt and opium.

The guerrillas who were to operate in this region were peasants by day and soldiers by night, using crude weapons easily concealed. Foreign observers flying over in an airplane or walking on the ground could see very little to support a contention that North Vietnamese soldiers were trespassing in Laos or that North Vietnam was sending arms across the border in violation of the Geneva cease-fire.

It will be recalled that in dealing with the mountain tribes of Laos, the French administrators had not interfered with the authority of the individual chiefs, wisely allowing the Kha, Meo, Yao, and Black, White, and Red Thai to pursue their own affairs under their traditional chiefs. These tribes had staged the only revolts against French rule in Laos. It was relatively easy for the Viet Minh to make contacts among the tribal peoples, and about the time of the Japanese surrender there were already agents in Savannakhet, Saravane, and Khammouane provinces sympathetic to their cause.

Ho Chi Minh carefully weighed American willingness to become involved in the affairs of Vietnam, Laos, and Cambodia. He was not absolutely sure that the Americans meant everything they said in their public speeches. If the post-1954 phase of the revolution started off in a low key, with maximum use of the front of the Lao "resistance government" and minimum overt involvement of the Vietnamese Communists, the United States would have no pretext for opposing him directly.

Limitations of the American Commitment

The SEATO treaty was geared to frontal invasion. It did not automatically commit the United States to go to the aid of Laos if the integrity of the Royal Lao Government was threatened by subversion. The nature of the commitment came out quite clearly during Dulles' testimony at the Senate hearings:

> Well, Article 4, paragraph 2, contemplates that if that situation arises or threatens, that we should consult together immediately in order to agree on measures which should be taken. That is an obligation for consultation. It is not an obligation for action.[8]

The problem of subversion in the treaty area was recognized immediately, but no real steps were taken to meet it head-on. Dulles did broach the idea of convening a conference of experienced leaders to thrash out means of countering subversion; the British had

[8] *Ibid.*, p. 25.

amassed a thick file of knowledge in Malaya, and President Magsaysay, in putting down the Huk rebellion in the Philippines, had demonstrated the ability of resourceful leadership to learn from its own mistakes.

Dulles said in his prepared remarks before the Senators:

> To go on now to the question of subversion, as I pointed out, we deal with that in this treaty more specifically than we have with any other treaty. We recognize the danger more clearly. I must admit that the mere fact of recognizing the danger does not mean that we automatically have found a way to meet the danger. Subversion in that area is a very difficult thing to combat. It is virulent, it is well organized, it is effectively prosecuted by trained persons, and the task of meeting that threat will tax our resources and ingenuity to the utmost.
>
> One reason why I am very anxious to have this treaty promptly considered by this committee is that I hope it will be possible for us, perhaps even without awaiting the final coming into force of the treaty, to have a meeting of the signatories of the treaty, at which we will begin to think of ways and means that might be made available to combat this threat of subversion. This threat is most acute at the moment in Vietnam, but, as I indicated, there are threats of the same character as to Laos, Cambodia, Thailand, and Malaya; and Burma and Indonesia are not free from that danger.
>
> Therefore, I think it is of the utmost importance that we should have an early meeting of the signatories in which we began to think of ways and means to meet this subversive threat which is recognized by the treaty as being a particular danger in this area.[9]

The Senate ratified the SEATO treaty in February, 1955. But the meeting with Magsaysay, who died later that year, never took place.

The composition of membership in the alliance presented a diversity of national interests that militated against effective common action. The SEATO member states had no unifying policy toward the lands they were to protect. France, the colonial power relinquishing her hold on Indochina in a spirit of defeatism induced by a war that had cost her 172,000 casualties and the elite of her officer corps, was pursuing a transitional policy of disengagement. The arrival in power of General de Gaulle in 1958 was to reinforce French determination to avoid involvement in use of the West's military resources to fight an endless war with no well-defined political goals. Britain, concerned primarily with the security of Malaya and Singapore, had no wish to become entangled in an armed defense of the former colonial possessions of France. As the American-European end of the SEATO alliance became more and more frayed, the

[9] *Ibid.*, p. 14.

conventional military capabilities of the United States—beginning with military advisers, leading to pilots and aircraft crews, leading in turn to the deployment of American troops—played an increasingly lonely role in the developing conflict.

The attitudes of the Asian member states reflected their small-power status and their geographical position. Pakistan was far away. The Philippines took the standoffish view traditional for an insular nation. Alone among the signatories, Thailand had a direct territorial stake in the question of who controlled Laos and Cambodia.

Thailand's motivation for becoming a founding member of SEATO, as we have seen, was its desire to commit the United States to come to its aid so that it would never again be in the lonely, helpless position it had faced when the Japanese occupied Southeast Asia in 1941. Thailand knew that if this commitment was not valid, it would rapidly have to adopt a "neutralist" foreign policy, just as Cambodia had done.

This dilemma was explained by a study group at Chatham House in London as follows:

> In assessing Siam's policy towards the Manila Treaty it should nevertheless be noted that the country's history during the past century demonstrates the flexibility of its foreign policy . . . should any signs of weakening appear on the part of the United States and its allies, a change of government might occur in Bangkok, and one more favorably inclined towards the Communist bloc might appear.[10]

Since Thailand signed the Manila Treaty, the confrontation between the United States and the Communist bloc in Laos has been the principal criterion by which the Bangkok government has judged the worth of its American alliance. Throughout the crises that were to recur in Laos between 1954 and 1962, the Bangkok government expressed forebodings about Communist gains as a polite means of reminding the Americans of this paramount fact. Finally, in March, 1962, the Bangkok government obtained from the United States a bilateral commitment to defend Thailand, which in effect removed Thai fears that the United States would not act in a crisis because of a rule adopted soon after the founding of SEATO that no action could be taken without the unanimous consent of the eight members.

This Thai attitude toward the achievement of its own security, an attitude that has been correctly called "mature and cautious,"[11]

[10] *Collective Defence in Southeast Asia* (London: R.I.I.A., 1956), p. 25.
[11] Modelski, *op. cit.*, p. 98.

quickly became one of the most important considerations in Washington's formulation of policy with regard to Laos. When future Thai policy depended on the demonstration of U.S. ability and willingness to meet the challenge of Communist expansion in Laos, Washington was under a continuing compulsion to take actions disproportionate to the intrinsic strategic value of Laos. In the effort to pose a "hard" opposition to Communist expansion in Laos, the United States used Thailand as a rear base: Supply depots were built, lines of communications extended to the Laos border, and strategic airfields constructed for jet aircraft.

In the decade following the Geneva Conference of 1954, there were compelling reasons on both the North Vietnamese side and the American side for actions in Laos that went beyond the requirements of achieving ends within Laos itself. These actions were to end up by making a mockery of the Geneva provisions for restoring peace in Indochina. There was to be no peace, and nowhere was the confrontation of wills between the United States and North Vietnam carried on with more stubbornness than in Laos.

Going well beyond its paper commitments to Laos, the United States took on the burden of underwriting the Royal Lao Government. With one eye on Thailand to the rear, the United States poured into Laos during that decade America's largest per capita foreign-aid disbursements in Southeast Asia.

Yet, this American involvement in Laos was drastically mismanaged. The experience acquired in countering subversion in the region was not translated into action, and the Royal Lao Army was forged on the very same pattern as the French army that had gone down to defeat at Dien Bien Phu. In a terrible repetition of history, the Lao army could not meet an aggression that was carried on clandestinely rather than frontally, that had the character of a rebellion by disaffected elements of the population rather than that of a foreign invasion, that bore a nationalist label rather than a Communist one. And when it came to a showdown, America's allies could not summon the unanimity on which action by SEATO depended.

The men who had installed themselves in Hanoi appreciated these facts from the start. The Americans would be able to bar the tiger from seizing its prey with one swift bound. But by cunning, dissimulation, and raw nerve, the tiger was soon to appear in the very midst of the people whom the SEATO powers had hoped to protect.

5.

Pathet Lao and a Red Prince

A few days after the Lao Issara announced its dissolution, in October, 1949, Souphanouvong set out from Bangkok on foot, leaving his wife and children to follow him by way of Hong Kong. He arrived some weeks later at the Viet Minh headquarters in Tonkin, then established at Tuyen Quang, seventy miles northwest of Hanoi in a zone held by guerrillas in relative security from the French. He was warmly welcomed by Ho Chi Minh, who held ambitious plans for the Lao Prince whom he had befriended some four years earlier.

A Lao civil servant and onetime confidant of the Prince, who was present at this meeting, asserts that Souphanouvong was seeking only arms and money, in that order, from the Viet Minh. Nevertheless, he also received some advice from Vo Nguyen Giap:

"Use the peasants as your eyes and ears and your main source of supply," he said. "Before cooking each meal, peasant women must take a handful of rice and put it in a basket. Even in hard times, they won't miss it, and you'd be surprised how soon it mounts up." As for the mountain tribesmen, Giap said, "Teach them to shoot, guide them in killing a French soldier and, by implicating them in a crime, you implicate them in the war."

Giap told Souphanouvong to keep away from towns. "People in towns have chairs, tables, shoes, beds—you can't eat those things. Country folk have rice, eggs, chickens, pigs. Remember, those who rule the countryside rule the country."

Giap, the history professor who in a few years was to win glory as the victor of Dien Bien Phu and become North Vietnam's Minister of Defense, made a profound impression on Souphanouvong. Both were academicians fighting a guerrilla war.

"Pathet Lao"

The Viet Minh sponsored Souphanouvong as head of a "Lao Liberation Committee," which was patterned on their own embryo administrative structure in those areas of Vietnam they already controlled and which distinguished his small following from the Lao who had chosen to collaborate with the French in Vientiane. On August 13, 1950, Souphanouvong presided over the "First Resistance Congress," convened in secrecy in Laos somewhere near the borders of Phong Saly, Sam Neua, and Luang Prabang provinces. The meeting was attended by "more than one hundred representatives of all strata and nationalities [i.e., tribal groups] and of various religious beliefs."[1]

The Congress, carefully steered by Viet Minh agents, organized a "national resistance government," with Souphanouvong as Prime Minister, grouping together a number of other Lao who had made independent contact with the Viet Minh, in some cases earlier than Souphanouvong, and who Ho felt would be valuable in furthering his plans in Laos.

The Congress adopted a twelve-point manifesto, at the bottom of which appeared the notation "Pathet Lao," literally "Land of the Lao," referring to the areas of Laos claimed to have been "liberated" from French rule. Pathet Lao was henceforth the name of the organization of which Souphanouvong was the titular head.

The twelve objectives in this revolutionary manifesto included the following:

> Driving out the French colonialists and opposing international imperialist intervention; forming an independent and united Pathet Lao and establishing a coalition government [with the French-sponsored government in Vientiane]; realizing democracy and freedom, realizing the equality of nationalities [tribal groups]; formally establishing the national army of Pathet Lao; implementing the national united front; developing industry, agriculture, and commerce; reducing taxes and rates of interest; wiping out illiteracy, developing national culture and uniting with the peoples of Vietnam and Khmer [Cambodia]."[2]

The Pathet Lao regarded themselves as successors to the Lao Issara, and adopted the October 12 date of the Lao Issara Provisional Constitution as the anniversary of the independence of Laos. The nationalist emphasis in all this was plain. But the Viet Minh

[1] *A Chronicle of Principal Events Relating to the Indo-China Question, 1940–1954* (Peking: World Culture Publishing House, 1954), pp. 34–35.
[2] *Ibid.*, p. 35.

adroitly merged the Pathet Lao goals with their own, so as to subordinate the Pathet Lao to themselves.

The concern of the Vietnamese Communists to manage the revolutions in Laos and Cambodia was shown as early as November 25, 1945, when the Vietnamese-dominated Indochinese Communist Party circulated to all regional executive committees a series of secret instructions under the title "Resistance and Reconstruction of the Fatherland (Instructions from the Central Executive Committee)." These instructions contained thirteen points appraising the international situation and defining an action program. Included in the latter was the formation of a united front against the French in Vietnam, Laos, and Cambodia. In the same month that these instructions were circulated, however, in accordance with his efforts to cultivate the non-Communist nationalists, Ho formally dissolved the Indochinese Communist Party.

It was reconstituted in February, 1951, as the Dang Lao Dong Viet Nam (Vietnamese Workers' Party). Souphanouvong attended the First Congress of the Lao Dong Party during February and March, as did a number of other Lao and Cambodian observers. The congress produced a platform containing the following significant clauses:

> The people of Vietnam must unite closely with the peoples of Laos and Cambodia and give them every assistance in the common struggle against imperialist aggression, for the complete liberation of Indochina and the defense of world peace.
> In the common interests of the three peoples, the people of Vietnam are willing to enter into long-term cooperation with the peoples of Laos and Cambodia, with a view to bringing about an independent, free, strong and prosperous federation of the states of Vietnam, Laos and Cambodia if the three peoples so desire.[3]

The Vietnamese Communist leadership's decision to establish a party calling itself specifically Vietnamese, rather than Indochinese, aroused considerable opposition among the middle-level cadres, who received the impression that the change sacrificed the interests of the Vietnamese beyond the Annamite Mountains. To allay these fears, the leadership of the Lao Dong Party explained that it was a well-known fact that the resistance against the French in Laos and Cambodia was being led by the Indochinese Communists (i.e., the Vietnamese Communists primarily), but that for local reasons in

[3] Quoted in Allan B. Cole (ed.), *Conflict in Indo-China and International Repercussions; A Documentary History, 1945–1955* (Ithaca, N.Y.: Cornell University Press, 1956), p. 105.

these two countries the resistance could not carry a Vietnamese label. After the victory had been won and the two countries liberated, the separate parties could once again be constituted into a single Indochinese Communist Party.

The Party explained the position fully to cadres by means of a circular. A copy of this document, marked "Top Secret" and dated November 1, 1951, was captured by the French. It stated:

> The creation of a separate party for each of the three states does not prejudice the revolutionary movement in Indochina. . . . The Vietnamese Party reserves the right to supervise the activities of its brother parties in Cambodia and Laos.
>
> The Central Executive Committee of the Vietnamese Workers' Party has designated a Cambodian and Laotian bureau charged with assisting the revolutionary movements in these countries. It organizes periodic assemblies of the three parties in order to discuss questions of common interest; it works toward the creation of a Vietnamese–Khmer–Laotian United Front. Militarily, Vietnam, Cambodia, and Laos constitute a combat zone; Vietnam has substantially assisted Cambodia and Laos militarily as well as from all other points of view.[4]

Actually, no "brother party" was created in Laos until January, 1956, when the Phak Khon Ngan (Workers' Party) was formed clandestinely behind the front of the Neo Lao Hak Sat (Lao Patriotic Front).

For about a year during 1951 and 1952, we pick up Souphanouvong's camouflaged trail in Communist China. Certainly he had returned to Indochina before the firming up of Viet Minh plans for action in Laos in the spring of 1953.

As has been mentioned, Lao agents were involved in the Viet Minh actions in Sam Neua and Luang Prabang provinces. They were the first handful of guerrillas of the embryo Pathet Lao "army" to appear upon the scene.

Souphanouvong's Lieutenants

The organization of the Pathet Lao armed forces was entrusted to the Defense Minister in the resistance "government," Kaysone Phomvihan. Born in Savannakhet in either 1920 or 1925, Kaysone was the son of a Lao mother and a Vietnamese father, who, like many Vietnamese in Laos, worked for the French administration. Kaysone entered the University of Hanoi for medical studies in the

[4] Quoted in Department of State, *The Situation in Laos* (Washington: September, 1959), pp. 2–3.

early 1940's, when Souphanouvong was employed by the Indochinese civil service in Central Vietnam. Kaysone became active in the nationalist activities of the Students' Union and did some youth work under the direction of the Indochinese Communist Party. He became an active sympathizer of the Viet Minh and received both political and military training from them.

Ho heard of him, and in 1945 dispatched him back to his home town of Savannakhet with an important mission. He was to infiltrate another Lao nationalist movement that held some prospect of being useful to the Viet Minh. The rival movement was headed by Oun Sananikone, a leading member of the powerful Sananikone family of Vientiane. Oun had gone to Thailand during World War II, and his group was associated with the Free Thai movement, which was sponsoring the idea of an independent "Greater Laos" incorporating the Lao peoples on both banks of the Mekong. After Oun's return to Laos, however, his faction lost its dynamism and the project for a "Greater Laos" eventually disappeared from the platforms of the Lao leaders.

When Souphanouvong arrived at Savannakhet in 1945, he found Kaysone and a small group of followers already there. A dispute threatened briefly to erupt over formal leadership of the Lao resistance movement, but Kaysone deferred to the higher-ranking Prince and joined his band with Souphanouvong's. When the latter joined the Lao Issara government in Vientiane, Kaysone remained outside, but followed the Prince to Bangkok. Between 1950 and 1954, as Minister of Defense in the resistance "government," Kaysone had the task of recruiting partisans for the Viet Minh-style guerrilla force of the Pathet Lao. He subsequently held the post of Commander in Chief of the Pathet Lao forces from 1954 to 1957, the important period when the movement was consolidating its base area. He has held no government titles since then, although he is believed to be the most powerful figure today in the Pathet Lao movement.

A gifted linguist, Kaysone speaks fluent Thai, Shan, French, and English, in addition to his native Lao and Vietnamese. He has a strong distaste for the perquisites of military rank. This may explain why Kaysone himself has never divested himself of his name, which is a Lao transliteration of the Vietnamese "Cai Song," meaning "Corporal Song," and has never been referred to by officer's rank.

Kaysone is active in the military councils of the Lao Dong Party. In October, 1959, some months after the arrest of Souphanouvong in Vientiane, he was unanimously elected Vice Chairman of the Neo

Lao Hak Sat. He has not been seen in public in non-Communist countries since May, 1958, when he was defeated in the National Assembly elections in Attopeu, allegedly because of electoral rigging against Neo Lao Hak Sat candidates.

The Viet Minh had succeeded in enlisting the support of the ethnic minorities of northern and western Tonkin, overcoming the age-old animosity between lowland Vietnamese and mountain tribes.[5] Now, in 1950, Souphanouvong's "resistance government" was able to acquire as ministers two tribal leaders of Laos, Sithone Komadam and Phay Dang.

Sithone Komadam was the son of the great Kha chieftain of southern Laos who had led the 1901–7 Kha revolt against the French and who had finally been captured by them and executed. Perhaps more than any other member of the Lao dissidents, Sithone hated colonial domination. Even when addressing European visitors, Sithone has been known to use an interpreter rather than speak French.

Born about 1906 in either Saravane or Attopeu Province, Sithone crossed over the mountains into southern Vietnam during World War II, and there came upon the militant Communist Tran Van Giau. Slipping back into Laos, Sithone made contact with both the Viet Minh leadership in Tonkin and the Lao Issara government in Vientiane. His name appeared on lists of the Lao Issara faithful that were published in Vientiane at this time, but he never appeared in the Lao capital.

In the 1950 "government," Sithone, who eluded the French in Laos instead of settling in the relative security of Souphanouvong's compound in Bangkok, was Minister without Portfolio. But his principal sphere of influence continued to be the south. Two British doctors who in 1962 stumbled unwittingly into his "domain" reported that he rode a small pony over the countryside and was in constant touch with his soldiers and commissars through an elaborate network of messengers, which no doubt also kept him in contact with the Pathet Lao headquarters in the north.

Phay Dang, the other tribal leader in the "resistance government," had guerrilla bands in the Meo villages of Xieng Khouang Province loyal to him and hostile to the French. At the time of the

[5] One of Ho's first acts when he came to power in North Vietnam was to create a Thai-Meo Autonomous Region along the entire length of the Tonkin border with Phong Saly and Sam Neua. News of this undoubtedly had an impact among the mountain peoples in Laos, as did the fact that the Second North Vietnamese National Assembly included 56 mountaineers among its 362 northern deputies.

French reoccupation of Thakhek in March, 1946, Phay Dang, then a village headman, set about organizing his guerrillas into what later became known as the Meo Resistance League. He described his efforts in an interview in 1957:

"I heard there had been a great battle and that the townspeople had fought very bravely against the French. I thought it would be very good if we could fight together against the same enemy. I went down to the plains myself and tried to find this prince. He had already left and was in Thailand. I sent him a message and the reply came back: 'Arouse the people. Create a strong organization. Later we will fight together.' So I returned to the mountains and began to organize all the [Meo] villages from our own base. . . . Every village appointed organizers and formed scouts and defense corps."[6]

Before the Meo Resistance League, the Meo had no formal political organization, as the lowland villagers had; their family ties had traditionally knit them closely together. The difficulties of organizing the Meo were immense. Not only were they a people of independent will, but they were a people who shifted their villages frequently, especially in times of trouble, unlike the lowland Lao. Phay Dang later described the impact made on the Meo by the first manifesto of the Pathet Lao:

When the program of the Front was distributed among our [Meo] people, they saw it answered their deepest wishes. Equality for all races. Nobody had ever spoken of this before. A united fight against the French. We had never thought it possible. Abolition of unjust taxes. The French had burned and plundered our villages, massacred our people, taken our women in collecting taxes in the past. Of course, there were difficulties. We could not immediately improve the lives of the people. But it was not long before the people could see the benefits of our alliance with the Lao and others. They felt the efforts made by the Front and government to improve their lives. In place of our poisoned arrows and flintlocks we began to get some modern arms, some automatics and light machineguns. Great efforts were made to get salt to our villages. The opium tax was abolished and other taxes lightened. We formed women's associations and a youth movement. At first, membership was slow. Each village is on an isolated mountaintop and it was difficult to get people together. But after a few months people saw this was a very good thing and they joined up with great enthusiasm. From the self-defense corps we set up guerrilla bases, first of all in our own province of Xieng Khouang and then in the neighboring ones. We have 40,000 [Meo] in our

6 Wilfred Burchett, *Mekong Upstream* (Hanoi: Red River Publishing House, 1957), p. 264.

province alone and later on we were able to form whole [Meo] companies from our guerrilla bases and attach them to the regular Pathet Lao forces formed by Souphanouvong.[7]

Souphanouvong's "resistance government" included, as Minister of Economy and Finance, Nouhak Phoumsavan, the young Lao later sent to the Geneva Conference by the Viet Minh. Nouhak remained in either Laos or Vietnam while Souphanouvong was in Bangkok, and meanwhile received intensive training from the Viet Minh.

The son of a peasant, Nouhak was educated only in primary school in his birthplace, Savannakhet. He was operating a bus line connecting Vinh, Savannakhet, and Thakhek when he first came in contact with the Viet Minh. They found Nouhak a valuable courier, and Nouhak threw in his lot with them.

In December, 1952, Nouhak was in the entourage of the Viet Minh delegation to the Peking Conference of the Asian and Pacific Regions. In May, 1954, he arrived at the Geneva Conference, after being given the additional portfolio of Pathet Lao Minister of Foreign Affairs.

When the first coalition government was eventually established in Vientiane in 1957 and the Pathet Lao "resistance government" was dissolved, Nouhak took up residence in Vientiane, and became a deputy to the National Assembly, representing Sam Neua. Later, in 1959, he was arrested, as was Souphanouvong, and escaped in the Prince's party in 1960. Nouhak headed the Pathet Lao delegation at the Ban Namone cease-fire talks in 1961. He is today the only ranking Pathet Lao leader from a peasant background.

As Deputy Prime Minister of the 1950 "resistance government," Souphanouvong picked a man who had been closely associated with him in Bangkok and who remains to this day one of his most trusted deputies, Phoumi Vongvichit. Born in 1910, the son of a Governor of Vientiane Province, Phoumi entered the Indochinese civil service and became secretary to the French Resident in Xieng Khouang. When the Pathet Lao took over administration of Sam Neua Province after the 1954 Geneva Conference, Phoumi was made Governor. In the first coalition formed in 1957, Phoumi, like Souphanouvong, entered the Cabinet at Vientiane. Phoumi became Minister of Cults, and as such skillfully indoctrinated a number of bonzes in the justness of the Communist view of world affairs.

Phoumi was dispatched to Geneva in 1961 to head the Pathet Lao delegation to the second conference on Laos. In the second

[7] *Ibid.,* p. 267.

coalition formed in Vientiane in 1962, Phoumi was again Souphanouvong's colleague in the Cabinet, this time as Minister of Information, Propaganda, and Tourism. He has a quiet, clerkish air, and handles the orthodox Communist jargon with perfection.

In his recruiting drive in the Mekong Valley in October, 1945, Souphanouvong enlisted certain members of the region's leading families. Two who joined the resistance against the French and fought side by side with Souphanouvong in his small Lao Issara army were Singkapo Chounlamany and Phoumi Nosavan.

Singkapo, scion of the leading family of Thakhek, which had provided administrative officials for Khammouane Province for three generations, abandoned both his wife and his teaching career to join Souphanouvong's guerrillas. Phoumi, a member of the powerful Voravong family of Savannakhet, was sent by Souphanouvong to learn guerrilla tactics from the Viet Minh, a training he completed in 1947. Phoumi was ambitious and determined on a military career.

When Souphanouvong took the Lao Issara dissidents into a tacit alliance with the Viet Minh in 1949, Singkapo and Phoumi were in the village of Do Luang, near the border of Laos and Central Vietnam. The two men had the alternative of staying on with the Prince in his new relationship with the Viet Minh or of journeying to Vientiane to cooperate with the French-sponsored government being set up there. The two men decided their fates by drawing matchsticks, it is said; the long matchstick signified Vientiane, and the short, Souphanouvong. Phoumi drew the long stick, the story goes, and Singkapo cursed his luck.

Singkapo had difficulty in relinquishing the bourgeois life, a price of membership in the Pathet Lao. Sent on travels abroad by the Pathet Lao high command, he gave disturbing signs of defecting to the Royal Government, and in Vientiane, his proclivity for nightclubbing got him in hot water. In May, 1955, Souphanouvong sent him to Communist China for some political reindoctrination. In 1961, he became a general in the Pathet Lao army. His second wife, like Souphanouvong's wife, was Vietnamese, and the two men have remained close associates.

Phoumi Nosavan was rewarded for his decision to return to Vientiane with rapid promotion in the territorial army the French were forming. He entered in October, 1950, as a lieutenant, and was soon fighting against the Viet Minh, who had instructed him in guerrilla tactics. By 1959, he was a brigadier general.

Securing a Base

In the mounting war with the French, Souphanouvong and his small band of Pathet Lao faithful dutifully followed in the footsteps of their mentors, the Viet Minh. In order to support their claim to represent a legitimate government fighting for independence, the Pathet Lao bent their efforts to establishing a "liberated" base area. A revealing newspaper article by Nouhak stated in 1953:

> We have not always had an extended operations base with which to support our long-term resistance.
>   During April of this year . . . we liberated nearly 40,000 square kilometers of territory, which included the entire province of Sam Neua, a large part of Xieng Khouang, and part of Luang Prabang and Phong Saly provinces. . . .
>   This victory gave us a vast, wide operational base full of obstacles, a base where paddy, forest products, and soil resources are abundant, a base which borders the free zone of the friendly country of Vietnam. In this place we will build up our armed forces, establish our territory, and reinforce our front.[8]

The passing reference to the Viet Minh hardly suggests that if 40,000 square kilometers of Lao territory were indeed "liberated" in April, 1953, it was done almost entirely by the Viet Minh guerrillas and not by the fledgling Pathet Lao, with their mixed leadership of displaced aristocrats, schoolteachers, and tribal chieftains. Describing the Pathet Lao administration established in the wake of the Viet Minh invasion, Phoui Sananikone told the 1954 Geneva Conference:

> Mr. Pham Van Dong has told us that a "free Lao administration" was being installed in the occupied zones. For the good of the inhabitants I wish it were so. But alas, that is far from being the case. This so-called Government does not exist apart from the Viet Minh, and has no seat other than the Viet Minh military command posts.[9]

The Geneva agreement of 1954 gave the Pathet Lao what they most needed: security of their base area in order to proceed with consolidation of their armed forces and to impose their iron-clad rule. The agreement provided for regrouping areas for the belligerents, and allocated the two provinces of Sam Neua and Phong Saly to the Pathet Lao for this purpose.

This was to be a temporary measure to separate the belligerents

[8] Broadcast by Vietnam News Agency on April 24, 1953, of an article in *Lao Itsala (Free Laos)*.
[9] Cmd. 9186, p. 155.

and make the cease-fire a reality. But in November, 1954, Souphanouvong declared: "The Pathet Lao forces . . . have proclaimed the power of the Pathet Lao in the two provinces of Sam Neua and Phong Saly."

The Pathet Lao proceeded to set up all the trappings of a permanent administration in Sam Neua and Phong Saly. They established schools and print shops to publish their own textbooks. They appointed village headmen and district officers. They meted out justice according to rules of Communist Party discipline. They recruited a local militia. They stored arms and ammunition for the day when the enemy, no longer the French but the Vientiane government and its American backers, would resist their "liberation" of additional territory.

The signatories at Geneva had set up an International Commission for Supervision and Control (ICC), composed of representatives of India, Poland, and Canada, to oversee on the spot the implementation of the accords. In Laos, however, the ICC met endless difficulties. Its efforts to inspect any part of the border region in order to supervise the withdrawal of "Vietnamese People's Volunteer Forces" and the demobilization of the Pathet Lao were systematically frustrated by the Pathet Lao's repeated failures to furnish facilities and liaison officers. On at least three occasions, the ICC complained in 1957, its inspection teams were fired on by Pathet Lao guerrillas. When members of one investigating team arrived unannounced in a village, they were promptly tied up. The Pathet Lao's standard explanation was that a "misunderstanding" had arisen because the ICC team had been taken for foreign agents.

The ICC's independent verification that the Vietnamese "volunteers" had withdrawn completely from Laos, as prescribed in Article 4 of the cease-fire agreement, was a farce, illustrated by the following extract from an official ICC report:

> It may be said that owing to difficult terrain and monsoon weather, particularly till the end of September, and mutual distrust between the two parties, and the fact that the Commission staff and its team did not get fully set up till early October, the withdrawals were not checked *in toto* by either the Joint Groups or the International Teams. . . . Finally, it is stressed that the Commission has had to rely to some extent on the assurances given by the two parties that they have completely withdrawn their forces in accordance with the terms of the Geneva Agreement.[10]

[10] Cmd. 9445, p. 15.

The Vientiane government complained that ten Vietnamese "volunteer" officers were stationed in Sam Neua Province after the 120-day withdrawal period and that two of them held official posts. An investigatory ICC team in Sam Neua could neither prove nor disprove the allegation.[11]

The clause providing for a check on all arms shipments into Laos was equally susceptible to violation. The ICC reported:

> In November 1955, the Commission's team at Sam Neua investigated the Royal Government's complaint which had been lodged in June 1955 regarding reported import of war materials from Vietnam into the province of Sam Neua, which they later alleged in August 1955 were stored in the village of Ban That. Due to non-availability of a helicopter and of a Pathet Lao liaison officer at various times, investigation of this complaint was delayed. The team stated that no depot of arms, ammunition or equipment was found in the village or in the area surrounding the village.[12]

Meanwhile, in the rugged jungle country of the northern border region, the Communists went ahead with their efforts. Supply lines were mounted and extended across the border at will, then dismounted as rapidly. Agents came and went without fear of being observed.

But if the ICC was powerless to investigate the situation in the two border provinces, first-hand accounts of it began to be heard from defectors and other Lao whose families were very much involved in what was happening.

These accounts were later substantiated by diaries written by Vietnamese *can bo* (cadres) serving in Laos and by a United Nations mission that, in the summer of 1959, directly questioned many inhabitants of Sam Neua Province. The evidence proved that the Pathet Lao, far from being the patriotic, nationalist movement its propaganda portrayed, was nothing but a tool of the North Vietnamese Lao Dong Party.

One of the earliest reliable accounts of North Vietnamese domination of the Pathet Lao is attributed to Major Kavinh Koenakorn, a onetime secretary to a Pathet Lao political delegation to the Royal Government, who defected to Vientiane in September, 1955. He reported that the Vietnamese had absolute control of the Pathet Lao organization at all levels, and that Pathet Lao officials could decide nothing but had to obey *can bo* orders. He described how, after 1954, families in the Pathet Lao-controlled areas were de-

[11] Cmd. 9630, p. 19.
[12] Cmnd. 314, p. 27.

liberately split up and women and children removed across the border by the North Vietnamese to serve as hostages and as potential recruits. (Souphanouvong enrolled two of his sons in schools in North Vietnam.) Many of those sent to North Vietnam were later returned to Sam Neua, where they constituted something of a fifth column.

Phoui Sananikone, at the Geneva Conference, accused the Viet Minh of imposing "relentless social coercion" in the Pathet Lao zones:

> In the province of Sam Neua, which has been occupied since April 1953, children are sent to Viet Nam for Communist indoctrination; the whole population up to the age of fifty-six (including children and pregnant women) is forced to do haulage and road work, while rice, salt, etc., are requisitioned unmercifully.[13]

A defector, in an interview published in November, 1955, said:

> I thought I was fighting in and for my own country, but the discipline imposed by the Viet Minh [North Vietnamese] kept us in constant danger of deportation. The least argument, the smallest mistake, was greeted by the fatal words: "to be sent to the instruction center." These instruction centers were in [North] Vietnam, and no one who went there ever came back.[14]

Intensive political indoctrination in Sam Neua was closely modeled on that carried out by the Viet Minh in Tonkin during the Indochina War. A mimeographed instruction sheet distributed to Pathet Lao cadres contained this catechism:

> Question: Have the [Lao] Issara recruited new forces since the cease-fire?
> Answer: Never, there are only volunteers.
> Question: Are the Issara requisitioning rice?
> Answer: No, the residents give it voluntarily.[15]

After the cease-fire had been signed in Geneva on July 20, 1954, one of Souvanna Phouma's first acts was to renew contact with his brother. He took a plane to Khang Khay, a village on the Plain of Jars, and there the two men had a cordial reunion after five years of separation.

On his return to Vientiane, the Prime Minister expressed his conviction that an agreement reintegrating the Pathet Lao into the

---

[13] Cmd. 9186, p. 155.
[14] Lao Presse bulletin, Vientiane, November 26, 1955.
[15] Sisouk na Champassak, *Storm Over Laos* (New York: Frederick A. Praeger, 1961), p. 38.

national community would soon be reached. He discounted the rumor that Souphanouvong had become a convinced Communist.

The Pathet Lao were now caught in a dilemma: Whether to consolidate their hold on their base area, in the expectation that force would prove the most effective means to power in Laos, or to press negotiations for a role in a coalition government, a course that would give them a minority voice in the Vientiane government but would almost certainly cost them their exclusive control over Sam Neua and Phong Saly.

Probably as a result of the influence of the North Vietnamese, who were primarily concerned over the security of their borders while the Lao Dong Party was consolidating its hold on the population, the first decision was in favor of consolation. Royal Army troops who probed into the two provinces in an effort to reassert Vientiane's jurisdiction there were threatened with ambush by Pathet Lao guerrillas.

The Geneva agreement to leave the procedure for reintegrating the two provinces to later negotiations between the Royal Government and the Pathet Lao enabled the latter to retain its positions there in the interval. The Pathet Lao used this time to build up a solid core of cadres, on the Viet Minh model. By mid-1956, more than 3,000 partisans had been recruited from the populations of Sam Neua and Phong Saly, neither of which totaled more than 100,000. These troops released hard-core cadres for missions in the other provinces of Laos, which were nominally under Vientiane's control. In 1956 alone, several hundred cadres were dispatched from these base areas.

The Pathet Lao were unwilling to take part in the general elections for the country's unicameral National Assembly, scheduled for 1955 by the Geneva provisions. Seeking pretexts for boycotting the voting, the Pathet Lao demanded changes in the basic electoral law, including lowering the qualifying age for candidates from thirty to twenty-five and extending the franchise to women, and continuance of their exclusive administration of Sam Neua and Phong Saly until after the elections. When the Royal Government rejected these demands, the Pathet Lao refused to participate in the elections. After being postponed for four months, voting was held on December 25. At this time, the Royal Government's control over the countryside of Sam Neua and Phong Saly was so poor that to get blank ballots to some localities, it had to resort to dropping them from airplanes.

The country-wide voting gave eight seats out of thirty-nine to left-leaning candidates outside the Pathet Lao. The Pathet Lao branded the results "illegal and invalid."[16]

Souvanna Phouma had relinquished the post of Prime Minister in October, 1954, and had been succeeded by Katay Don Sasorith, a southerner and former Minister of Finance in the Lao Issara government. When he took office, Katay spoke hopefully of prevailing upon Souphanouvong's nationalism and bringing the Pathet Lao back into the national community:

> If it is left to the Lao, it can be worked out. . . . I believe Souphanouvong is a Lao nationalist. It is possible to cooperate with these people if we can get them away from the Viet Minh.[17]

No start could be made toward negotiating the Pathet Lao's reintegration into the national community, as envisaged at Geneva, until the insecurity in the two northern provinces had been settled. But Pathet Lao continued to resist attempts by the Royal Army to establish Vientiane's authority in these provinces; this would have prevented consolidation of the Pathet Lao base area, which was necessary to North Vietnam.

As a starting point, negotiations were limited to a regrouping of separate forces in the two provinces. Talks opened at the end of June, 1955, to the accompaniment of a Pathet Lao attack on the main government outpost in Sam Neua Province. After a long deadlock, agreement was reached on the regrouping of Royal Army troops, and a cease-fire line had almost been decided on when the Pathet Lao attacked and captured two of the government outposts whose status was being discussed. In October, a new cease-fire agreement was drawn up, which, since it prohibited reinforcements, could be said to favor the Pathet Lao; but again the negotiations on the details of the separation of the two sides broke down. Meanwhile, the Pathet Lao maintained their pressure by means of guerrilla pinpricks.

Later in 1955, Katay attempted to negotiate a political settlement with Pathet Lao emissaries in Rangoon, but without result. Finally the ICC, in a resolution adopted on January 7, 1956, advised the Pathet Lao that the Geneva accords meant that it was "the sovereign right of the Royal Government to establish its administration in the two northern provinces and this right is undisputed."

16 Cmnd. 314, pp. 6–9.
17 *New York Herald Tribune,* January 9, 1955.

Coalition in Vientiane and Party Underground

When Souvanna Phouma returned to office as Prime Minister in March, 1956, after a sixteen-month interval, the atmosphere for political negotiations with the Pathet Lao improved considerably. He announced that reintegration of the Pathet Lao was the most important domestic task facing his new government, and he indicated that he was prepared to go outside the borders of Laos, to Hanoi and to Peking, to achieve it.

Meanwhile, however, an important meeting in Sam Neua had created a basic change in the Pathet Lao organization and brought a new departure in Pathet Lao policy toward Vientiane.

A conference of 160 leading Pathet Lao cadres, said to represent a diversity of ethnic minorities, political parties, religious bodies, and popular organizations, met in secrecy at the beginning of 1956. On January 6 they adopted a political manifesto that stressed the desirability of forming a united front, and by implication held out the possibility of a coalition with the Royal Government. A new organization was created to implement this program. It was called the Neo Lao Hak Sat (Lao Patriotic Front).

More significant, however, was the simultaneous creation of the Phak Khon Ngan (Workers' Party), the nucleus of a true Communist Party of Laos. It was modeled closely on the Lao Dong Party of North Vietnam.

Reports indicate that the top leaders of the Phak Khon Ngan hold simultaneous membership in the Lao Dong Party. The organizational structure of the Phak Khon Ngan follows the Marxist-Leninist principle of "democratic centralism." At the lowest levels are cells, which meet secretly at regular intervals to learn of the current Party line. To cloak its activities on the operational, that is, the village, level, the Phak Khon Ngan implements its programs through a number of fronts, the most important of which is the Neo Lao Hak Sat (NLHS). Indeed, the NLHS, which appears as a mass political party, serves as a pool for recruits to the hard-core Phak Khon Ngan.

The recruits are put through a probationary period of indoctrination and training, during which they are carefully screened. The cadre training system includes a command school for the military, another for political and military cadres, and an additional one for ethnic minorities. New members are admitted at a ceremony in which they swear unquestioning obedience to all orders received from their superior in the Party hierarchy, without regard for the race of the person issuing the order.

The Phak Khon Ngan determines what line the NLHS should take on broad political issues. The Pathet Lao guerrilla network implements this line by means of coercion and terrorism. (The parallel with Communist organization in South Vietnam is striking. There, a hard-core and clandestine Marxist-Leninist party, the Vietnam People's Revolutionary Party, was set up to operate behind the National Front for the Liberation of South Vietnam, created in December, 1960. The top leaders of the Vietnam People's Revolutionary Party are reported to have close secret membership ties with the Lao Dong Party of North Vietnam. The armed insurgents in South Vietnam enforce the line of the National Front.)

For the Asian Communist movements, 1955–56 was a peaceable period, during which they used parliamentary tactics and accommodation with nationalist movements and governments. In South Vietnam, the passing of the July, 1956, date set at Geneva for the elections throughout both portions of Vietnam did not trigger the start of insurgency. The date passed without action because Ngo Dinh Diem, having won a referendum in the south for the post of head of state over the French puppet, Bao Dai, and crushed his major political opponents by force, refused to participate in Vietnam-wide elections. His refusal might have been taken by Hanoi as a provocation. But the insurgency did not begin until well after July, 1956, although the groundwork for such an eventuality had been laid when the Viet Minh withdrew from the south in 1954.[18]

In Laos, there was a noticeable decrease in the frequency of incidents between Royal Army troops and Pathet Lao guerrillas in Sam Neua and Phong Saly, and an easing of military pressure on government strongpoints. In this more favorable atmosphere, discussions between the two sides got under way in Vientiane on August 1, 1956.

The Pathet Lao proved themselves to be hard bargainers. It soon became clear Pathet Lao representation in a coalition government was the price for settlement of the factionalism within the country in accordance with Souvanna Phouma's hopes.

When it appeared that Souvanna Phouma would not allow himself to be swayed by the American Ambassador in Vientiane, J. Graham Parsons, who advised against such a coalition and pointed out that it had not been stipulated at Geneva,[19] Souphanouvong

[18] "Toward the end of 1957 and the beginning of 1958, the first armed self-defense units of the southern people came into existence." (*Hoc Tap* [*Studies*], Hanoi, February, 1964.)

[19] Parsons later remarked frankly: "I struggled for sixteen months to prevent a coalition." (*Hearings*, I, p. 195.) For complete identification of Congressional hearings, see Bibliography.

himself arrived in the capital to take charge of the Pathet Lao delegation.

Complete agreement on the details of the settlement was not reached until more than a year later, in November, 1957. Then Souvanna Phouma and Souphanouvong signed two documents, one political and one military, and declared their satisfaction at the prospect of "complete and early success of general reconciliation."

Two Pathet Lao leaders were taken into the Vientiane government: Souphanouvong, as Minister of Plans, Reconstruction, and Urbanism; and Phoumi Vongvichit, as Minister of Cults. The NLHS was to be permitted to operate as a political party, and supplementary elections to the National Assembly were to be held within four months.

Sam Neua and Phong Saly provinces were formally turned over to the authority of the King on November 18. The Pathet Lao retained a considerable voice in the new administration set up in these provinces. A Vientiane governor was appointed in Sam Neua, with a Pathet Lao deputy; a Pathet Lao governor was appointed in Phong Saly, with a Vientiane deputy. The mayor of Sam Neua town was a Pathet Lao, and the mayor of Phong Saly town a Vientiane official. Half the mayors and other officials of the two provinces were to be appointed from the Pathet Lao and half from Vientiane.

The military agreement provided that the Royal Government would take over the "entire personnel" and "entire equipment" of the Pathet Lao forces. But further clauses provided that, because of budgetary limitations, the number of Pathet Lao troops to be integrated into the Royal Army, whose size had been set at 23,650 men, would be limited to 1,500, including officers, noncoms, and men. The men to be integrated into the Royal Army would be selected by the Pathet Lao, and the remaining Pathet Lao troops would be demobilized.

At a ceremony held on February 18, 1958, at the Plain of Jars, 1,501 Pathet Lao soldiers were formally integrated into the Royal Army. This left 4,280 to be demobilized in the next few days. The rapid growth in the Pathet Lao forces since the 1954 cease-fire was explained to ICC observers by a Pathet Lao spokesman as the result of the incorporation of "volunteers." Shrewdly, the Pathet Lao leadership had selected the 1,501 from its best fighting men, many of them from the mountain tribes, and formed them into two battalions with their own weapons and officers while they said they were awaiting actual integration into Royal Army units.

The ICC sent off a report on March 5 stating that "complete integration of former Pathet Lao military personnel into the Lao National Army has been achieved."[20] But subsequent events were to show that ceremonial integration was very different from absorption of the Pathet Lao soldiers into the ranks of the army. Soon disputes broke out over the Pathet Lao's allotment of officer ranks in the Royal Army. Other difficulties arose. The issue of these soldiers was to drag on until May, 1959—and then it was to have a most unexpected denouement.

To the Vientiane government, the problem posed by the partisans of the old Lao Issara independence movement at last appeared solved. In agreeing to integrate the Pathet Lao partisans into the national army and to accord their political leaders a minority voice in the Cabinet, Vientiane was reasoning along these lines: It would bring the "outsiders" on the inside by granting them responsibility in the affairs of the nation. Their acceptance of this responsibility would weaken their ties with North Vietnam. The Pathet Lao could not have it both ways; they could not participate in Cabinet decisions and at the same time foster their private rebellious movement in the jungle. So went the Vientiane logic.

Work at the Village Level

Through the systematic assignment of cadres by provinces, districts, and villages, the NLHS organized a country-wide network of cells. The cells provided a means for mobilizing popular support for the NLHS political program, which was decided upon in the secrecy of the Phak Khon Ngan and then passed down to the NLHS leaders for implementation. Conversely, the intimate knowledge of village happenings acquired by the cadres at the cell level provided a constant flow of intelligence to the central directorate.

The cell network as it existed toward the end of 1958 was analyzed by the anti-Communist newspaper *Lao Hakxa Sat*.[21] Horizontally, it was organized into study groups, family groups, and associations; vertically, the front organizations. Study groups were formed by hard-core, well-indoctrinated cadres, who gathered around themselves sympathizers who, by persuasion, coercion, or outright terrorism, were gradually rendered more and more susceptible to the NLHS political line. Some of these study groups would

[20] Cmnd. 541, p. 74.
[21] *Lao Hakxa Sat* (*National Guardian*) (Vientiane), No. 5, November 1–14, 1958.

split, forming other study groups in neighboring villages and districts.

The newspaper attributed the success of the study-group organizers to their personal ascendancy, their dedication, and their tireless activity in gaining undisputed leadership and control. The hard-core organizers guided discussions and sponsored motions in accordance with a program that was carefully prepared at a higher echelon.

At the study-group level, there was little or no concern with a knowledge of Marxism-Leninism. On the contrary, the emphasis was on practical, down-to-earth matters that were readily comprehensible to the villagers and would be sure to enlist their support.

Instead of analyzing the struggle against "imperialism," NLHS propaganda pointed to the American aid program as evidence of a scheme to exploit Laos for foreign purposes. Potential converts were sent from their villages on trips to Vientiane so that they could get an eyeful of the luxurious homes and cars that Lao Government officials had bought with money meant to help Laos become economically independent. Because of Laos' sparse population, land reform was given little importance. As Phoui Sananikone commented: "The redistribution of land certainly figures on the program of popular movements in many Asian countries; but for anyone who knows Laos and its economic problems, it is almost cruel irony to talk of dividing up the land when there are too few inhabitants to cultivate the immense areas available."

The family group made use of the traditionally strong family ties among the Lao. It comprised between five and ten families led by a "responsible" (cadre), almost always a convinced Communist. The families of a group were summoned to a compulsory meeting every five days. At these meetings, the cadres gradually developed self-criticism and guided the participants' minds along lines of rigorous discipline. Besides using the family groups as effective channels for disseminating propaganda, the Communists also learned from them what was going on in the village. These family groups were reported to have been instrumental in preparing victories for several of the NLHS candidates who contested the elections prescribed in the November, 1957, reintegration agreement.

"Through intimidation and punitive measures, members are forced to participate willingly or otherwise," the *Lao Hakxa Sat* article said. "In the long run, apathy on the part of the more willing ones and inertia on the part of the others combine to place the population under the complete control of the cadres and make them obedient to their orders."

The front organizations grouped together persons of similar age or profession into associations of peasants, women, youth, and young girls. Through regular association meetings, through self-criticism conducted at these meetings, through shows of strength by "volunteer" militia forces, the Communists softened up the population. It was virtually impossible to resign from one of these associations.

The associations provided the Communists with a valuable picture of what was going on in the minds of the villagers. For example, in a family of four, the father might belong to the Peasants' Federation (Samakhom Sao Hai Na), the mother to the Women's Federation (Samakhom Mae Nying Lao), the daughter to the Young Girls' Association (Youvannari), and the son to the Youth Federation (Samakhom Sao Num). Each member of the family was subjected to propaganda that, although adapted to each group's requirements, was aimed at a single objective. By conducting self-criticism sessions, the cadres soon learned all the undercurrents of the village, the people's state of mind, the danger signs pointing to the germination of rebellion. The child was led to denounce his parents, the wife her husband.

The strong organizational apparatus facilitated action that had been decided upon in secrecy at the center of the web, involving disobedience to the orders given by the traditional village headman (nai ban). In this resistance, the front organizations played a key role.

Through passive resistance, slanders, and rumors, honest village headmen quickly became discouraged and were led to resign. Alternatively, the population of a village, encouraged by one of the front organizations, might make a collective petition asking the district officer (chao muong) to change the village headman. This type of action was designed to effect the replacement of "undesirable" leaders by NLHS sympathizers.

In other instances, the population might be incited against village "capitalists," those whose standard of living was above average. Through boycotts and intimidation, the cadres forced such people to leave the village and seek asylum in the larger towns, where they felt safe. In some villages, certain inhabitants were made responsible for destroying all government propaganda arriving in the village, others for housing strangers and keeping them under surveillance.

All this elaborate organization was enforced by threats, made concrete by clandestine armed groups that appeared in the villages from time to time. Sometimes these groups passed death sentences, sometimes they passed out first or second warnings. As a last measure, assassination proved a highly effective way of undercutting the will to resist and of ensuring the obedience of the peasants.

Since the villagers could not easily disentangle themselves from the front organizations of which they were members, these organizations were able to mete out punishment to any who persisted in resisting the Party's orders. Three categories of punishment were known to the villagers, each more severe than the previous one. These were isolation, re-education, and trial by secret tribunal.

Under the first type, the offender was completely isolated from his fellow villagers. They were not permitted to give him food or shelter, and his family could not see or talk to him. He was treated as an outcast. Under the second type, the offender was removed from the village and placed in a special camp, where he was informed of his mistakes and "re-educated." The most severe form of punishment was the trial by secret tribunal; if the offender did not return to his home, the other villagers deduced the verdict.

Coercion was one tactic used by the NLHS in organizing the population; the other, applied with equal skill, was persuasion. A Royal Government report in July, 1957, observed:

> The Pathet Lao propagandist knows how to present himself as a friend who helps and advises and works with his own hands. He acts disinterestedly, shows honesty and enthusiasm and knows how to get along with a minimum of comfort.
>
> The success of his work lies in those qualities and in the fact that he is always there . . . and does not fear the ephemeral effect of the mobile information teams of the Royal Lao Government.
>
> The proof of the success of the propaganda methods of the Pathet Lao cadres can best be seen in the fact that they have succeeded in having the Lao population accept the Vietnamese as "brothers."[22]

Buddhism and its institutions confronted the NLHS with an interesting tactical dilemma. As Buddhism is strong among the lowland Lao and the bonzes form a considerable part of the population and wield great influence on Lao customs and habits, the NLHS was attracted by the possibility of using this influence for political ends.

Attempts were made by the NLHS to enlist the support of the bonzes and to bring them to the NLHS point of view on political

[22] Quoted in Bernard B. Fall, "Informal Communications in Southeast Asia" (Washington: 1960), mimeographed, pt. 2, pp. 32–33.

matters, particularly during the tenure of Phoumi Vongvichit as Minister of Cults. The fact that Souphanouvong is a devout Buddhist has been of assistance in this effort, as indicated by a Lao bonze in Vientiane:

> He visits the monks at the wat and tells them of his troubles and the hardships suffered by his army when they were fighting in the forest. The soldiers were not paid any salary, and they had to beg rice in the villages. I like Souphanouvong and the Pathet Lao because they are honest people. Most of the monks sympathize with the Pathet Lao in their difficulties.[23]

However, because the NLHS leaders and the Pathet Lao forces included a strong component of ethnic minorities, they could not take an unequivocal stand on Buddhism. In the mountain country, the people are not Buddhists but make sacrifices to the spirits of the forest; they regard the bonzes who come to their upland villages preaching Buddhism as subversive agents. In many such villages controlled by the Pathet Lao, the bonzes have been chased out by the population, and Buddhist temples have been desecrated.

The effect of the softening-up action carried on by the Pathet Lao cadres in the villages was first to make the villagers less amenable to the central government's orders, and then to estrange them completely from the government. They arrived at the point where they believed that the web of fronts and groups in which they were enmeshed was really their government. The French described this state as *pourriture*—rottenness.

The basic source for statements from the leadership of the NLHS was the official NLHS newspaper, *Lao Hak Sat,* until it was banned by the Royal Government on May 16, 1959. After this, a clandestine edition was quoted from with regularity by Hanoi and Peking. Important statements of attitude or policy were quoted from *Lao Hak Sat* immediately after publication, a surprising feat in a country whose communications are primitive. Even more amazing, Hanoi and Peking have quoted from *Lao Hak Sat* a full day before its publication in Vientiane. Crediting such statements to the Pathet Lao had several advantages for Hanoi and Peking: It enhanced the guerrilla movement's international prestige, and it permitted Hanoi and Peking to avoid committing themselves on many thorny issues.

A favorite Communist theme in the early days of the Pathet Lao

[23] Quoted in Joel M. Halpern, *Government, Politics, and Social Structure in Laos* (Southeast Asia Studies, Monograph Series, No. 4 [New Haven, Conn.: Yale University Press, 1964]).

movement was that the Royal Government, by prosecuting an armed campaign against the guerrillas, was violating Article 15 of the Geneva cease-fire agreement. This had provided that "each party undertakes to refrain from any reprisals or discrimination against persons or organizations for their activities during the hostilities [of the Indochina War] and also undertakes to guarantee their democratic freedom." Because the Pathet Lao was organized before Geneva, its leadership could claim a valid grievance against Vientiane's efforts to reassert its authority over all the territory of Laos.

After the summer of 1959, the Communist portrayal of the Pathet Lao changed drastically. From being portrayed as one legitimate faction among many, the Pathet Lao became one of two opposing sides in a civil war. Gradually their views came to be represented as those of "the people of Laos" and the views of the Vientiane government as those of a minority. By then, the Pathet Lao was equipped with a powerful radio transmitter, which broadcast the views of the leadership on a station calling itself Radio Pathet Lao. This, too, was part of what Giap had called "people's war."

The Second National Congress of the Neo Lao Hak Sat, held in Sam Neua Province from April 6 to 11, 1964, elected a Central Committee of sixty-three members. This Central Committee then re-elected Souphanouvong as Chairman and elected other officers. They are: Vice Chairmen: Sithone Komadam, Phay Dang, and Kaysone Phomvihan; members of the Standing Committee: Nouhak Phoumsavan, Khamtay Siphandon, Phoun Sipraseuth, Sisomphou, Nhia Veu, and Kham Moun; and Secretary-General: Phoumi Vongvichit.[24] By 1964, the membership of the Phak Khon Ngan was placed at 700 members.

Souphanouvong told the author, in December, 1962, that the day-to-day work of the NLHS is handled by about twenty subcommittees of the Central Committee, and that he was chairman of more than half of these committees and personally presided over them. This helps to explain Souphanouvong's lengthy absences at undisclosed locations in the mountains of Laos.

The actual distribution of decision-making authority within the movement, however, departs from this neat hierarchical structure. It is bound up with the ties with the Lao Dong Party.

Although Souphanouvong has been titular leader of the Pathet

[24] Radio Pathet Lao, quoted by Radio Hanoi, April 11, 1964. For the action program adopted at this Congress, see Appendix VI.

Lao movement since its founding, it is uncertain how much weight he carries in the inner councils of the NLHS, and more particularly in those of the Phak Khon Ngan. Unlike Kaysone, Souphanouvong has never been reported as belonging to that exclusive elite of the Phak Khon Ngan who hold simultaneous membership in the Lao Dong Party.

The Vietnamese Communists have paid particular attention to securing absolute control over the Workers' Party in Laos. The fact that the titular leader of the front behind which the Party operates is a prince of the royal blood, and the fact that the program adopted by this front in 1964 failed to mention the incorporation of Laos in an eventual Communist-dominated federation with Vietnam and Cambodia, afford a glimpse of the distance that separates the word of the front and the intentions of the Party.

6.

The First Coalition

The 1954 cease-fire agreements defined who held what in Indo-china. They established a *status quo* that the Conference partici-pants pledged themselves to honor by renouncing military conquest as a means of effecting territorial changes. The United States, in the tremendous striking power of the Seventh Fleet in the Western Pacific, held the key to enforcing this *status quo*.

The leaders of Laos saw clearly that their country's independence hinged on whether their larger neighbors and the big powers respected the pledge to renounce military expansion into Laos. Disturbances among neighboring countries had always had reper-cussions in Laos. In the centuries of wars waged by the princely states of Southeast Asia, the Kingdom of Luang Prabang had been swept this way and that, first the vassal of Annam and then of Siam. The French Protectorate, far from removing these destructive cur-rents, had brought them even more intimately into contact with the Kingdom.

In 1954, Laos benefited from a balance of interests that pre-vented any of its neighbors from launching a war of conquest on its soil. To avoid upsetting this balance, Laos sought to avoid aligning itself with either the Communist bloc or the non-Communist bloc.

The international situation looked favorable for this effort. The Chinese had embarked upon a policy of wooing Asian neutrals, and any pledge that Chou En-lai might have given at Geneva to respect the sovereignty of the Royal Government of Laos in return for exclusion of an American military presence in Indochina fitted in well with this policy. Communist China was not to take an active hand in Laos for more than six years. Peking had been anxious to extricate itself from the Korean War, and saw no need to become embroiled in another war with the United States in an area that, unlike Korea, did not contain American garrisons. And the Americans had no need of military positions in Laos, since their power was based on the ships of the Seventh Fleet, backed up by bases on Okinawa and in the Philippines.

The North Vietnamese position was less obvious than that of the Chinese, and it was here that the Royal Lao Government had to look for a threat to its sovereignty. However, North Vietnam, the newest and weakest member of the Communist bloc, was clearly under Chinese pressure to keep on good terms with Vientiane.

Scarcely a year after the Geneva Conference came the Bandung Conference of Afro-Asian states. This provided a good indication that the Chinese were pressuring the North Vietnamese to normalize their relations with the neutral, non-Communist government in Vientiane. A meeting of the Lao and North Vietnamese delegates to Bandung was brought about on April 23, 1955, in the presence of both Chou En-lai and Indian Prime Minister Jawaharlal Nehru.

At this meeting, Chou and Pham Van Dong, North Vietnam's Foreign Minister, gave verbal assurance of noninterference in Laos. Further, Pham Van Dong concluded a written agreement with the Lao delegation covering future relations between their two governments. The text of this agreement read:

> First, the Government of the Democratic Republic of Vietnam considers that the settlement which is due to take place between the Royal Government of Laos and the "Pathet Lao," by virtue of the Geneva agreements, is a question of internal order which the Royal Government of Laos and "Pathet Lao" are entirely free to solve in the best way possible in the higher interests of the country and people of Laos.
>
> Second, the Government of the Democratic Republic of Vietnam and the Royal Government of Laos will develop and harmonize the good neighborly relations which tie and should tie these countries to each other, within the framework of the Five Principles defined in the Sino-Indian Agreement of April 29, 1954.[1]

The North Vietnamese could well afford to make this statement; their principal preoccupation was the reunification of their own country, and the frustration of this objective had not yet made Laos of vital military importance to them.

The combination of correct relations with all its neighbors and

[1] Quoted in George McTurnan Kahin, *The Asian-African Conference* (Ithaca, N.Y.: Cornell University Press, 1956), p. 27.

the good will of the great powers was the *sine qua non* of peace in Laos. This the leaders in Vientiane energetically set out to achieve. In demonstration of its neutral posture vis-à-vis the Cold War, the Vientiane government permitted no embassy of either Communist China or Nationalist China, North Vietnam or South Vietnam, but strove to maintain friendly contacts with all of them. This was a variation of the Indian and Indonesian patterns of maintaining consuls in both Hanoi and Saigon.

Laos was walking a tightrope. The most vigorous proponent of this policy balance was Prince Souvanna Phouma. On becoming Prime Minister again at the beginning of 1956, he declared: "We will oppose any foreign interference in our own affairs. We will strive to maintain the best possible relations with our friends and our allies [i.e., France], and especially with our neighbors."[2]

Determined to keep Laos out of the Cold War, Souvanna Phouma visited Peking and Hanoi in August, 1956. In a joint statement with Chou En-lai, the Prince pledged his government to carry out a policy of "peace and neutrality," to subscribe to no new military alliance so long as Laos' security was not menaced, and to allow no foreign military bases other than as provided in the 1954 accords. Informally, Souvanna Phouma assured Mao Tse-tung that Laos desired friendly relations with Peking, although it could not permit diplomatic representation because of the continuing rivalry between Peking and Taipei. According to Souvanna Phouma's own account, Mao replied that his government was content with Laos' nonrecognition of both Peking and Taipei.

A few days later, Souvanna Phouma was received equally cordially in Hanoi. In a joint statement with North Vietnamese Government leaders, he gave assurances that Laos would not permit foreign powers to set up military bases on its territory. A short while later, Souvanna Phouma was received in the capital of South Vietnam with every display of good will.

Shortly after the establishment of the coalition in Vientiane, Chou En-lai voiced his satisfaction before the National People's Congress in Peking:

> The establishment of a coalition government in the kingdom of Laos and the settlement of the question of the provinces of Sam Neua and Phong Saly were signs that great progress had been made in the implementation of the Geneva Agreement on Laos. The Chinese Government welcomes the peaceful unification of the Kingdom of Laos on the basis of the Geneva Agreement, which provides a more favor-

2 *Le Journal d'Extrême-Orient* (Saigon), February 29, 1956.

able condition for the independent development of Laos. Although the United States has not given up its attempt to drive Laos into the Manila Treaty [SEATO], Laos, like Cambodia, adheres to a policy of peace and neutrality.[3]

A few months after this Souvanna Phouma once again made his policy quite clear. Also, he gave one of his many indications that he was fully aware of the danger represented by Communist subversion and was determined not to allow it to endanger the course of neutrality:

> In the political field, the new government will strive to consolidate its prestige and maintain the Lao tradition to safeguard freedom and the complete independence of Laos. It will do all it can to check the Communists' sabotaging activities and the spread of Communist thoughts and ideas. Our neutral policy applies only to the military field. Politically speaking, we still adopt a system of constitutional monarchy and practice democracy. We have decided to maintain friendly relations with democratic nations.[4]

Security or Insecurity?

The preservation of the independence of Laos and Cambodia, and the support of non-Communist governments in those countries, had been the objective of Secretary of State John Foster Dulles since the Geneva Conference, as we have seen. In the aftermath of the cease-fire, Dulles had determined that these countries might be defended by a regional alliance guaranteeing collective action in case of aggression and the deterrent of over-all American nuclear striking power.

It became obvious immediately that aid programs would be required if the Royal Lao Government was to maintain its authority, even after the fighting on its soil had stopped and the Viet Minh had withdrawn. The aid that the United States had been furnishing under the 1950 agreements was continued, and a reinforced American aid mission, United States Operations Mission (USOM), began operations in Vientiane on January 1, 1955. In an exchange of notes the following July, the validity of the basic agreements was reaffirmed.[5]

French aid to Laos also continued in the forms of the military training mission permitted by the Geneva agreements and the provi-

---

[3] New China News Agency (Peking), February 11, 1958.

[4] Agence France-Presse, June 15, 1958.

[5] *Economic Cooperation. Agreement Between the United States of America and Laos* (Department of State, Treaties and Other International Acts Series, No. 3664 [Washington: Government Printing Office, 1956]).

sion of teachers and other assistance in the fields of education and cultural exchanges. Britain also undertook limited technical aid to Vientiane under the Colombo Plan.

Following the signing of the SEATO treaty in September, 1954, Secretary of Defense Charles E. Wilson requested the Joint Chiefs of Staff to set forth their views on the optimum size of the Lao armed forces that the United States should support to further the goals of the Mutual Security Program. The consensus of the Joint Chiefs was that, with the end of actual fighting in Indochina and with the inclusion of Laos under the "umbrella" provided by SEATO, it would be best to reduce the Lao Territorial army from its wartime strength of 15,000 men to the level needed for routine internal policing. In November, 1954, the Joint Chiefs advised the Secretary of Defense, "No force levels are recommended for this country."[6]

A key factor influencing the Joint Chiefs' decision was the prohibition inherent in the Geneva agreements against U.S. establishment of a Military Assistance Advisory Group (MAAG) in Laos to supervise the training of the armed forces. The State Department advised that the United States would respect this prohibition. The Defense Department thereupon concluded that in Laos it would be impossible to ensure effective training on the spot, unlike in South Vietnam, where a MAAG had been operating since 1950, and recommended against supporting a Lao army.

Within months after the Geneva cease-fire, it became apparent that the Pathet Lao were acting as a political force as well as a military force. In their two northern provinces, Pathet Lao cadres were not only recruiting young men but also drumming up popular support for the manifesto issued by Souphanouvong's "resistance government" in 1950, whose objectives included formation of a coalition government with Vientiane.

At this point, the Royal Government in Vientiane had no civic action program; it did not even have a Ministry of Rural Affairs. The army, which included many of the country's best-educated men, was now the only national organization that could enlist support for the central government. Thus the army, besides its policing function, would have the higher mission of awakening patriotism, unifying the nation, and lending substance to its independence.

Asked to reconsider their decision in January, 1955, the Joint Chiefs advised that their views on support of a Lao army had not changed. They stated that mutual-security support of a Lao army

[6] *Hearings*, II, p. 8.

could not be recommended "from the military point of view," but acquiesced in the provision of such support "should political considerations be overriding."[7] These views were communicated from Wilson to Dulles with the comment that Wilson would acquiesce in a program of support for a Lao army "for political reasons."

That same month, the State Department requested the American diplomatic mission in Vientiane to draw up its recommendation for the size of a Lao army. The mission in Vientiane, taking into account the potential political influence of such an army and the stimulus to the economy that army salaries would provide, came up with a recommendation for 23,600 men.

A year later, in January, 1956, the Joint Chiefs were asked to consider a small increase in the size of the Lao army. Again they acquiesced, this time on the basis that it seemed indicated "from a psychological, political, and morale aspect." Referring to the earlier correspondence, however, the Joint Chiefs stated that "their views . . . are still valid."[8] The Royal Army was increased to 25,000 men.

During 1955, it will be recalled, the Royal Army's probes into the Pathet Lao-occupied provinces of Sam Neua and Phong Saly had been forcibly rebuffed, with some casualties. By January, 1956, the Royal Government was encountering real difficulty in reasserting its authority there.

Now, by putting into the hands of the Royal Government a military weapon to meet a political threat, the United States had created the issue of "American imperialism" in Laos. Hanoi and Peking could not have done it better. The harassment of the Royal Army by the Pathet Lao was no military threat to the Royal Government; the objective of the Pathet Lao was political power. The weakness of the Royal Government was its political inefficacy in the countryside. The United States had done nothing to assist that government in asserting its authority. In areas of the country accessible to the Pathet Lao political cadres, the Royal Army became synonymous with repression.

A Congressional committee reported:

U.S. support of a 25,000-man army, of the entire military budget, and of segments of the civilian economy is, in fact, based on a political determination, made by the Department of State contrary to the recommendations of the Joint Chiefs of Staff. In Laos, the only coun-

[7] *Ibid.*
[8] *Ibid.*

try in the world where the United States supports the military budget 100 per cent, military judgments have been disregarded.[9]

As late as 1958, Defense Department documents continued to list the Lao army as being "not within force objectives." By 1959, executive-branch papers were speaking of an additional mission for the Royal Army, which originally had been intended only to maintain internal security. The army was then assigned the added mission of resisting outside aggression (against a regular North Vietnamese army of 300,000!). By 1960, executive-branch documents indicated that the military program in Laos had "just grown" on the Defense Department without military justification.[10]

On the basis of available documentation on the origin of United States support for the Royal Army, it seems farcical to argue, as did an official statement of the American Embassy in Vientiane, dated April 25, 1958, that Laos, with the advent of independence,

> inherited [sic] a 25,000-man army, which it desired to maintain in order to guard against potential Communist aggression originating in North Vietnam and the Pathet Lao provinces to the north. As it turned out, it was well that this army was maintained, for fighting soon broke out.

The thinking of the intelligent Lao leaders in Vientiane was more realistic. They saw the need for a small armed force to secure law and order on Lao territory, put down rebellion should it occur, and prevent lawless bands from marauding in the villages. This also had been the view of the Geneva powers when they agreed to permit Laos to retain a French military training mission and to procure arms for its own defense. In the event of an invasion, Laos would be compelled to seek international help. Prince Somsanith, for instance, one of the most intelligent of the Lao leaders, said categorically after his tenure as Prime Minister that what Laos needed was a police force, not an army.

The tendency of high-ranking State Department officials to assign to the U.S.-supported army in Laos functions far in excess of routine policing caused understandable uneasiness among the Vientiane leaders. They deplored the American habit of referring to the "containment" of Communist power by a string of national armies in the countries on China's periphery. To equate an army intended to maintain internal security in Laos with one ready to go to war against North Vietnam, and possibly even China, seemed sheer folly to these

[9] *Ibid.* Italics in original.
[10] *Ibid.*

men. Moreover, a "collective security" that provoked their neighbors by upsetting the delicate *status quo* of 1954 was, in their view, no security at all. It was the opposite—insecurity.

They recognized the extreme danger of being caught by a rebellion à la Giap, supported from North Vietnam, the guerrilla type of warfare that a conventional army could not deal with—just as the 450,000-man French Union Forces could not deal with the Viet Minh.

Nevertheless, with the United States equipping it and financing it to the last penny, the Royal Lao Army was built up, by 1959, to two paratroop battalions, one artillery battalion, one armored reconnaissance battalion, twelve infantry battalions, and twelve volunteer infantry battalions. This army was saddled with a Transportation Corps, an Ordnance Corps, a Quartermaster Corps, Military Police, and the other impedimenta of a fighting force in which jeeps have replaced elephants. The armed forces also included a "navy" of river patrol boats and an air force of six C-47 transports and a handful of light reconnaissance aircraft. These were officially described as "small by Western standards, but sufficient for the job at hand."[11]

The fact that Laos has few roads, most of which are unserviceable during the six months of the rainy season, appears not to have greatly influenced planning. The army's jeeps and trucks were hardly suited to ferreting out insurgents in remote villages accessible by little more than footpaths.

Even more serious, however, was the fact that the American-supported army was based on the lowland Lao, who inhabited the valleys, and ignored the mountain tribes, who inhabited the uplands that formed most of the country and, more particularly, its border regions. The Pathet Lao made a point of recruiting entire units of the ethnic minorities, but for years the Royal Army made no major effort to incorporate the Kha, Black Thai, or Meo. The situation changed in 1961, when their fighting qualities and strategic geographical distribution were finally recognized by the American Special Forces.

Also, there were serious deficiencies in the preparation given the officers of the Royal Army. During the first few years, little attention was paid to counterguerrilla training. Promising junior officers were sent off to staff school in the United States and France to study tactics for set-piece battles with neat front lines, thrusts, and flanking

[11] *Briefing Notes on the Royal Kingdom of Laos* (Vientiane: U.S. Information Service, May, 1959), p. E-2.

movements. Soon, Laos boasted five generals but possessed few officers or noncoms who could lead a squad of rangers on a week's jungle patrol.

Having justified American support for a Lao army on political grounds, the State Department went halfway toward meeting the Joint Chiefs' cautions that such support would be wasted if it was not coupled with on-the-spot training by Americans. The State Department set up an American military mission in disguise in Vientiane. This mission, known as the Programs Evaluation Office (PEO), was attached to the U.S. Operations Mission. All its members wore civilian clothes and were officially described as "technicians." Officially, their training activities were under the over-all responsibility of the French Military Mission.[12]

The head of the PEO was a U.S. Army general who had been removed from the roster of active officers. Because he wore civilian clothes, his presence in Laos became known only in 1961, when a *New York Times* reporter tracked down the whereabouts of Brigadier General John A. Heintges, a career officer who had distinguished himself in Europe in World War II and who had seemingly vanished into thin air after 1959, when, it became known, he had taken up his unpublicized duties in Laos.

The PEO's task was a monumental one. At the height of the Indochina War, the French had trained and equipped a Lao Territorial army of 15,000, with many French officers and noncoms acting as a cadre for the Lao troops. But the PEO had to form an army completely staffed and officered by the Lao.

The problems in administering this program were immense. It was necessary to station teams of PEO technicians at Luang Prabang, Paksane, Savannakhet, and Pakse as well as at Vientiane. Army recruitment was haphazard. Pay envelopes were mysteriously rerouted during their long journey from Vientiane to the soldiers in the field. Fully three years after the PEO was established, tables of organization and equipment were still being drawn up. Programming was based on sketchy Lao listings of troop units and unmethodical estimates of strength.

The American economic-aid program in Laos was built around the Royal Army. The existence of an army of this size in a country with virtually no productive capacity and little experience with a money economy created economic problems, and to deal with them, a program of considerable proportions had to be implemented.

[12] Department of State, *The Situation in Laos* (Washington: September, 1959), p. 23.

Without hard goods to soak up the salary payments to the army, a runaway inflation would have ensued. The solution was to finance a goods import program in order to maintain the value of the Lao currency, the kip.

Each month, the United States Government made a multimillion-dollar deposit in a New York bank account in the name of the Royal Lao Government. The latter then placed in circulation the equivalent value in kip, which was officially pegged at 35 to the dollar. The dollars were used to pay for hard goods that were then imported into Laos by commercial importers under a licensing system operated by the Lao government.

These funds came from Congressional appropriations under the Mutual Security Program. Although the PEO was attached to USOM, the PEO had sole jurisdiction of the spending of these funds. An official Embassy document stated:

> Most of this local currency generated by the dollar-aid program is not utilized by USOM in its own operations, nor has USOM the responsibility for the use to which these funds are put, since most of them go for the support of the Lao military establishment.[13]

The PEO also decided the military equipment supplied to the Royal Army. Funds for this also came out of the Mutual Security Program under the title Military Assistance Program. The amounts of the various categories of the American aid program can be seen from the figures in Table 1.

The PEO not only controlled the bulk of the aid funds spent in Laos, but also possessed its exclusive channel of communication to Washington, through the Commander in Chief, Pacific Forces (CINCPAC), whose headquarters were in Hawaii, and the Defense Department. At times this caused conflict with the authority of the Ambassador, who was the head of the "country team" of official Americans in Vientiane, and the State Department. In one instance, the PEO promised the Lao Defense Ministry a salary increase for the army. The move was approved by CINCPAC and sent back to the Defense Department in Washington. The State Department, fearing an inflationary effect on the Lao economy, cabled a protest. The increase, however, went through on schedule. The Central Intelligence Agency, whose functions extended from the field of intelligence gathering into actual operations, also maintained its own channels of communications to Washington.

The arrival in Vientiane of hundreds of Americans to implement

[13] *Briefing Notes on the Royal Kingdom of Laos,* p. D-5.

TABLE 1

U.S. FOREIGN AID TO LAOS, FISCAL YEARS 1955–63*
(*In Millions of Dollars*)

Fiscal Year	For Development Grants and Technical Cooperation	For Budget Support[a]	For Military Equipment[b]	Total
1955	$	$ 40.9	$	$ 40.9
1956	1.0	47.3	27.4	75.7
1957	1.5	42.9	4.3	48.7
1958	1.7	29.8	5.4	36.9
1959	1.7	23.4	7.5	32.6
1960	1.2	40.9	13.4	55.5
1961	1.4	29.1	33.4	63.9
1962	—.6	27.5	37.1	64.0
1963	....	38.5	24.0	62.5
	$7.9	$320.3	$152.5	$480.7

* *Source:* Agency for International Development.
a Principally to pay salaries of army and civil administration.
b Referred to in official publications as Military Assistance Program (MAP).
Note: Figures do not include funds for assistance under PL 480, which were minor, or expenditures of the CIA, which are secret. Military Equipment figures represent net deliveries, but other figures represent dollar obligations; in some years, actual expenditures were substantially lower.

this large program created a swarm of activity that caused no little astonishment in a country accustomed to thinking of foreigners in terms of the easygoing French. People who had always lived in wooden houses open to the ventilation of the breeze and with wide verandas on all sides looked on dubiously as Americans shut themselves up in air-conditioned cubicles. The Lao marveled at the Americans, who, in order to run the air conditioners, did not hesitate to set up a generating station, which required the transport of barrels of diesel fuel, which necessitated building a railway line to the Mekong. American know-how took care of everything.

The money fed into the economy of Laos to pay for the army— amounting to the highest per-capita influx of American aid into any Southeast Asian country, as can be seen from Table 2—went for importing an extraordinary variety of goods in order to soak up paper money and prevent a runaway inflation. Soon the shops along Vientiane's two paved thoroughfares began to look like the open-air market at the landing wharf of the Hong Kong–Macao ferry, with their shiny new aluminum pails, flashlights, cheap suitcases, and

TABLE 2

U.S. FOREIGN AID TO COUNTRIES OF SOUTHEAST ASIA, FISCAL YEARS 1946–63

Country	Population	Total[a] (In Millions of Dollars)	Per Capita
Laos[b]	2,500,000	$ 481	$192.3
South Vietnam[b]	14,617,000	2,656	181.7
Cambodia[b]	4,952,000	367	74.1
Philippines	30,200,000	1,851	61.3
Thailand	28,000,000	869	31.0
Indonesia	100,000,000	881	8.8
Burma	22,000,000	108	4.9
Malaysia	10,500,000	25	2.4

[a] Source: Agency for International Development, Statistics and Reports Division, U.S. Foreign Assistance and Assistance from International Organizations—Obligations and Loan Authorizations (Washington: 1964).

[b] Figures are for fiscal years 1955–63 only.

other bric-a-brac. Defending the range of goods allowed into Laos under the American commercial import program, the Embassy declared:

Our [Economic Aid] Mission in Vientiane advises that there are only three Cadillacs in Laos, all models predating the aid program, and that only 30 Buicks, all lowest priced models, have been imported with funds derived from the aid program. It is known that licenses for a reasonable quantity of fishhooks and thermos jugs were issued. It is thought probably that festival decorations used in the celebration of the 2500th anniversary of Buddha were imported although not paid for with U.S. aid funds. There is no record of any automobile covers being included. It is known that feather dusters, sporting goods, fishing tackle, thermos jugs, decorations and musical instruments were included in the country's import plan, but insofar as the use of U.S. funds is concerned the Mission advises that quantities of these items imported were not significant.[14]

It is a matter of conjecture what a "reasonable quantity" of fishhooks is in a country where the people fish by dipping broad nets suspended on poles.

The import trade in Laos was concentrated in the hands of the Chinese merchants, who had access to the free-money markets outside the country and who had influence in the Lao Government. While the import program operated on the officially pegged rate of 35 kip to the dollar, free-market operators in Bangkok and Hong Kong gave up to 110 kip to the dollar. This great disparity led to

[14] Mimeographed statement dated April 25, 1958.

speculation in foreign exchange in which the hard goods themselves became merely the medium for defrauding the import program. This involved importing dollar-financed goods and then exporting them for resale for hard currencies, which in turn could be turned to importing more goods. In the later stages, the importers did not even bother to transport the goods to Laos, a costly business on the single railway from Bangkok, but merely bribed a customs official to issue a receipt for them, and resold them in Bangkok.

Under the weight of the commodity import program, the imbalance in Laos' trade increased dramatically, as shown in Table 3.

TABLE 3

LAO BALANCE OF TRADE, 1939–58*
(*In Millions of Kip*)

	Imports	Exports
1939	4.3	0.6
1949	65.4	7.3
1958	1,040.9	54.7
1962	1,929.6	62.0

* *Source:* Joel M. Halpern, *Economic and Related Statistics Dealing with Laos* (Los Angeles: University of California, Department of Anthropology and Sociology, Laos Project Paper No. 11, 1961), extracted from Table 35, p. 39; *Far Eastern Economic Review* (Hong Kong), January 9, 1964, p. 52.

Despite American efforts to support the kip, its value on the free market declined steadily. In small market towns outside Vientiane, the price of 100 kilograms of polished rice rose from 450 kip in 1955, to 600 kip in 1956, to 950 kip in 1957; in the same period, the price of one can of kerosene rose from 110 to 260 kip; and that of one chicken from 20 to 80 kip. American Ambassador Parsons later attributed this inflationary trend to the Lao's loss of confidence in the stability of the kip following the initiation of negotiations between Souvanna Phouma and the Pathet Lao.[15] This explanation, however, appeared to be wide of the mark.

The profit to be reaped from discrepancies between the official and unofficial kip rate was so tempting that even Americans were implicated in malpractices in connection with the administration of the aid program. Subsequent disclosures made at Congressional hearings on the program in Washington compromised the reputations of several Americans and undermined the confidence of those Lao who

[15] *Hearings,* I, p. 232.

were more interested in preserving their country's independence than in lining their pockets.

The abuses of the import program had several other deleterious effects. The proliferating luxurious villas and large automobiles in the capital were in marked contrast to the rudimentary furnishings of the country at large. No traveler coming to Vientiane from the provinces could fail to be astonished by what he saw. The American aid program was obviously increasing the gap between the haves and the have-nots, and as a result it was creating grievances rather than eliminating them.

As pointed out by one observer:

> Corruption and extortion in the customs, banking, foreign trade, police, and other administrative departments were commonplace. Black market deals in American aid dollars reached such proportions that the Pathet Lao needed no propaganda to turn the rural population against the townspeople. The Chinese of Hong Kong and Bangkok and a few Lao officials profited from the American aid, while the poor Lao for whom it was intended stood by helplessly. Official Vientiane of course knew nothing about this prodigious fraud, although the entire city seemed to be involved.[16]

Enrichment of the small Lao elite in the capital undermined the Lao tradition of service, which counted the accumulation of wealth a perquisite of office but not a goal in itself. In an effort to counteract the corrupting effect of newfound wealth on public officials, especially younger ones, the government in 1959 issued an edict requiring civil servants to attend religious services.

With the sudden advent of the cash economy came new responsibilities of finance and taxation. The realization that the growing apparatus of ministerial offices depended upon the economic power of a foreign nation made many Lao feel that their country had less independence now than under the Protectorate.

The American program concentrated on financing the import of hard goods in order to prevent a runaway inflation, and neglected aid to the countryside, which would have had permanent effects. Of the $480.7 million obligated to Laos in fiscal years 1955–63, only $1.9 million was spent on improving agriculture—that is, less than 1 per cent of aid funds were spent in a field of activity that provided the livelihood of 96 per cent of the population. Of course, the agricultural economy of Laos indirectly benefited from the import program.

Except for emergency airdropping of rice to alleviate shortages in

16 Sisouk na Champassak, *op. cit.,* p. 64.

villages caused by the Indochina War, no village aid program was undertaken in earnest until the autumn of 1957, nearly two years after the USOM had been established. Prior to this, there had been experimental attempts to train young Lao to discover the basic needs of villages in terms of agriculture, education, health, and sanitation. Later, American specialists had been stationed in six provincial capitals to gather information and initiate some assistance on a limited scale. But in the 10,000 villages of Laos, the people had no intimation that a vast bureaucratic machine had arrived on the banks of the Mekong to help them overcome their age-old problems of malnutrition and illiteracy, disease and isolation.

Even where it did show up in the form of development projects instead of in sterile salary payments, American aid did little to improve the infrastructure of the country. American officials made a show of opening a newly surfaced road north of Vientiane in 1959, but in reality this was the completion of repair work on a stretch of the Royal Road, which had been ceremoniously inaugurated by the French Governor General on March 17, 1942.

The Lao administrators who, under the Protectorate, had gone around to the villages on bicycle and on foot, had graduated to the automobile, and paid fewer and fewer visits to the backwoods. In Vientiane, they moved serenely from diplomatic reception to diplomatic reception. Forfeiting their authority in the countryside, they retreated into the confines of the capital, where they played a political game of musical chairs for Cabinet posts.

From the neglected villages, officials in the provincial capitals began receiving reports that the Pathet Lao, who had already expanded their network of cells to cover virtually the whole country, were preparing to make a major issue of the widening gap between the haves and the have-nots in the coming elections.

It will be recalled that the agreements signed in November, 1957, by the Royal Government and the Pathet Lao had stipulated that supplementary elections would be held within four months with participation of the NLHS. Twenty additional seats in the National Assembly were to be contested, bringing its total membership to fifty-nine. (An extra contest would be held to elect a replacement for one member who had died.) The additional seats were to be contested in widely scattered parts of the country in accordance with a revised electoral map of Laos. Women would vote for the first time, satisfying a demand frequently advanced by the Pathet Lao. The elections were set for May 4, 1958.

The American Ambassador in Vientiane, aware that the NLHS

candidates would exploit any shortcomings of the aid program, initiated a crash program—dubbed "Operation Booster Shot"—to assist the villages. It was accurately described by a Congressional committee in 1959:

> Basically, this activity was a village aid program. The physical condition of the population in most remote areas was reported to be very bad. Few of the villages could be reached by road, and in most cases aid from Vientiane would have to be sent in primarily by air. In fact, most of it would have to be air-dropped due to a lack of airstrips usable by cargo-carrying planes. . . .
>
> The program took the form of more than 90 work projects, including well digging, erection of small irrigation and flood control dams, repair of schools and temples, repair of roads and airfields, and construction of hospitals; and the dropping of some 1,300 tons of food, medical and construction supplies and other useful commodities.
>
> The program did not overcome the Communist election slogans, related to the U.S. aid program, of "governmental corruption," "government indifference," or "U.S. domination."[17]

Operation Booster Shot did, however, for the first time bring meaningful aid to thousands of Lao besides the handful of officials and merchants in Vientiane who had been its principal beneficiaries up to then. But it was terribly late to attempt to undo the effective propaganda and coercion that the Pathet Lao cadres had been producing since 1954.

Thirteen NLHS candidates ran in the elections, and nine won. Another four seats went to the Santiphab (Peace) Party, formed in 1957 by Quinim Pholsena, a protégé of Souvanna Phouma, and which favored establishing contacts with Communist-bloc countries. Thus, "leftist" candidates had won a majority of the seats contested. Even more revealing, the NLHS candidates had won in widely scattered districts in both the north and the south. The progovernment forces had hopelessly weakened their cause by running eighty-five candidates for the twenty-one seats at stake.

Prince Souphanouvong, who showed up at the voting tent in Vientiane wearing patent-leather shoes and a dapper business suit with a kerchief tucked in his breast pocket, received 37,389 votes—more than any other candidate in the country. When the new members of the National Assembly convened a few days later, he was elected chairman.

Shaken by the success of the NLHS candidates in exploiting the issue of American aid, certain members of Souvanna Phouma's

17 *Hearings,* II, pp. 45–46.

Cabinet began talking about Laos' neutral course in very different terms from those Souvanna Phouma had been using. Phoui Sanani-kone, the veteran of Geneva who was now Minister of Foreign Affairs, declared that Laos' neutrality "does not imply a neutrality on the ideological plane: We are anti-Communists." He further constricted his definition of neutrality by adding: "Today, since there is a balance of forces, to be neutral means not to take part in any military alliance."[18] Obviously, he referred to SEATO; Laos was still allied to France in her bilateral mutual-security arrangement.

Phoui was implying that neutrality in foreign relations did not preclude forceful measures at home against Communist agents. In September, 1958, after he had succeeded Souvanna Phouma as Prime Minister, he declared:

> Like all Buddhists, the Lao have the habit of practicing tolerance. . . . However, events have made it clear to us that what matters is no longer philosophic considerations, but the defense of our cultural heritage and our love of freedom, which are being endangered by a subversive proselytism.[19]

In Souvanna Phouma's mind, holding the elections marked the fulfillment of the obligations Laos had undertaken at Geneva. The Prince stated that his government regarded as "fully accomplished" the obligations that Phoui had announced four years previously. He declared that Laos pledged itself anew not to enter into military alliances and not to seek military aid from foreign sources "except for the purpose of its effective territorial defense."[20]

On July 20, 1958, the International Control Commission adjourned sine die over the objections of its Polish member and amid a chorus of protest from Hanoi and Peking. The adjournment coincided with a mounting crisis in the Lao Cabinet.

Souvanna Phouma's government had been under constant American pressure since he had entered negotiations with the Pathet Lao for a coalition. Following the electoral successes of the NLHS, the United States, using as a pretext the mounting evidence of corruption in the import program and the need for a monetary reform, held up the normal monthly deposit of dollars in the Lao Government's bank account in New York.

Souvanna Phouma soon had a full-scale parliamentary crisis on

[18] *L'Indépendant* (Vientiane), June 17, 1958.
[19] *Le Journal d'Extrême-Orient,* September 2, 1958.
[20] Cmnd. 541, p. 121.

his hands—which was exploited by a group of would-be Young Turks, organized as the "Committee for the Defense of the National Interests" (CDNI). Describing themselves in their statutes and manifesto as a mass civic group, not a formal political party, the CDNI members favored reform in the civil service and, more importantly, a "hard" line in dealing with the Pathet Lao. Communist propaganda portrayed them as lackeys of American interests.

At all events, Souvanna Phouma was denied confidence by the National Assembly on the issue of monetary reform and resigned as Prime Minister on July 23.

Failure of the Experiment

The first coalition was at an end. It had been little more than an experiment, and its short life had been beset by turmoil and external pressures. A new Cabinet, formed by Phoui and voted into office by the National Assembly on August 18, excluded the NLHS ministers Souphanouvong and Phoumi Vongvichit and included four members of the CDNI who were not members of the Assembly. Souvanna Phouma became Ambassador to France.

One of Phoui's first official acts was to put an end to most of the abuses in the American aid program. Under American guidance, he instituted a monetary reform that revalued the kip at 80 to the dollar, and abolished the notorious system of import licenses.

In world affairs, Phoui made it clear, he favored keeping Laos on a neutral path. He warned that he would not brook the implantation on Lao soil of what he termed "Communist ideology." He was, he said, no less eager than Souvanna Phouma to integrate the Pathet Lao into the national community, but he was seriously worried by their links with a foreign country (i.e., North Vietnam).

Early in his tenure as Prime Minister, in the autumn of 1958, Phoui strayed from Souvanna Phouma's cautious avoidance of relations with the Communist or anti-Communist governments of the divided countries of Vietnam and China. Phoui established relations on a consular level with the anti-Communist governments.

Ngo Dinh Nhu, political counselor and brother of the South Vietnamese President, visited Vientiane in September, 1958, and was followed shortly by the South Vietnamese Foreign Minister. At the beginning of 1959, both South Vietnam and Nationalist China opened consulates in the Lao capital. On the other hand, Soviet overtures to open relations with Vientiane, which had been made as early as July, 1956, were not followed up.

All these developments, beginning with the adjournment of the ICC, were unfavorable to the North Vietnamese, who saw in them the prospect of a Vientiane government increasingly under American influence and therefore increasingly hostile to them. They had no representation in Vientiane, and had to depend on the Pathet Lao to influence developments in their favor and on the occasional direct contacts provided by visits such as Souvanna Phouma's in 1956.

North Vietnamese statements interpreted the ICC's adjournment as upsetting the *status quo* established at Geneva. Because their paramount objective was to reunify Vietnam under their direction, they could construe this upsetting of the Geneva arrangements only as a setback.

An official statement in Hanoi by the Vice Minister of Foreign Affairs, Ung Van Khiem, made it clear even before the ICC took the decisive vote to adjourn that North Vietnam regarded as "essential" the continued presence of the ICC in Laos.

> Peace in Indochina is indivisible: this was recognized during the discussions at the Geneva Conference and confirmed by the spirit of the final declaration, especially in Para. 4 and 5. In the light of Art. 39, 46 and 25 of the Geneva agreements concerning respectively Laos, Vietnam, and Cambodia, it is clear that the three international commissions should continue their activities as long as the political problems are not completely solved in the three countries [i.e., as long as Vietnam is not reunified]. In the present situation in Indochina, the winding up of the activities of the ICC in one country, Laos for instance, without taking into account the settlement of the political problems in the other two countries, would have dangerous repercussions on the effective implementation of the Geneva agreements and on the activities of the ICC as a whole. Such winding up runs counter to the spirit and letter of the Geneva agreements.[21]

This line on maintaining the ICC was faithfully echoed by Souphanouvong and other Pathet Lao spokesmen, the very men who had done the most to make the ICC's task impossible by preventing it from carrying out investigations in the border area. The NLHS newspaper declared:

> After the elections, the ICC will still have to continue its task . . . with a view to safeguarding peace in Laos at a time when peace in Indochina still is threatened, and the foreign reactionaries are still plotting to drag Laos into the Southeast Asian aggressive bloc. The

[21] Quoted by Vietnam News Agency (Hanoi), May 31, 1958.

presence of the ICC in Laos is therefore necessary, and conforms to the present practical situation.[22]

Significantly, Hanoi and Peking did not repeat two other themes that were taken up by the NLHS. The NLHS newspaper accused Souvanna Phouma's government, just a few weeks before its fall, of failure "to carry out a policy of neutrality in the real sense of the word," i.e., to establish relations with the Communist countries. The newspaper also protested the submission to the National Assembly of a draft decree providing for "the arrest, fining, and deprivation of political rights of those who had a tendency to favor a Communist system."[23]

The adjournment of the ICC in Laos coincided with renewed evidence of the Hanoi regime's concern about the refusal of the Ngo Dinh Diem regime to discuss reunification. Two years after the date for the scheduled Vietnam-wide elections had passed, there still appeared no possibility of this reunification. That the men in Hanoi were preoccupied with this problem is shown by an authoritative article written in May, 1958, by North Vietnam's Prime Minister, Pham Van Dong, who stated:

It is clear that the maneuvers of the American imperialists in South Vietnam are part of their over-all plan to sabotage peace and intervene in the domestic affairs of other countries. That is why the struggle of the Vietnamese people and the Government of the Democratic Republic of Vietnam against American intervention in the affairs of South Vietnam and for the country's reunification is inseparable from the general struggle of the peoples for peace and national independence.

The American invaders have insolently violated the Geneva agreements. They have prevented the calling of a consultative conference of representatives from North and South Vietnam to discuss the holding of free general elections. They have brought new war materials and military personnel into South Vietnam and built military bases; they have included South Vietnam in the "defense zone" of SEATO. They are now trying to compel it to join this aggressive bloc.

The Government of the Democratic Republic of Vietnam and the Vietnamese people are fully determined to resist the intrigues of the American imperialists, whose interference in the affairs of South Vietnam is the main cause of the present territorial division of the country and the chief obstacle to reunification. . . .[24]

[22] *Lao Hak Sat* (Vientiane), quoted by Vietnam News Agency, May 11, 1958.
[23] *Ibid.,* July 13, 1958.
[24] "The Foreign Policy of the Democratic Republic of Vietnam," *International Affairs* (Moscow), July, 1958, p. 20.

Whether or not free elections might have been held, as envisaged in the Geneva agreements, is not our concern here. What this article reveals is the charge by North Vietnam that the Americans were using South Vietnam as a "military base" and preventing reunification. Whatever understanding may have prevailed at the moment the agreements were signed, it was clear by the summer of 1958 that this understanding no longer existed. From this point, the actions on both sides, in both Vietnam and Laos, become a gradual escalation.

In late July and early August, the Vietnam News Agency, Hanoi's official mouthpiece, published a series of articles under the title "Imperialist Schemes in Vietnam Against Peace and Reunification." These amounted to a staff study of American military assistance to the Saigon regime, and they were obviously intended to alert the Lao Dong Party's cadres in the south to the possibility that a decision to mount an all-out guerrilla war against the Diem regime was imminent. The Party had had the foresight to leave caches of arms in the south when the bulk of the Viet Minh forces withdrew after the armistice. It had also pulled back into the north a large number of native southerners, who were subsequently indoctrinated and then infiltrated back into the south as guerrilla leaders.

Several approaches had been made on an official level to the Diem regime to initiate negotiations on the reunification issue, and on December 22, 1958, a final attempt was made when Pham Van Dong proposed in a letter the "normalization of relations" between North and South. No reply was received. Ho and Giap decided to take the reunification of their country into their own hands.

To maintain its contacts in the south, to infiltrate trained cadres from the north, and to receive back from the south couriers and recruits for indoctrination, the Lao Dong Party depended on trails through the mountains of eastern Laos, along which men and supplies could be moved with near-perfect concealment. The trails departed from points far north along the Laos-Vietnam border, and came to be known collectively as the Ho Chi Minh Trail. It was a two months' march through Laos into South Vietnam.

Phoui's government had come into office in Vientiane on a dual pledge of reform and firm measures against subversive agents at home. The breakup of the coalition had nullified the November, 1957, agreements between the Royal Government and the Pathet Lao. Phoui made it clear he regarded the Pathet Lao as agents of North Vietnam, and implied that he would have no compunction about using the Royal Army to clear out centers of Pathet Lao strength, on the pattern of the Katay Don Sasorith government in

1955. Such a move would mean that Royal Army troops would be patrolling right up to the borders of North Vietnam and interfering with North Vietnamese use of the trails in the eastern mountains of Laos.

Developments took an ominous turn when, in December, North Vietnam began accusing Phoui's government of perpetrating a series of air and ground violations of their common border, all of which Phoui stoutly denied, and between December 23 and 29, Hanoi dispatched across the border two companies of regular North Vietnamese soldiers. Some six miles inside Laos, the troops, estimated at 280 men, dug entrenchments and took up positions at the villages of Ban Taroua, Ban Tapang, and Ban Kapai, near the town of Tchepone in Savannakhet Province in the highly sensitive area just west of the demarcation line between North and South Vietnam.

The North Vietnamese lay claim to a frontier strip in that area, which they call the Canton of Huong Lap. However, the Royal Lao Government maintains that the map used at Geneva leaves no room for disputing its sovereignty over the area.

The accusations of ground violations are a characteristic tactic employed by Asian Communists when they are preparing their own military initiatives. Such accusations serve to confuse the proper location of blame for intrusions into another country. The accusations of air violations, however, are harder to explain. The air force at the disposal of the Lao Government included no fighter aircraft and appeared eminently unsuited to staging missions over North Vietnam. A clue may be had in accusations made by Chinese Communist organs toward the end of 1958 that American aircraft were flying over southern China, especially Yünnan Province. If the two sets of accusations are related, their explanation may lie in flights of American reconnaissance aircraft which the North Vietnamese identified as belonging to the Royal Lao Government.

The most logical explanation of the North Vietnamese dispatching of troops across the border near Tchepone seems to be that the North Vietnamese wished to emphasize, on the ground, their determination to keep Royal Government troops out of the area, and, in Vientiane, the desirability of adhering to the November, 1957, agreement, failing which, the North Vietnamese would support the Pathet Lao on the pattern of the precoalition period.

If the North Vietnamese action was intended as a warning, however, Phoui was not to be intimidated. Addressing the National Assembly in Vientiane, Phoui spoke of "a new and very grave, if not critical, situation" on the border and accused North Vietnam by name of interfering in the internal affairs of Laos. In addition, Phoui's government announced that it would bring the border violation to the attention of the United Nations.

On January 15, 1959, the National Assembly granted Phoui special powers to govern for one year without recourse to the votes of the deputies. A few days later, Phoui reshuffled his Cabinet, for the first time giving minor posts to three army officers. One of these was Colonel Phoumi Nosavan, who since his series of rapid promotions had associated himself closely with the Young Turks of the CDNI.

Phoui also declared that he was exploring means of dismembering the NLHS as a subversive organization. Several NLHS deputies in Vientiane, judging these indications not propitious and made uneasy by CDNI-inspired rumors of an imminent army coup, left town hastily in the direction of the North Vietnam frontier. In addition, according to Phoui, "in the provinces of Sam Neua and Xieng Khouang several important Neo Lao Hak Sat cadres and their families sought refuge in the Democratic Republic of Vietnam in order to get in touch with those Lao cadres who had refused to be integrated into the national community and are currently undergoing training from the North Vietnamese authorities."

In response to a vociferous campaign by Hanoi and Peking to have the ICC reconvened to deal with the charges and counter-charges of border violations, Phoui announced at a news conference on February 11: "The Royal Government considers that the agreement on the cessation of hostilities in Laos has been completely fulfilled." More specifically, he added that his government could not accept the view that Laos was bound by the terms of Geneva as long as a political settlement had not been reached in Vietnam. "No government worthy of the name," the Prime Minister said, "may mortgage the political future of its country on the basis of the situation existing in a neighboring country."

Phoui made it clear that he was accusing North Vietnam of activities that threatened his government's authority. "A neighboring country of the Kingdom," he charged, was waging a campaign against Laos "by acts of intimidation of all sorts, including the violation and occupation of its territory."[25]

Phoui's accusation was for the North Vietnamese the last in a long series of worsening developments in Laos. Gone was the ICC,

[25] Unclassified telegram from American Embassy, Vientiane, February 11, 1959.

whose presence in Laos had been turned into a greater disadvantage for the anti-Communists than for the Communists. A South Vietnamese consulate had been established in Vientiane. The coalition had broken up. Phoui's threat to move against the NLHS politically and against the Pathet Lao militarily heralded the scrapping of the November, 1957, agreement. Now Phoui's declaration that his government no longer considered itself bound by the terms of the Geneva cease-fire foreshadowed the possibility of unrestricted military aid from the West, and perhaps even alliances. The *status quo* established at Geneva was being scrapped. The United Nations, of which North Vietnam was not a member, was being brought into the picture as the potential arbiter of the conflict in Laos. All this jeopardized the favorable position of the Hanoi regime that had gradually developed with the increasing Pathet Lao strength and organization across the border.

The trump card remaining in North Vietnam's hand was the 1,500 Pathet Lao soldiers, forming two battalions, still awaiting assignment to the national army. Delays had been caused first by the Pathet Lao's demand for a preposterously high proportion of officers in the merged army, and second by a dispute over the rank to be awarded the senior Pathet Lao officer, Colonel Phoumi's old friend from Thakhek, Singkapo Chounlamany, who had also risen to colonel in the Pathet Lao army.

While negotiations between Vientiane and the Pathet Lao dragged on inconclusively, the Pathet Lao soldiers settled down to domestic life in the two camps in which they had been living since the signing of the November, 1957, agreement. One was in a valley south of Luang Prabang and the other was a former French Foreign Legion camp on the Plain of Jars, the Thong Mai Hin camp.

In mid-May, the Vientiane government adopted a firm attitude toward the two Pathet Lao battalions, and gave them an ultimatum: They must, within the next twenty-four hours, accept integration into the national army on the government's terms or else surrender and resign from the army. On May 17, the First Battalion south of Luang Prabang agreed to integration. A letter from Prince Souphanouvong, found on the person of the battalion commander and written some weeks earlier, instructed him to delay integration until after the next general elections. Evidently, Souphanouvong had intended the Pathet Lao troops to delay integrating as long as possible. But, in the face of the government's sudden ultimatum, he changed his instructions and ordered compliance with Phoui's integration ultimatum.

With the Second Battalion at the Plain of Jars, it was a different story. During eighteen months of living in camp, the Pathet Lao guerrillas and their families, largely Black Thai, Meo, and Kha, had been the object of increasingly lax surveillance. The Lao guards at the gates to the camp passed along food and water to the guerrillas and even, out of compassion, allowed some persons to slip in or out.

But on the morning of May 19 the guards were shocked out of their complacency. Overnight, the entire camp had been emptied. Its occupants—men, women, and children—had vanished, taking with them all their belongings.[26]

Upon learning of this colossal blunder, General Ouan Ratikon, who had been in charge of the government's efforts to negotiate the integration of the Pathet Lao troops, flew to the Plain of Jars and took command. He ordered the dropping of paratroopers along the battalion's presumed escape route and the scattering of leaflets bearing a reprint of Souphanouvong's last-minute message to the First Battalion ordering compliance with the integration demand.

In Vientiane, Souphanouvong and the other remaining NLHS members were placed under house arrest. There is evidence that the Second Battalion's escape was authorized not by Souphanouvong but by another, higher echelon in the Pathet Lao command, probably in Sam Neua or in Hanoi. The orders may very well have bypassed Souphanouvong completely, and it is possible he was not even aware of the battalion's intention to escape into the forest.

In any case, the Second Battalion's commander, by alternating rear-guard skirmishes with bogus offers to negotiate, succeeded in getting his troops safely beyond the reach of General Ouan's paratroopers. The Second Battalion disappeared from view. By the standards of many another country, this overt treachery was sufficient cause for the Pathet Lao leaders still in Vientiane to be lined up against a wall and shot. But to the Buddhist Lao, such reprisals are unheard of. Souphanouvong was released from house arrest on June 6.

Phoui's government announced that the soldiers of the Second Battalion would henceforth be treated as deserters. It was now the beginning of the rainy season, and Vientiane observers predicted a temporary halt in military activity. But subsequent events demonstrated the folly of trying to forecast the future in Laos.

[26] Sisouk na Champassak, *op. cit.,* p. 80.

7.

The Failure of the "Hard" Policy

The escape of the crack fighters of the Second Pathet Lao Battalion under the noses of their guards in the spring of 1959 shattered, overnight, the accords worked out so patiently by Prince Souvanna Phouma with the Neo Lao Hak Sat. Once this became apparent, the Pathet Lao acted to reinstate their power in the provinces of Sam Neua and Phong Saly.

They did so with the active encouragement of the North Vietnamese, who had reason to be alarmed by the decisiveness exhibited by the anti-Communist Phoui Sananikone government. On June 8, Radio Hanoi reported: "The first number of a newspaper addressed to the people and published by the Pathet Lao battalion in flight has reached Hanoi. The newspaper explains that as the reintegration agreements have not been respected, the battalion is obliged to defend itself." The battalion completed its return to "its former revolutionary bases," according to the Hanoi newspaper *Nhan Dan* (*The People*), on June 10. On May 20, the North Vietnamese news agency had referred to the "civil war," portending further foreign assistance and the danger of escalating military shipments in Laos.

Ominously, beginning about mid-July, small detachments of guerrillas struck at isolated government outposts deep in the jungles of Sam Neua Province. The attackers were found to be Black Thai tribesmen who inhabit areas astride the Laos-North Vietnam border. It was uncertain whether they were members of the Second Battalion.

In accord with General Giap's precepts, each attack mounted a superior local force against a Royal Army garrison. Although, over-all, the Pathet Lao were numerically inferior, the Royal Army forces were scattered in companies and platoons across the length and breadth of Laos.

Nor was the morale of the Royal Army equal to that of the attackers. In Sam Neua Province, the troops garrisoning mud forts (the defenses of the towns consisted of mud forts and trenchworks; the soldiers lived in thatched huts, and sometimes wooden barracks) were supplemented by local "self-defense forces." These militia were considerably less reliable than the regular troops, and in the thick of an attack often went over to the Pathet Lao. This happened, for instance, in the village of Muong Son, thirty-five miles west of the town of Sam Neua, where the lieutenant in command of the Royal Army company defending the village was shot in the back by militiamen who deserted during a Pathet Lao attack on July 20.

As far back as the memories of the village elders go, combatants in the jungles of Laos had tricked the enemy by making him think he was about to be overwhelmed by a large, well-equipped army. Before launching an assault on a village, the attackers commonly sent messengers ahead into the villages, in the guise of travelers, to buy rice or opium in order to create rumors of a massive concentration of troops beyond the mountains. Usually the attacks were launched just before daybreak with a concentrated mortar barrage or volley of rifle fire. Often the attackers heightened the impression of massive numerical superiority by shouting at the top of their voice or by blowing bugles. The Pathet Lao guerrillas repeated this pattern in village after village. At the first blast of the bugles, the handful of terrorized defenders usually fled into the darkness of the surrounding jungle.

A further difficulty for the army garrisons was that they had little or no communication with their rear areas, since contact was limited largely to messengers or liaison planes. They were susceptible to the illusion that they were cut off, that they could not summon and receive reinforcements in time. Thus they frequently resorted to a standing order for garrisons under attack by superior forces to abandon posts and make their way through the jungle to the next post, there to regroup and prepare for a counterattack.

These conditions made the renewed guerrilla campaign in Laos a very fluid thing indeed. At the height of the monsoon season, when nine days out of ten were overcast and rain poured down, Vientiane went for weeks without definite word about the military situation along the North Vietnam border. Alarming rumors spread.

The situation looked threatening. Sop Nao, a village at the head of the traditional invasion route from Vietnam by way of the Dien

Bien Phu valley, was briefly occupied by guerrillas. The town of Sam Neua, a collection of shops and houses bordering a dirt road that led nowhere, with a population of about 3,000, was reported encircled by roving bands of guerrillas.

To the credit of the tiny Lao air force, its Beavers and C-47's succeeded in operating a hazardous airlift to the single grass airstrip a mile from Sam Neua. They brought troop reinforcements and ammunition, food and clothing, and above all reassurance for the panic-stricken population crowding the airstrip in the desperate fear that an entire North Vietnamese army was about to sweep down on the town.

On July 23, in response to a request from Prime Minister Phoui Sananikone, the United States announced it was furnishing additional technicians to conduct an emergency training program that would expand the Royal Army from 25,000 to 29,000 men. The technicians would remain in Laos for six months (the period was later extended in view of the continuing "crisis") and would wear civilian clothes. In the following two weeks, about a hundred of these technicians entered Laos, along with new equipment, including tanks and trucks, to replace worn-out Royal Army items.

In reply to a Soviet accusation that Phoui was handing over control of the Royal Army to the United States, a State Department spokesman declared, "The Lao army is controlled exclusively by the sovereign government of Laos." The American statement was only too true. The United States, despite its gifts of weapons and money, never controlled the Lao army. The tanks it gave the Lao army were to have far more effect in staging a *coup d'état* in Vientiane than in fighting the guerrillas in the roadless jungles of Sam Neua Province. This is the best evidence of how little control the United States exerted over the Lao army.

On July 29, a government communiqué stated that a grave situation had arisen in Sam Neua Province: "According to the latest reports reaching Vientiane, it seems established that the rebel bands operating in the Sam Neua sector do not belong to the rebel battalion from the Plain of Jars but represent new elements entirely equipped, armed, and stiffened [*encadrés*] by the Democratic Republic of Vietnam."

It had been decided, the communiqué stated, to charge certain NLHS leaders "whose collusion with the foreigner is established" with offenses against the security of the state. Prince Souphanouvong, under house arrest since the previous May, was removed from his comfortable single-story villa on the bank of the Mekong to the Phone Kheng police camp on the northern outskirts of town. Also detained in barracks were fifteen others, including Colonel Singkapo, Phoumi Vongvichit, Nouhak Phoumsavan, Sithone Komadam, Phoun Sipraseuth, and the editor of *Lao Hak Sat*.

Because of the threatening military situation, Phoui's government on August 4 proclaimed a state of emergency in five provinces—Phong Saly, Sam Neua, Xieng Khouang, Khammouane, and Savannakhet. On the same day it requested United Nations Secretary-General Dag Hammarskjöld to inform members of the situation and stressed the role of North Vietnam.

Hanoi and Peking propaganda immediately raised a barrage of objections to involving the United Nations, of which they were not members, in any peace-keeping role in Laos. This campaign was coupled with renewed calls for reactivation of the ICC and reference of the crisis to the Geneva Co-Chairmen, Britain and Russia. On August 8, a program was published in Peking and said to have been issued a week previously by the NLHS. It made nine points, including a demand for a coalition Lao government in which the NLHS would be represented.

Phoui's message to the United Nations was followed by a lull in guerrilla activity that lasted approximately a fortnight. But toward the end of August, the pinprick attacks began again in widely scattered areas of Laos adjoining the Vietnam border.

On September 4, Phoui sent a second message to the United Nations, stating categorically that North Vietnamese soldiers were fighting on Lao soil. He referred to the attacks of the previous month, and declared that "on August 30, a fresh attack, more violent than the previous ones, was launched against the posts of Muong Het and Xieng Kho. Elements from the Democratic Republic of Vietnam took part in the attack, which was supported by artillery fire from the other side of the frontier."

Muong Het and Xieng Kho are in the Ma River valley, approximately thirty miles north of the town of Sam Neua. The former was defended by 250 armed men, mostly militia. Xieng Kho's garrison was smaller. Simultaneous attacks had been mounted on two other posts in the same region, Sop Sai and Sop Bau, the latter defended by only 30 militiamen.

The clandestine nature of the military actions and the inaccessibility of the fighting area made it difficult to gauge the extent of the North Vietnamese involvement on the ground. The case against North Vietnam was seriously handicapped because Phoui's references to North Vietnamese "elements" were not substantiated by the capture of any foreign troops in these actions.

Phoui's government was facing a critical situation, but it was due more to the government's weaknesses than to the strength of the enemy forces. Now, the West was being told of the internal weakness of the Lao Government and its vulnerability to invasion at any time by the North Vietnamese, after five years of assurances that American aid was building up a strong and enlightened Laos that would be a bastion against Communist encroachment.

The scale of the fighting was considerably exaggerated by the Western press. The more than fifty newspaper correspondents who surged into Vientiane focused on the dramatic aspects of the situation, the minor armed clashes over a wide area that, when recounted in a coordinated story, made headlines. Their dispatches gave little or no description of the Communist infestation of northeastern Laos or of the years of insidious subversion of the Royal Government's authority there.

Reporters from Western countries, confronted with a guerrilla war, attempted to describe it with the standard military vocabulary. Terms like "advance," "front," "main line of defense," "move up," "fall back," and "storm" hopelessly distorted the picture for Western readers. One observer later drew up a glossary of military terms for Laos. A fortress was defined as a "mud fort in a clearing defended by at least six men," and a siege was a "concentrated attack lasting more than five minutes." Unfortunately, only a few correspondents got anywhere near Sam Neua during the rainy season and could appreciate the accuracy of these definitions.

The single biggest impetus to the apparent urgency of the military situation was given by the groundless reports circulated by Lao military officers, unwittingly or deliberately. Most of them were based on scanty radio reports from faraway Sam Neua, and these in turn derived from isolated jungle posts linked by runners. Although some of these posts may have correctly assessed their own predicament, they had no way of relating it to the situation outside their own immediate area. On the basis of such reports, Lao officers in Vientiane hypothesized North Vietnamese battalions marching through Laos in a manner reminiscent of the Viet Minh invasions of 1953 and 1954.

The Security Council met on September 7 to consider Phoui's charges against North Vietnam, and later that month dispatched an investigatory subcommittee to Laos. With this, the urgency created by the Royal Government's charges abated. The members of the subcommittee took a plane to Sam Neua Province, where they interrogated a number of prisoners and refugees, several of whom were Black Thai. In its report, the subcommittee stated:

> Practically all witnesses (40 out of 41) stated that the hostile elements received support from the territory of the DRV [North Vietnam] consisting mainly of equipment, arms, ammunition, supplies, and the help of political cadres.[1]

The subcommittee reported that the Lao government placed its casualties in the fighting between July 16 and October 11 at 99 killed, 96 wounded, and 125 missing.

At Phoui's request, a United Nations economic mission also visited Laos. Its report, while not exactly encouraging, was, in fact, the most objective survey of the country's economic needs ever made. As a result, the U.N. undertook some small-scale technical-assistance schemes, most of them in the field of public health, in order to fill some gaps in the American aid program. (As the mission report pointed out, only 8 per cent of American funds had gone to building roads, schools, and other developments.)

In the midst of these disturbing events in his Kingdom, Sisavang Vong died at Luang Prabang. At the time of his death, he was, at seventy-four, the oldest reigning monarch in the world. A beloved sovereign, Sisavang Vong had enjoyed the pleasures of royal life, receiving visitors to his palace on the bank of the Mekong or sailing off to France to take his cure at Vittel. During the dark days of 1953, when his capital was threatened by the Viet Minh, his stubbornly determined presence there in the face of French advice to retire to safety surely ranks among the splendid episodes of his Kingdom's history.

His successor, Savang Vatthana, was of a more austere, less flamboyant character. Educated at the Ecole de Science Politique in Paris, he had read widely and had traveled throughout the world. But from the first days of his reign, he was assailed by a host of troubles.

The disturbances of the summer of 1959 had demonstrated that the North Vietnamese, who were not members of the United Nations or any other significant international body and who possessed the most meager material resources, could nevertheless stir up a crisis in the neighboring kingdom when it suited their purposes, get all the capitals of the world stirred up, and then, with just as much

---

[1] *Report of the Security Council Sub-Committee under Resolution of 7 September 1959* (United Nations Security Council s/4236, November 5, 1959), p. 31.

control, tamp down the crisis. This exercise must have confirmed their judgment that the United States had learned nothing from the French experience.

An Abortive Putsch

Before the expiration of Phoui's one year of special powers, he announced his intention of reshuffling his Cabinet. The principal change he contemplated was the removal of ministers who belonged to the CDNI, the most important of whom were Khampan Panya, Minister of Foreign Affairs, and Phoumi Nosavan, Secretary of State for National Defense. When Phoui renounced his special powers, the National Assembly met in extraordinary session. On December 17, the deputies voted to prolong the Assembly's four-year mandate (which was to expire on December 25) until the new general elections, scheduled for the following April. The CDNI, whose main backers were high-ranking army officers, opposed Phoui and argued that an attempt to prolong the Assembly's mandate would be unconstitutional; they claimed that until the elections the country should be governed by a provisional Cabinet named by the King.

On December 30, Phoui submitted his resignation to King Savang Vatthana, in the belief that the National Assembly, which had closed its extraordinary session on December 25, would retain its mandate until the coming elections. However, during the early hours of December 31, soldiers acting on the orders of all five generals of the Royal Army occupied the principal public buildings in Vientiane. Four armored cars took up positions surrounding the residence of the King, who was in Vientiane for the extraordinary National Assembly session. Not a shot was fired.

Simultaneously, the radio station proclaimed that the King had accepted Phoui's resignation and that the army had taken over maintenance of public law and order until a new, legally constituted government could be named. The National Assembly, the communiqué said, was now considered dissolved, and all actions taken by this body after December 25 were considered null and void.

The King's presence in Vientiane enabled the generals to have frequent audiences with him, at which they protested their devotion to the throne and to the Constitution. None of the five was more energetic in these protestations than Brigadier General Phoumi Nosavan. Phoumi's four colleagues were Major General Sounthone Pathammavong, the chief of staff; Brigadier General Sing Ratanasamay, his adjutant; Brigadier General Ouan Ratikon, commandant of the armed forces; and Brigadier General Amkha Soukhavong, his adjutant.

The generals were careful to point out that they were acting to preserve constitutionality by preventing the National Assembly from illegally extending its mandate, and that they had no political ambitions. Their putsch was a natural consequence of their genuine disgust at the political situation. They wanted action. They were also disturbed that the elimination of CDNI influence from the Cabinet might lead to a reconciliation with the Pathet Lao, who had reacted to Phoui's reshuffle by stating their willingness to enter into "peaceful consultations" to settle their dispute "at any time." Had they, the generals of the Royal Army, not spent the last six months battling a rebellion whose leaders were sympathetic to the Communists? And here were these civilian politicians, many of them old-time masters at corruption and graft, arguing hotly about how long their terms should run. Was this not madness?

Besides frustration, another factor motivating the generals was their conviction that they alone could prepare the country to resist the Communist menace. The army has a peculiar status in Laos. It is the only organization that reaches every part of the territory and that involves the life of virtually every Lao family. It is the country's greatest unifier, a catalyst with the potential of making the diverse peoples of Laos feel as if they belonged to a single nation. The army may be slipshod and lazy, but without it there would be little to make the villages feel the existence of the monarchy, the flag, and the government.

Also, in economically underdeveloped Laos, the national army represents a reservoir of manual skills and practical training. Unlike a Western army, which puts to use skills acquired in civilian life, the Lao army receives men with virtually no training whatsoever and is compelled to instruct them. This is another reason why service in the army commands prestige in Laos.

Third, the army is the Lao economy's only sizable source of circulating currency. In the army, many Lao are paid in cash for the first time. In their native villages, they had usually worked for remuneration in kind, such as rice, lodging, or a marriage into a good family. The Lao soldier with his monthly pay, equivalent to about $10, is a rich man compared to his peasant brothers who still live in a barter economy.

For the inhabitants of Indochina, the military has long been a remunerative way of life. Many of the top-ranking officers of the

Royal Army (and of the Pathet Lao, too) served as noncoms or officers in the Lao Territorial army attached to the French Expeditionary Corps.

Phoumi Nosavan was among these. Inducted for service with the French in the Indochina War, he had in 1957 spent a year at the French War College and graduated with honors. Soft-spoken and not particularly impressive at first sight, he possessed both a clear head and a tenacity that contributed to his rapid advancement in the Lao officer corps.

Like the other four generals involved in the attempted putsch of December, 1959, General Phoumi was in deep sympathy with the reforms advocated by the CDNI, a sympathy that appears to have been encouraged by his contacts with the U.S. Central Intelligence Agency.

General Phoumi had a genuine desire to see Laos free itself from the shackles of underdevelopment, and in this narrow sense he was indeed a patriot, albeit a patriot who saw no objection to accepting, under various guises, large amounts of money from a foreign power.

The general was strongly influenced by Marshal Sarit Thanarat, Thailand's Prime Minister, whom General Phoumi called uncle. Under a benign army dictatorship instituted by Marshal Sarit, Thailand had achieved an economic stability and prosperity that was the envy of Southeast Asia. Phoumi was also deeply impressed by General de Gaulle.

The CIA chose to support General Phoumi because the army was the only organization that could put through a program of development in a country where there were no effective political parties, where basic education was still lacking, where malaria and malnutrition were rampant, and where the most lucrative, if unofficial, export was opium. There was every indication that liberal democracy could not overcome such obstacles. The army, however, could provide a disciplined leadership for economic progress, even as the Communist parties professed themselves determined to provide in the underdeveloped countries.

If American policy required a strongman in Laos, General Phoumi was unquestionably the leading candidate. Of all the generals, he had the most drive. However, certain American officials did not share the CIA's optimistic evaluation of the capabilities of General Phoumi and the Lao army. After the putsch, Horace Smith, who had succeeded Parsons as Ambassador in Vientiane in 1958, bluntly told the author that General Phoumi was using anti-Communism, through the device of the CDNI, to further his own personal ambitions. A year later, when American policy found itself at a dead end and actually jeopardizing the whole Western position in Southeast Asia through a most unhealthy polarization in Laos, it was not for any lack of on-the-spot information.

Communist propaganda has pictured General Phoumi as an American puppet. That is quite wrong. Whatever encouragement he may have received at the outset from the CIA, General Phoumi later showed plainly that he was willing to resist pressures mounted by the entire apparatus of American diplomacy. In 1962, when even the CIA had been disabused of its high hopes for Phoumi and all U.S. agencies supported formation of a coalition government under Souvanna Phouma, the General proved to be a most stubborn and uncooperative man. Oddly enough, he grew in stature in Laos by this show of resistance against the Americans, and this played a not inconsiderable part in earning him a place in the troika under Souvanna Phouma.

The generals had badly underestimated adverse reaction outside their own country to their attempted putsch. Actually, they probably fully intended to hold the elections that were constitutionally due the following April and then to return power to a civilian Cabinet.

However, any such plans were abandoned when the British and French ambassadors, concerned lest a military dictatorship be interpreted as the final scrapping of the Geneva cease-fire, sought out Ambassador Smith, as well as the Australian chargé d'affaires, and went in a common front to the King. They told him that he had been misinformed if he believed that such a military dictatorship would receive the approbation of the countries with which Laos maintained relations. They advised him of their unanimous desire to see the constitutional process preserved. Immediately afterward, a telegram to the same effect arrived from the Secretary-General of the United Nations. The generals were constrained to pull back.

King Savang Vatthana thereupon named Kou Abhay, the aged and venerable head of the King's Council, as Prime Minister. On January 7, 1960, a new provisional civilian Cabinet entrusted with preparing general elections was formed. The only military man in the Cabinet was General Phoumi. As Minister of National Defense, Phoumi exercised considerable influence because his ministry controlled more than 80 per cent of the Lao budget. Although he had not come out top man, he had not done badly.

Electoral Rigging

The elections, set for the first Sunday in April, confronted Kou's government with the problem Souvanna Phouma's government had faced two years earlier: NLHS candidates, contesting the fifty-nine seats to be filled, might sweep to another victory on the strength of the undisrupted, ruthless guerrilla organization in the countryside. Yet, barring the NLHS candidates from the ballots would be a serious, open breach of the Lao government's pledge at Geneva to conciliate all factions. The government could take at least some comfort from the fact that the NLHS deputies who had been arrested the previous year were still awaiting trial in their police barracks outside Vientiane and thus would not be able to run.

In a blow aimed at other potential NLHS candidates, the government decreed higher educational standards and larger financial deposits for candidates. The educational requirement hit the NLHS particularly hard because, aside from its titular chief, very few of its cadres had any formal education at all; indeed, most of them were illiterate. Of the nine NLHS deputies elected in 1958, only three besides Souphanouvong met the new requirements.

Also, the electoral map of Laos was completely redrawn once again so as to gerrymander those districts, in the south especially, where it was thought the NLHS candidates stood a chance of winning a large vote, as they had done in 1958.

In the face of these obstacles, only nine NLHS candidates ran in the election. The government proudly announced that it had magnanimously permitted Souphanouvong to issue instructions, from his prison barracks, for the NLHS candidates to contest the election according to the rules and do the best they could.

Beneath the façade of contesting the elections against government-supported candidates, the tireless Pathet Lao political and guerrilla cadres went about their work at the village level. Even while guerrilla raids on government outposts decreased in frequency at the beginning of 1960, Vientiane's control over thousands of villages throughout the country was being systematically subverted.

The Pathet Lao technique was to turn to their own advantage the centuries-old system of local administration. From the capital, the established hierarchy of government radiated out to the provincial governors (*chao khoueng*) and thence to the district officers (*chao muong*). There it stopped. That was the extent of the centrally appointed officials.

To implement its measures, the government depended on the

district officers to pass orders on to the village headman (*nai ban*). But the village headman was not appointed by the central government; he was elected by the village. So to prevent the central government's authority from reaching to the village, all the Pathet Lao had to do was to get their own agent elected village headman.

Conversely, the central government depended on the village headman to inform the district officer of local grievances. If it did not know what grievances the villages had, it could not respond to them. Tradition in Laos did not encourage the elevation to headman of a forward-looking young man. Although the village election was theoretically a democratic affair, with candidacy open to all, the post usually went to the village elder, the man who owned the most land and buffaloes, the man whose daughters were most sought in marriage because they guaranteed maximum advancement in the social scale.

If a village headman was not responsive to local grievances, the district officer had even less reason to concern himself with village demands. Secure in his government job, he was usually not even a native of the district he administered.

Nor were the deputies elected to the National Assembly a more effective channel of communications between village and capital. Most deputies were members of the Kingdom's leading families, elected as an honor. They were rarely schoolteachers or men who had made a reputation for honesty or efficiency in the district in which they were elected.

Just as the Chinese Communist Party had done in the 1930's and 1940's, the Pathet Lao now concentrated on placing their own agents on the village level. In China, the appointive authority had stopped at the *hsien,* or district. It was the township, or *hsiang,* that was all-important in the effort to substitute Communist authority for non-Communist.

In China, the intermediary between district and township had for centuries been the landed gentry, most of whom lived in the chief town of the district, gathering their rents from their surrounding lands. This class of people was lacking in Laos, however, where most of the peasants owned their own land and where they could increase their holdings merely by clearing a new patch of jungle. The absence of a landed gentry made it easier for the Pathet Lao to isolate the village from higher authority, but made it more difficult for them to incite peasant resentment over the alleged wrongs committed by the ruling class.

The Pathet Lao undertook a course of subversion that was a

calculated combination of persuasion and coercion. Their cadres would live for six months in a village, observing its routine of everyday life and its channels of leadership. During this time, they would determine which man most suited their purposes. Usually he was a relatively young man. Next, the Pathet Lao cadres set about winning this man away from his allegiance to traditional authority. They impressed upon him that the Pathet Lao guerrilla network, which they portrayed as the defenders of "the people," operated in the countryside under the very noses of the government's troops, which they portrayed as molesters of "the people."

Another Pathet Lao technique was to incite dissatisfaction in the village with the traditional authority. Hard-core Pathet Lao guerrillas made the village unsafe for the district officer to visit, except under escort, and then the village cadres spread the word that the central government was neglecting the welfare of the village. Foreign aid, they said, was going to enrich a handful of well-placed men in Vientiane, while the village had no prospect of ever advancing itself under this government.

The Pathet Lao impressed on their agent-to-be the prospect of becoming the real chief of his village once the cause of "the people" had triumphed. If the incumbent chief was an exceptionally young or dynamic man, the Pathet Lao frequently concentrated on his deputy, fomenting a rivalry between the two men and trying to embroil the chief in unpopular measures that would work against him and in favor of his deputy. If a village was of special importance to the Pathet Lao, they sent their agent-to-be to Hanoi or even Peking free of charge for a year's "education." Also, they sent his children to North Vietnamese or Chinese schools, making them in effect hostages for the cooperation of their parents.

Working persistently and shrewdly, the Pathet Lao, through propaganda, split loyalties, and calculated intimidation, gradually arrived at the point where their words carried more weight than those of the central government. In all this, their minute knowledge of village life served them well.

Coercion was also put to effective use by the Pathet Lao. On occasion, the power of the guerrilla organization was impressed on the villagers by the assassination of a key anti-Pathet Lao figure well known to the inhabitants. Such acts persuaded the district officer of the inadvisability of cooperating too enthusiastically with the central government in its heavy-handed attempts to root out the Pathet Lao. On the very Sunday on which the 1960 elections were held, a Meo district officer accused by the guerrillas of meddling too much in the affairs of his villages was ambushed and killed while riding in his jeep between two villages near Nong Het in Xieng Khouang Province. One American observer called the Pathet Lao technique "a propaganda sentence punctuated by a terrorist period." As the 1960 election campaign approached its climax, Royal Army units that had been concentrated in the north during the previous summer were dispatched to the south for mopping-up operations against Pathet Lao guerrillas, to make the countryside safe for balloting. In the course of these operations, the troops meted out discipline as a warning in villages suspected of harboring Pathet Lao cadres. Sometimes the discipline was imposed on an individual basis; not infrequently, however, a whole village was set afire. The Pathet Lao cadres in certain villages turned the mopping-up operation to their advantage by arranging anonymous denunciations of Communist complicity against villagers who had caused them particular trouble. The result of this countryside campaign was not the mopping up of the Pathet Lao but the alienation of the peasantry.

Meanwhile, the energies of the central government were monopolized by the election preparations. Satisfaction prevailed in Vientiane during those incredibly hot days of April when the sun melted the asphalt in the streets and the dry south wind lifted the loose sand from the Mekong's dry bed and whirled it, in tiny cyclones, into the baked city, foreshadowing the breaking of the monsoon. The country was once again quiet. Members of the interim Cabinet, having successfully arranged the electoral campaign, relaxed on veranda chairs in the evening twilight and concluded that perhaps Laos was not condemned to perpetual chaos after all: The nation was in good hands; there was no National Assembly to raise embarrassing constitutional issues, and speculation about who would head the next government had not yet really begun.

The government's measures to ensure that no NLHS deputies were elected had been effective. On election day, it was clear from the first that there would be a landslide for the progovernment candidates, despite their habitual large number (almost three candidates for each seat) and their self-defeating family rivalries.

The results were incredible. In Sam Neua, the Pathet Lao base area, the NLHS candidate, a former governor of the province, was reported to have received a total of 13 votes to the successful candidate's 6,508.

In each of the six electoral districts of Champassak Province, progovernment candidates were reported to have received 90 per cent or more of the votes cast. In one of these districts, the leader of the Santiphab Party, Quinim Pholsena, was defeated by 17,175 votes to 721. In another, the NLHS candidate was credited with 4 votes to the opposition's 18,189, although there were at least 5 members of his immediate family eligible to vote for him. The single NLHS candidate in Savannakhet Province was reported defeated by a margin of 7,414 to 881.

Plainly, the election had been rigged. Whether the soldiers guarding the polling places had exerted pressure or whether the vote totals had been falsified, the leaders of the minority Santiphab Party and the National Union Party were clearly justified in charging a fraud.

The real story of these elections emerged slowly. An observer who visited Sam Neua two days before the election saw Royal Army soldiers dropping progovernment campaign leaflets from planes. The NLHS candidate told him that he was fully aware that the legal opposition did not stand a chance but nonetheless was determined to go through with the election in accordance with Souphanouvong's instructions.

An example of the heavy-handed tactics was the telegram addressed by the Interior Ministry to civil servants in Pakse, capital of Champassak Province. It named the six progovernment candidates in the province and instructed civil servants to give them "financial, material, and moral support"—or face disciplinary sanctions.

CIA agents participated in the election rigging, with or without the authority of the American Ambassador. A Foreign Service officer flatly told an observer in Savannakhet that, prior to the voting, he had seen CIA agents distribute bagfuls of money to village headmen; the inescapable conclusion was that the United States had been buying votes.

For an intelligent opposition leader like Souphanouvong, the 1960 general election in Laos was more than a travesty of democracy. It was proof positive that the West can stage-manage an election just as efficiently as the Communists can.

Stiffer Attitudes in Hanoi and Peking

During the first few months of 1960, while overt guerrilla activity remained in a low key in Laos, the Vietnamese Communists sprang a major armed action in South Vietnam. To thousands of Viet Minh cadres who had been waiting out the years since 1954 in the villages of the south, this was the start of the violent phase of the struggle for reunification. The increasing risks to which the Lao Dong Party was willing to have its southern cadres expose themselves gave supreme importance to the possession of secure communications by means of trails through the mountains of Laos.

Hanoi's new line of increased force to achieve reunification with the south was formalized at the Third Congress of the Lao Dong Party in September, 1960. Le Duan, a high-ranking member of its Politburo and a native of the south himself, declared that the two strategic tasks for the party in the years ahead were the carrying out of a Socialist revolution in the north, on the one hand, and "the eradication of the colonial and semifeudal regime in South Vietnam and the realization of national reunification," on the other.

Three months later, a clandestine radio transmitter in South Vietnam broadcast news of the formation of the National Liberation Front of South Vietnam, which it described as a loose alliance of peasants, industrial workers, intellectuals, defectors from the Saigon regime's army and civil service, and representatives of all religious and ethnic minorities. At the end of 1961, in South Vietnam, a secret People's Revolutionary Party was formed. It was described as a Marxist-Leninist party with the mission of leading the National Front.

The relationship of these organs to Hanoi was later made clear in a document captured from local insurgents in May, 1962, that informed cadres that "The independent existence of the People's Revolutionary Party is only apparent. In reality, the party is the Lao Dong Party of Vietnam, united in north and south, under the direction of the Party Central Committee whose chairman is President Ho."

Meanwhile, for reasons quite independent of North Vietnam's strategic interests in Laos, an ominous shift was taking place in Communist China's attitude toward the political situation in Laos. The Chinese had reacted quickly and unfavorably to the adjournment of the ICC, which came when the leaders in Peking were outraged at Soviet Premier Khrushchev's behavior over Lebanon and Jordan in July, 1958, particularly his eagerness to arrange negotiations with the Western powers and to invite India to a summit conference. The following month, the Chinese instigated the Quemoy crisis.

The events in Laos the following year found Peking in a more intransigent mood than Chou En-lai had expressed to the National

People's Congress, in February, 1958. The crisis with India over the Tibetan revolt, and the U.S.S.R.'s tearing up of the two-year-old technical-assistance agreement in nuclear research, increased the Peking leaders' isolation in the Communist world and heightened their scornful determination to assert their influence.

The evolution of Peking's attitude toward Laos from hands-off-so-long-as-there-are-no-American-bases-there to a barely concealed concern for its own security was in accordance with the increasing doctrinal emphasis in Peking on support for "national liberation movements," which was becoming manifest in the period 1957–60.

It is particularly significant that the Chinese introduced the term "civil war" into the Laos situation in the spring of 1959, even before the North Vietnamese. In the disciplined and coordinated realm of Communist propaganda, the application of a term of such far-reaching implications as "civil war" to a situation in a neighboring country is unlikely to be haphazard or random.

"Civil war" was used for the first time on May 18 in a formal statement on the Laos situation by Peking's Ministry of Foreign Affairs. Barely two days later, Hanoi adopted the term, which thereafter was part of the North Vietnamese vocabulary in describing the summer's fighting.

To Peking, the developments unfolding in Laos increasingly assumed the pattern of an anticolonialist struggle, with growing American influence supplying the "colonialist" imprint. More and more, Peking had been supporting—verbally, only—the cause of anticolonialism. In the Middle East crisis of 1958, the walls of every Chinese village had been plastered with huge posters proclaiming "The Chinese people support the Lebanese and the Jordanians in their anticolonial struggle!" and "Hands off Lebanon!" (Actually, few Chinese knew where Lebanon and Jordan were.) But this verbal support was backed up by the threat, more or less veiled, of help in the form of supplies or army "volunteers" on the Korea pattern. This loud championship of the anticolonial struggle, in furtherance of the Communist revolution, was of immense importance in Peking's growing quarrel with Moscow.

As early as May, 1958, at the 8th Party Congress, Chinese Communist Party Vice Chairman Liu Shao-chi spoke of the "uninterrupted revolution." A few months later it was disclosed that millions of Chinese peasants were being militantly organized into rural communes designed to raise the country by its own bootstraps and make the transition to a Communist society. And in the theoretical journal *Red Flag* in April, 1960, Peking warned that all "revolutionary"

Leninists should support colonial revolutions "without the slightest reservations."

Peking had expressed its growing concern over what was happening in Laos:

> Disregarding the wishes of the people of Indochina for peace, the United States arbitrarily included these countries in the sphere of "defense" of SEATO. . . . The United States formally set up her foreign aid mission in Laos as an organization to carry out her military, political, and economic aggression. . . . A stream of arms and ammunition came into Laos from the United States and a large number of U.S. military personnel in the guise of "technical personnel" or "employees" arrived to control the armed forces and military bases of Laos. To completely wreck the Geneva agreements, the United States used all manner of base and underhand methods and indulged in open interference in Laos' political affairs. . . . The scrapping of the Geneva agreements by the Lao authorities at the insistence of the United States has now created a grave situation in Laos and menaced peace in the countries of Indochina and the Far East.[2]

The American military aid agreement with the Phoui Sananikone government, especially, was taken by the Chinese to be a violation of the conditions under which in 1954 they had accepted the status of Laos and Cambodia. The chief Chinese delegate to the second Geneva Conference was later to say in reference to the provision of military training to the Lao army, "Our agreement to this right for France was an indication of confidence in France. If we then foresaw that France would arbitrarily transfer this right to the United States, we definitely would not have agreed to this right for France."[3]

On August 12, 1959, a spokesman of the Chinese Foreign Ministry took the Laos issue one step further than the Chinese had ever taken it before by implying that the security of China was involved. "The Chinese Government and people," the spokesman said, "are watching closely the daily deteriorating situation in Laos. All activities of the U.S. Government and the Laotian authorities violating the Geneva agreements and creating tension in Indochina, and further menacing the security of China, will certainly face the firm opposition of the Chinese Government and people. The U.S. Government and the Laotian authorities must bear full responsibility for the consequences of their activities."

Despite their hints of direct involvement in the Laos "civil war" in the summer of 1959, the Chinese Communists had taken no *action* toward involvement. Nevertheless, the statements from Peking

2 *Jenmin Jih Pao* (*People's Daily,* Peking), June 3, 1959.
3 New China News Agency, Geneva, August 2, 1961.

raised once again in Washington the bogey of a massive invasion of Laos by Communist forces.

In the summer of 1959, the United States, despite the nuclear capability vested in the aircraft of the Seventh Fleet patrolling the western Pacific, began to envisage the possibility of having to engage in a ground campaign in Laos. With very little publicity, a stand-by force of American soldiers and their logistical support, known as Task Force 116, was set up on Okinawa, under the command of General Donald M. Weller. It would be assigned to intervene in Laos if the need arose.

In setting up this task force, the United States was moving dangerously near the very situation that, as Dulles had assured the Senate, American policy was designed to avoid—the unilateral commitment of American ground troops to Indochina.

Souphanouvong's Escape

Prince Souphanouvong and his NLHS colleagues, who had been arrested at the height of the "aggression" panic in 1959, had since been vegetating in the Phone Kheng police camp just outside Vientiane. Souphanouvong passed the time reading Greek classics. His colleagues in detention were seven other NLHS deputies—Phoumi Vongvichit, Nouhak Phoumsavan, Sithone Komadam, Phoun Sipraseuth, and three others—Colonel Singkapo, the military commander who had been engaged in the abortive negotiations with Phoui's government for reintegration into the Royal Army, and seven lesser personalities suspected of carrying on activities on behalf of the NLHS.

After the government's announcement that the suspects would be charged with offenses against the security of the state, defense lawyers had been appointed, and a trial date set. However, it soon became apparent that the detention of the NLHS deputies was acutely embarrassing to the government. The trial date came and went. It was not even certain whether prosecution of these NLHS deputies would serve the government's purpose of dismembering the NLHS. Despite the government's announcement that four other NLHS leaders—Kaysone Phomvihan, Phay Dang, Khamtay Siphandon, and Souk Vongsak (a deputy from Luang Prabang who had fled Vientiane before the "aggression" crisis)—would be tried in absentia, all of them were still at large and in a position to call upon North Vietnam for aid. In this light, Souphanouvong represented a "moderate" among the NLHS leaders.

Moreover, the trial, if held, would be certain to produce statements for the defense that would prove exceedingly embarrassing to the Vientiane government. The main defense attorney was the leader of the Santiphab Party, Quinim Pholsena, a humorless man who had been a member of the Constituent Assembly in 1947. He would relish the opportunity to further his inordinate ambitions by a successful defense of the "Red Prince"—Souphanouvong.

Souphanouvong, the defense argument would run, had spent ten years in the jungle fighting to free Laos from the fetters of colonialism, while General Phoumi had been living in luxury on a fat salary paid by the Americans. Who, then, was patriot and who traitor?

Several foreign embassies advised Vientiane strongly against holding the trial, and three successive governments had been only too glad to demur. Souphanouvong had passed these ten months conducting a long-range attempt to win the loyalty of his prison guards, an attempt that he described as successful in an account published in the Hanoi newspaper *Nhan Dan* in May, 1961.

Before the politicians of Vientiane could find a solution to their dilemma over the trial, the NLHS "traitors" found one for them. In the early morning hours of May 24, 1960, amid the raging of a violent tropical thunderstorm that flung almost solid sheets of water across the jungles, Souphanouvong and his co-prisoners escaped from Phone Kheng, taking their guards with them. When the day guards arrived on duty at 6 A.M., they found the barracks deserted.

While in prison, Souphanouvong had maintained contact with the rest of the Pathet Lao leadership by means of smuggled messages. We have already seen that, by means of such messages, he ordered NLHS candidates throughout Laos to engage in the 1960 electoral campaign despite indications they could not win. How much actual authority Souphanouvong exercised during his captivity remains unclear, but it is fairly clear that the influence of the "Vietnamese faction" in the Pathet Lao, represented by people like Kaysone, grew during this period.

Once free, Souphanouvong did not hurry to rejoin the top command in Sam Neua or to travel to Hanoi. During the next five months, according to his own account, he traveled 300 miles on foot, visiting Pathet Lao strongholds in each province. He says he finally arrived in Sam Neua on November 7, 1960. By that time he was tired out from his long trek and noticeably weakened by illness.

Coup d'État

The matter of deciding upon the composition of the Cabinet had dragged on for weeks since the April election. It was obvious that

General Phoumi, while not a member of the National Assembly, would have the largest say in any Cabinet formed during CDNI control over the deputies' votes. The general exuded optimism about the political course the country was taking; he called the election results "better than expected."

The Cabinet list presented to the National Assembly included General Phoumi as Minister of National Defense. The Prime Minister was Prince Somsanith, who had been elected a deputy unopposed and who had acquired a reputation for honesty during his tenure as Governor of Nam Tha Province, when he claimed to have visited all the province's 200 villages—not once, but twice or more —on foot.

Nevertheless, the situation in Laos was not good, especially in the military. The great vacuum left by the French between the Mekong and the Annamite Mountains still had not been filled. Confusion, corruption, and an acute lack of soldierly qualities inherent in the Lao had conspired to frustrate American efforts to create an effective fighting force, in the Western sense of the term. PEO instructors complained that the Lao seemed unable to master the techniques of modern warfare. Lao officers sent for training to Thailand did not even bother to show up for classes.

On the Lao side, serious questions were being raised about the value of the American military-aid program and the lack of economic development resulting from concentration on military objectives. The principal newspaper in Vientiane, the organ of Phoui Sananikone's political party, described the trucks and jeeps which the Americans had given the Lao, many of which lay rusting in vacant lots, as *"un tas de ferraille"* ("a heap of scrap metal").

Among the officers of the Royal Army, the generals' attempted putsch had set a dangerous precedent, whetting appetites for political power. Phoumi's adoption of civilian dress and of the other prerogatives of ministerial position in Vientiane was alienating a growing number of middle-rank Lao officers. This was especially so after the renewal of fighting against the Pathet Lao, when many of these officers recalled that they had never seen General Phoumi anywhere near a battlefield. Although the generals and a small coterie of staff officers in Vientiane associated themselves with the self-styled Young Turks of the CDNI, by no means the entire Lao army lent its support to these professed reformists in their comfortable villas by the Mekong.

Discontent among the 600 men and officers of the Second Paratroop Battalion attained such proportions that news of it reached

King Savang Vatthana. This battalion, the best unit in the Royal Army, had borne the brunt of the fighting against the guerrillas. During the crisis of 1959, its young commander, Captain Kong Le, had led the battalion into action in Sam Neua Province. After that, his battalion had undertaken a series of mopping-up operations in southern Laos in preparation for the elections.

Kong Le and his three companies of devoted soldiers had then been posted to Vientiane, where they expected to have a brief respite from fighting. There they were housed in ramshackle buildings on some outlying mud flats. Kong Le protested to the Ministry of National Defense about the conditions in which his battle-weary men were compelled to live; he demanded that a large and relatively lavish mansion that had just been completed to house the family of Chief of Staff General Sounthone Pathammavong be turned over to the Second Battalion.

In response to these remonstrations by Kong Le, the Ministry informed the battalion on Friday, August 5, that a work order had been approved for construction of new barracks for the men. On Monday, the men expected to begin work on the new site of their camp. Instead, they were abruptly ordered on operations the following morning to clean up a suspected pocket of Pathet Lao guerrillas thirty miles west of Vientiane. On Monday, also, General Phoumi and the entire Cabinet emplaned for Luang Prabang to discuss with King Savang Vatthana plans for the state funeral of King Sisavang Vong, whose body had remained embalmed in a large sandalwood bier since October, 1959. While at the Royal Palace, General Phoumi assured the monarch that the rumored dissension in the army had been taken care of.

Only hours later, Kong Le's battle-dressed paratroopers climbed in jeeps and, at three the following morning, rolled out of their encampment, presumably bound for the airport. Instead, the paratroopers fanned out across the town and occupied all strategic points: the offices of the Prime Minister and all other government Ministers, the electric power station, the radio station, and the telegraph office. They parked jeeps on the airport runways to prevent any aircraft from landing, and set up roadblocks along all approaches to the capital. They took over the large Chinaimo army camp downstream from Vientiane, and commandeered its armored cars and tanks.

The whole operation went off like clockwork. Few shots were fired, and except for two resisting guards at General Sounthone's house, there were no casualties.

Vientiane Radio began announcing a series of terse communiqués formulated in perfect French. Their import was that the Second Paratroop Battalion had assumed full civil and military powers in Laos. When Vientiane's population turned out on the streets at daybreak, they were confronted all over town by squads of paratroopers in green-and-brown camouflage uniforms and red berets.

8.

Return to Neutrality

Vientiane, under the paratroopers, came alive with activity. Squads of determined-looking men, bearing rifles almost too big for them, guarded all public buildings. Jeeps and trucks loaded with cheering soldiers hurtled through the streets. At some corners, armored cars were parked in the shade of serene flame trees, the crews lounging on the turrets reading newspapers or mimeographed pamphlets. Some drank beer from their canteens (they were under orders to pay full price for their beer and to refuse even a free cigarette from a civilian). On the fifteen-mile drive into the capital from the Mekong ferry crossing downstream, the author's taxi was stopped at two roadblocks manned by paratroopers, who made the passengers, including three bonzes, get out so the car could be searched.

Until now, the Lao army had never been rated very highly. Even the deployment of four armored cars in the generals' putsch attempted the previous January had had a faintly ludicrous air to it. But there was nothing ludicrous about the control Kong Le's Second Paratroop Battalion now exercised over Vientiane. These men possessed an efficiency and, above all, an enthusiasm that had been almost unknown before.

Ironically, the boxes of ammunition toted by Kong Le's hustling soldiers and the trucks they rode in were emblazoned with the Stars and Stripes and clasped hands, the insignia of the American aid program. Nevertheless, they proclaimed their determination to put an end to "foreign interference" in Laos, an expression they obviously directed against the United States and its activities in the little Kingdom over the past six years.

The Little Captain

The man behind this transformation was tiny in stature (5 feet 1 inch tall), shy in speaking, innocent of politics, and naïve to the point of being credulous. A more unlikely strongman could hardly be imagined.

Kong Le, the son of a Kha tribesman from southern Laos, was born in Muong Phalane in central Savannakhet Province. He claims to have one older brother, two younger brothers, and a sister, who has remained in Savannakhet. He has been married at least three times. His first wife was a Black Thai, who bore him five children. Nothing is known about his second wife. In 1959, he took for his third wife the niece of General Ouan Ratikon.

Kong Le's military career began in 1948 or 1949, when, after one year of formal schooling in the Savannakhet *lycée,* he was recruited by the French to fight the Viet Minh. He rose through the ranks and was promoted to captain in the Territorial army on January 8, 1952. He became an adept field officer, probably the best in the Lao army. The British military attaché shortly after the coup described him as "having an instinct possessed by all great captains, but in need of more formal training in matters of tactics."

In 1954, he was in command of a detachment of thirty men in Luang Prabang. In October, 1957, he was sent to the Ranger School for field-grade officers in the Philippines, under the American training program for officers in the Royal Lao Army. There he met Kamlon Thongpant, a Lao officer who shared his growing misgivings about the mounting American influence in their homeland. The two officers soon decided to attempt a coup against the Lao government, and they used their remaining few months in the Philippines to work out their plans. In January, 1958, they returned home, and the Second Paratroop Battalion was formed under Kong Le's command. "From that moment on, I chose the men," Kong Le recalled later. Carefully keeping his motives secret, Kong Le sounded out a number of fellow officers on their attitudes toward the war against the Pathet Lao. Those officers he judged would be in sympathy with a coup to restore national unity, he had placed in his unit. He chose seventeen such officers, and confided to them his plan to overthrow the government. At the same time, he worked to mold his battalion into a functioning unit whose efficiency and loyalty he could count upon implicitly.

In Vientiane, the commander positioned his co-conspirators at strategic locations: Kamlon, also a captain, commanded a small group of men from the battalion at a point on the road to Paksane, north of the town; Ketsana Vongsouvan, a loyal lieutenant, had charge of another such group near the Chinaimo army camp, on the eastern outskirts of Vientiane. Two other lieutenants, Soulivan Sihavara and Deuan Siphaseuth, were also assigned to strategic points. Kong Le, with the main body of the battalion, made his headquarters at the Sikhay military camp, near the Vientiane airport.

Throughout that June and July, a Coup d'État Committee conducted regular meetings to plan the details of the uprising against the Somsanith government.

The objective of the plotters was simple: They wanted to rid the country of a regime that they believed was leading Laos into a new form of colonization, this time under the United States. The fact that Kong Le had never attracted much attention from the Vientiane politicians and their American advisers was of considerable help to him in keeping his plans secret. While he and his paratroopers had been hacking through dense jungles to locate Pathet Lao guerrillas, men like General Ouan Ratikon had sat in their offices amid wall maps covered with red and blue arrows and explained the anti-Communist campaign. It was a General Ouan, not a Captain Kong Le, who had the privilege of conferring with the Commander in Chief of American Pacific Forces in Hawaii.

Quinim Pholsena, the Santiphab Party leader, perhaps the only civilian to be taken into the confidence of the Coup d'État Committee, warned Kong Le that his military skills could not solve the political problems that would arise following the coup. Quinim advised him to consult Souvanna Phouma. The Prince was again in Vientiane, having returned from his ambassadorship in Paris. He had run unopposed in Luang Prabang for the National Assembly in April, 1960, and had been elected chairman. However, the Prince was not made privy to the coup plot.

The success of the coup brought an abrupt end to the obscurity in which Kong Le had lived. Overnight, he became a magnetic public figure, as the people responded enthusiastically to his simplicity and earnestness. For virtually the first time, the Royal Lao Army had a hero. Vientiane students organized themselves in support of the paratrooper junta, and Lao students left schools in France and the United States to return home and join the small group around Kong Le. It was an extraordinary episode in a country traditionally apathetic about politics.

A number of rumors circulated about the new hero. His good

luck in the thick of fighting was said to be uncanny, and inspired the widespread notion that he wore an amulet. As proof of his amazing luck, an actual incident was cited: At the battle of the Ca Dinh River against superior forces of General Phoumi Nosavan in November, 1960, Kong Le's personal bodyguard had been seriously wounded but Kong Le himself had escaped untouched. Various rumors that he had died also received wide circulation. When he was enduring great hardship on the Plain of Jars, it was rumored that he had been killed in a mutiny of his men; another time he was reported to have been caught in a fatal ambush by Meo guerrillas.

Kong Le, plucked from the familiar milieu of his trusted soldiers and thrust in the public limelight, acted with a strange mixture of humility and flamboyance. He delighted in pleasing the people; while in Vientiane he passed out hundreds of photographs of himself in his captain's uniform.

Inexperienced in political oratory, he addressed the crowds in simple, homespun terms, reducing the most complex international situations to easily grasped ideas.

At a public rally at the Vientiane sports stadium on August 11, two days after the coup, he expressed in broad terms his goals: an end to the government's military campaign against the Pathet Lao ("I am tired of seeing Lao fight Lao") and an end to corruption in the army, the bureaucracy, and the National Assembly ("I am willing to die for Laos, but not to cover up incompetence and corruption"). He told the people:

> During my period of military service, all Lao governments and the Royal Army have informed us that there were enemies outside Laos ready to enter and cause agitation within our country. But I and my friends, in our work together, have never seen such enemies coming to make trouble. We have only seen Lao killing Lao without cause.
>
> In my experience, many past Lao governments have told us they wished to follow a neutral course, but they never did so. My group and I decided to sacrifice everything, even our lives, in order to bring neutrality and peace to our nation.

A mimeographed leaflet he ordered distributed at this time defended the course taken by the military: "If we did nothing, our country would have become prey to others, just as in former times we were a prey to the French." One wonders if Kong Le comprehended even dimly the dangerous precedent he had set for Laos. Never before had the power of the army been so dramatically demonstrated.

Kong Le expressed a rarely voiced indignation at the worst abuses of the American aid program, again the subject of rumors about corruption. "I like honesty," Kong Le told the stadium audience. Then he charged that the members of the Somsanith government had been "bought as slaves," and that this government, which had "foolishly led the people" to become involved with the American dollar, had to be destroyed.

Kong Le ended the rally with a strong plea that Souvanna Phouma, whom he described as a man who "can restore control" and "return the country to normal," be named by the King as Prime Minister. It was Souvanna Phouma's government that had stood for reconciliation among all the Lao in 1956 and 1957 and had resisted the American Ambassador to achieve this.

Communiqués attributed to Kong Le and broadcast on the radio defined the aims of the *coup d'état* as the protection of nation, religion, monarchy, and Constitution. In order to achieve these goals, the communiqués declared, the Coup d'État Committee intended to recognize human rights; revamp the internal affairs of the National Assembly; eliminate corruption in government and reorganize the administration; abolish all foreign military intervention and remove foreign bases; strictly adhere to the United Nations Charter, maintain a neutral policy, and promote friendly relations with neighboring countries; and accept from all countries aid without strings attached.[1] At first, Kong Le signed his name as "Chief of the Revolutionary Party," then as "Chief of the Revolutionary Committee," and finally as "Chief of the Coup d'État." Despite the free use of the word revolutionary, there was no intention of opposing the monarchy.

Within hours after seizing control of Vientiane, Kong Le demanded that Somsanith and his fellow Cabinet ministers return to Vientiane from Luang Prabang. Ensconced with his band of faithful officers in the colonial-style yellow stucco building that housed the Prime Minister's office, Kong Le declared over a loudspeaker outside the office that Somsanith's failure to appear would be interpreted as a "hostile act."

On August 13, with no repentant Cabinet ministers yet in sight, a small crowd assembled outside the Prime Minister's office to demand action to force the removal of the Somsanith government. Students and *fonctionnaires* mingled in front of the building, where they were joined by a long line of saffron-robed bonzes. Then the crowd, led by a number of paratroopers, marched in some disorder and merriment out of the yard and up the street toward the National

[1] See texts in Appendix IV.

Assembly, picking up adherents along the way. By the time it reached the Assembly building, the mob numbered more than 1,000. Some carried crudely painted banners proclaiming "Down with U.S. Imperialism!" and showing Uncle Sam passing out bagfuls of money. But there were no acts of hostility toward American residents in Vientiane.

At the entrance to the Assembly building, the demonstrators were met by Souvanna Phouma, dressed impeccably and puffing on his pipe, making his first public appearance since the coup. He addressed the crowd briefly, urging moderation, and was loudly cheered. Then he withdrew and, behind closed doors, presided over a National Assembly meeting. As the hours dragged on, the crowd outside became restive. Egged on by paratroopers who had been posted around the building, ostensibly to safeguard the deputies, some demonstrators brought up sound trucks and threatened to storm the building. However, the only damage inflicted was a broken pane of glass in the front door. When the session ended, it was announced that the deputies had passed a vote of censure against the Somsanith government.

Meanwhile, a series of radio communications had been transmitted between Vientiane and Luang Prabang. The result was that on the afternoon of the demonstration, an Air Laos airliner—a 1939, four-engine Boeing Stratoliner, a make of plane curiously suited for short hops over the country's precipitous mountains— roared over the capital. When it rolled to a stop on the airfield, General Ouan Ratikon alighted. He surveyed the battle-ready paratroopers encircling the airfield, and announced he had been commissioned to determine the coup leaders' "true intentions" and report them back to Luang Prabang. Apparently, General Ouan on his return convinced Somsanith that the coup was a serious undertaking, for the latter resigned the following day. He then returned to Vientiane, accompanied only by Ngon Sananikone, the Minister of Economy.

General Phoumi, the Defense Minister, however, was having none of this mutiny. Upon learning of the coup, he had flown from Luang Prabang to Bangkok for hasty consultations with Prime Minister Marshal Sarit Thanarat, and thence to the town of Savannakhet. There, he was joined by twenty-one Cabinet members and National Assembly deputies. Under General Phoumi's leadership, they formed a Counter Coup d'État Committee, and on August 16, they sent a C-47 over Vientiane to drop leaflets announcing the new group. Two days later, a transmitter in Savannakhet began making regular broadcasts denouncing the Second Paratroop Battalion as traitors and saying there would be a march on Vientiane by loyalist soldiers.

Neutrality Again

In the meantime, however, the thirty-four remaining members of the National Assembly removed from the Cabinet the CDNI leaders (to whom they owed their seats won in the rigged elections of the previous April). A new Cabinet, formed exclusively of men who had not held posts under Somsanith and headed by Souvanna Phouma as Prime Minister, was unanimously approved by the Assembly.

The new government, said Souvanna Phouma, was committed to a policy of "true and wise neutrality." He pledged himself to "respect all Laos' obligations, including the Geneva agreements." This reversed his 1958 declaration that he regarded Laos' commitments at Geneva as "fully accomplished." His change in position reflected the unsettled nature of the Pathet Lao rebellion.

In its nine days under military administration, Vientiane had functioned smoothly and efficiently. The post and telegraph services, closed down in the predawn hours of August 9, had reopened four days later. A paratrooper had moved into the Immigration Office, long a chief source of the corruption associated with "squeeze" and "key money," and had begun issuing residence and travel permits. The Vietnamese population of the town, who had been lying low because of the high price of keeping their papers in order, had flocked to the Immigration Office in large numbers as soon as word had got around that permits were being issued with dispatch and for nothing more than the legal fee.

On August 17, the paratroopers handed over their administrative functions to the newly formed Cabinet and vacated the Prime Minister's office. The civil servants resumed their shuffling of dossiers in a dozen different ministries and the administrative life of the capital returned to the sleepy inefficiency to which it was accustomed.

If Souvanna Phouma had not been in the capital, Kong Le's coup might well have led up a blind alley. It was probably because of Souvanna Phouma's insistence that Kong Le respected legal procedures once he had seized power.

Kong Le had had another stroke of luck. New PEO deliveries had filled Vientiane warehouses with new and reconditioned weapons, and the paratroopers immediately put these depots under guard. In addition, there was plenty of ready cash in Vientiane's National Bank, which dispensed the pay for the whole army. Thus, Kong Le's troops were in an excellent position to ward off any opposition movement from the provinces.

Souvanna Phouma, however, was determined to effect a reconciliation with the ousted Cabinet members. This necessitated a settlement with General Phoumi, whose independent position in Savannakhet carried the dangerous overtones of a civil war between two factions of the Royal Army. Souvanna Phouma was also eager to obtain the King's approval of the new Cabinet.

With these objectives in mind, Souvanna Phouma flew in a borrowed U.S. Army liaison plane on August 23 to the French air base at Séno, and proceeded by car to Savannakhet. He was accompanied by General Ouan and Captain Kamlon. The Prince spent the entire day talking with General Phoumi, to whom he proposed that a meeting of both factions of the National Assembly be held in Luang Prabang, considered neutral ground, with the objective of reconciling policy differences and forming a coalition government. General Phoumi supported his plan and agreed to attend such a meeting.

Six days later, the proposed meeting opened in Luang Prabang, attended by thirty-four deputies who had accompanied Souvanna Phouma from Vientiane and twenty-one who had flown north from Savannakhet with General Phoumi. The setting was the spacious house of the Governor of Luang Prabang Province. Both men addressed a united session of the National Assembly.

Souvanna Phouma and General Phoumi then embarked on a series of tête-à-têtes in the office of the Provincial Governor. These lasted for almost two days, at the end of which Prince Somsanith appeared at the Royal Palace to tender his resignation to the King. This was accepted forthwith, and the King named Souvanna Phouma as Prime Minister, empowered to form a new Cabinet.

In the resulting Cabinet, General Phoumi had a major role as Deputy Prime Minister and Interior Minister, and several posts were restored to members of the old Somsanith government. Quinim Pholsena, who at Kong Le's insistence had been included in the August 17 Cabinet, was given the minor post of Information Minister, whose official duties consisted mainly of censoring press cables, but who was to play a much more important role after Souvanna Phouma initiated dealings with the Pathet Lao.

General Phoumi, emerging from the session clad in a crisp new green fatigue uniform without any insignia of rank, announced that the new government would grant amnesty to Kong Le and his battalion.

He and Souvanna Phouma announced in a two-paragraph communiqué that they were agreed on the need to re-establish peace and concord among all Lao and to preserve constitutional legality. It was the first of many such communiqués. Whatever the differences among the Lao leaders, they were never so great as to prevent the declaration of agreements "in principle" among all factions.

By the afternoon of August 31, everything appeared settled. The new government seemed to have the blessing of the Western powers, whose embassies had dispatched their first secretaries to witness the National Assembly deputies' unanimous ratification of the Cabinet. Most important, Souvanna Phouma had the obvious sympathy of the new United States Ambassador, Winthrop G. Brown, a New Englander who had arrived in Vientiane just the week before the coup. On his return to Vientiane, Souvanna Phouma reported his evaluation of the American position: "The Ambassador assures me that the United States remains absolutely neutral in this matter."

On that fateful afternoon, General Phoumi clambered aboard his mud-splattered C-47 to fly back to Savannakhet "to clear up remaining business" there, he explained. Speaking in his usual soft French, which reporters had to lean forward to hear, he said, "I hope that with the authority commanded by Prince Souvanna Phouma everything will be arranged. Otherwise, there is nothing."

Yet General Phoumi never showed up in Vientiane. Instead, as if indicating passive disapproval, he shut himself up in Savannakhet.

Perhaps the deciding factor was a rash broadcast by Kong Le on the last afternoon of the negotiations in Luang Prabang. On learning of the composition of the new Cabinet, he had rushed to the radio station and, in an emotion-filled voice, declared that his men were determined to oppose the return to power of "corrupt officials" who wished to pursue the civil war. He said his men would rather "die to the last one." Later, Kong Le was severely reprimanded for this outburst by Souvanna Phouma.

Many members of the defunct Somsanith government were genuinely fearful of returning to a Vientiane controlled by paratroopers. This was made clear by a remark made to the author by Education Minister Nhouy Abhay. As he boarded Souvanna Phouma's plane to return home (he had been in Paris when the coup occurred and had flown directly to Luang Prabang), he smiled and said, only half joking, "You see, I am the only one who has nothing to fear!" Indeed, most of the former ministers who decently could stayed away from Vientiane.

In Vientiane, it was no longer fashionable to be living in the largest house or driving the largest car. The author was startled to see a Lao businessman friend driving around the capital in a battered Morris Minor. He had put his shiny black Mercedes in his garage for safekeeping, he explained with a twinkle in his eye. *"C'est plus prudent!"*

The probable reason for General Phoumi's remaining in Savannakhet was that he was advised by members of his entourage there that his compromise with Souvanna Phouma, which granted him a Cabinet post but not control over the vital Defense Ministry, was not to his advantage. It would be smarter, he was likely told, to gamble his future on opposing Kong Le in Vientiane by force of arms.

It would take time to mobilize an army to march against the 600 paratroopers and other less reliable units defending Vientiane. But Prince Boun Oum na Champassak, the venerated southern leader, was loyal to the Counter Coup d'État Committee, and so the Phoumists could count on the support of the army units stationed in the lower Mekong Valley. The provincial governors were another matter. Most of those in the north had sent telegrams of support to Souvanna Phouma. Even so, the Phoumists might gain allies in northern Laos, because Souvanna Phouma's contacts with the provincial governors there were more formal than personal.

Colonel Khammouane Boupha, the Governor of Phong Saly, equivocated between expressing his loyalty to either Souvanna Phouma or General Phoumi, and at the same time arranged to remain on good terms with the Pathet Lao.

General Phoumi, of course aware of Kong Le's superiority in matériel, saw a possibility of overcoming this. If he undertook a struggle against the *coup d'état,* he was certain to receive support from Thailand, which had been alarmed by the overthrow of Somsanith, and from powerful interests within the agencies of American diplomacy. Marshal Sarit held the belief that a coalition government in Laos would open the door to the Communists on his border, and some American officials shared this belief. The Phoumists' capture on August 22 of the town of Paksane, on the banks of the Mekong, only ninety miles east of Vientiane, undoubtedly served to reassure the General's backers that an armed expedition against Vientiane was worth the gamble.

There remained the Pathet Lao.

Voice from the Jungle

Prince Souphanouvong learned of Kong Le's *coup d'état* while on his trek from Vientiane to Sam Neua. A statement attributed to him was broadcast by the clandestine Radio Pathet Lao in one of its first transmissions, on August 24. It applauded the coup and pledged "full support" to the policy of neutrality and reconciliation enunciated by the new government in Vientiane. Also, it urged that diplomatic relations be established with neighboring countries as soon as possible. However, it demanded that no concessions be made to the Phoumists. Once again, as when Phoui eliminated the CDNI from his Cabinet in December, 1959, the Pathet Lao had quickly opened the door to a new coalition.

Souvanna Phouma, when he returned from the Luang Prabang meeting, had issued an appeal to the Pathet Lao to place their confidence in him and send representatives to Vientiane to resume negotiations to end the civil war. This struggle had not been decided in fifteen months of campaigning across the length and breadth of Laos. In his statement, he assured the Pathet Lao: "I shall turn all my efforts toward ending this fraticidal struggle and re-establishing the union we formed in 1957."

Undoubtedly, the Pathet Lao were banking on the failure of the Prime Minister's attempt to come to terms with the Phoumists. The Pathet Lao reaction to the appeal for a resumption of negotiations was speedy. However, it came in a New China News Agency dispatch datelined Hanoi and quoting the "minimum conditions" that the Central Committee of the NLHS had decided upon for again entering into negotiations. These conditions were: immediate dismissal of the Phoumists from the government; termination of the civil war and a halt to mopping-up operations; release of prisoners detained for pro-Pathet Lao activities and restoration of their democratic rights; pursuit of a policy of "real peace and neutrality"; establishment of diplomatic relations with all countries; and acceptance of aid from "all countries willing to extend assistance to Laos with no political and military strings attached."

As was their custom, the Pathet Lao immediately set about strengthening their hand for these negotiations by a series of military initiatives.

In the first few days in September, Black Thai guerrillas began infiltrating across the Ma River to re-establish Pathet Lao control in the villages of northern San Neua Province, and again took over Sop Nao in the Dien Bien Phu valley after brief skirmishes with Royal

Army troops. Pathet Lao guerrillas also reoccupied vantage points in the limestone mountains east of Thakhek, where thousands of natural caves had afforded the Viet Minh an impregnable hideout during the Indochina War. Other bands blew up a number of bridges south of Pakse on the road linking Laos and Cambodia.

In Sam Neua town, the garrison commander, Colonel Khamkong Vongnarath, was under pressure from both Vientiane and Savannakhet for the allegiance of his two infantry battalions, numbering some 1,500 men. He resolved the dilemma by taking an ambivalent position: He proclaimed his determination to take orders only from Savannakhet but welcomed aid in any form from any quarter for the defense of the town. On September 28, the Pathet Lao attacked in force. Colonel Khamkong's soldiers put up a hopeless siege defense against the attackers, who held the mountain heights overlooking the valley, and then broke out of the town after sabotaging its landing strip. They retreated southwestward toward the Plain of Jars over the same rugged trails that the French garrison troops had taken seven years previously. In possession of the town, the Pathet Lao established their usual administrative committee and began the patient process of educating the inhabitants to the benefits of "liberation." They reinstated Thao Ma, a former private secretary of Souphanouvong and once the highest-ranking Pathet Lao official in the province (by virtue of the 1957 reintegration agreement), as Acting Governor.

On October 2, Pathet Lao pursuers overtook Colonel Khamkong's retreating troops at Muong Peun, twenty miles southwest of Sam Neua town. Khamkong's men surrendered, handing over their American weapons and ammunition. (Six Catholic missionaries— three Frenchmen, two Canadians, and an American, Father Lucien Bouchard of South Attleboro, Massachusetts—managed to avoid capture and made their way back to Vientiane in five days of walking.)

On receiving news of these Pathet Lao victories, Souvanna Phouma dispatched Quinim to make contact with the Pathet Lao commanders in the area and to attempt to reassert Vientiane's authority there. He bitterly blamed the fighting at Sam Neua and Muong Peun on the Phoumists, and contemptuously advised the military to "go back to their tents instead of seeking high positions for the advancement of their personal ambitions," a remark directed against General Phoumi. After a final unsuccessful attempt to arrange a meeting with General Phoumi, he formally dropped the latter from his Cabinet.

Arms and Money for General Phoumi

Meanwhile, on September 10, General Phoumi broadcast from Savannakhet that a Revolutionary Committee, headed by Prince Boun Oum, had been set up to succeed the Counter Coup d'État Committee. The Prince, in the same broadcast, declared: "In order to restore peace and tranquillity in the country, to protect the King and religion and the freedom of the people, we revolutionaries, in the name of the citizens of Laos, hereby declare that we seize power and abrogate all constitutional rights of the present government from this date." This unilateral suspension of the Constitution was later to embarrass Boun Oum's government when it wanted to take office by legal process in Vientiane.

On September 19, Radio Pathet Lao announced that guerrilla forces loyal to Prince Souphanouvong had been ordered to avoid clashes with troops loyal to Souvanna Phouma, and suggested that soldiers of the two factions should, wherever possible, join in fighting Phoumist troops.

General Ouan Ratikon, who had returned to Vientiane, offered his services to Souvanna Phouma's government, and been placed over Kong Le as commander of all troops loyal to Vientiane, formally warned Phoumist commanders that they faced prosecution as mutineers unless they disassociated themselves from the Revolutionary Committee. In mid-September, Kong Le's paratroopers, outnumbered 4 to 1, routed the Phoumist occupiers of Paksane, under Colonel Bounleuth Sanichan. Later that month, they pushed them down the Mekong Valley to the south bank of the Ca Dinh River, where a front stabilized temporarily.

It was plain that General Phoumi was rapidly building up his matériel and manpower for a march on Vientiane. From mid-September, Savannakhet was the scene of an increased number of landings and takeoffs by unmarked C-46 and C-47 transports, manned by American crews. These planes belonged to Air America, Inc., a civilian charter company with U.S. Air Force organizational support and under contract to the U.S. Government. The aircraft, giving the Phoumist forces a badly needed logistical supply system, ferried military supplies from Bangkok to Savannakhet, the headquarters of the Revolutionary Committee, and shuttled between Savannakhet and outlying garrisons loyal to General Phoumi.

The Phoumist forces were substantially augmented by 200 paratroopers, originally intended to form a First Paratroop Battalion, who had newly completed training in Thailand. They had been returned by the PEO to southern Laos despite the Prime Minister's request that they be sent to the Plain of Jars, where a tug of war was under way for the allegiance of Colonel Khamhou Bhoutsarath, commander of the Second Military Region with headquarters at Xieng Khouang. The Xieng Khouang garrison had proclaimed its loyalty to Souvanna Phouma after the fall of Sam Neua to the Pathet Lao. But in mid-October the garrison switched to General Phoumi, largely due to the influence of the Meo leader Toubhy Lyfong. He opposed Vientiane's prospective negotiations with the Pathet Lao, and had flown from Vientiane to Xieng Khouang a few days before they were to begin. (Despite heavy fortification by the Phoumists, Xieng Khouang was recaptured by Kong Le with Pathet Lao assistance in January, 1961.)

Souvanna Phouma's difficulties were measurably increased by Thailand's imposition of an unofficial blockade on Vientiane. This was a product of Marshal Sarit's opposition to Souvanna Phouma's government, which he feared would make a deal with the Communists and outflank him. By far the greater portion of Vientiane's supplies came across the Mekong from Thailand, so that cutting off this traffic soon had a drastic effect on the capital's economy. The railhead in the Thailand town of Nong Khai was particularly important in the supplying of petroleum products, which accounted for 26 per cent of the value of Laos' total imports. After the flow of these had been cut off, Souvanna Phouma resorted to obtaining petroleum products elsewhere, first from Burma and then from the Soviet Union, which had responded favorably to feelers to open an embassy in Vientiane. In this way, the blockade, inspired by Marshal Sarit's fear of Communism, actually played into the hands of the Communist powers. Their best interests were served by a Souvanna Phouma so weakened and isolated that he would turn to them in desperation. Insofar as it affected the movement of rice and vegetables, the blockade was not completely effective: The Thai peasants had traditionally ferried their produce across the Mekong in sampans, and they were not going to let a bureaucratic edict interfere with their small profit. Although rice prices on the Vientiane market nearly doubled during the blockade, no serious shortages ever developed.

A feeling of nervousness pervaded Vientiane, heightened by sporadic shooting incidents and isolated acts of sabotage perpetrated by night raiding parties. In one such incident, a half-dozen mortar shells were lobbed into the vicinity of the power station, and the United Nations representative in Vientiane, Edouard Zellweger, said that he had seen flashes of firing coming from the Thailand bank of the river opposite his house. However, the mortar fire might have come from a boat in midstream. Thailand formally denied implication in the affair.

In these circumstances, Souvanna Phouma was less and less inclined to enter into any bargain with General Phoumi. When King Savang Vatthana requested the two men to meet in Luang Prabang and General Phoumi suggested formation of a three-cornered coalition by Prince Boun Oum, Prince Souvanna Phouma, and Prince Souphanouvong, these moves were politely rejected by Souvanna Phouma.

The announcement at the end of September that a Soviet Embassy would be established in Vientiane produced near panic in the State Department. A rapid series of maneuvers and announcements ensued, one effect of which was to alert the Soviet Union to the possibilities opened up by the lack of control exercised by the United States over a delicate foreign-policy situation in an election campaign.

Negotiations with the Pathet Lao

These developments in the military, economic, and political fields moved toward a climax about the middle of October. At this moment, the Pathet Lao, having buttressed their bargaining position by once more consolidating their control over their base area in northern Laos, opened the way for the negotiations with Vientiane. The trio of Pathet Lao negotiators, Nouhak Phoumsavan, Phoumi Vongvichit, and Singkapo Chounlamany,[2] had slipped back into the capital. On October 11, in the starkly furnished conference room of the Prime Minister's office, decorated only with a portrait of the King, Souvanna Phouma and the Pathet Lao emissaries exchanged the customary Buddhist greeting of clasped hands and a slight bow of the head, and sat down at a makeshift wooden table.

---

[2] An intriguing sidelight is provided by remarks attributed to Singkapo by Wilfred G. Burchett in a later interview. Singkapo said that Souphanouvong, on learning of Kong Le's coup, detached Singkapo from the walking party. " 'It was decided I should go back and re-establish contact. I was to travel light and fast. What had taken us three months to cover I did in seven days and nights of travel, stopping only for snatches of sleep. I got back to a point close enough to Vientiane to establish contact with Kong Le and he sent a helicopter to pick me up.' " (*The Furtive War: The United States in Vietnam and Laos* [New York: International Publishers, 1963], p. 188.) But Kong Le, in August, 1960, had no helicopters. Interestingly, four months later, in December, the Thai border police photographed a wrecked Soviet-built helicopter that had been abandoned only a few hours earlier, in Loei Province, upstream and across the Mekong from Vientiane.

The resumption of negotiations between the Royal Government and the Pathet Lao appeared in Washington to confirm the worst fears of a number of high-ranking State Department officials who were less convinced of Souvanna Phouma's trustworthiness than was Ambassador Brown. The coup had come as a complete surprise, and therefore the State Department had no prepared policy on how to deal with its aftermath. The American Embassy in Vientiane had no biography of Kong Le (whether or not the CIA had such a document is uncertain). On the defensive because of its lack of preparation, the State Department devoted itself to denying French assertions that the coup had fundamentally transformed the situation in Laos by shattering the illusion that the Royal Army would defeat the Pathet Lao rebels. Attention at the State Department was also focused on protesting to the Thais that the United States was still as resolved as ever to support the anti-Communist struggle. How exactly this was to be done when the Royal Government was in the process of negotiating with the pro-Communists was, however, problematical.

Messages from the State Department in the days following the coup advised Ambassador Brown to take such action as would remove Kong Le from the scene as expeditiously as possible. The messages, however, gave no specific orders as to how Brown should effect this. In any case, it became impossible to eliminate Kong Le and restore the *status quo* after Prince Somsanith resigned. Some suitable accommodation, then, had to be worked out with Kong Le. However, Brown made no overtures to Kong Le, feeling that he was too swept up in his immediate administrative problems to be accessible and that he would be cool to any American proposals.

As the days went on, the State Department messages to Brown became less and less coherent. Conflicting suggestions would appear within the same telegram. The State Department felt that Kong Le should be gotten rid of, but it had no means to achieve this; there was no over-all policy directive permitting speedy, deliberate action against Kong Le, who was not a Communist.

With Souvanna Phouma, on the other hand, Brown early established cordial relations. He felt that the calm, self-assured Prince was the best hope for keeping Laos from being swept by a Communist revolution manufactured by the Kingdom's more powerful militant neighbors. He proposed to the State Department that the United States throw its support to the new government. But Brown was unable to muster the backing in Washington necessary if the Prince's leadership was to assert itself in the face of the growing challenge from the Pathet Lao and the expanding influence of the Soviet Union, China, and North Vietnam.

Displaying more decisiveness than the State Department (possibly these agencies were less subject to the disruptive effects of the Presidential election campaign then in full swing), the Pentagon and the Central Intelligence Agency in Washington set in motion actions consistent with their past efforts in Laos and with their interpretation of the current situation—they immediately began building up General Phoumi.

The Pentagon's support for General Phoumi was motivated by the conviction that the entire American defense posture in Southeast Asia, and more particularly in South Vietnam and Thailand, depended on unconditional support to anti-Communists in Laos (and, conversely, the conviction that U.S. support for a government that was negotiating with Communist insurgents and preparing to take them in would provoke disastrous repercussions in these countries). But there was a flaw in this logic. The American military was acutely aware that the Royal Lao Army was not a first-class fighting force, that it was up against a cunning and patient enemy, and that its chances of victory were remote. Even so, the deleterious effects of abandoning General Phoumi appeared to the Pentagon considerably more nightmarish than those of continuing to back his forces in a heretofore fruitless war.

The CIA was in a position to size up the situation with considerable accuracy. For years, its field agents had been submitting precise, first-hand reports about the balance of forces. Of all the agencies represented in Laos, the CIA had the closest contact with the villages in the hinterland; its men spent more time in the field than the Embassy or the PEO personnel and they had excellent sources of information among both the Lao and the mountain people. They could not be deluded about the factual weaknesses and strengths of the American position in Laos. The CIA recognized that General Phoumi was no paragon of virtue. But he and his fellow generals represented the army, and the army was still the only cohesive country-wide organization comparable to the Pathet Lao and the NLHS.

Ambassador Brown gave the various American agencies in Vientiane relatively free play in forming their opinions about the situation and recommending actions. At the same time, however, he made it clear that he wished to be kept informed about dissenting recommendations.

American support for the factions in Laos was implemented by the aid program. Unexpectedly, the first statement that the aid program had been affected by these developments came from General Williston B. Palmer, the Pentagon's Director of Military Assistance. During a brief stopover at the Saigon airport on October 1, he announced that aid to Laos was being stopped because of the three-way split in Laos.

This statement was denied two days later in Vientiane on Brown's order. General Palmer's statement, an Embassy spokesman declared, had been made "without instructions from or knowledge of the Washington agencies concerned." The spokesman added, "In fact, United States military aid to Laos has not been suspended," but acknowledged that delivery of supplies to Kong Le's paratroopers had virtually ceased since the coup. This was understandable; the United States had been reluctant to make deliveries to what appeared to be a mutinous band of soldiers.

On October 7, Souvanna Phouma declared that the United States had suspended its cash-grant aid to his government. On the same day, a State Department spokesman in Washington confirmed that payment of funds for the September army salaries had not been made to the Vientiane government. Souvanna Phouma's government was immediately in jeopardy.

Simultaneously, Washington announced that former Ambassador J. Graham Parsons, now Assistant Secretary of State for Far Eastern Affairs, was being dispatched in haste for consultations with Souvanna Phouma. Upon disembarking at the Vientiane airport on October 12, Parsons made it unmistakably clear that resumption of American cash-grant aid to Souvanna Phouma's government depended on the attitude Souvanna Phouma took toward pending political questions, most urgent of which was the negotiations with the Pathet Lao that had commenced the previous day.

Parsons entered the talks with Souvanna Phouma with three principal objectives: (1) He wanted to get the Prime Minister to break off his negotiations with the Pathet Lao forthwith; the discussion on this was delicate, since Souvanna Phouma attributed the breakup of the first coalition in 1958 largely to Parsons' reports to Washington that the coalition would open the way to Communist control. (2) Parsons wanted Souvanna Phouma to guarantee that he would enter into negotiations with General Phoumi. The Prime Minister replied that if resuming talks with the Phoumists was so urgent, it was up to General Phoumi to come to Vientiane. (3) Parsons wanted Souvanna Phouma to move the capital from Vientiane to Luang Prabang, presumably because Washington felt that there the King would exert a conservative influence on the government.

On none of these points would Souvanna Phouma make concessions. Next day, Parsons flew to Luang Prabang for an audience with King Savang Vatthana. Souvanna Phouma angrily interpreted this as an effort to go over his head. Now any agreement with the Americans was unthinkable. Yielding to any U.S. request at this juncture would finish his political career.

Souvanna Phouma's bargaining position was bolstered by the arrival in Vientiane on October 13 of a burly Russian named Aleksandr N. Abramov. He was the first ambassador of a Communist country to enter Laos. After his initial meeting with Souvanna Phouma, Abramov emerged smiling broadly. Asked for the Soviet position on Parsons' trip, Abramov replied, still smiling: "I would have liked to meet Mr. Parsons, but he left in such a hurry."

Parsons had now gone on to Bangkok, accompanied by Ambassador Brown, and the two diplomats spent the next few days looking for some way out of the impasse. Souvanna Phouma's position in relation to the Pathet Lao was reviewed. General Phoumi was weighed against Souvanna Phouma. Finally, they worked out a course of action that was a compromise between all-out support for General Phoumi and all-out toleration of Souvanna Phouma's predilection for coexistence with the Pathet Lao.

On his return to Vientiane, the sympathetic Brown suggested to Souvanna Phouma that the Prince would not want the Pathet Lao guerrillas to take over the country while the non-Communist forces were squabbling among themselves. Brown then pointed out that General Phoumi shared this wish. Next, Brown proposed that the Prime Minister agree to deliveries of American military equipment to General Phoumi at Savannakhet. In return, the cash-grant aid to Vientiane would be resumed.

Souvanna Phouma assented to this gentlemen's agreement with Brown on one condition—none of the military equipment delivered to General Phoumi must be used against Souvanna Phouma's commander, Kong Le; it must be used against the Pathet Lao only. Souvanna Phouma, in agreeing to this proposition, full of risks to himself, did so to demonstrate to Parsons and the rest of the State Department that he was a patriot. Indeed, after this there was no more talk by American officials about Souvanna Phouma's neglect of his country's best interests.

On October 17, the State Department announced the resumption of cash-grant aid to Souvanna Phouma's government. Eleven days later an agreement "in principle" was announced between Souvanna Phouma and Abramov for Soviet aid to his government, but there was no evidence that the Soviets could establish a large-scale aid program on short order. In fact, the first shipment of petroleum supplies from the Soviet Union did not arrive in Vientiane until December 3. The Soviet aid program, moreover, did not include cash grants. Up to the day Kong Le's troops left Vientiane, he paid them with funds from American aid.

The promised aid to General Phoumi began arriving in large quantities. Included were funds, logistical support, and technical aid. Besides the Savannakhet transmitter, American technical aid provided for the operation of clandestine radio stations that were used by the Phoumists to encourage defections from Kong Le's troops and other forces loyal to Souvanna Phouma, without attacking the Prince by name. The main fault with the gentlemen's agreement between Souvanna Phouma and Brown was that making American aid available to General Phoumi also indicated that he had official American support. From there, he hypothesized that he could use this support to oust Souvanna Phouma; after all, he himself had made no promises. The United States was thus in the position of furnishing assistance to a rebel movement against a government with which it maintained diplomatic relations.

General Ouan Ratikon, who had flown to Luang Prabang with Souvanna Phouma, had remained there after the Prince returned to Vientiane. Weeks went by, and still General Ouan did not return. Finally, Souvanna Phouma confirmed rumors that were circulating in Vientiane. General Ouan had defected to the Phoumists. To succeed him, Souvanna Phouma named Sounthone Pathammavong, the only general left in Vientiane.

General Sing Ratanasamay, Lao military attaché in Paris, returned to Laos and went to Savannakhet to join General Phoumi. By mid-November, the Phoumists had three of Laos' five generals. A fourth, General Amkha Soukhavong, the only Christian general in the Royal Army, was kidnaped by Phoumist agents while on a mission for Souvanna Phouma in Xieng Khouang. He was flown to prison in Savannakhet, and was not released until May, 1963.

On November 11 came the hardest blow of all. In Luang Prabang, the Third Infantry Battalion mutinied against Souvanna Phouma's authority and declared for General Phoumi. A detachment of three companies of militia commanded by Captain Southep, a protégé of General Ouan, was dispatched to join forces with two Pathet Lao columns, whereupon the combined units were to encircle Luang Prabang and force the surrender of the Third Battalion. But halfway on the march to Luang Prabang, the militia detachment set up camp at Muong Kassy and waited. Kong Le's queries to Captain Southep were met with silence. The reason was that Southep, too, was a Phoumist. He was secretly monitoring Kong Le's radio messages to Phong Saly and other provincial capitals, and passing the information to Phoumist agents. He had had the foresight to take with him from Vientiane a stolen set of codebooks.

General Phoumi, meanwhile, was building up his main force in the Mekong Valley. Advance units, when sufficiently trained and indoctrinated, probed Kong Le's defense line on the Ca Dinh River on the left bank of the Mekong. In one such action, Phoumist patrols crossed the Ca Dinh and a pitched battle developed, during which the Phoumists brought artillery batteries into play for the first time. Kong Le's two companies of troops, without artillery support, fell back in confusion.

Souvanna Phouma was in dire straits. His relations with the Royal Palace had been edgy since the Phoumist coup of November 11 in Luang Prabang, following which Souvanna Phouma had publicly warned that he would not be bound by the King's decisions if the monarch was not a free agent. He divided his time among harried Cabinet meetings, consultations with loyal officers, and trips to villages in northern Vientiane Province, an area known to be heavily under the influence of the Pathet Lao "administrative committee" network. When he exhorted a crowd of villagers to grow more vegetables to defeat the blockade instead of attending Pathet Lao meetings, he was loudly cheered, and even Pathet Lao soldiers in their mustard-colored fatigues drifted into the villages to listen to him. On more than one occasion, he turned a hostile crowd, obviously cued by Pathet Lao agents, into a cheering mob of sympathizers calling out his own slogans of "Peace and Neutrality!" and "Reconciliation!" Nevertheless, his political position in Vientiane became increasingly isolated, while in the countryside his authority was eroded from both left and right.

There were reports that thousands of rifles and carbines from the warehouses in Vientiane had been distributed, on Kong Le's orders, in the Vientiane region to a "people's militia," of which a large proportion were Pathet Lao agents. Phoumi Vongvichit, still carrying on negotiations with Souvanna Phouma's government, told the author on November 30 that "as armed forces of the people, the Pathet Lao fighting units have up to the present made use only of arms and matériel which they have received from the people, or else seized from the hands of their enemy, the rebel lackeys of the American imperialists." He also indicated that the Pathet Lao command regarded its position as much more advantageous now than it had been in 1957. Any new coalition agreement "would have to be based on the agreements signed in the past and at the same time," he stressed, "be adapted to the present situation in the country."

The inroads that the Pathet Lao had made since the coup into the village organization of even Vientiane Province is well illustrated by detailed accusations broadcast by Radio Savannakhet on November 30, 1960:

> Village headmen in Phone Hong district [about forty miles north of Vientiane] were informed of the creation of village committees in their areas. This was directed by Thao Chan together with five armed men to supervise the organization. The newly created committees will have full authority to deal with affairs of their villages. At Ban Nasai and Na Phoh, the Neo Lao Hak Sat village committees take no recognition of the officially elected headmen despite the respect paid them by the local residents.
>
> On November 19, the *Chao Muong* [District Officer] of Phone Hong sent a messenger to the NLHS [in a nearby village completely dominated by the Pathet Lao] asking them to come to discuss the situation. They came in. He asked them not to spread false rumors or incite the people. The leader of the NLHS replied that they did so in compliance with the popular will.
>
> At Ban Liang San, more than two hundred soldiers have been training the villagers for the "people's militia." These soldiers are being fed by the village headmen [of the area]. No one could refuse, since the soldiers always say, "We must all be united."

The Pathet Lao had greatly strengthened their ground position under their unofficial cease-fire agreement with Souvanna Phouma. At the beginning of November, they had captured Ban Ban as part of the process of re-establishing their control over the whole tier of districts along the North Vietnam border. Moreover, as early as October, intelligence reports had disclosed the infiltration of North Vietnamese Army elements into the ranks of Pathet Lao units, to serve as "stiffeners." The number of these "stiffeners" was to increase steadily throughout the winter and into the spring of 1961. In Hanoi, Ho Chi Minh was reported to have approached Gopala Menon, the Indian chairman of the ICC in Vietnam, and urged the reactivation of the commission in Laos.

Leaving behind the Pathet Lao emissaries, with whom he had been making little progress in negotiating a solution, Souvanna Phouma left Vientiane on November 18 and flew to Sam Neua for talks with his brother, who had on several occasions refused to make a trip to Vientiane. The two men embraced each other warmly on the balcony of Souphanouvong's villa.

In two days of talks in Sam Neua, Souvanna Phouma obtained his brother's agreement to take part in a coalition that would include representatives of the Vientiane government, the Pathet Lao, and the Phoumists. The only limitation on this suggested coalition Cabinet was that it would exclude military officers as ministers, a stipulation that reflected the Pathet Lao's refusal to deal with General Phoumi. There appeared little probability that General Phoumi, who had previously declined an offer to participate in a coalition on much more favorable terms, would now accept this one. Nevertheless, Souvanna Phouma sent a delegation of National Assembly deputies to Savannakhet a few days later in an effort to persuade the General to call off his plan to seize Vientiane by force.

On December 2, the National Assembly delegation came back from their unsuccessful mission to Savannakhet. Their return led to the ugliest pro-Communist demonstration yet staged in Vientiane. A small core of agitators, mainly students, incited a crowd to bottle up inside the parliament building the thirty National Assembly deputies remaining in Vientiane and to chant slogans denouncing negotiations with General Phoumi.

Soviet Airlift

The next day, Abramov, at the ceremonial inauguration of Soviet flights transporting oil from Hanoi to Vientiane, used the occasion to cite Khrushchev on "the need for abolishing colonialism and foreign intervention." But his words elicited only a perfunctory round of applause from the small group of spectators, who saw irony in them. A row of saffron-robed bonzes chanted *sotto voce,* and the portly Abramov awkwardly squatted down on his haunches and joined his palms in Buddhist greeting. The Russian civilian pilots, in their heavy clothing, looked singularly uncomfortable as they peered at the corrugated-iron shacks and the jungle beyond, shimmering in the midday heat.

The Russians, in undertaking to supply one of the belligerents in Laos, were simply following the precedent set by the United States. Appropriately, the World War II-vintage planes they put on the Laos–North Vietnam run had just come from an airlift operation in the Congo.

With Vientiane apparently in imminent danger of attack from the Phoumists, whose forces were reported to be approaching up the Mekong Valley, Souvanna Phouma for the first time made a flat request to Ambassador Brown that aid to General Phoumi be stopped. The American Embassy, realizing that General Phoumi fully intended to violate the American guarantees given Souvanna Phouma in mid-October, obtained assurances from the Defense Department that technical, logistical, and material assistance to the Revolutionary Committee would be stopped. Brown was able to report to the Prime Minister after a delay of two days that no such assistance had been furnished since November 30.

"The Lao Won't Fight"

It had long been an axiom that the Buddhist Lao would not fight. Their religion forbade them to kill even animals. Their way of life was serene rather than belligerent. Their nature was peaceable, and they had a knack for compromise that always came to their rescue and avoided conflict.

The French in Vientiane had adopted this axiom as a favorite explanation for the failure of the American effort to equip and train the Royal Lao Army to put down the Pathet Lao revolt. But French officers who fought in the Indochina War declared that small units of Lao soldiers, properly trained and under skilled leadership, fought well on the offensive. That the axiom contained a certain amount of truth was accepted by the American military advisers of the PEO although many agreed that the explanation might be more complex than a Buddhist aversion to killing.

The fact remains that the Lao capital, in the next few days of December, was to witness a battle that would kill an estimated 600 people and injure another 1,000. What is the explanation?

It is that the soldiers of both Kong Le's battalion and General Phoumi's forces were armed to the teeth with modern rifles, machine guns, mortars, and artillery. When fired in the confined quarters of the streets of Vientiane, with their thin, wooden houses and shops, these weapons could not but spread death and destruction.

The author saw soldiers repeatedly change sides in the course of the battle. Squads of frightened-looking infantry made a hasty retreat along the side of a deserted street although no one was advancing against them. In fact, throughout much of the battle the combatant forces were separated by a no man's land more than four city blocks wide, which shifted back and forth in the general direction of where the enemy's positions were reported to be.

Both sides poured out a deafening volume of fire across this area, and made up for any lack of bravery by keeping fingers pressed on triggers. Indeed, the attitude on both sides was that the enemy had to be repelled at all costs but the individual soldiers wanted no responsibility for any bloodshed. This explains the wide distances between opposing forces, the heavy dependence on mortar and artillery fire, and the absence of hand-to-hand fighting.

The battle was preceded by an abortive countercoup led by the commander of the Vientiane Military Region, Colonel Kouprasith Abhay. Taking advantage of the approach of the Phoumist troops, he and his men on the morning of December 8 effected a sortie from their Chinaimo camp, where they had been more or less confined since August. They forced Kong Le and his red-armbanded men to withdraw westward, and seized control of the capital with little resistance. In leaflets distributed to the populace, the colonel's soldiers, who wore white armbands, claimed that their countercoup was aimed at forestalling a Pathet Lao takeover rather than against Souvanna Phouma, for whom Kouprasith declared his full support.

Kong Le and his men established a temporary headquarters at the airfield, where the Prime Minister visited just before nightfall. He had already paid a call on Kouprasith and now had the pledge of both men to hold their respective positions until daybreak. But in the morning, red armbands were everywhere. Under cover of night, Kong Le's men had moved in and had occupied the town once again, without so much as firing a shot. Whether Kouprasith's men had merely abandoned their untenable positions voluntarily or had been driven from them by the threat of serious fighting is not clear. They returned to the Chinaimo army camp, where they awaited a more opportune moment to strike against Kong Le.

For Souvanna Phouma, the situation had deteriorated so badly that he despaired of a solution. His last shred of hope that the Pathet Lao and Savannakhet factions might still come to terms, with him as a conciliator, disappeared on December 9.

Several planeloads of Savannakhet troops dropped on the eastern outskirts of the town had rendezvoused with Kouprasith, giving rise to wild rumors, all untrue, that General Phoumi might launch his impending offensive that very night.

In the empty hallways of the building that housed his office, Souvanna Phouma found a typist to peck out a final communiqué declaring in effect that the end had come: "By reason of the situation created by the misunderstanding that has arisen between military factions in the Vientiane region, the Government is obliged to delegate all its civil and military powers to the High Command of the Army effective at 9 A.M. today, December 9, 1960, in order to preserve security and the functioning of public services." This was not a resignation from office; it was simply a delegation of powers to General Sounthone Pathammavong, the senior army officer in Vientiane.

After a last-minute effort to bring about a meeting near Vientiane of Colonel Kouprasith and General Sounthone, Prince Souvanna Phouma turned his black Peugeot sedan toward the airport for the last time. Without making any further statement, he left Vientiane shortly before six in the evening and landed in the Cambodian capital of Phnom Penh about two hours later, a voluntary exile.

The Die Is Cast

Quinim Pholsena, Souvanna Phouma's senior remaining Cabinet minister, slipped out of Vientiane on the morning of December 10 aboard a Soviet Ilyushin transport bound for Hanoi. In twenty-four hours in the North Vietnamese capital, he made a firm deal with the Russians: In exchange for a formal alliance between Kong Le's troops and the Pathet Lao, the Russians would airlift into Laos arms and supplies for the resistance against General Phoumi's American-supplied troops.

The Russians, seeing the opportunity afforded them by the possibility of supporting Souvanna Phouma and his able military commander, Kong Le, against the imminent attack of the Phoumist rebels, apparently arrived at their decision in a week of urgent consultations in Moscow at the beginning of December. Quinim's signature merely formalized the bargain.

The alliance with the Pathet Lao would permit Kong Le to withdraw his men, with their jeeps, trucks, and armored cars, safely into the hinterland should the Phoumists capture Vientiane. The airlift of Soviet supplies, especially food and gasoline, would permit Kong Le's men to continue operating as a fighting force even though they were cut off from American supplies, and the provision of heavy weapons would give them a capability equal to that of the Phoumists. For the Pathet Lao, the airlift meant a share in Soviet weapons and ammunition, enabling Prince Souphanouvong to re-equip his guerrillas for regular combat operations. The entire complexion of the Laos confrontation had changed.

On the runway at the Vientiane airport by the afternoon of December 11, in full view of American observers, olive-drab Ilyushins were unloading six 105-mm. howitzers complete with ammunition and North Vietnamese gun crews to man them (neither Kong Le nor the Pathet Lao had any cannoneers).

General Sounthone, finding himself incapable of steering the ship of state through such perilous waters, abruptly announced that he was turning back full powers to what remained of the civilian government, namely Quinim.

Kong Le, again headquartered in the Prime Minister's office, was making final preparations for the defense of the capital. On the eve of the battle, he walked quietly about the tree-shaded yard of the stucco building, talking to small groups of paratroopers who sat in their jeeps beside boxes of ammunition and supplies. In his left hand, the diminutive captain twirled a grenade.

The first fighting in the town broke out shortly after one in the afternoon on Tuesday, December 13, on the eastern outskirts near the Chinaimo camp. It was the siesta hour. Houses were shuttered and the people inside as the din of crackling rifle fire, machine guns, and mortar explosions increased in intensity.

Outside the bookshop where Quinim Pholsena, the Acting Prime Minister, lived, a jeep pulled up and tooted its horn. Quinim appeared, flustered and in great haste. The soldiers in their bulky field jackets took him aboard. But the jeep would not start. The soldiers pushed it for about 100 yards, then abandoned it. Another jeep was commandeered to take Quinim to the airport. There he boarded an Ilyushin transport for Hanoi. With him, he took 25 million kip (about $312,500) in cash, for which he left a signed receipt at the National Bank.

From Chinaimo, Colonel Kouprasith sent tanks and armored cars along the road into the town. He also dispatched three river boats upstream to an island opposite the center of the town, from the cover of which they could train fire on defenders retreating slowly down the main streets, which paralleled the river.

The entire length of the left bank, a thoroughfare where the Lao were accustomed to take leisurely Sunday walks, suddenly became a dusty line of firing troops. Lao soldiers fired blindly and incessantly in the general area where an enemy might be hiding; there was ammunition aplenty. An occasional tank rumbled up to take a position on the embankment and fire a round or two, either downstream or directly across the mile-wide Mekong into the Thai village on the other side, causing some casualties, mostly civilians.

Carefully located machine-gun nests manned by Kong Le's soldiers stubbornly held up advances by whole companies of Kouprasith's troops. On the afternoon of the first day, the Colonel's troops occupied the entire twenty-block center of the town, but they failed to search the surrounding houses for pockets of resistance. That night they were driven back, almost to the eastern town limits, by the paratroopers, who had a far better knowledge of night fighting, and whose jeeps circulated freely in the reoccupied center on December 14.

From the fierce resistance put up by the paratroopers, it was apparent that the battle was going to be a long one. During brief lulls in the firing in daytime, the civilian population cautiously opened their doors to steal a look outside. They saw streets littered with fallen telephone wires and tree branches. Heaps of empty mortar shells cluttered street intersections, along with ammunition boxes bearing the clasped-hands emblem of the American aid mission. Almost every building in Vientiane bore scars from small-arms fire and mortar fragments.

One of the first buildings to go was the Immigration Office; it had served as a riflemen's nest and was the target for a direct mortar hit. The army headquarters was also destroyed. Diagonally across the street from it, the American Embassy lost its old building, containing the Ambassador's office, when the eaves caught fire from a neighboring flaming shed. However, a newly added wing escaped destruction.

At night, no civilians ventured out, because any moving thing was likely to draw fire. Tracer bullets painted great red arcs in the sky, and an occasional jeep whined frantically by in the deserted streets.

The amiable proprietor of the Constellation Hotel, André Cavalerie, a Corsican who had seen much turmoil in China and Indochina, explained that the reason he had firmly locked the front doors during the battle was to keep his staff of waiters and houseboys inside rather than to keep soldiers outside. "I opened the doors just now and lost five boys," he complained during a brief lull in the firing.

By the afternoon of December 14, when it looked as if Kouprasith lacked sufficient strength to gain control of the city, General Phoumi's forces had reached the city and were able to join battle. The Phoumists emplaced their artillery pieces on a slight rise near the National Assembly building on the northeastern fringe of the town, and began shelling the airport at a range of approximately three miles. Kong Le's artillery pieces, manned by the North Vietnamese, retaliated by shelling the Chinaimo army camp, in an artillery duel that lasted until the battle ended. At night, when small-arms fire subsided and the stillness was punctuated by only occasional machine-gun bursts, the distant pounding of artillery fire and the whistling of shells overhead continued.

The Vientiane radio station had gone off the air, and the cable office had shut down as soon as the fighting began. Now the only links with the outside world were the American, British, and French embassies. Ambassador Brown remained in the U.S. Embassy throughout the fighting. Several streets away at the Settha Palace Hotel, Soviet Ambassador Abramov had taken shelter, and he, too, remained throughout the battle. (Afterward he flew to Bangkok aboard a British military aircraft and thence to Phnom Penh.) A mile-high column of black smoke rose into the cloud-studded, blue tropical sky over the crippled town.

On December 16, Kong Le's troops, inferior in numbers and armament despite the Soviet deliveries, began an orderly withdrawal from the western end of the town, taking all their military equipment with them. Seventy-six hours after the first shot had been fired, the last Kong Le paratrooper trudged out of the town.

A strange quiet settled over the littered streets of the capital. Not until forty-eight hours after the end of the fighting did the leaders of the Revolutionary Committee, General Phoumi and Prince Boun Oum, make their appearance. While still in Savannakhet, the headquarters of the Revolutionary Committee, they had laid the groundwork for forming their own government.

Forty deputies out of the total fifty-nine in the National Assembly had arrived in Savannakhet by December 11. Next day, this majority met in session to pass a vote of censure against the Souvanna Phouma Cabinet. This was followed shortly by a royal proclamation from Luang Prabang entrusting the Revolutionary Committee with the "temporary conduct" of the Kingdom's affairs.

At his refuge in Cambodia, Souvanna Phouma spoke bitterly against the United States. In an interview, he said of Ambassador Parsons, a man with whom he had never had good personal relations:

> He understood nothing about Asia and nothing about Laos. The Assistant Secretary of State is the most nefarious and reprehensible of men. He is the ignominious architect of disastrous American policy toward Laos. He and others like him are responsible for the recent shedding of Lao blood.[3]

The next day in Washington, a new Administration was inaugurated. Soon it would face the same agonizing decision—whether or not to send American troops to Indochina—that had been faced by the Eisenhower Administration in 1954.

[3] *The New York Times,* January 20, 1961.

9.

Two Prime Ministers

It was an ironic twist of fate that Eisenhower, whose immediate objective on assuming the Presidency in 1953 had been to extricate the United States from the Korean War, spent his last days in office wrestling with another critical situation in Asia.

In late December, 1960, the President's top diplomatic, military, and intelligence advisers began a series of White House meetings to review the situation in Laos after six years of consistent United States support of anti-Communists. This was the picture that confronted them:

The Pathet Lao forces, which had numbered a few hundred poorly armed guerrillas at the 1954 cease-fire, had increased to several thousand; moreover, they had gained as allies the crack paratroopers of Captain Kong Le, who had been driven out of Vientiane but not defeated and who possessed brand-new American weapons taken from the capital's warehouses. The Soviet Union had posted an ambassador to Laos and was openly running an airlift from North Vietnam to supply weapons, ammunition, and food to Kong Le and the Pathet Lao. The United States had alienated Souvanna Phouma and committed itself to support a largely military government that was avowedly anti-Communist and thus had no claim to the magic mantle of "neutrality." Meanwhile, Souvanna Phouma, clinging to that mantle and claiming still to be the legal Prime Minister, had been befriended by the Communist powers. Effective authority was being exercised in his name by Quinim Pholsena, who was much less favorably disposed to the West and frankly anti-American.

In short, the American policy of attempting to contain Communist expansion in Laos by inadequate ground action (supporting the efforts of the Royal Lao Army) and strategic deterrence (the threat to commit American troops) had failed; while there had been no invasion by Communist forces, seven years of subversion had achieved virtually the effect of an invasion.

Soviet Support of Souvanna Phouma

The Soviets were apparently taken aback by Souvanna Phouma's departure from Vientiane on December 9. Now their claim that their actions were in support of the legitimate government was being jeopardized by the distinct possibility that Souvanna Phouma, who was tentatively staying in Phnom Penh, might resign, which he could do with a simple message to the King. The Prince was bitter at the United States for following what he considered a short-sighted, hopeless policy, and he was especially angry at his own military commanders for pursuing, hell-bent, a course of action that made street fighting and its heavy toll of civilian lives inevitable. Disgusted with the whole tragic episode, he probably would not tarry long in Phnom Penh but would fly to Paris to rejoin his wife and children in a comfortable retirement from political life.

A reliable American source affirms that the Prince dispatched a telegram to the Royal Palace on December 11, informing the King of his reasons for leaving Laos and placing himself "at the disposition" of the monarch. But because of the fighting, the telegram was not delivered in Luang Prabang until weeks later, on January 9. By that time he had made up his mind to stick it out.

The Soviets, aware that their best interests lay in persuading Souvanna Phouma to remain as Prime Minister despite the loss of Vientiane to the Phoumist rebels, acted with dispatch. A Soviet note on December 13 assailed the United States for backing General Phoumi, declaring that:

> if two or three months ago the Government of the United States made some effort to camouflage its unlawful actions in Laos, lately the United States has in effect become a party to military operations on the side of the rebels against the lawful government of Laos and the Laotian people.
>
> Flouting the sovereign rights of the Laotian Government headed by Prince Souvanna Phouma, the United States now openly supports the rebel group of Nosavan, supplying it with arms, military equipment, ammunition and money. . . .
>
> United States military advisers and instructors not only train the rebels but also directly supervise their military operations against the troops of the legitimate Laotian Government. The United States

Government also makes extensive use of Thailand, its ally in the military SEATO pact, which makes the territory of its country available for active military operations against the Government units and effects a brutal economic blockade of Laos. . . .

All this is a glaring violation by the Government of the United States of Article 12 of the Final Declaration of the 1954 Geneva Conference on Indochina, which contains an undertaking by every participant in the aforesaid Conference, including the United States, to respect the sovereignty, independence, unity, and territorial integrity of Laos and to refrain from any interference in its internal affairs.

On December 17, the State Department categorically rejected these charges and declared that "the responsibility for the present fratricidal war in Laos . . . rests squarely and solely upon the Soviet Government and its partners." It further stated:

The United States has repeatedly made clear its consistent policy of supporting the Kingdom of Laos in its determination to maintain its independence and integrity. Such support will continue. The United States has warned against efforts to seize control of or to subvert that free nation.

The note defended the supplying of American weapons to the Royal Lao Army, and declared that "such American advisers as have been in the country either administering the American military aid program or in the Franco-American training program are located at various training sites and supply depots and have not led any military actions."

Two days later, the State Department announced immediate resumption of military assistance to the Revolutionary Committee headed by General Phoumi and Prince Boun Oum, which had been entrusted by the King with the temporary conduct of the Kingdom's affairs.

During this interchange of notes, Ambassador Abramov, who was now also in Phnom Penh, gave Souvanna Phouma the Soviets' assurances that they would continue to regard him as the legal Prime Minister unless he resigned. Quinim Pholsena and Phoumi Vongvichit flew to Phnom Penh aboard a Soviet Ilyushin transport and pleaded with the Prince to stay on. Quinim brought word that he was maintaining a skeleton Cabinet in northern Laos in expectation of the Prince's return.

On December 22, in Moscow, following reports from Vientiane that Boun Oum had formed a Cabinet, First Deputy Foreign Minister V. V. Kuznetsov handed the British Ambassador a second Soviet note on Laos. It contained these two important paragraphs:

In conformity with universally recognized international standards, only the legitimate Lao Government is entitled to request any assistance from other states and to receive such assistance from them. In the light of this, the actions of the U.S. Government in rendering active military, material-technical and financial assistance to the rebels —actions which go to the length of the actual participation of servicemen of the United States and its allies in the military operations of the rebels against the legitimate Lao Government—are nothing but a flagrant violation of international law and the Geneva agreements on Laos under which the participants of the Geneva Conference of 1954 pledged themselves not to interfere in the internal affairs of Laos.

The Soviet Government believes that the Government of Great Britain is aware of the fact that the national Lao Government headed by Prince Souvanna Phouma has announced that it is continuing to function, that it is the legitimate government of Laos and that it regards the formation of a "government" led by Boun Oum as an act against the constitution.

Nine days after this Soviet note was delivered, the author interviewed Souvanna Phouma. The Prince immediately declared that the National Assembly's censure of him, on December 12, was not valid because it had been voted during an extraordinary session held in neither the royal capital nor the administrative capital, but in Savannakhet. He regarded the King's dealing with the Revolutionary Committee as maladroit and beyond the royal authority. An underlying factor here was the long-standing personal rivalry between the vice-regal branch of the royal family and the royal family itself, which had lain barely beneath the surface since formation of the Lao Issara in 1945.

The Prince said that he had not submitted his resignation to the King and made no mention of sending to Luang Prabang a telegram indicating his willingness to resign. He contended that he was still Prime Minister. The 1947 Constitution offered no guideposts. It did not indicate how soon a Prime Minister must resign after losing the confidence of the National Assembly, but merely stated, in Article 22, that the "vote of a motion of censure involves the resignation of the entire Government."

In Vientiane on that same day, December 31, a Lao source reported that "five battalions" of North Vietnamese troops had crossed the border into Laos near Route Coloniale 7 and were attacking Nong Het. The newly formed Cabinet of Prince Boun Oum distributed the information in a press communiqué, and Delegate Sisouk na Champassak relayed it to United Nations Secretary-General Dag Hammärskjold in an interview arranged by the U.S.

Simultaneously, the State Department announced it had turned down an appeal from India to support the reactivation of the International Control Commission in Laos. The U.S. was also unresponsive to a proposal, on January 1, from Prince Sihanouk of Cambodia for an international conference on Laos, to be attended by all the countries that had participated in the 1954 Conference, plus the three ICC countries and Laos' neighbors Burma and Thailand.

The National Assembly deputies returned to Vientiane and vainly awaited news from Phnom Penh that Souvanna Phouma had resigned. Finally, they decided to overlook Boun Oum's suspension of the Constitution on September 10, and unanimously endorsed the Prince's Cabinet on January 4. It consisted entirely of Phoumist politicians, whom Souvanna Phouma labeled a "bunch of clowns." General Phoumi was the new Deputy Prime Minister and Minister of Defense. Six ministers, including those of Finance and Interior, were relatives of Boun Oum, who now installed himself and his retinue of relatives, servants, and hangers-on in the spacious suburban villa formerly occupied by General Sounthone Pathammavong.

Once again, the United States threw its support to the most feudal elements of the country, extending recognition to the Boun Oum government. Britain, France, and Canada also acknowledged it. The Soviet Union and India continued to recognize Souvanna Phouma; Communist China, North Vietnam, and Poland, which had no formal diplomatic relations with Laos, supported Souvanna Phouma.

Shift of Course

It was clear that Laos was not a bastion of the Free World. The United States was confronted by the prospect of having tied itself to a minority government whose constitutionality was in doubt and whose only source of internal support was an army incapable of victory. The time for sitting tight was past. Action had to be taken at once.

John F. Kennedy, in the first few days of January, declined to be associated with the departing Administration's handling of the deteriorating situation in Laos. On January 7, the Eisenhower Administration published a White Paper on Laos, setting forth a sharply revised line of thinking:

The United States believes that it can best contribute to a solution of the Laos problem:

First, by attempting to further international recognition and understanding of the true nature of Communist intentions and actions in Laos;

Second, by the United States itself continuing clearly to show that it has no intention and no desire to establish a Western military position in Laos;

Third, by joining with other free nations to support and maintain the independence of Laos through whatever measures seem most promising.[1]

Translated from diplomatic parlance, this statement meant three things:

First, the United States wanted to make known how much aid the Kong Le–Pathet Lao alliance was getting from the Soviet airlift and the encadrement of North Vietnamese regulars. However, the U.S. had to stop short of calling this aid a violation of international agreements, since many countries felt that the United States itself had violated such agreements. This outside aid consisted of supplies transported in unarmed aircraft, unmarked except for serial numbers, belonging to the Soviet Union and piloted by Soviet crews in civilian clothes; this set-up closely resembled that of General Phoumi, who since September had received aid delivered by Air America aircraft under contract to the United States Government and piloted by American crews. The outside Communist personnel were North Vietnamese instructors and technicians; the American equivalents were PEO advisers and technicians, who had been training the Royal Army since 1955. United States condemnation of the Communist bloc for intervention in Laos would find little, if any, international support. Moreover, the Communist position on the ground was stronger than could be accounted for by the receipt of outside aid. Both Eisenhower and Kennedy appreciated this fact.

Second, the United States wanted to avoid an escalation of the commitment in Laos. Despite the Communist gains in the previous six years, it did not want to "establish a Western military position in Laos"—i.e., to garrison Laos with American troops.

Third, "whatever measures seem most promising" to maintain the independence of Laos prepared the ground for American support of a Vientiane coalition government including the Pathet Lao. Though purposely vague, this paragraph was by far the most significant of the three. It represented, at long last, a step forward

[1] Department of State Press Release No. 9, January 7, 1961.

out of the bog in which American policy toward post-1954 Indochina had been mired.

The Eisenhower Administration policy-makers, meeting in Washington in the last days of December and early January, agreed that Laos could not be forfeited to the North Vietnamese without serious consequences for the American position throughout Asia. They also agreed that direct American intervention was as unpalatable in 1960 as it had been in 1954, the last time the situation in Indochina had reached such a critical point. A coalition was the one remaining alternative that, it was hoped, would neither turn Laos over to the North Vietnamese Communists nor involve American troops in action in Indochina.

What were the facts on the ground that had to be considered? Militarily, American power in the Pacific—i.e., the Seventh Fleet—was as preponderant as always, and the gap between this power and that of North Vietnam was as wide as in 1954, if not even wider. However, American power had to be brought to bear effectively (as it had not been from 1954 to 1960). The war under way in Laos was still General Giap's textbook "people's war" (as it had been in 1954), and this warfare must be understood (as it had not been from 1954 to 1960). Lastly, the West continued to hold many political advantages, the chief one being that, basically, Souvanna Phouma still faced to the West.

These realities on the ground, it is obvious in retrospect, had been lost sight of by Eisenhower's policy-makers. The North Vietnamese-stimulated crisis atmosphere of 1959 had led to the American involvement with General Phoumi. This in turn limited the Administration's freedom of action and when in the autumn of 1960 the more serious crisis arose, bringing direct Communist intervention into the picture, the United States was boxed in a corner. The new men of the Kennedy Administration had a clearer perspective on the realities previously referred to, and they proceeded to make them once again the basis of American actions in Laos.

Kong Le's Daring Stroke

General Phoumi's troops, after taking Vientiane, were slow to pursue Kong Le's paratroopers, who had staged an orderly withdrawal from the smoking capital along the Royal Road. Where normally only ox carts, bicycles, and an occasional bus traveled, now the paratroopers' U.S.-supplied jeeps and 2½-ton trucks churned northward.

At the outset, an altercation took place between Kong Le and a subordinate, Lieutenant Deuan Siphaseuth. Deuan, who had had no troops under his command, had left Kong Le's ranks to join Colonel Kouprasith at the Chinaimo army camp before the Colonel's abortive countercoup of December 8. After its failure, Deuan had rejoined Kong Le, who had accepted him back without asking questions. Deuan was in sharp disagreement with Kong Le, pressing strongly for a counterattack against Vientiane after December 16, but he was overruled.

Rear-guard paratroopers protected the retreating column from any advance patrols of General Phoumi's forces. However, the General made no serious effort to attack from the rear or to cut off the paratroopers' retreat by dropping paratroopers into the hills ahead. Kong Le, after he had moved his trucks and five remaining 105-mm. artillery pieces (one of the original six had been knocked out in Vientiane) across the Lik River, destroyed the bridge to prevent pursuit.

Soviet Ilyushin transports, no longer able to land supplies for Kong Le at the Vientiane airport, now parachuted weapons, ammunition, and food rations onto a whitewashed drop-zone in the rice paddies near Phone Hong, a village 40 miles north of the capital. When Kong Le's column was in the foothills, the Soviet planes landed and made parachute drops at the small field at Vang Vieng. American intelligence estimated that Soviet aircraft flew 184 missions into Laos between December 15 and January 2.[2] Light Czech-made liaison planes ferried officers and advisers back and forth at will between Vang Vieng, Sam Neua town, and Hanoi.

As Kong Le moved northward, the mountainous terrain increasingly favored him. Each day it became more unlikely that General Phoumi's column, which had laboriously ferried its armored cars across the Lik, could strike a telling blow; confined to the road, unable to maneuver, the Phoumist column was vulnerable to land mines, which Kong Le's troops used with effect, and to guerrilla harassment from the Pathet Lao.

At Sala Phou Khoun, the Royal Road reaches a fork; to the left lies Luang Prabang, to the right the Plain of Jars. Kong Le's objective was the latter, with its all-weather landing field, heavily fortified by the Phoumist troops. With lightning rapidity, he trucked an advance striking force past Sala Phou Khoun and onto the western rim of the rolling plain. Closely coordinated attacks by Pathet Lao guerrillas created the necessary diversion from the opposite direction, along the northeastern periphery. A concen-

[2] Department of State Press Release No. 2, January 4, 1961.

trated bombardment by Kong Le's artillery against the Phoumists sent them fleeing from their exposed positions and into the surrounding hills, leaving most of their supplies to the attackers. Several planeloads of Phoumist paratroopers, flown in to retrieve the situation, were dropped over the rugged area, but becoming scattered, joined the general panic. U.S. military advisers with the Phoumists were evacuated by Air America transports. As the last C-46 banked away from the airfield, the first of the airlift Ilyushins skimmed over the green hills.

Xieng Khouang town, twenty miles southeast of the Plain of Jars airfield, soon fell to the Pathet Lao. However, its military commander, Lieutenant Colonel Vang Pao, a Meo, conducted an orderly evacuation of his troops into the surrounding mountains.

Kong Le's daring stroke had gained control of the most important military complex in northern Laos. He and his Pathet Lao allies now possessed a base area linked by airlift and the old Route Coloniale (called, since 1950, Route Nationale) 7 with North Vietnam. (See Map 3.)

Soviet Motives

The Plain of Jars was transformed into a vast armed camp. A British observer on a visit there in February reported that "the overwhelming impression . . . is that of massive military assistance" from the Communist bloc.

What were the reasons behind the Soviet Union's sudden commitment to supply, openly and directly, the Kong Le–Pathet Lao alliance with aid in such immense quantities as to enable the Pathet Lao forces to make the basic transformation from guerrillas to regular forces? Why did the Soviet Union involve itself in such a distant battle, an action that gave the lie to simultaneous Soviet professions of peaceful coexistence and concern over the possibility that the Laos crisis might escalate into a larger war? Why did the Soviets undertake to rescue Souvanna Phouma from the dire straits in which U.S. pressure had placed him?

There is one answer to these multiple questions: The Soviet Union was acting out of the imperative need to retain the allegiance of North Vietnam in the developing quarrel with China.

The position of the North Vietnamese leadership in Communist-bloc affairs in the autumn of 1960 resembled that of the Viet Minh leadership vis-à-vis the Chinese, French, and nationalists when these four factions were contending for power in Hanoi in 1945 and 1946. Although relatively weak at the start, the Vietnamese Communists, in both cases, had gained strength by adroitly shifting their deciding weight in disputes.

Ho Chi Minh's position had been precarious, but not necessarily disadvantageous, ever since Mao Tse-tung had come to power in Peking in 1949. A common background in revolutionary activity had created a strong bond between the two Asian Communist leaders, and thousands of North Vietnamese cadres had been trained by the Chinese Communists during the eight-year war against the French. Chinese aid to the Viet Minh had been considerable (American-made artillery supplied by the Chinese had been crucial in the Viet Minh's successful siege of Dien Bien Phu), although the Vietnamese had repaid at least a part of this wartime aid in rice and salt, and sought to preserve the distinction between their regime and the Chinese.

The Soviet Union, on the other hand, had shown little concern about North Vietnam. It had lagged behind China in recognizing Ho's government, in 1950. Stalin was deeply involved in European political maneuvers, and these sometimes worked to the detriment of the Viet Minh struggle against the French. Such maladroit Soviet moves as its proposal, on January 24, 1957, to seat both North and South Vietnam in the United Nations prolonged the coolness between Hanoi and Moscow and, conversely, strengthened the solidarity between Ho and Mao, both rulers of divided countries with rival regimes supported by the "imperialists."

This rapport between the two countries continued into 1956, when Hanoi carried out a Chinese-style land reform, which was directly supervised by Chinese cadres. This was a disastrous economic failure, and marked a turning point in Hanoi-Peking relations. The Vietnamese did not follow in 1958 when the Chinese initiated their "Great Leap Forward" and the communes. As Chinese influence decreased, Moscow's increased, amid promises of Soviet largesse for North Vietnam's industrial rebuilding program.

These shifting influences were reflected in the emergence within the Lao Dong Party of pro-Soviet and pro-Chinese factions, which subtly competed for predominance under Ho's watchful eye. The rivalry between these two factions grew increasingly violent, until by the end of 1960, it shook the Lao Dong Party to its foundations

In November of that year, Ho flew to Moscow for a meeting of eighty-one Communist parties from all over the world. While there, he apparently attempted to mediate the dispute between

China and Russia. But the differences that separated Khrushchev and Mao had become so great that they were no longer susceptible to mediation, even by such a veteran Comintern hand as Ho. During this period, the Chinese viewpoint was exerting a renewed attraction in Hanoi. The North Vietnamese, by 1960 embarked on an armed struggle to topple the Ngo Dinh Diem regime in the south and reunify their country, had more sympathy for Mao's militant arguments for Communist guerrilla warfare against the American presence in Asia, Africa, and Latin America than they had for Khrushchev's efforts to reach a *détente* with the West.

The Soviet Union, aware of this advantage held by the Red Chinese, acted to offset it by granting North Vietnam, in August, 1960, large credits to finance an ambitious expansion of industry. In December, the U.S.S.R. capped its persuasive efforts by initiating the airlift from North Vietnam to the pro-Communist forces fighting the "imperialists" in Laos. The Soviet Union had calculated that this move would preclude accusations by Lao Dong Party militants that the U.S.S.R.'s conciliatory policy was betraying the Communist cause, and would prevent the Lao Dong Party from throwing its entire support to the Chinese Communist Party.

Souvanna Phouma in the Center

Still in Phnom Penh, Souvanna Phouma watched with sardonic satisfaction the State Department's ineffectual attempts to persuade the Soviet Union to call off the airlift. He remained bitter at the flagrant failure of the U.S. to back up its assurances that American military supplies turned over to the Phoumists would not be used against Kong Le's forces. Speaking to James Wilde, a Canadian working for *The New York Times,* he said in an interview published by that newspaper on January 20, 1961, "What I shall never forgive the United States for, however, is the fact that it betrayed me, that it double-crossed me and my government." He felt it was up to the big powers to find a solution, because the Lao had lost control of the situation.

Two weeks later, Souvanna Phouma told Takashi Oka of the *Christian Science Monitor* of his desire to complete the task of forming a coalition government, which had been interrupted by General Phoumi's seizure of Vientiane. This would require patience, however. He expressed hesitancy about returning to Laos; as an exile, he compelled others to come to him, since he was certain the present opposition of the Boun Oum regime and the Pathet

Lao would lead only to continued strife and greater foreign interference in Laos. If he returned to Vientiane, he would appear to
lend his support to the Boun Oum government, which he considered illegal. If he went to northern Laos, he would be placing
himself as a hostage in the eager hands of the Pathet Lao. The best
solution was an exploratory trip, and he spoke hopefully of visiting
Kong Le on the Plain of Jars, and Colonel Khammouane Boupha,
the Phong Saly warlord, who claimed his forces were loyal to Souvanna Phouma. "As with Kong Le, there is a certain accommodation with the Pathet Lao, but the royal troops stay royal troops,"
the Prince remarked.

He said that in any genuine plebiscite, 95 per cent of the vote
would be for nationalist candidates, and the remainder for the
Pathet Lao and the pro-Americans. He called for an international
conference to frame a big-power guarantee of Laos' neutrality, with
the three Lao factions forming a united delegation. His own centrist
position would pull together the two extremist wings, the Pathet
Lao and the Phoumists.

"The Americans say I am a Communist," the Prince observed.
"All this is heartbreaking. How can they think I am a Communist?
I am looking for a way to keep Laos non-Communist." His remarks
became more pointed: "To be pro-West, on the other hand, does
not necessarily mean to be pro-American. To be anti-American
does not mean to be pro-Communist. When we say we are anti-
American, we are against the American policies of the moment. We
are anti-American because these Americans don't understand Laos,
they have regard only for their own interests."

To refute the American charge that he was blind to the danger
from the north, he cited the ancient, deep-seated Lao fear of the
Chinese. In 1945, he recalled, after the Potsdam Agreement had
stipulated that Chinese Nationalists would occupy northern Laos,
inhabitants of Luang Prabang started building canoes and rafts to
flee downstream when the Chinese army of occupation was still
200 miles away.

On February 20, Souvanna Phouma flew to the Plain of Jars,
where he was greeted by the skeletal Cabinet that Quinim Pholsena
had informed him would await his return. It was made up of three
men: Khamsouk Keola, Acting Prime Minister; Quinim Pholsena,
Minister of Foreign Affairs, Defense, and Finance; and Chao
Sisoumang, who held the portfolios of Interior, Economy, and
Social Welfare, and the remaining minor portfolios. These men had
established themselves in the limited accommodations available in

Khang Khay, a village of about 1,000 souls. Not far from the Prime Minister's office, a full Soviet Embassy had been set up.

At Phong Savan, a great opium-trading center on the road between Khang Khay and the Plain of Jars airfield, lived a dozen Russian aircraft technicians, who serviced the airlift planes. They were lodged in what had been the Snow Leopard Inn but was now the Friendship Hotel. At opposite ends of Phong Savan's main street, Czech and North Vietnamese information offices had been established. And in near-by Xieng Khouang town were billeted an "economic and cultural delegation" from Peking.

At the Plain of Jars airfield, North Vietnamese technicians proudly manned the old French control tower to direct the Soviet airlift planes. Near Phong Savan, the North Vietnamese had set up a tent hospital to care for Pathet Lao wounded. The Plain of Jars was becoming a mirror image of the PEO compound in Vientiane.

Among those who greeted Souvanna Phouma was his army commander, Kong Le. His troops wore American uniforms, distinguishing them from the Pathet Lao, who wore mustard-colored uniforms. Kong Le's American weapons and vehicles were supplemented by generous quantities of Soviet-type small arms and Molotova trucks and armored cars.

Soviet 37-mm. radar-directed antiaircraft guns were set up around the Plain of Jars, and Vietnamese instructors were training Kong Le's troops in their use. Their crews meant business: They shot down a reconnaissance American C-47 attached to the air attaché's office in Saigon, killing seven and capturing the one survivor. The American Embassy in Saigon falsely claimed that the plane had been on a routine liaison flight between Vientiane and Saigon.

Harvard Fighters and Special Forces

With the political and military initiative wholly in the hands of the Communists, the Kennedy Administration sought as best it could to limit the damage in Laos to consolidation by the Kong Le–Pathet Lao alliance of control over the entire eastern half of the country. In early January, the U.S. sent the Phoumist forces six AT-6 Harvard trainer aircraft armed with machine guns and equipped to fire rockets and drop bombs. These were manned by Lao pilots trained in Thailand. The introduction of these six planes effected a small but noticeable escalation of the conflict, and the Soviet Union protested to the United States when the planes strafed the Kong Le–Pathet Lao forces along the Royal Road. The AT-6's were not used against the airlift's Ilyushin-14's. A tacit agreement between Washington and Moscow required airlift planes to be unarmed.

More significantly, the U.S. replaced General Heintges' PEO infantrymen with a contingent of about 400 Special Forces personnel from Okinawa, to act as cadres for the Phoumist troops. Called White Star Mobile Training Teams, they were under the command of a tough American of Finnish extraction, Lieutenant Colonel Aito Keravuri. They were particularly effective in working with Colonel Vang Pao's Meo fighters, who had reorganized themselves into guerrilla bands in the mountains surrounding the Plain of Jars. The White Star detachments lived and fought for long periods in the field under miserable conditions, and showed that the Meo added a new dimension to the protracted Laos conflict.

However, these efforts by Washington no longer had the previous objective of *militarily defeating* the Pathet Lao, an objective that had been rendered infinitely more difficult than before because of the massive Soviet assistance to the Pathet Lao. Now the American objective was to keep the Mekong Valley out of Pathet Lao control, thus easing the pressure on the Thai government, and consolidating a bargaining position vis-à-vis the Communist bloc in the increasingly likely event of a new international conference.

Despite its limited objective, the U.S. endowed its efforts with an ever-greater urgency because of the rapid build-up in Communist strength and the State Department's failure to get the Soviets to halt the airlift. Reports reached Vientiane of well-armed Pathet Lao columns on the march over much of northern Laos, particularly in Luang Prabang and Phong Saly provinces. Barely twenty miles north of Vientiane, there occurred clashes involving guerrillas permanently based in a mountain resort called Phou Khao Khouei.

General Phoumi's armored column was moving northward from Vientiane at a distressingly slow pace, balked by land mines and trees felled across the narrow road, sometimes for hundreds of yards at a stretch. Correspondents who visited the "front" found the Phoumist troops catching fish in mountain streams by exploding grenades underwater. They had neither the dedication of Kong Le's paratroopers nor the merciless discipline of the Pathet Lao. Sentries were posted here and there; whenever they heard a burst of small-arms fire in the near-by forest, they would fire several random shots and then flee back to the main camp.

Vietnamese Cadres

The Phoumist soldiers' disinclination to engage the enemy was due partly to rumors that the opposing forces included regular North Vietnamese troop units. Soldiers from the North Vietnamese 335th Division had been reported present in northern Laos since the previous October. After January, an increasing number and variety were reported. Also reported were elements of the 316th Division, 120th Independent Regiment, and 359th Frontier Guard Regiment.[3] Both the 316th and the 335th divisions were veteran units formed largely of mountain tribesmen. The 316th had captured Sam Neua from the French in the spring of 1953, and had fought in the battle of Dien Bien Phu.

Further evidence of North Vietnamese soldiers in Laos came from diaries kept in Vietnamese that were captured by the Phoumist troops. One carried the bearer's oath "to respect the people, to aid the people, and to defend the people," and described the "soldier of the People's Army" as he who "defends the sovereignty, national territory and security of the Democratic Republic of Vietnam"—an indication that North Vietnamese soldiers sent into Laos were told that they were defending their homeland from possible attack by the Americans.

In the midst of this foreign involvement, King Savang Vatthana on February 19 addressed a message to his people. He harked back to King Sisavang Vong's stubborn refusal to be intimidated by the Viet Minh invasions of 1953 and 1954:

> Lao people, our country is the most peaceful country in the world. . . . the people of our country have always strictly applied the teachings of Buddha concerning forgiveness, gentleness and charity. At no time has there ever arisen in the minds of the Lao people the idea of coveting another's wealth, of quarreling with their neighbors, much less of fighting them. And yet, during the past twenty years, our country has known neither peace nor security.
>
> Our august father, a magnanimous sovereign, witnessed several foreign invasions. He faced them with courage. Since our accession to the throne, enemies of all sorts have tried to cross our frontiers,

[3] Department of State, *A Threat to the Peace: North Viet-Nam's Effort to Conquer South Viet-Nam* (Washington: Government Printing Office, 1961), Part 1, p. 39. See also Government of the Republic of Vietnam, *Violations of the Geneva Agreements by the Viet-Minh Communists* (Saigon: Ministry of Foreign Affairs, 1961), p. 35. The latter source mentions two other independent regiments, the 270th and the 148th; and states that from the 335th Division, the 83rd Regiment operates in northern Laos, the 280th Regiment in central Laos, and the 673rd Regiment in southern Laos.

to destroy our people and to destroy our religion and our nation's aura of peace and concord.

Lao people, the misfortunes which have befallen us have been the result of disunity among the Lao on the one hand and of foreign interference on the other. Foreign countries do not care either about our interests or peace; they are concerned only with their own interests.

The King coupled this exhortation with a declaration of Laos' neutrality. Speaking before the Boun Oum Cabinet and assembled foreign diplomats, he proposed that Burma, Cambodia, and Malaya form a commission to visit Laos "to establish that this country threatens no one and aspires solely to peace." He said: "This commission would have as its mission the denouncing of all foreign intervention, direct or indirect, open or camouflaged, which would result in the imperiling of the Kingdom's independence, integrity, and neutrality." This proposal, according to a diplomatic informant, was drafted behind the scenes by the State Department, which was perturbed by the sparse international recognition accorded the Boun Oum government and by the continued insistence of Cambodia on the convening of an international conference to discuss the situation in Laos.

The initiative for a new commission was almost immediately rejected by the Communist countries and by two of the proposed members, Cambodia and Burma, on the grounds that acceptance would imply taking a position for Boun Oum against Souvanna Phouma, in other words in an internal state matter. The Cambodian reply made it clear that foreign intervention on behalf of the one Lao government was no less reprehensible than intervention on behalf of the other. But the King had raised his voice in favor of reconciliation and he had not specifically condemned Souvanna Phouma (there had been, after all, an explosive reaction in 1945 to his father's condemnation of Souvanna Phouma's elder brother). It was the King's message more than any other factor that decided Souvanna Phouma to leave Phnom Penh the following day in an Ilyushin transport and begin his exploratory visit to Khang Khay.

After this visit, the Prince established contact with Vientiane through emissaries, and at the beginning of March, he and General Phoumi confounded foreign observers by meeting in Phnom Penh. Their exchange was cordial. In a joint communiqué issued on March 10, they stated that they "strongly oppose foreign interference and refuse to allow the Kingdom and its people to bear the cost of a deadly struggle for influence in which they have no part."

Washington reacted with tentative approval, of particular significance because the communiqué called for an international conference to untangle the complicated situation in Laos.

For three days, neither Radio Hanoi nor Radio Peking mentioned the March 10 communiqué. Then, apparently because of the American endorsement, both North Vietnam and China sharply denounced the communiqué as evidence of an imperialist plot to hoodwink Souvanna Phouma. Perhaps as a result of their unfavorable response, Souvanna Phouma issued a more cautious statement when the meetings with General Phoumi ended on March 15.

An international conference became the Prince's watchword. In Hong Kong the following day, about to set off on a world tour, he called it "the only solution." On March 22, Moscow Radio broadcast an interview in which Souvanna Phouma called for a cease-fire in Laos to precede the conference, apparently to mollify the United States, which refused to participate in any conference so long as the Pathet Lao were still making gains on the ground in Laos.

The North Vietnamese flatly opposed any cease-fire that would limit the military gains they were making, but voiced support for the proposed conference. Peking took the same line.

The Pathet Lao, encadred by the North Vietnamese, struck sharply in the first days of March, spreading terror and confusion down the Royal Road. On March 9, the Vientiane government announced that Sala Phou Khoun, the vital road junction between Luang Prabang and Vientiane, had fallen. Within the next twenty-four hours, the entire road as far as Muong Kassy had been taken by the Pathet Lao. Entire companies of Phoumist troops panicked, throwing away their arms and fleeing for safety to the surrounding mountains. All idea of a Phoumist offensive against the Plain of Jars was abandoned. The new situation was more threatening than the 1959 "crisis" had ever been.

Bitter fighting developed at the head of the valley north of Vang Vieng, where Phoumist troops made a stand. Among those captured by the Pathet Lao was the son of Phoumist General Sing Ratanasamay. A shrapnel-wounded soldier taken prisoner by the Phoumists, who called himself Private Boun Kong, a common enough name in Laos, turned out to be Vi Van Sang, a member of the 925th Independent Regiment of the North Vietnamese Army. He said he belonged to one of two 42-man sections of mortar and machine-gun specialists who had been ordered into Laos on February 19. They had marched for four days along Route Coloniale 7 to the area of Nong Het, and thence traveled by truck convoy to the Plain of Jars, where they had been attached to the 6th Pathet Lao Battalion.

The Phoumists' situation worsened from day to day. The Ilyushins parachuted some of Kong Le's paratroopers into attack positions to help the Pathet Lao break through the disorganized Phoumist lines. On March 23, North Vietnamese assault troops led a successful Pathet Lao attack on Kam Keut in Khammouane Province. By the end of the month, the pro-Communist forces controlled portions of six provinces: Phong Saly, Sam Neua, Luang Prabang, Xieng Khouang, Vientiane, and Khammouane.

The Pathet Lao–North Vietnamese initiatives, undertaken without any Soviet assurance of unconditional support for North Vietnam in the event of American retaliation (in this period, not a single Soviet statement promised such support to North Vietnam), had strengthened the Soviet bargaining position vis-à-vis the West.

American Intervention Weighed

The critical deterioration of the Western position in Laos confronted President Kennedy during his first hundred days in office with a dilemma that had confronted the White House in the dark spring of 1954: whether or not to send American troops to the jungles of Indochina, and if so, in what numbers, and how, and where. Dulles had been tragically correct in his thesis, enunciated at the height of the Dien Bien Phu crisis, that if the United States took a firm stand to resist the Communists with force, American intervention would be increasingly costly as time went on. The decision lay with the United States, but its effects would be felt not only in Laos, but in the rest of Asia and Europe where the United States had alliances. The Communist powers were watching Kennedy for the slightest hint of weakness in the Laos situation. Irresolution carried with it the penalty of forfeiting the Western position in Laos and perhaps Indochina and the rest of Southeast Asia.

Kennedy met with his top advisers to consider the alternatives to continued reliance on the Phoumist troops. The prospects were not good. Admiral Harry D. Felt, Commander in Chief of U.S. forces in the Pacific, dispelled any illusions about the complexity of the logistics problems. In the event of large-scale movement of North Vietnamese troops into Laos in response to the commitment of American troops there, the enemy supply line would be short, the American line long. An official calculation disclosed that the

United States had hardly enough conventional equipment and ammunition at hand, in the spring of 1961, to fight a limited war in Indochina. Kennedy knew—having learned "with stunned amazement" a few weeks after taking office—that if he sent 10,000 men to Southeast Asia, his own country would have practically no strategic Army reserve left for other contingencies.[4]

After deliberation, seventeen steps to progressive commitment were reportedly decided on. The number of steps actually taken would depend on how hard the United States was pressed.

A Marine helicopter repair base was set up in northeastern Thailand at the all-weather airfield at Udorn, and an initial flight of helicopters was posted there from the vast deployment of the Seventh Fleet. Gasoline, ammunition, and weapons were stocked in advance bases along the Mekong. Lieutenant General Thomas J. Trapnell, commander of the 18th Airborne Corps, part of the Strategic Army Command at Fort Bragg, North Carolina, was sent to Laos to reconnoiter the fighting conditions in the field.

On Okinawa, Task Force 116 was placed on alert. Troops included two regiments and headquarters of the Third Marine Division with Marine Air Group 16 (between 15,000 and 20,000 men), the Second Airborne Battle Group of the 503rd Infantry Combat Team (1,900 men), and the First Special Forces Group (300 men). These could be airlifted rapidly to Laos aboard C-130 turboprop transports, which were capable of landing on relatively rough fields.

If Task Force 116 was put in action, its mission would be to seize the key points of Mahaxay and Tchepone, with its vital airfield, and these would become the cleats for a line between the Laos-Vietnam border at the Seventeenth Parallel on the east and the Thai border at just about Thakhek on the west. Below that line, American forces would protect the southern "panhandle" of Laos, including Route Nationale 9, against Communist control.

If this plan was implemented, a large area would require garrisoning by American troops. The troops would be vulnerable to guerrilla action. In combat against the North Vietnamese, they would be fighting on the defensive against an enemy highly skilled in attritional warfare and intimately familiar with the terrain.

Yet the commitment of American forces to Laos would be the logical outcome of the polarization of forces within Laos. U.S. policy in Laos since 1954 had put up a bold front to the Commu-

---

[4] Major General Chester V. Clifton, *Hail to the Chief* (Association of the United States Army, January, 1964).

nists. Now that front was being probed. And the will to carry that policy to its conclusion was tempered by the sober calculation that, in the event of fighting, there was no reason to think that the Americans would be any better off than the French had been when compelled to withdraw their men, tanks, and planes from the Red River Delta.

The grave consequences of an open American commitment in Indochina weighed heavily on President Kennedy. Having assessed the dangers and worked out with his advisers the contingency plans, he went before the television cameras on March 23 to enlist the support of the American people and to notify the Soviet Premier that the United States was leaving an honorable way out of the crisis that confronted them both. The way out was embodied in an American declaration of support for a British proposal, made in Moscow that very day, for a joint British-Soviet appeal to both sides in Laos for a cease-fire, reactivation of the ICC in Laos, and an international conference on Laos after the cease-fire had become effective.

In his television address, the President said:

First, we strongly and unreservedly support the goal of a neutral and independent Laos, tied to no outside power or group of powers, threatening no one, and free from any domination. Our support for the present duly constituted government is aimed entirely and exclusively at that result. And if in the past there has been any possible ground for misunderstanding of our desire for a truly neutral Laos, there should be none now.

Secondly, if there is to be a peaceful solution, there must be a cessation of the present armed attacks by externally supported Communists. If these attacks do not stop, those who support a truly neutral Laos will have to consider their response. . . .

No one should doubt our resolution on this point. We are faced with a clear and one-sided threat of a change in the internationally agreed position of Laos. This threat runs counter to the will of the Laotian people, who wish only to be independent and neutral. It is posed rather by the military operations of internal dissident elements directed from outside the country. This is what must end if peace is to be achieved in Southeast Asia.

Thirdly, we are earnestly in favor of constructive negotiation among the nations concerned and among the leaders of Laos which can help Laos back to the pathway of independence and genuine neutrality. We strongly support the present British proposal of a prompt end of hostilities and prompt negotiation.

My fellow Americans, Laos is far away from America, but the world is small. Its two million people live in a country three times the size of Austria. The security of all Southeast Asia will be endangered if Laos loses its neutral independence. Its own safety runs with the safety of us all—in real neutrality observed by all.

I want to make it clear to the American people and to all the world that all we want in Laos is peace, not war; a truly neutral government, not a cold war pawn; a settlement concluded at the conference table and not on the battlefield.[5]

The situation was handled with remarkable skill. No crisis of tension was created in the American electorate. The pros and cons of American intervention were not brought into public debate, as in 1954. There were no public threatening statements by military officers such as Admiral Radford. Instead, preparations were made quietly and deliberately; ships put to sea and troops were alerted. The Soviets were informed of these moves, but without any hysterical warnings from Washington. The domino theory still applied to Indochina; the stakes were just as high. And many underlying hesitancies were still there, as in 1954. Admiral Arleigh Burke, Navy Chief of Staff, sent by the President to brief a bipartisan group of Congressional leaders, found them opposed to intervention but, in the interest of national security, prepared to back the President in any decision.

Kennedy, with his intuitive awareness of the country's mood, paced his actions to the needs of the crisis without exacerbating matters by stimulating public debate, and therefore public uncertainty, over the Administration's course. This was no mean accomplishment.

As Kennedy put it, there were contradictions in American feeling—an extreme desire to stand up to the Communists but a strong reluctance to become involved in any military action. He was acutely aware of the political consequences of either action or inaction, and especially of the old Republican charge of "Democratic wars." But he had no doubt that the nation would follow the President if he ordered men into combat.[6]

It was of the utmost importance that North Vietnam, especially, understand the firmness of the American resolve to prevent a Communist takeover in Laos. But the United States unfortunately had no diplomats in Hanoi or in Peking. In this situation, Kennedy had to depend upon Moscow's channels of communication with Hanoi

[5] *Public Papers of the Presidents, 1961* (Washington: Government Printing Office, 1962), p. 214.

[6] Conversation with Chalmers M. Roberts, reported in *The Washington Post,* November 30, 1963.

and Peking. The President and Secretary of State Dean Rusk met constantly with Soviet Foreign Minister Gromyko in Washington, and Kennedy sent his Ambassador in the Soviet Union halfway across Siberia to deliver a personal message to Khrushchev, who was visiting Novosibirsk.

Khrushchev's Dilemma

Kennedy's course of action had put Khrushchev on tenterhooks. Like Kennedy, he faced the very real prospect of being dragged willy-nilly into a most unprofitable confrontation far from home. Supporting his Asian allies in a war against the United States would produce serious risks and would limit his ability to exploit issues much closer to home and of much greater interest, such as Berlin.

Khrushchev had to explain to the North Vietnamese the precise degree of American firmness as he understood it from Kennedy himself. Moreover, he had to do this without appearing as an appeaser to the North Vietnamese. While details of the exchanges between Moscow and Hanoi and between Peking and Hanoi are not yet known, the available evidence indicates the outlines of the arguments on all sides. Khrushchev was compelled to weigh his moves against his American policy and against his Communist-bloc policy. Khrushchev could agree to a cease-fire in Laos with little sacrifice to himself. His reasoning with the North Vietnamese probably ran like this: In order to prevent the Americans from intervening in Laos, it is necessary to agree to a cease-fire; we are supporting Souvanna Phouma, who is the legal Prime Minister of Laos, and in the long run this policy will achieve the same ends as a military victory by the Pathet Lao.

For the North Vietnamese, however, a cease-fire meant considerable sacrifice. Their men, fighting with the Pathet Lao, were on the way to "liberating" Laos from foreign domination, a task at which they had been working patiently for fifteen years. Giap's analysis of "imperialist" behavior in his theory of "people's war" foresaw that the risk of retaliatory action against the base area (in this case, North Vietnam) would increase as the struggle became more acute; the most dangerous time was at the brink of victory. Therefore, the North Vietnamese were in no mood to follow Khrushchev's advice blindly. Also, the Vietnamese Communists harbored a deep-rooted suspicion of the Russians, the origin of which went back to Ho Chi Minh's days in the Comintern. Stalin had been dead wrong, in the 1920's, in advising the Chinese Communists to cooperate with Chiang Kai-shek. Ho had been there. *He knew.* Why should he now place any greater stock in Khrushchev's advice?

The Politburo of the Lao Dong Party probably calculated that the Americans, despite their threatening moves, would not actually intervene in Laos unless the Mekong Valley fell to the Pathet Lao. By a shrewd projection of the well-known official American reluctance to commit garrison troops to mainland Southeast Asia and the primary American preoccupation with the security of Thailand, the Vietnamese Communists probably judged that they could carry on their covert activities in the uplands of Laos with relatively little fear of provoking American intervention.

Peking was holding up to Hanoi, by public statements and no doubt by secret communications, developments in Laos as proof positive of the correctness of the militant line in advancing Communist control over the revolutionary movements in the underdeveloped countries. In this view, the American military preparations were the latest confirmation of "U.S. imperialism" as the "international gendarme" that rushed troops here, there, and everywhere in a vain effort to police the world.

The Peking government had another concern in Laos. Remnants of the defeated Kuomintang armies, forced out of China by the Communist takeover in 1949, had since subsisted in the mountains of northern Burma and reportedly had been supplied with arms by aircraft from Taipei. When in 1961, the Burmese Government used force to dislodge them, several thousand of these armed men drifted eastward into Thailand and Laos. No one knew exactly how many there were or what their movements were. On March 14, 1961, however, Lucien Coudoux, a journalist, saw approximately 1,200 of these irregulars at Ban Houei Sai, on the Laos side of the Mekong, crossing the river into Thailand; they carried American rifles, machine guns, mortars, and bazookas. A month later, an official of the Chinese Nationalist Consulate in Vientiane reported that Nationalist aircraft had airlifted 4,000 Kuomintang troops from Nam Tha to Ban Houei Sai.[7] The reasons for this move may be disclosed in future publications of diplomatic correspondence; now it appears extremely likely that it was closely tied to American efforts to persuade the Soviets to cooperate in reaching a settlement in Laos.

Even at the height of the military crisis in the spring of 1961, Peking refrained from hinting at committing its own troops in Laos

[7] United Press International dispatch, April 12, 1961.

except for one statement. That was made by Foreign Minister Chen Yi at the Djakarta airport on April 2. He said that if SEATO forces intervened in Laos, China would send troops if requested to do so by Souvanna Phouma. There was little risk in this statement, since neither proviso was likely.

Caught between considerations of Communist solidarity and the desire to avoid entanglement in a thoroughly unprofitable situation, Khrushchev temporized. Days went by, and Moscow made no response to the British proposal for a joint British-Soviet appeal for a cease-fire and the convening of a conference. Khrushchev was careful not to identify himself too closely with the drive forward of the Communist-supported forces in Laos; the Soviet press did not accord prominent attention to the Pathet Lao advances and made no mention of the Soviet airlift.

At long last, on March 27, *Pravda* dropped a hint that the Soviet Union would agree to call for a cease-fire in Laos *before* an international conference. "It is quite evident," *Pravda* commented, "that the realistic way to the solution of the Laos problem lies not in aggravating the situation in the area of Laos, not in preparing military intervention, but in peace talks and in the calling of an international conference and the renewal of the work of the ICC." The foreign ministers of the SEATO powers, who had opened their annual meeting that very day in Bangkok, breathed a sigh of relief. It was obvious that if there were to be "peace talks" between the factions in Laos, someone had to order the pro-Communists to stop shooting.

Then the Soviets did a remarkable thing. On April 4, they beamed a program in the Vietnamese language *only*—declaring that the Soviet Union did not demand a cease-fire in Laos as a "precondition" to an international conference and that the conference was the "main point" of the Soviet plan. However, the broadcast added, "a cease-fire in Laos will help to create a favorable atmosphere for negotiations." This was tantamount to a direct appeal to North Vietnam, and to an admission that the Soviets recognized that only the North Vietnamese had the power to control the ground fighting in Laos and thus to call a cease-fire. The North Vietnamese, however, were being advised by the Chinese not to sacrifice their gains in Laos by agreeing to a cease-fire.

A long commentary in the official Peking *People's Daily* on April 1 had expressed serious concern about American military bases near its own southern border, and made it clear that the Chinese opposed a cease-fire in Laos, whether it was proposed by the United States *or* by the Soviet Union:

According to what has been disclosed by U.S. press reports alone, scores of U.S. warships, several hundred aircraft, and thousands of troops have completed redeployment and entered into a state of war readiness. . . . With a view to rescuing the rebel clique and expanding the civil war in Laos, the United States has built an air force base capable of handling large aircraft at Udorn in Thailand, only 50 miles away from Vientiane across the Mekong River . . .
Can it be said that all these deployments made by the U.S. government are aimed at promoting a cease-fire in Laos? Is it not more true to the fact to say that it is adding fuel to the fire and ready to expand the civil war in Laos?

The paper went on to issue forceful verbal support: The fight that was being waged in Laos was a just one. The fight that the North Vietnamese were engaged in was just.

The SEATO Paper Tiger

The annual meeting of the SEATO Council of Ministers, in Bangkok, came on March 27, just at the peak of Pathet Lao fortunes, and so was widely viewed as a forum in which to iron out differences in views on collective action in Laos. In fact, nothing of the sort occurred. There was no decision to act.

The meeting acquainted Secretary of State Dean Rusk with the extent of SEATO opposition to collective action. French Foreign Minister Maurice Couve de Murville, whose intelligence corroborated American estimates of North Vietnamese backing of the Pathet Lao, made clear France's unwillingness to embark on a second Indochina War. British Foreign Secretary Lord Home, still awaiting a reply from Moscow on the cease-fire proposal, was of course unable to support SEATO intervention.

Clearly, there would be no joint intervention. If Laos required outside help, the United States alone would have to shoulder the burden. SEATO had shown itself to be a paper tiger.

Radio Hanoi and Radio Peking had been busily laying down preconditions for a cease-fire, notably including the withdrawal of American military advisers from Laos. Yet it was to be another month before Moscow had gained enough freedom of action from its Vietnamese and Chinese allies to join London in an appeal to the rival Lao factions to cease fire.

The Pathet Lao continued their military offensive. On March 31, they captured Tha Thom, in southern Xieng Khouang Province, in an attack mounted by paratroopers dropped by Soviet transports and ground troops believed to include regular North Vietnamese cadres. The defenders were routed, and some of them fled almost as far as Paksane on the Mekong before regrouping.

Again, on April 3 and 7, the Ilyushins dropped several companies of Kong Le's paratroopers near Vang Vieng, an act that prompted the State Department to announce it was considering a "strong statement" to Moscow. The paratroopers rendezvoused with Pathet Lao partisans, and on April 22 the combined force surged out of the mountains above Vang Vieng. By this maneuver, they cut off the Phoumist forces, whose company included four American advisers, and scattered the remainder as far south as the Lik River.

The conversations between the State Department and the Russians were stymied by the Soviet demand for withdrawal of American military personnel from Laos and the American demand for a halt to the Russian airlift. Early in April, the State Department depicted the extent of this airlift in alarming terms. On April 19, the United States transformed its military advisory personnel in Laos from civilian PEO status to uniformed MAAG status. The State Department defended this move by again holding that the U.S. was not bound by the 1954 Geneva agreements, which it had not signed.

The middle of April brought the disastrous Bay of Pigs invasion in Cuba. Kennedy, who took "full responsibility" for it, henceforth adopted a new approach to the Laos problem. Previously, he had taken a vital interest in every detail of the contingency planning; afterward, according to a reliable source who observed his behavior during this critical time, the President showed less interest in the military map work of positioning potential American troop strong-points in Laos.

Pathet Lao columns on the march in northern Laos, especially in Luang Prabang Province, were helping consolidate the pro-Communists' political control over large regions inhabited by sparse populations, mostly mountain tribesmen. Typically, the village of Ban Nam Bac on the Hou River, about halfway down the old invasion route from Dien Bien Phu to Luang Prabang, went under Pathet Lao control with barely a skirmish. Emissaries then set out for the valleys farther west in order to spread the word that "liberation" was near.

Toward the end of April, the garrison at the mountain village of Muong Sai, a great opium-trading center, came under a "rolling" mortar barrage—that is, rounds aimed on successive lines that moved horizontally across the town, from one end to the other. Most of the houses were set afire, but the civilian population had already fled into the hills. From the accuracy of the fire, it was obvious that it was the work of expert gunners; from its volume, the garrison at Muong Sai realized that it was heavily outnumbered and outgunned.

After the mortar barrage came concentrated fire from small arms, machine guns, recoilless rifles, and everything else that could fire a bullet. Once again the insurgents attacked at daybreak with telling effect. By evening, the smoking ruins of Muong Sai were in their hands, and the Pathet Lao infantry was mopping up resistance to make the place safe for the political officers attached to the attacking units.

Meanwhile, diplomatic interchanges had resulted in a compromise formula that would preserve "face" for Khrushchev among his Asian allies and that would ensure a cease-fire before the conference met, as the Western powers insisted. The international conference had been agreed to *before* a cease-fire prevailed in Laos, but would not meet until *after* the cease-fire took effect. The withdrawal of American troops and cessation of the Russian airlift operations were temporarily left unsettled.

On April 24, three separate messages went out from London and Moscow. The first informed the "military authorities, parties and organizations in Laos" that an international conference would convene at Geneva on May 12, and called upon them to cease firing before then and to send "appropriate representatives" to negotiate a cease-fire agreement. The second invited to the conference the governments of the thirteen nations originally suggested by Prince Sihanouk—all the countries that had participated in the 1954 Conference, plus the three ICC countries and Laos' neighbors Burma and Thailand—in addition to Laos (if and when the two rival governments led by Souvanna Phouma and General Phoumi once again merged). The third, addressed to India, with copies to Canada and Poland, sought reactivation of the ICC in Laos.

Predictably, these moves won immediate backing from Hanoi and Peking.

The government of the Democratic Republic of Vietnam hopes that the measures put forward by the Co-Chairmen will bring about peace in Laos and create conditions for the Lao people to build for themselves a peaceful, neutral, independent and unified Laos.[8]

An official Chinese government statement declared:

The Chinese government fully supports the appeals of the Co-Chairmen of the Geneva Conference to the parties concerned in Laos to

[8] Radio Hanoi, April 25, 1961.

cease fire before the convocation of the international conference and their appeal to the representatives of the parties concerned in Laos to enter into negotiations for concluding an agreement on questions connected with the cease-fire.[9]

Military commanders on both sides in Laos issued cease-fire orders to take effect May 3 at 8 A.M. For the Pathet Lao, the cease-fire order was issued by radio from Sam Neua and was signed by General Khamtay Siphandon, "Commander in Chief of the Neo Lao Hak Sat Armed Forces." The cease-fire was vague in the extreme, making no stipulations to halt troop movements or to specify territorial controls. While soldiers of both factions remained stationary along the Royal Road, the Pathet Lao on the morning of May 3 attacked and captured the village of Muong Phalane in Savannakhet Province, enabling them later to seize the vital airfield at Tchepone. General Phoumi's troops reoccupied the village of Ban Hat Bo in the valley above Paksane after the cease-fire had gone into effect.

The first contingent of ICC personnel was soon on its way to Laos. The delicate question of which government the commission should be accredited to had been resolved by assigning a separate group to each capital. The Indian chairman, Samar Sen, established his headquarters in Vientiane on May 8, but the ICC group traveling to Souvanna Phouma's capital of Khang Khay on the Plain of Jars was subjected to several days' delay.

An ICC message was sent to Souvanna Phouma from Saigon, where the ICC plane had stopped over. Because there were no direct communications between Saigon and Khang Khay, the message was dispatched to Hanoi for forwarding. Surprisingly, the North Vietnamese telegraphers reported that they could not deliver the message because no one in Hanoi knew where to find the Prince. An effort to reach the Prince through Pathet Lao liaison officers on the stabilized "front" at the Lik River was similarly frustrated.

Hanoi's ignorance of Souvanna Phouma's whereabouts was all the more extraordinary inasmuch as he had passed through the North Vietnamese capital only a few days previously on his return home from his world tour.

When the planeload of ICC personnel finally arrived at the Plain of Jars, they were taken in hand by the Communist-appointed provincial governor and lodged in the town of Xieng Khouang, far away from Khang Khay, where they might stumble on some of

[9] New China News Agency, Peking, April 26, 1961. Marshal Chen Yi later asserted at Geneva that a cease-fire had never been a precondition to the holding of the conference.

the Vietnamese military advisers who were shuttling around the countryside with such telling effect. When the author visited Xieng Khouang at the beginning of June, an ICC officer told him that the commission members were not allowed to deal directly with Souvanna Phouma.

An ironic scene occurred at the Vientiane airport when arriving ICC personnel were debarking from their plane. Right next to them landed a helicopter carrying evacuated Lao soldiers wounded in fighting six days after the cease-fire deadline. The American helicopter pilots employed by Air America still reported being shot at regularly. When four AT-6's took off with rockets slung under their wings and returned without rockets, only one reasonable conclusion could be drawn.

Not until several days after the May 3 broadcast of the cease-fire order did the opposing sides actually establish liaison with each other. The initial, wary contact between the opposing military forces occurred on the banks of the Lik River, where the "front" had stabilized with the Pathet Lao and Kong Le forces in control of the north bank and the Phoumists dug in on the south bank. On May 5, after an exchange of messenger-borne letters, a Phoumist officer, Lieutenant Colonel Siho Lamphouthacoul, crossed the makeshift foot bridge, alongside the blown-up road bridge, and met a junior-grade Pathet Lao officer in the shade of a candy-striped tent fashioned out of parachutes. Next day, they met in an abandoned house by the roadside (the civilian population had fled into the hills). Two Lao flags fluttered from a pole in the breeze.

As in Korea, the Communists demanded that the truce talks be held in territory they controlled. This demand and others of a similar nature were to lend to these talks an uncomfortable Cold War chill.

10.

Negotiations: Ban Namone and Geneva

The cease-fire proclaimed on May 3, 1961, marked a definite transition of Western policy from a military to a political orientation. Six weeks earlier, at the end of March, the United States had come within a hairsbreadth of deciding to commit American ground and air forces to Laos. If the Pathet Lao had exploited their military and psychological advantage in the spring of 1961 and compelled the Phoumist government to relinquish its control over any of the Mekong Valley towns, the United States almost certainly would have intervened. Instead, the Pathet Lao spun out their advantage by consolidating their control over much of the upcountry and heightening the general impression of their formidable strength.

American intervention would have scrapped, overnight, the 1954 agreements, and with them the hope of an unallied Laos forming a demilitarized zone between the Sino-Soviet bloc and the main Southeast Asian position of Western influence (in Thailand), and the possibility of preserving Laos' independence without committing a single American soldier. Scrapping these agreements would have shifted the basis of American policy from the concept of an "umbrella" provided by superior reserve striking power to one of forward commitment and possibly limited warfare on the pattern of Korea.

Even though both sides had flouted the Geneva agreements by clandestinely pouring military hardware and "advisers" into Laos, the concept of an unallied Laos was still salvageable. The task was to avoid intervention, not to run headlong into it. In order to transform the cease-fire into a situation advantageous to the U.S., American thinking about Laos had to be readjusted.

This readjustment, first indicated in January by the State Department White Paper on Laos, was provoked by the Soviet airlift, which of course had been a predictable response to American aid to the Phoumists by airlift and other means.

Just as American aid to the Phoumist government in Vientiane gave the United States a measure of influence over that government, so Russian aid to the Souvanna Phouma government in Khang Khay gave the Soviet Union leverage on the pro-Communist forces. The Soviet airlift had enabled the Pathet Lao to upgrade themselves from a motley guerrilla band to a regular armed force of considerable weight. But after this transformation, the Pathet Lao could no longer function on the crude matériel from home workshops and village factories. Their sophisticated Soviet weaponry required resupply from the arsenals of Kiev and Minsk. In short, the Pathet Lao were now dependent on the Soviet airlift. Therein lay the key to transforming the cease-fire into a political settlement acceptable to the United States.

Soviet military supplies were being flown into Laos under an agreement with the Khang Khay government. If the Pathet Lao received a large share of these supplies, it was because of their alliance with Kong Le, which permitted them to claim that they supported this government. Officially, Soviet aid was helping the Royal Lao Army commanded by Kong Le, not the Pathet Lao, and the Royal Government headed by Souvanna Phouma, not the NLHS headed by Souphanouvong. There was no indication that if the United States abandoned the Phoumists and threw its support to Souvanna Phouma, the Soviet Union would hold out for more than a government headed by Souvanna Phouma in which the NLHS had representation. Pathet Lao military gains that threatened to embroil the Soviets in a confrontation with the United States were viewed by the U.S.S.R. as counterproductive, even if made under the guise of revolutionary warfare. The Soviet Union had other interests that weighed more heavily than Laos. At this point, Soviet motivations diverged from North Vietnamese and Chinese motivations, opening up the possibility of a political settlement.

Soviet reluctance to become embroiled with the United States in a revolutionary war in small, faraway Laos had become, by 1961, a major point of contention between Khrushchev and Mao Tse-tung. Soviet feelers for a *détente* with the incoming Kennedy Administration had seriously displeased Peking. This was made plain by the

Chinese response to Kennedy's accession to the Presidency. The Soviets welcomed the new Administration, saying that the change in
American leadership held out the promise of a new era in relations
between the socialist and capitalist worlds. But the Chinese greeted
the advent of Kennedy with an outpouring of vitriolic propaganda
pegged to the theme that "Kennedy is more dangerous than Eisenhower," not less so, as Khrushchev supposed. As 1961 opened,
Peking and Moscow were poles apart on how to deal with the
Americans, and this question was set forth with particular clarity
in Laos.

In a speech on January 6, Khrushchev specified his interpretation
of the obligation to aid revolutions in the underdeveloped countries.
He argued that the Communist bloc must provide aid to "national
liberation movements" fighting "wars of liberation," which originate
as popular insurrections, not wars between states. However, Communist-bloc countries should not internationalize "wars of liberation," for this would lead to dangerous escalation. Instead, they
should prevent the foreign "imperialist" powers from intervening by
threatening to intervene in turn. In this way, they would ensure the
victory of "the people." In terms of Laos, this meant that the Soviets
favored supporting the Pathet Lao in a "war of liberation," but did
not favor support so extensive as that of North Vietnam, a Communist-bloc country that was taking the initiative in driving the
"imperialists" out of Laos.

This was an important distinction. It explained how the Soviet
Union could maintain good relations with nationalists like Souvanna
Phouma and Prince Sihanouk of Cambodia. Eventually, their countries might become "people's democracies," but for the time being
the first objective of the Communist bloc should be to hasten the
elimination of foreign "imperialists" from these countries.

Cambodia had best fulfilled expectations of the 1954 Conference
that the Indochina states would adopt neutral positions in the Cold
War. Sihanouk had become an ardent advocate of this course. His
country was more prosperous than Laos, but much weaker than its
two other neighbors: Cambodia's army had about 30,000 men, South
Vietnam's 150,000, and Thailand's 90,000. Although Cambodia
did not border a Communist country, it was relatively easy for Communist agents to infiltrate, especially across its mountainous northeastern provinces adjoining Pathet Lao-held areas of southern Laos.
Cambodia had less than 5 million people, including large Vietnamese
and Chinese minorities numbering approximately 300,000 each.

Sihanouk kept his country peaceful by maintaining friendly relations with major foreign powers. The Cambodian capital had embassies of the United States, Britain, France, the Soviet Union, and Communist China. The presence of these embassies served to guarantee Cambodia's security from Thai irredentism and from Vietnamese imperialism.

From the American point of view, Cambodia was the Indochinese state that had received the least aid—far less than either of the pro-Western regimes of Laos and South Vietnam[1]—and the only one completely free of warfare. No Communist insurgents were leading a "people's war" to overthrow Sihanouk's popular government, and an American felt secure traveling in any part of the country.

The word "neutralist" is commonly used to refer to the happy position achieved by Sihanouk, in which a small, weak country cautiously walks a tightrope between two opposing powerful blocs. The author, however, prefers to avoid applying the word to Laos. "Neutralism" is a word coined by certain French newspapers in the dark, Cold War period of 1949–50. It designated a political tendency to extricate oneself from a definite alignment with one bloc of countries against another bloc of countries. However, neutralism did not become a serious policy until General de Gaulle had restored France to a respected place in the council of nations. Then, with a sound economic base and a military no longer tied down in colonial wars, France could advocate neutralism because it was at last strong enough to determine its own future, no longer to be dictated to by either Cold War bloc.

The situation of Laos is obviously different and will remain so. A small country in an economically and militarily precarious position vis-à-vis more powerful neighbors, Laos must depend on an *external* balance of forces. It is not strong enough to compel its neighbors to recognize its right to pursue any foreign policy it chooses, as De Gaulle can do in Europe. To convey the concept of a Laos that is not aligned with one bloc or the other, the author has chosen to refer to Laos as *neutralized* by international agreement rather than as *neutralist* by its own volition and power. The author has also avoided using the term "neutralist" to identify one faction in Laos that has sought to steer a middle course between two others, which are loosely referred to as "leftist" and "rightist" in allusion to the foreign powers supporting them.

The suggestion that Laos be neutralized by international agree-

[1] See Table 2, p. 105.

ment was made as early as September 29, 1960, when in a speech before the General Assembly of the United Nations Prince Sihanouk declared:

> While this situation owes its origin undeniably to foreign interference from the two blocs, it is obvious that to avoid the risk of a show of strength, the only reasonable and valid solution to eliminate this new and dangerous trouble-spot is the neutralization of Laos backed by international guarantees of its unity and territorial integrity.

The American-launched trial balloon in favor of the Boun Oum government and an inspection commission composed of Burma, Malaya, and Cambodia had come down without positive result. In its wake, American policy began to adjust itself to the need to neutralize Laos. But to achieve this, it was necessary to deal with Prince Souvanna Phouma.

Kennedy delegated Averell Harriman to explore the possibility of joint Soviet-American support for a Lao Government, headed by Souvanna Phouma, that would be neither Communist nor anti-Communist. Harriman had gained some experience in dealing with the Russians as American Ambassador to the Soviet Union. On March 29, he reported to the President on conversations he had had with Souvanna Phouma in New Delhi and Paris. Harriman felt it was encouraging for the United States that the Prince continued to regard himself as the central wheel in a three-wheeled mechanism. Souvanna Phouma, Harriman commented, "is a factor that has to be dealt with, and I think he should be in any government. He thinks he ought to be Prime Minister. Whether that should be or not, I don't know, but he certainly should be in any government."

Harriman felt that the best hope for preserving Laos' independence from North Vietnam lay in American support for a neutralized Laos under a coalition government guaranteed by both the Soviet Union and the Western powers. He thought that a coalition government could be formed in Laos without leading to a Communist takeover. Despite Soviet probing for weak spots, Harriman said, "I think Mr. Khrushchev doesn't want war. He's made that very plain."

Actually, Washington had no alternative to a coalition including the Pathet Lao except intervention with American troops, if it was not to see Laos become a North Vietnamese satellite and U.S. influence in Southeast Asia wane and perhaps disappear. Britain and France would oppose SEATO intervention in Laos, as the Bangkok meeting had shown all too clearly, and for the United States, a military venture in Southeast Asia was not worth the risk of jeopardizing European partnerships. The "decision" to accept a coalition in Laos was virtually thrust upon the Kennedy Administration.

The Soviet Union, unwilling to risk war over Laos, was agreeable to a coalition in Laos. But it remained to be seen how the Pathet Lao could be made to accept the coalition government. They were under the direction of Hanoi. Their troops were dependent on the Soviet airlift for supplies, but this was a temporary dependence, and Hanoi was to make it as brief as possible.

Truce Talks

Ban Namone, the village finally agreed upon as the site of the cease-fire talks, consists of some seventy wooden houses built on stilts, and is situated on the Royal Road about thirty-five miles north of the Lik River. It is a peaceful spot. In early May, just at the beginning of the rainy season, the air between showers is cooler than in the plain of Vientiane and has a bright, clear quality. Towering white cumulus clouds appear over the green hills at about noon, and by late afternoon turn a menacing gray that heralds the daily rainstorm. From the surrounding forests, columns of blue smoke evidence the slash-and-burn agriculture of the mountain tribesmen. A few small paddy fields afforded landing space for helicopters, and a mud-floored bamboo schoolhouse, decorated with Lao flags, became the meeting room.

The Pathet Lao, by their own description, were the fighting units of a political party whose program supported Souvanna Phouma but that held no membership in his government. Since the cease-fire was to be signed by the forces of the two rival "governments" of Laos, there was little legal justification for Pathet Lao participation in framing the cease-fire. However, no objection was made to the Pathet Lao demand for an equal role in the talks.

Souvanna Phouma's delegation was headed by Pheng Phongsavan, a close associate who had been a member of the Prince's 1953 Cabinet. The Pathet Lao delegation was led by Nouhak Phoumsavan, the Lao who had traveled to Geneva in 1954 on a Vietnamese passport. The Phoumist delegation, led by General Sing Ratanasamay, comprised only military officers, because Vientiane had assumed that the talks would deal solely with implementing the cease-fire.

The close coordination between the centrist and Pathet Lao delegations became evident when, in a statement issued from Souvanna Phouma's capital on May 8, Pheng and Nouhak declared that "military talks must be held [and] at the same time political talks should be held in order to broaden the Royal Government and reorganize it into a coalition government and form a unified Government delegation to the forthcoming international conference at Geneva."[2]

Despite this last-minute surprise, the three delegations convened in the schoolhouse at Ban Namone for their first meeting on May 11, with the centrists occupying the head of a U-shaped table. In attendance were the ICC military observers. No records were kept, except for notes made by Western journalists after the meeting. (Correspondents from the Soviet Union, North Vietnam, and China arrived a few days later.) The meeting was cordial and lasted one hour. At its conclusion, the ICC felt sufficiently encouraged to telegraph Geneva that a cease-fire was in effect, which overstated the case. This gave the Western delegations the green light to open the international conference on Laos.

At the second meeting two days later, the representatives of the three factions signed a typed statement confirming that military commanders all around had ordered their troops to cease fire. However, there was no pinpointing of troop locations, specifying of ground controlled by the various forces, or indicating of whether the cease-fire prohibited troop movements behind the points of contact or the airlifting of supplies that was going on at Vientiane and the Plain of Jars.

The cease-fire thus disposed of, the meeting broke up amid considerable conviviality. The Pathet Lao delegates, seemingly forgetting their vitriolic propaganda against the "Phoumi–Boun Oum clique," fraternized jovially with the Phoumists, and Nouhak clapped his arm around the shoulders of General Sing. Members of the three delegations toasted each other in glasses of hot tea poured from thermos flasks, exchanging news about their families and trading letters for delivery.

At a two-hour meeting the following day, the Vientiane delegates agreed to the introduction of political matters, and were roundly cheered by Pheng and Nouhak. The latter declared that "the most urgent question is to form a provisional coalition government." The meeting broke up with the appearance of a cold chicken buffet lunch.

In a united front, Pheng and Nouhak now insisted that the talks take up the formation of a coalition government, the abrogation of agreements by the Boun Oum government (the target was the American MAAG), and the rewriting of electoral regulations restricting NLHS activities. Nouhak expressed the hope that a coali-

[2] New China News Agency, Xieng Khouang, May 8, 1961.

tion might be formed shortly so that it could determine the responsibilities of the ICC, which had yet to travel outside either of the
two "capitals" to verify the cease-fire. Obviously, the objective was
to keep the ICC—which could act only on instructions from the
Co-Chairmen or by unanimous request of the three Lao factions—
in a state of prolonged inactivity.

On May 17, the negotiators announced they had agreed to form a
provisional coalition government that would organize elections for
the National Assembly. Two days later, however, in the face of
flagrant cease-fire violations, the Vientiane delegation insisted that
the delegates drop the political negotiations and concentrate immediately on enforcing the cease-fire.

Their concern had been aroused by continued Pathet Lao pressure on a Meo entrenchment on a mountaintop at Padong, only a
few miles south of the Plain of Jars. Since April, increasing numbers
of Pathet Lao had been committed to action in this sector. Several
artillery bombardments had succeeded each other, one heavier than
the last. On May 15, the defenders estimated, 100 shells fell on
Padong, in the forty-eight hours of May 26–27, some 400 shells.
Lulls between these bombardments suggested that the Pathet Lao,
aided by North Vietnamese, were using coolie labor to move their
75-mm. mountain guns up rugged slopes to closer positions, as at
Dien Bien Phu.

On May 30, an Air America helicopter maneuvering in mist to
land at Padong crashed, killing the two American crew members
and critically injuring an American attached to MAAG. A few days
earlier, another Air America helicopter had made a forced landing
because of engine failure and its two crew members and an American journalist on board, Grant Wolfkill, had been rounded up by
local partisans and turned over to the Pathet Lao.

Pathet Lao pressure was also being felt elsewhere. Guerrilla activity north of Luang Prabang and against boats on the Mekong
had served to blockade food supplies to the royal capital, and in a
month prices in the local market had doubled.

The delegates agreed on May 26 to setting up three military sub-
delegations, which would meet at the same time as the main delegations but in a small woodshed near the schoolhouse, in order
to work out implementation of the cease-fire. The Pathet Lao
continued to refuse to permit the ICC to do any verifying. ICC requests to travel into areas where there had been complaints of cease-
fire violations were refused, on the ground that transport facilities
were inadequate. An ICC suggestion for joint efforts to draw up a

map clearly indicating troop positions was also turned down by the Pathet Lao.

The Pathet Lao recommended that the ICC send field teams to verify the cease-fire at Ban Hin Heup and at Kiu Ka Cham, farther north on the Luang Prabang road, places where there had been virtually no firing since May 3. However, ICC suggestions of visits to Padong and other Meo strong points in Sam Neua Province, as well as southern Laos, were rejected by the Pathet Lao. They saw no need for ICC inspection of areas wholly "liberated by the patriotic forces," where "bandits" were being mopped up. Later, when the Phoumists unexpectedly insisted that Pathet Lao actions at Padong violated the cease-fire, the Pathet Lao charged that the Meo and their American advisers had been parachuted into their positions after the cease-fire had gone into effect. This claim was obviously spurious, because correspondents had visited the Meo and their hardy commander, Vang Pao, as early as March.

The Meo outposts in Xieng Khouang and Sam Neua provinces were sustained by supplies ferried in by Air America C-46's and C-47's, whose courageous crews risked death almost daily in these hazardous missions to Laos' most rugged terrain.

Meanwhile, the main body of delegates in the schoolhouse listened for hours as Nouhak declared that he favored discussion of restoration of democratic rights in Laos, equality for all minority groups, unification of the armed forces, and other such generalities.

On June 7, the Vientiane delegation formally requested the other two delegations to permit the ICC to send a field team to Padong to investigate the situation. Nouhak agreed "in principle."

After the meeting, the Phoumists flew by helicopter back to Vientiane, where they were met with shocking news: Padong had been abandoned the previous evening. The Phoumists charged that eight companies of mixed Lao and Vietnamese troops had been engaged in the siege of Padong.

At Ban Namone on June 14, the Indian observer at the military talks, Major General Shiv Dayal Singh, rose from a wooden bench and, over Pathet Lao opposition, read a letter addressed by the commission to the three factions. The letter reminded the delegates that "at the meeting held at Ban Namone on 7 June 1961 all parties agreed in principle that the Commission should go and examine the situation in some sensitive areas," and requested the delegates to suggest sites for investigation and provide necessary facilities, in what was by now a familiar ICC plea. Angered by this active participation by the ICC, the Pathet Lao successfully demanded that the ICC remove its observers permanently from the sessions at Ban Namone.

The Ban Namone talks revealed the perspective in which the Pathet Lao viewed the situation in Laos. The Pathet Lao talked of themselves and the followers of Souvanna Phouma as the supporters of "the people." They did not refer to their armed forces in the language of soldiers, as the Phoumists did, but called them the "people's patriotic defense forces." These forces never launched an offensive; they cleared up "bandits" dropped in the "liberated areas" by U.S. "imperialists." The "small minority" represented by the "Phoumi-Boun Oum clique" were preventing peace from being restored in the Kingdom. Whenever the Phoumist delegates requested a recess to consider some new Pathet Lao demand, they were accused of obstructing the peace talks in order to give the Americans time to ready their final plans for aggressive intervention in Laos. The Pathet Lao made the loudest outcries against breaches of the cease-fire, but blocked any on-the-spot inspection by the ICC; they vigorously protested Phoumist attacks, but flagrantly mounted offensive operations against the Meo around the Plain of Jars; and they decried foreign intervention, but depended on massive outside aid.

Counting Swans at Geneva

The relative ground positions in Laos were reflected in the attitudes of the various delegations who gathered at Geneva on May 16 for the Conference of foreign ministers on Laos. The North Vietnamese and Chinese delegations, bolstered by the military advantage gained by the Pathet Lao, anticipated squeezing the maximum political concessions from the frustrated supporters of General Phoumi. The United States was prepared to engage in a long holding operation.

The Conference opened in the familiar atmosphere of mutual suspicion. The United States strenuously but unsuccessfully objected to the seating of a Pathet Lao delegation as a full participant. However, these objections were seriously weakened by the precedent set at Ban Namone. The first session was attended by Quinim Pholsena and Phoumi Vongvichit representing the centrists and the Pathet Lao, respectively, and boycotted by Phoui Sananikone, representing the Phoumists, in protest against the seating of the Pathet Lao. At a subsequent meeting, Phoui came up with the mischievous suggestion that leaders of the fifteen other political parties in Laos should also be seated. His idea was not adopted.

The delegates recessed for the summit meeting of Kennedy and Khrushchev at Vienna. The joint statement issued by the two leaders on June 4 showed how close their interests were in Laos:

> The President and the Chairman reaffirmed their support of a neutral and independent Laos under a government chosen by the Laotians themselves, and of international agreements for insuring that neutrality and independence, and in this connection they have recognized the importance of an effective cease-fire.[3]

The aura of optimism emanating from this statement was short-lived, however. News of the fall of Padong, reaching Geneva almost immediately after the Conference had resumed, threw the meetings into deadlock. The United States let it be known that it was considering pulling out of the Conference in view of the flagrance of the Pathet Lao violation of the cease-fire. The Chinese thereupon accused the United States of delaying, even sabotaging, the Conference. The Chinese were prepared for a long stay in Geneva: They had taken six-month leases on a villa and limousines. For a while, the delegates were uncertain whether plenary sessions would be resumed. Soviet Foreign Minister Andrei Gromyko gave vent to the general impatience: "One cannot sit indefinitely on the shores of Lake Geneva counting swans."

The atmosphere improved toward the end of June, as the result of a princely summit meeting in Zurich. There, Souvanna Phouma, Souphanouvong, and Boun Oum reached agreement in principle on forming a coalition including all three factions. The princes also decided that the ICC observers should be readmitted to the Ban Namone talks and that the Phoumists should end their boycott of the Geneva sessions.

The Geneva delegates resumed their meetings, and proceeded by fits and starts toward a common declaration of the neutrality of Laos. A major reason for the slow pace was that the delegations were working under no fixed deadline, as they had in 1954. Consequently, there was less bargaining *en coulisse*. This suited the Chinese particularly. They exploited every possible angle inside the Conference in order to maintain a steady propaganda barrage against the United States.

By the end of the year, the Chinese had withdrawn their objections to majority vote within the ICC and had softened their recalcitrant stand on clauses governing the withdrawal of foreign troops and military personnel, banning the introduction of fresh

[3] *Public Papers of the Presidents, 1961*, p. 438.

troops, eliminating military bases in Laos, and ruling out the use of Lao territory as a corridor or staging area for direct or indirect aggression against unspecified countries.

The ICC mandate was perhaps the biggest stumbling block. Debate on the exact relationship between the ICC and the future Lao government continued, on and off, for several months.

The United States believed that it could enlist Russian influence on the Chinese and Vietnamese in support of a practicable *modus vivendi* in Laos if only the U.S. gave full backing to Souvanna Phouma's political program. Acting on this premise, the U.S. took initial cautious steps to give assurances to the Prince. By making its sentiments clearly understood without actually committing itself to any promises, the State Department attempted to gain his confidence without losing that of General Phoumi. Following the initial approach in March, an invitation to Washington had been extended to Souvanna Phouma on April 9, but this had not been taken up.

General Phoumi's Obstinacy

The delicate task proved more difficult than the State Department had expected. General Phoumi, seeing that his position was being cut away from under him, reacted with displeasure to the maneuver and lapsed into an obstinate silence. Since the State Department's actions were largely predicated on considerations of Sino-Soviet rivalries that he could not fathom, the General's reluctance to be removed as Vice Prime Minister, and perhaps from the Cabinet entirely, is understandable.

Moreover, General Phoumi undoubtedly harbored the illusion that the CIA, with which he had had close contacts in the past and which he had always known to have the last word, would once again outweigh the counsels of the Ambassador. A meeting of himself, Admiral Harry D. Felt, and Brigadier General Andrew Jackson Boyle, the MAAG commander, in early October perhaps strengthened his feeling that not all the agencies of the United States government wholeheartedly supported the State Department.

Nevertheless, it was clear that the State Department was having none of General Phoumi and his annoying reluctance to enter a coalition with the centrists and the Pathet Lao. Harriman, now Assistant Secretary of State for Far Eastern Affairs, held two days of talks with Souvanna Phouma in Rangoon in mid-September, after which he stated that the State Department wanted to get the three princes into a coalition Cabinet. "But it's up to Prince Boun Oum to make his own decision," he added.

Harriman then flew to Luang Prabang for an audience with the King, who had privately expressed his fears that Laos would be judged by the Geneva Conference as by an international tribunal. In Vientiane, the following day, Harriman held a two-hour interview with Prince Boun Oum and General Phoumi. He listened with ill-concealed impatience to their reasons for refusing to cooperate at this late hour with Souvanna Phouma.

It was increasingly urgent to form some kind of stable coalition. Souvanna Phouma was under ever-greater pressure to give a freer hand to the North Vietnamese and Chinese through "aid agreements," which threatened to undermine all remaining Western pretensions to influence in Laos.

Souvanna Phouma in Khang Khay was certainly aware of the role of North Vietnamese military personnel in the Pathet Lao and in Kong Le's forces. He was in a singularly poor position to protest the presence of these "advisers and technicians" to North Vietnamese representatives, who would remind him that he had once tolerated American advisers and technicians in Vientiane.

Beginning with his visit to Hanoi in April, 1961, Souvanna Phouma had signed a series of agreements with North Vietnam. These dealt with economic and cultural cooperation (April 28), exchange of press correspondents and photographs (June 7), cooperation in broadcasting (June 7), exchange of specialists and foreign training grants (July 13), commercial relations (July 13), exchange of payments (July 13), and town planning for Khang Khay (September 13).

These agreements permitted the North Vietnamese to run trucks in and out of Lao territory controlled by the merged Pathet Lao and Kong Le forces. The trucks could be on an official mission, bringing construction workers and materials in conjunction with the town planning for Khang Khay. There was no control over whether they carried military personnel and supplies as well. The Soviet airlift was soon extended to Tchepone, which was in "liberated" territory and had to be defended against the threat of Phoumist attacks.

By August, 1961, the United States estimated the North Vietnamese forces in Laos to include 1,000 combat troops and support personnel in Sam Neua; between 1,200 and 1,500 troops at Ban Liang, two miles northeast of Khang Khay, available for combat missions; up to 300 advisers to Pathet Lao battalions and 100 combat-tactics instructors on the Plain of Jars; 300 security personnel and antiaircraft gunners on the Plain of Jars and at Ban Liang;

and 50 tank and armored-car crew members. These figures were indicated in a mimeographed statement circulated at Geneva by the American delegation.

No public mention of these troops was made by Hanoi, of course. Even in the closed-door sessions of the Conference, Hanoi refused to acknowledge their presence in Laos.

In Laos, the ripening of the upland rice crop in September would afford the Pathet Lao the fresh food stocks they needed in the villages to resume fighting on a broad scale. Also, the onset of the dry season would again make the trails passable.

Commenting on the still fluid situation at the end of September, the Peking *People's Daily* on September 25, 1961, said that "a resumption of the war in Laos is poised like an arrow on a drawn bow."

Just before the Ban Namone talks ended in September, the delegates arranged for a meeting of the three princes in Vientiane. At this gathering, the princes decided that Souvanna Phouma would seek the King's authority to form a new government, and worked out the Cabinet representation for the three factions. But General Phoumi became dissatisfied with the distribution of Cabinet posts and prevented any further progress toward formation of a coalition.

Despite American efforts to bring the sides together, the meeting in Vientiane broke up without result. On the last day of the year, the Vientiane radio broadcast a lengthy diatribe against Souphanouvong, thus deepening the prevalent gloom.

Siege at Nam Tha

From the beginning of January, 1962, there were indications that the North Vietnamese were hoping to mount a set-piece battle that would humiliate General Phoumi's army and crush Vientiane's opposition to a three-way coalition. Intelligence reports mentioned the finding of telltale caches of rice and other supplies all over northern Laos. By the middle of January, a battalion of North Vietnamese foot soldiers were known to be operating in the region of the Beng River valley; they probably used Pathet Lao-occupied Muong Sai as a base.

Northern Laos appeared to be the logical setting for the decisive Pathet Lao victory wanted by the Vietnamese. A Phoumist defeat there would exclude Vientiane troops from a band of territory along the border of China, which was then building the first road into Laos from Yünnan Province under an agreement announced by the New China News Agency on January 13. Also, a triumph could be achieved there with the maximum shock but without throwing pro-Communist forces into the Mekong Valley and risking American (or Thai) retaliation.

Suspicions of a forthcoming attack received further confirmation when a mixed force of Vietnamese and Pathet Lao attacked and reoccupied the village of Ban Na Mo, thirty miles northwest of Muong Sai, displaying such vigor that the defending garrison retreated in haste a full ten miles south.

Twenty miles west along a rugged trail lay the provincial capital of Nam Tha, a town of 1,800 that had always remained free of Pathet Lao influences. Lying in a wide bowl-like valley at the junction of four rivers pointing in the four directions of the compass, Nam Tha surely reminded the North Vietnamese of Dien Bien Phu. Indeed, a private who had been at Ban Na Mo and who kept a diary in Vietnamese, observed, "Our troops, following the instructions of Uncle Ho, have come here to bring our contribution to the construction of a Dien Bien [Phu]."

From the latter part of January on, the indefatigable Vietnamese dug a network of trenches on the heights just east of Nam Tha. It was excellent field training for the Pathet Lao. On January 25, under cover of mortar fire, their patrols overran one or two leading Phoumist outposts, enabling them to advance their trench network to within twelve miles of Nam Tha. Town officials formed a militia and armed it with old rifles from whatever stocks were available.

General Phoumi decided to reinforce the garrison with Lao troops, a tactic about which American military advisers expressed private reservations. This was a region where no Lao lived; the local inhabitants belonged to the Thai tribes or the smaller Pu Noi tribe. On January 27, General Phoumi flew in a first group of reinforcements to Nam Tha, who landed on the single tiny airstrip. The garrison swelled to 5,000 men. General Phoumi's commander in the Nam Tha sector, Major General Bounleuth Sanichan, watching additional reinforcements arrive, told correspondents confidently, "Nam Tha has never been captured by the Pathet Lao before. We will bring up as many reinforcements as required to stop them."

Pilots winging low over the mountain heights dominating the wide valley reported seeing the Vietnamese trundle into position three 120-mm. mortars (these would be used later to interdict the airstrip). On January 30, for the first time, an American supply plane was hit by ground fire while taking off. The Phoumists flew in four 105-mm. howitzers and twelve 75-mm. mountain guns.

The Pathet Lao released the text of a letter they had sent to the Geneva Co-Chairmen in which they accused the Vientiane regime of "spreading rumors" that they were violating the cease-fire. The Pathet Lao "cannot stand idly by," the letter warned. "When necessary, they will take appropriate measures in self-defense and hit back at the invaders," it said, without specifying Nam Tha, which had never been in Pathet Lao territory.

(A book published in Hanoi in 1962 under the authorship of a certain Quang Minh contains a map giving the positions occupied by the Pathet Lao at the time of the cease-fire of May 3, 1961. On that map, Nam Tha appears well within the area not yet "liberated" by the Pathet Lao.)

The Pathet Lao and their Vietnamese supporters began the siege in earnest in February. On the first day of the month, the airstrip was hit by mortar shells for the first time. On the third, the shelling reached the town itself, causing panic among those who had not already fled into the hills.

"The enemy is in a precarious position. Our troops are above him and dominate him," the Vietnamese platoon soldier recorded in his diary. "Today we celebrated the Tet [Vietnamese New Year, which fell at the beginning of February] with a bombardment of the airstrip, which is burning and enveloping the countryside in thick black smoke."

He recorded two bombardments on New Year's Day, three the day before, and four the day before that. "The airstrip is finished. The planes which have already landed there cannot take off."

The Vietnamese had managed to set up a mortar on a mountain slope nearer than the others to Nam Tha on the southeast. Despite repeated swoops by General Phoumi's AT-6's against this position, the mortar continued to shell the airstrip with deadly accuracy. Meanwhile, the Vietnamese had been extending their network of trenches on the heights to the northeast and southeast, so that they were gradually forming a ring around the town.

The shelling of the town by mortar increased noticeably on February 12, and in the following three days General Phoumi rushed in several hundred fresh paratroopers. These landed in a drop zone on the western outskirts of the town. Only 4,500 yards away was the Vietnamese trenchwork. Sporadic shelling continued throughout the month, but on March 1, an on-the-spot MAAG unit reported that the Vietnamese eased off and even moved back some of their mortars.

On March 13, Phoumi Vongvichit, who had returned to the Plain of Jars from Geneva, issued a statement saying that Souvanna

Phouma, as the Prime Minister-designate of the coalition government, is "entitled to reserve the important portfolios for his own party of neutrals." This surprisingly conciliatory statement appeared aimed at General Phoumi himself. General Phoumi continued in his obstinate unwillingness to cooperate on the proposed coalition and in his refusal to concede to Souvanna Phouma the important ministries of Defense and Interior. In an effort to force an accommodation, the U.S. shut off its cash grants to the General at the beginning of February.

The deadlock persisted. The Pathet Lao gained ground. Alarmed by the increasingly suicidal character of General Phoumi's stubbornness, Harriman hurried off to Bangkok, where Marshal Sarit, who had reluctantly accepted American determination on a coalition including the Pathet Lao, was prevailed upon to meet with General Phoumi and Harriman. The Thais, while they looked upon the coalition proposal as a risky bet, had no alternative to offer, short of garrisoning Laos with American troops—something they were not in a position to order.

The meeting took place at the town of Nong Khai on the Thai side of the Mekong, on March 24. Amid considerable diplomatic trepidation, Marshal Sarit talked in low tones in Thai for about twenty minutes, explaining patiently why it was advisable for General Phoumi to accede to the coalition. He did not look at Phoumi. When he had finished, the General replied in French, enumerating the reasons for his reluctance. After several minutes of this, Harriman, apparently not realizing that the General's speech was the necessary prelude to his acceptance without loss of face of Marshal Sarit's advice, lost patience and interrupted him. He said flatly that the General was wrong and intimated that the Phoumist forces were finished in Laos if they did not agree to the coalition.

Back in Vientiane, Harriman had further conversations with General Phoumi in what one of the General's aides termed an "animated and occasionally venomous" atmosphere. Shortly after this, a State Department official who had accompanied Harriman to Laos, William H. Sullivan, showed up in Khang Khay, Souvanna Phouma's "capital." There, he gave reassurances to Souvanna Phouma that the United States was doing everything possible to expedite the formation of a coalition.

Sullivan's trip to Khang Khay, when it was disclosed in Vientiane, did little to improve the atmosphere. Harriman termed General Phoumi a soldier who was out of step and said he was leading his country to destruction. The agencies of the United States Govern-

ment were now in a peculiar reversal of the positions they had occupied in 1960. The State Department was refusing economic aid
to a regime that the Defense Department was supporting with arms
and advisers. In 1960, the State Department had supported a
regime in Vientiane with economic aid while the Defense Department had actively worked against it by providing military aid to a
rebel faction.

On May 2, with the rainy season already imminent, the Vietnamese launched a major probe against Nam Tha's defenses from
the southeastern quarter of the perimeter. It was repulsed by the
defenders, who by now were cut off from any means of supply except parachute drops.

The following day, the first anniversary of the cease-fire among
the three factions, a combined Pathet Lao and Vietnamese force
surprised the garrison of Muong Sing, some twenty-five miles west
of Nam Tha, a two days' march by trail. They captured it after only
slight resistance from one company of Phoumist troops. This effectively interdicted General Phoumi's last usable airfield of any size
in northern Laos.

On May 4, the Vietnamese captured a defense outpost only 2,500
yards east of Nam Tha. At 3 A.M. on May 6, a concerted mortar
barrage opened on Nam Tha. Using flares to coordinate their movements in the predawn darkness, four battalions opened an attack
on the lightly defended northwest quarter of the perimeter. Meanwhile, other forces swarmed down on the town from their trenches
on the heights to the east, southeast, and northeast, pouring a hail
of small-arms fire into the mud breastworks in which General
Bounleuth's defenders had been pinned during the three-month
siege.

First one sector caved in, then another. The twelve-man American White Star team was evacuated by helicopter at 7:30 A.M.
Six hours after the start of the Vietnamese attack, the 5,000 defenders were withdrawing in panic-stricken disorder.

A Phoumist picked up the diary from the lifeless body of the
Vietnamese soldier who had written of his platoon's New Year's
celebration and his implicit loyalty to Uncle Ho. On the next to
last page was the following entry:

OUR ARMY

We are the men who, years ago, vanquished the enemy at Dien
Bien [Phu], fighters who for years have struggled and overcome every
obstacle and every danger without discouragement.

On every front we are the first-line troops.
With every day that passes, we are proud of our Army.

The disorganized crowd of General Bounleuth's soldiers streamed southward to the Mekong, 100 miles away. Some did not stop there, but hired boatmen to take them across, where they were interned by the Thai Border Police.

The violation of the cease-fire by the Pathet Lao was patent. The rout of the Phoumist troops was complete. Expressing concern for Thailand's security, President Kennedy announced that, at the invitation of the Thai Government, he had ordered American ground and air units to take up positions at Udorn and elsewhere in northeastern Thailand. As he phrased it later:

> The dispatch of United States forces to Thailand was considered desirable because of recent attacks in Laos by Communist forces, and the subsequent movement of Communist military units toward the border of Thailand.[4]

A White Star patrol back up the trail to Nam Tha found only scattered bands of Pathet Lao guerrillas and no North Vietnamese. So far as the author was able to determine, there was no movement of "Communist military units" toward the Mekong. The significant thing about the Nam Tha debacle was that it was the first instance in which it was credible that Communist forces *were* intent on moving into the Mekong Valley. In the confusion surrounding the whereabouts of the Pathet Lao forces and the question of North Vietnamese and even Chinese presence in the area, the swift American reaction cheered the Thais. They were reassured of the validity of the American commitment to go to Thailand's aid in a crisis even without SEATO. It was safe to assume that the American reaction to a genuine Communist move would be similar to that of May, 1962. While this understanding between Washington and Bangkok stood, the Thai government might not turn to "neutralism," no matter what happened in the upcountry of Laos.

President Kennedy, discussing the reasons for the dispatch of troops to Thailand at his news conference on May 17, showed the Administration's uncertainty about Communist intentions when he gave the following answer:

> We're concerned about the breach of the cease-fire, the sign of deterioration in Laos, which brought Communist forces to the border of Thailand up in the—near the Mekong River section of—not too

[4] *Public Papers of the Presidents, 1962* (Washington: Government Printing Office, 1963), p. 396.

far from Nam Tha, and we did not know whether this was an indication of a general breach of the cease-fire which, of course, would immediately imperil Thailand.[5]

The New China News Agency, on May 12, actually distributed a report to the effect that Ban Houei Sai itself had been "liberated." The alleged liberation was subsequently forgotten by the Chinese. In Vientiane six months later, Souphanouvong revealed that a difference of opinion had existed within the NLHS Central Committee as to whether the Pathet Lao should press all the way to the Mekong after the collapse of Phoumist resistance. Presumably, this course of action was urged by Kaysone and the "Vietnamese faction."

In Vientiane, the Phoumists sent a telegram to Souvanna Phouma in Paris, informing him that they agreed that he could appoint his own followers to the key ministries of Defense and Interior. The Prince made plans to return to Laos immediately. So did Prince Boun Oum and General Phoumi, who were in the middle of a trip to a number of Asian capitals in quest of financial aid for the Royal Lao Government. They had received short shrift in Bangkok, as General Phoumi's conduct of the Nam Tha defense had left the Thai leaders thoroughly alarmed at the prospect that they might be dragged into a war in Laos with such allies. None of the other so-called anti-Communist governments in Asia, except South Korea, was willing to make any substantial offer of assistance to them.

Boun Oum's government had reacted to the cut-off of American cash grants by ordering the National Bank to place in circulation its considerable stock of printed banknotes. The result was that the dollar backing of the Lao currency dropped from 90 per cent in January to about 60 per cent in June, a change that produced a 20-per-cent increase in the price of food.

The Troika Under Way

The most important of a long series of princely summit meetings convened on the Plain of Jars at the beginning of June. Souvanna Phouma, borrowing a trick from Mendès-France, said that whether or not there was agreement, on June 15 he intended to return to Paris, where his daughter, Princess Moune, was to be married to a French nobleman.

Under this deadline, agreement was reached on June 11 on the division of powers in the coalition, which had been the main stum

[5] *Ibid.,* p. 403.

bling block. The three princes affixed their signatures to the document almost exactly thirteen months after the Ban Namone talks.

Souvanna Phouma was to be Prime Minister. General Phoumi retained one of two posts of Deputy Prime Minister, and Souphanouvong held the other. Boun Oum, who had intimated his desire to return to the relative peace of southern Laos, announced his retirement from politics.

Under the key Paragraph 5 of the agreement, either Deputy Prime Minister was empowered to veto a decision in Cabinet session. This arrangement, which soon became known as a troika, after the Russian three-horse sleigh, required unanimity among the three factions for important proposals.

Other portfolios were divided up among the three factions by mutual agreement. Phoumi Vongvichit joined Souphanouvong in the Cabinet, as he had done in 1957. He assumed the portfolio of Information, Propaganda, and Tourism. The Pathet Lao were also represented by two secretaries of state, who had lesser power than full ministers. Souvanna Phouma retained the key portfolio of Defense, and his associate Pheng Phongsavan became Interior Minister.

On June 23, Boun Oum formally presented his resignation, and the following day Souvanna Phouma, who had been officially charged by the King with forming the new government, took the oath of office in Vientiane. There still remained to be decided the role to be played by the National Assembly in relation to the new Cabinet, which was provisional and had the main task of working for reunification of the country. Reintegration of the separate administrations and armies of the three factions was the troika's main challenge. After that, it was expected that national elections would be organized to elect a new National Assembly and in turn permit the formation of a permanent Cabinet.

At the first meeting of the provisional troika Cabinet, Phoumi Vongvichit jarred the proceedings by unilaterally announcing to the press that it had been decided to protest the presence of American troops across the Mekong in Thailand. The troops were, in any case, shortly to be withdrawn, having served their function. But amid all the doubts and rude shocks, there was more good will than ill will at the launching of the venture in troika government; Souphanouvong showed up at the American Embassy on the Fourth of July to drink a toast to President Kennedy and the friendship of the American people.

Meanwhile in Geneva, Foreign Minister Quinim Pholsena had

presented to the Conference delegates a statement outlining Laos' neutrality. This was incorporated into a Declaration signed by the thirteen other foreign ministers present.

On July 23, after fourteen months of plenary and restricted sessions, all the foreign ministers signed the Protocol, which established a new *status quo* in the strife-ridden little kingdom.[6] Souvanna Phouma was present for the ceremony.

The signing of the agreements was interpreted differently in Moscow and Peking. The official Soviet reaction was that this conclusion of so many months' ardent bargaining proved once again that negotiations could settle even the thorniest international issues dividing the socialist world and the capitalist world. The Peking *People's Daily,* on the other hand, described them as "a major victory of the people of Laos in their struggle for independence, unity, peace, and neutrality of their homeland."

> The agreements reached at the international Geneva Conference on Laos show once again that international disputes can be settled through negotiations. But these agreements have by no means been won easily. The conference was convened only after a struggle. And these agreements were reached only after a serious and complex principled struggle.[7]

Few of the signatories harbored many illusions as to the durability of the settlement at Geneva. Looking ahead beyond the agreement, the Chinese foresaw the complete "liberation" of Laos, that is, the final elimination from Laos of all Western influence.

Chinese verbal support for the activities of North Vietnam's agents in Laos was to be repaid handsomely within the coming year in the ever-sharpening Sino-Soviet quarrel. Ho Chi Minh, for his part, had indebted himself to his powerful neighbor without having had occasion to see his neighbor's mettle tested. The impression that the Chinese had come out of the episode on top of the heap was strengthened by a revealing incident inside a closed session at Geneva. In the midst of a Chinese tirade against the activities of the United States in Laos, the acting chief American delegate, William H. Sullivan, arose to object strenuously. If China believed that the Americans and the Russians were going to fight China's wars for it in Laos, so that the Chinese could effect a costless takeover, Sullivan declared, then the Chinese were making a major miscalculation. At this, the Soviet delegate interrupted to suggest

[6] Texts of Declaration and Protocol in Appendix V.
[7] *People's Daily,* July 24, 1962.

that it was Sullivan who was committing the major miscalculation in underestimating the solidarity between the Soviet Union and the Chinese People's Republic.

It was a strange new world in which the ship of American diplomacy was navigating.

11.

The Second Coalition

The Laos civil war had become far more than that because each side had become closely identified with the interests of one or more foreign powers. It was the purpose of the 1961–62 Geneva Conference to neutralize Laos by providing the coalition government with certain international guarantees that would minimize foreign intervention.

The effective neutralization of Laos did not go against the interests of any of the Conference participants; nevertheless, there was considerable doubt all around that effective neutralization could be achieved. There was continuing bitter hostility in United States relations with Communist China and North Vietnam. There was rivalry between Communist China and the Soviet Union involving the question of the risks to be taken in expanding Communist control in the underdeveloped countries.

Communist China and North Vietnam were insistent on the theme of American "aggression" against Laos. The Chinese Communists pressed for an international condemnation of American actions in Laos, arguing that the conflict in Laos was a matter basically to be settled by the Lao themselves. In this context, the seating of the Pathet Lao faction at the Conference was a major victory for the Chinese Communists. The West, never able to produce convincing proof of either Chinese Communist or North Vietnamese intervention in Laos, was compelled to match accusation for accusation. The West sought the adoption of effective controls on future intervention, an effort that met stiff opposition and was not altogether successful.

Thus, the Declaration and Protocol on the Neutrality of Laos, signed in Geneva on July 23, 1962, was viewed negatively by the

United States and positively by North Vietnam and Communist China. For all the big powers, the agreement was more a face-saving device to freeze the *status quo* than a foundation for stability in the area. For the North Vietnamese, it was a device for hamstringing American policy in Southeast Asia and a useful precedent for an agreement to freeze the *status quo* in South Vietnam. Ho judged that the Declaration and Protocol on the Neutrality of Laos would not constitute a serious obstacle to pursuit of his long-term objectives in Indochina.

The Geneva Agreements of 1962

The 1954 Conference had produced a cease-fire agreement between the commander of the French Union forces, including Lao Territorial units, and the commander of the Viet Minh forces, acting on behalf of the Pathet Lao. In addition, the Conference had produced two unilateral declarations by the Royal Lao Government promising that Laos would follow a strictly neutral course in foreign affairs, and a declaration binding all the participants to respect this neutral course.

The 1962 documents, signed by all the Conference participants, pledged the signatories not to impair the sovereignty, independence, neutrality, unity, or territorial integrity of Laos. They agreed to refrain from interfering in the internal affairs of the Kingdom. They would not attach political strings to aid to the coalition government. They would not entice Laos into any military alliance, specifically SEATO, or establish military bases on Lao territory. They would not introduce foreign troops or military personnel into Laos. And within seventy-five days, they would withdraw those present under the guise of advisers and technicians.

In view of the specificness of the 1962 documents, and of the commitments made by the participants in the second Conference, it might appear at first sight that the 1962 agreement held out a better prospect of removing Laos from the currents of big-power manipulation and neighborly spoliation than had the 1954 agreement. As we have seen, the 1954 agreement had not been observed in its spirit by either Communists or non-Communists.

Unfortunately, the second agreement was no more effective than the first, partly because the ICC's mandate had been diluted at the insistence of the Communist powers, and partly because the ICC was now dealing with a coalition of three separate factions, each of which possessed its own territorial administration and armed forces. The 1962 provisions for neutralizing Laos were full of loopholes.

As in 1954, the ICC, again composed of India, Canada, and Poland, was entrusted with supervising the implementation of the provisions. Its work, however, could be sabotaged at the whim of either the Communists or the non-Communists.

Unlike 1954, there was no provision for stationing fixed ICC inspection teams in the countryside to keep track of foreign troops and arms, although the Western delegates had fought hard to have such a provision included in the Protocol. A Franco-American proposal would have allowed the ICC to set up both fixed and mobile inspection teams with "free and unrestricted access" to all parts of Laos and "full freedom to inspect, at any time, all aerodromes, installations or establishments and all units, organizations and activities which are or might be of a military nature." In contrast, a Soviet draft would have had the ICC, "in agreement with the Government of Laos, set up suitable groups" to control the withdrawal of foreign military personnel, but made no mention of subsequent introductions of foreign soldiers.

Since the ICC inspection teams set up in 1954 had been effectively blocked by Pathet Lao subversion, the Protocol's failure to provide for fixed teams did not appear to be an irretrievable loss for the West. The Protocol did specify that ICC teams could be dispatched by helicopter for a "length of stay . . . determined in relation to the requirements of the particular investigation."

A concerted Western effort eliminated the word "agreement" to designate the relationship between the ICC and the Lao government. It was argued that "agreement" might be interpreted to mean that the ICC could not take any step without government permission. In the final version, the Protocol stated that theICC was to act with the "concurrence" of the government. Since the troika Cabinet gave the Pathet Lao an effective veto over government decisions, the Communists still could obstruct ICC operations. However, some legalists pointed out that the clauses were so worded as to make it appear that the Lao government had given its "concurrence" when it signed the Protocol.

The ICC was further weakened by limitations on its authority to make decisions. Once the ICC, on Royal Government request or concurrence, had undertaken an investigation, questions relating to initiating and carrying it out could be adopted by majority vote of the Commission. But the conclusions and recommendations resulting from such an investigation had to be adopted unanimously.

Unanimous ICC decisions were also required on questions relating to violations of the cease-fire or of provisions for withdrawal of foreign troops or prohibition of foreign troops, military personnel, and armaments. Under the 1954 agreements, the ICC had needed only a majority vote in making any recommendation except those concerning violations believed to threaten a resumption of hostilities between the French and the Viet Minh (or Pathet Lao).

These difficulties were somewhat mitigated by the Protocol's creating a closer liaison between the ICC and the Co-Chairmen than had been provided in 1954. The ICC was charged with immediately reporting to the Co-Chairmen any Protocol violations, in addition to preparing its periodic reports on the general situation.

Diplomatic Implications of Neutrality

In keeping with the international nature of its sponsorship, the newly established troika government in Vientiane declared that it was prepared to exchange diplomatic representation with all friendly countries. In Souvanna Phouma's view, this meant that if both Communist China and Nationalist China wished to maintain embassies in Vientiane, they would be free to do so. The same applied to both North Vietnam and South Vietnam. However, each of the rival Chinese governments felt that maintaining its ambassador accredited to a state to which its rival was likewise accredited would be tantamount to acknowledging that there were two Chinas, one governed from Peking and the other from Taipei. Therefore, each would refuse to accept the existence of two Chinese embassies in Vientiane. The two rival Vietnamese governments (which had followed a slightly modified version of the Chinese tactic, both maintaining consulates in India, for instance), refused to permit the establishment of dual diplomatic representation in Vientiane at ambassadorial level, and the South Vietnamese Ambassador withdrew.

Exactly a month before the 1962 Geneva agreement was signed, Peking had announced, on June 23, that it had arranged with Souvanna Phouma to exchange ambassadors following installation of the coalition. Not surprisingly, Liu Chun, the head of Communist China's cultural and economic mission on the Plain of Jars, an expert on ethnic-minority questions, was named Peking's first ambassador to Vientiane.

In August, when Souvanna Phouma returned from his trip to Geneva and Washington, where he conferred with President Kennedy, the presence in Vientiane of the Communist Chinese Liu Chun and of Dr. Han Lih-wu, long the Nationalist Chinese Ambassador to Thailand and accredited to Laos since the days of the Boun Oum government, created a minor diplomatic crisis. Liu

Chun, although he had not yet presented his credentials to King Savang Vatthana, appeared at the airport to greet the returning Prime Minister. Over the protests of a Lao protocol officer, Liu Chun joined the diplomatic queue at the side of the Soviet Ambassador. When Souvanna Phouma, moving slowly up the line and shaking hands, approached Dr. Han of Nationalist China, Liu Chun thrust himself forward between the two, claiming loudly that he, and not Dr. Han, was the representative of the 650 million Chinese. Souvanna Phouma took this calmly, but the Phoumist security officer at the airport refused to allow Liu Chun to drive back into the town flying his yellow-starred red flag, and a heated two-hour dispute ensued. Prince Souphanouvong intervened to suggest that the Communist Chinese ambassador remove the flag for the sake of expediency. Eventually Souvanna Phouma prohibited the flying of the flag until Liu Chun had presented his credentials, but allowed him to proceed home with his flag flying.

Subsequently Taipei announced that it was severing relations with Laos. South Vietnam followed a similar course after the arrival in Vientiane of the new North Vietnamese Ambassador, Le Van Hien, a minister in Ho Chi Minh's original 1945 government.

Hanoi hailed the establishment of its embassy in Vientiane as a great triumph for North Vietnamese diplomacy. Its press and radio told the North Vietnamese that this was a hard-earned victory, coming after eight years of imperialist machinations had frustrated their efforts to gain representation in the neighboring kingdom.

As time went on, the diplomacy of both Peking and Hanoi increasingly took on the aspects of a double game. While their ambassadors maintained correct relations with Souvanna Phouma in the Lao capital, their military advisers played a more ominous role at Khang Khay, the Pathet Lao headquarters. These agents enjoyed a complete monopoly, since there were no Russians with the Pathet Lao.

Souvanna Phouma established diplomatic relations with a number of East European countries, including Czechoslovakia and Yugoslavia. In this, he was following the example of Prince Sihanouk, who believed that having as many embassies as possible in his capital furthered his country's neutrality.

The restored confidence between Souvanna Phouma and the United States was manifest after he had had a series of meetings with President Kennedy and the new men in the State Department. When asked later how he viewed American intentions, the Prince replied with a wave of his arm, "Oh, with these people, it's entirely different."

Much of the Prince's optimism could be attributed to the new American Ambassador who had reached Vientiane in July. Leonard Unger, a forty-four-year-old career diplomat, had spent the previous four years in Bangkok, part of the time as deputy chief of mission, and could speak enough Thai to make a speech understood by the Lao. Unger possessed another advantage: His superior officer in Washington—Averell Harriman—was receptive to his ideas. Unger's predecessor had had to manage without this advantage.

The economic situation facing Souvanna Phouma was not good. The spread between the official kip rate of 80 to the dollar and the black-market rate was steadily growing. At the end of 1961, the black-market rate stood at 120 to the dollar. Then, following the cut-off of U.S. cash grants, Boun Oum placed in circulation large quantities of paper money not backed by dollar deposits in the United States. By the summer of 1963, the progressive reduction in dollar backing of the kip notes in circulation (which had increased in the same period from 2.7 billion kip to 6.1 billion kip) had pushed the black-market rate to 360 to the dollar.

Inflation hit particularly hard in Vientiane and the other Mekong Valley towns, which were dependent upon Thailand for rice and vegetables. In Vientiane, the consumer price index for a Lao family rose from 115 (with 1959 representing a base of 100) in 1961, to 268 in mid-1963. The countryside, which lived largely by a barter economy and in isolation from the Mekong Valley towns, was not affected by the inflation. The fighting was only an indirect cause of the inflation in that it led to uncertainty about continued American backing for the currency of the Royal Government.

On January 1, 1964, the coalition government, compelled to effect the first devaluation since 1958, pegged the kip at 240 to the dollar. A smooth transition to the new official value was made possible by public assurances from the United States, Britain, France, and Australia of their backing for a $7.8-million stabilization fund (the United States provided $4.0 million, Britain $1.7 million, France $1.7 million, and Australia $0.4 million) separate from the month-to-month budget support, which the United States promised to continue.

The extent of the government's deficit can be judged from the figures presented by Souvanna Phouma in the autumn of 1963, when conditions had returned to relatively average norms, for the fiscal year 1964. Expenditures were estimated at 6.386 billion kip (of which 3.469 billion kip were for military expenditures and 2.917 billion kip for civilian), and receipts at only 1.480 billion kip. The difference represented the amount of foreign aid on which Laos was dependent for its continued day-to-day existence.

The deficit was met by the continuation of the U.S. budget-support program. However, U.S. cash-grant aid, which had been in effect since the 1958 monetary reform, was scrapped. A commercial import program was inaugurated, designed to bring into Laos strictly controlled types and quantities of hard goods to soak up the paper money circulated by salaries. This program was to provide budget support of roughly $10 million per year. Mindful of the corruption under the previous import program, the United States tied the new program to a strict licensing system, coupled with enforced customs checks on goods entering the country. But these safeguards produced a mass of red tape that subjected imports to considerable delays. In a period of continuing inflation, such a licensing system was unworkable, especially since even the closest watch on the long river border could not prevent some re-exporting of goods brought in. The new system was abandoned and another devised.

The economic situation was complicated by the peculiar fact that the country had two sets of currency in circulation. There was, first of all, the Vientiane-issued kip-note currency, which was backed, in varying degrees, by the dollar. There was also a whole series of kip currency with no hard-currency backing that Souvanna Phouma's regime in Khang Khay had paid out to administration officials and troops on the Plain of Jars. These notes, rough imitations of the Vientiane notes printed by the American Banknote Company and the English firm of Thomas De La Rue, Ltd., had been printed in Czechoslovakia. The government had the problem of removing from circulation these notes, whose value on the free market was a good deal less than the Vientiane notes.

The coalition had to decide what to do about the aid agreements entered into with foreign governments by the two separate regimes of Souvanna Phouma at Khang Khay and Boun Oum at Vientiane. This was one of the first matters to be discussed in the Cabinet meetings. It was decided to honor all previous aid agreements that were not prohibited by the Geneva Protocol because of their military nature. The decision was announced by Souphanouvong on August 6: "The coalition Government will continue to maintain commitments with the Soviet Union, China, and North Vietnam, as it will with the United States."

The Chinese were pushing ahead with construction of roads linking Yünnan Province with Phong Saly and Nam Tha. The first indication that the Chinese had offered to construct the roads had come during Souvanna Phouma's visit to Peking in April, 1961, and actual work had begun late that year. Later, details of this vast construction project, involving several thousand Chinese laborers, were given by a New China News Agency dispatch from Peking on January 13, 1962.

The North Vietnamese had concluded a number of similar assistance agreements with Souvanna Phouma during his tenure as Prime Minister on the Plain of Jars. Besides those already referred to, these included: an agreement for aid during 1962 (signed on December 15, 1961); a protocol for reconstruction and construction of roads over the Annamite Mountains; a protocol on general conditions for delivery of goods; a protocol on general conditions of North Vietnamese "technical specialists" in Laos; a protocol on general conditions of Lao students and trainees in North Vietnam (all signed on March 10, 1962); and a protocol on aid for public health in 1962 (signed on June 9, 1962).

The official Lao Presse news agency reported on December 10, 1962, the completion of construction and repair work on four roads over the Annamite Mountains: one over the historic northern passage from the Dien Bien Phu valley as far as Sop Nao; one from the Vietnam border to Sam Neua town; one from the pass at Nape to the town of Kam Keut; and the fourth from the Mu Gia Pass to Nhommarath. The report made no mention of Route Nationale 7, which linked the Plain of Jars and the Vietnamese seaport of Vinh and which American air reconnaissance showed had also been repaired for heavy-duty traffic by the end of 1962. "The Vietnamese technicians and laborers who have been working on the repair of these roads are returning and will continue to return until they are all back in Vietnam," the agency reported.

These agreements were confirmed by dispatching General Phoumi to Peking and Hanoi, in his capacity as Finance Minister of the coalition, to countersign the documents previously signed by Souvanna Phouma. The road construction provided for in these agreements was so obviously of permanent strategic advantage to China and North Vietnam that it raises the question of why the General consented to validate these accords. Actually, he had little choice in the matter; he could not afford to scrap the principle of honoring previous bilateral agreements. Agreements signed by the Boun Oum government, one in particular, were of equal strategic significance to his own faction.

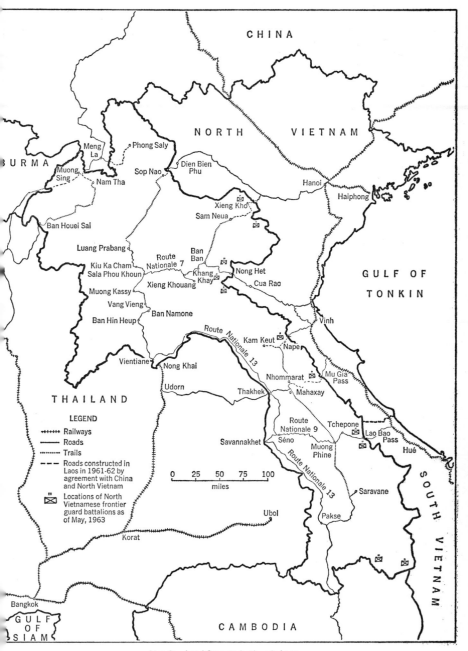

CHINA

NORTH   VIETNAM

BURMA

Meng
La   Phong Saly
Muong
Sing   Nam Tha   Sop Nao   Dien Bien
Phu   Hanoi

Ban Houei Sai   Haiphong

Xieng Kho

Sam Neua   GULF OF

Luang Prabang   Ban
Ban   TONKIN
Kiu Ka Cham   Route
Sala Phou Khoun   Nationale 7   Khang   Nong Het
Xieng Khouang   Khay
Muong Kassy   Cua Rao

Vang Vieng
Ban Hin Heup   Ban Namone

Route Nationale 13   Kam Keut
Nape   Vinh

Vientiane
Nong Khai   Nhommarat   Mu Gia
Pass
Udorn   Thakhek   Mahaxay

THAILAND

LEGEND   Route   Tchepone
Nationale 9   Lao Bao
+++++ Railways   Pass
───── Roads   Savannakhet   Séno   Muong   Hué
·········· Trails   Phine
── ── Roads constructed in
Laos in 1961-62 by   Route Nationale 13
agreement with China
and North Vietnam   Saravane
Locations of North
Vietnamese frontier
guard battalions as
of May, 1963   Ubol

0   25   50   75   100   Pakse
miles

Korat   SOUTH VIETNAM

Bangkok
GULF
OF
SIAM   CAMBODIA

Map 3.   Land Communications in Laos

(The General, however, reportedly balked at countersigning additional agreements that would have permitted free trade across the Laos-North Vietnam border, thus allowing the North Vietnamese to send agents across the border at their pleasure, and the arming of North Vietnamese convoys into Laos against attacks by Meo guerrillas.)

The coalition government also received promises of aid for economic development from other quarters. The Soviet Union proposed to build a new hospital in Vientiane and a 50-kilowatt radio transmitting station to supplement the existing American-supplied 5-kilowatt station. France set about installing a modern telephone system in Vientiane. Japan sent technicians to supervise construction of a water-distribution system in the capital.

The advent of the first Communist-bloc aid in Vientiane led to the usual unanticipated results. Souvanna Phouma agreed to furnish fuel for the Soviet-built transport planes that the Soviets placed at his disposal, and housing for the Russian pilots who were training the Lao to fly the planes (there was no room for the Russians at the Soviet embassy). Since the money for the petroleum supplies and the rent for the house occupied by the Russians came from the Lao government budget, this meant that in effect the United States was paying to house Russians and fuel Russian planes.

Floating Partition

The single most important reality of the troika coalition period was that the three separate factions continued to control the administration and military security of their own areas. These areas were not fixed. There were no front lines. Patrols of Phoumist soldiers often brushed with Pathet Lao patrols, and these brushes meant continued skirmishing in the countryside. A village in Pathet Lao hands one week might well be occupied the following week by Phoumist troops, whose stay was bound to be just as brief.

The *de facto* partition of the kingdom gave rise to seemingly insoluble differences. There was, for instance, the matter of authorizing armed guards from each faction to enter Vientiane to ensure the security of their political leaders. Since the days of the Boun Oum government, law and order in Vientiane had been preserved by the National Police Force of 3,000 men and an independent paramilitary organization known as the Department of National Coordination, which possessed its own force of 1,800 men organized into three battalions. When the coalition was formed, the centrists insisted on bringing back to Vientiane a certain number of their own security forces, and the Pathet Lao demanded an equal force of their own that would have immunity to arrest and reprisal.

Allocating the strength for each faction required considerable time and bargaining. General Phoumi assured Souvanna Phouma of the good behavior of the men of the Department of National Co-ordination (which also had responsibility for checking immigration papers). The Pathet Lao ministers were permitted a guard force of 100 men, who settled down in a row of houses near the American Embassy compound, where, encouraged by Souphanouvong, they began planting gardens and growing their own vegetables.

The task of maintaining liaison with the ICC was initially farmed out to a tripartite cease-fire commission, but it became apparent that this body, which operated on the same troika principle as the Cabinet, could reach no major decisions. Soon, all decision-making was back in the hands of the Cabinet, and the ICC tended to deal more and more with Souvanna Phouma himself.

The ICC spurred the three factions to take steps toward unifying the administration and the armies. Although agreement in principle was reached on the three factions' contributions to a unified army, the shooting incidents in the countryside, where the cease-fire was frayed in the extreme, gave a truer impression of the state of affairs. The question of preparing general elections for a new National Assembly had not even been broached.

In the *de facto* partition, General Phoumi's trump card was the continued legality of Air America, whose airlift permitted thousands of Meo tribesmen to remain outside the clutches of the Pathet Lao. By the summer of 1963, this airlift was dropping forty tons of supplies a day in flights all over Laos, including Pathet Lao-controlled areas. Air America's contract was with the American economic-aid mission in Vientiane. The mission, in turn, operated under an agreement with the Royal Government.

The Pathet Lao continually accused the United States of intervention in Laos and of obstructing the implementation of the Geneva Protocol, and charged the Phoumist faction with violating the cease-fire. At a meeting in Sam Neua Province of the NLHS Central Committee in the last week of September, Kaysone Phomvihan demanded the withdrawal from Laos of both the American economic-aid mission and the U.S. Information Service, which he claimed were a cover for military advisers in civilian clothes. His demand did not elicit any action, however, from the Soviet government, Co-Chairman of the Geneva Conference. The reason was that the

Soviets were finding their own involvement in Laos a source of increasing embarrassment.

In the first week of October, Souvanna Phouma sent identical letters to Soviet Ambassador Afanasseyev and American Ambassador Unger asking for logistical support in flying supplies to isolated pockets of centrist troops, who heretofore had received all their supplies by means of the Soviet airlift. This of course referred to Kong Le's troops.

The Prime Minister's request surprised Western observers, who had assumed that the arrangements between Kong Le and his Pathet Lao counterparts for sharing airlifted supplies had been working smoothly. For many months, Kong Le's troops had been armed exclusively with Soviet-type weapons and depended on resupply from Communist-bloc stocks to keep in combat preparedness.

Soon there were other hints of trouble in the Kong Le–Pathet Lao alliance. Reports were received of dissatisfaction among Kong Le's soldiers, who claimed they were running short of food and clothing. In some cases, it was reported, the discontent had been stimulated by Pathet Lao agents who had infiltrated the centrist army during its vigorous recruiting on the Plain of Jars. Finally, Kong Le discovered signs of treachery by his Pathet Lao allies: Two centrist soldiers stationed at the quartermaster depot in Vinh, North Vietnam, to supervise distribution of Communist-bloc supplies to the centrist and Pathet Lao forces in Laos had been subverted by the North Vietnamese and had falsified records to divert to the Pathet Lao thousands of tons of ammunition, parachutes, and other matériel earmarked for Kong Le. In a rage, Kong Le ordered the two back to the Plain of Jars and had them placed under arrest. The Soviet Union, which had been the source of most of the matériel, knew nothing of the misallocation of supplies until the process had been going on for some time.

When Souvanna Phouma appealed for help in getting badly needed supplies to his troops on the Plain of Jars, the Soviet Embassy immediately promised him the use of transport planes that had been flying the airlift from Hanoi to the Plain of Jars. The North Vietnamese, for reasons of their own, backed the Pathet Lao policy of subverting Kong Le's centrist troops. This policy depended on isolation of the centrists. Therefore, the promised Soviet aircraft did not show up in Vientiane for several weeks.

The American Embassy realized that subversion of Kong Le's forces would reduce the centrist faction to impotence (Souvanna Phouma had little enough backing in the country as it was, without losing his army on the Plain of Jars) and a return to the disastrous bipolar situation of the previous two years. Taking into calculation the dilemma in which the Soviets had been placed by their contradictory needs to support Souvanna Phouma and to retain the good will of the North Vietnamese, and the paramount American interest in preserving the three-sided coalition, Unger immediately authorized Air America aircraft to ship supplies to Kong Le in accordance with Souvanna Phouma's request.

The Pathet Lao, who still retained their headquarters on the Plain of Jars together with Kong Le, had reason to be displeased by the abrupt termination of the Soviet airlift, revealed by General Singkapo Chounlamany in an interview on November 6.[1] They had even more reason to be displeased by the new role of Air America, which had upset their calculations. While their agents commandeered a portion of the blankets and medicines flown to Kong Le by Air America, their military spokesmen claimed the airlift was illegal and threatened to shoot down the Air America aircraft with the antiaircraft batteries that ringed the Plain. By this time, however, the North Vietnamese had completed repair work on Route Nationale 7 and could truck military supplies overland to the Pathet Lao. Souvanna Phouma, for the time being, protested against neither the use of the North Vietnam road for import of military supplies nor the Pathet Lao threat to fire on airlift planes, believing that such protests might well lead to the complete breakdown of the coalition, a development he wished to avoid at all costs.

Prisoners captured by each side in the fighting in 1961 and 1962 were exchanged within the time limit set by the Geneva Protocol. The Pathet Lao turned this exchange to their advantage by unloading at Vientiane airport three Vietnamese whom they claimed had infiltrated into Laos from South Vietnam and been captured near Tchepone. The trio were in an unhappy position because the South Vietnamese Embassy refused to have anything to do with them, claiming that they were North Vietnamese agents in disguise. Even if they were from the South, intense "re-education" during their captivity had obviously ended their usefulness to Saigon.

Stepped-Up Commitments

Since their Party Congress in September, 1960, the Vietnamese Communists, using guerrilla pressure, had been making slow but steady progress toward reunifying their country by overthrowing the Saigon regime of President Ngo Dinh Diem. The insurgency in

[1] With Ray Herndon of United Press International.

the South, fed by widespread popular resentment against a narrow and dictatorial government backed by the United States (i.e., foreigners), was given new impetus.

Ho Chi Minh's strategy in the South was following closely the pattern set by the Viet Minh in the Indochina War and by Ho's use of the Pathet Lao to achieve his long-term objectives in Laos. He realized that, given sufficient international concern over the explosiveness of the situation in South Vietnam, a "neutralist" government might take power in Saigon, either by a coup, as in Laos, or by a cease-fire and an international conference. Such a conference would open up the prospect of resumption of contacts between the two halves of the country, including trade that would give the North access once again to the rich rice surpluses of the Mekong Delta.

The United States realized the dangers of an unsuccessful involvement in the South Vietnam fighting. Coming on the heels of the experience in Laos, a withdrawal of the American presence in South Vietnam under guerrilla pressure would just about put the seal of infallibility on General Giap's method of "people's war." The United States was just becoming aware of the implications of this type of conflict, in an age where nuclear weapons were canceled out as suicidal, for the underdeveloped nations of Asia, Africa, and Latin America. In April, 1961, Truong Chinh, an important member of the Central Committee of the Lao Dong Party, wrote in the Hanoi journal *Hoc Tap* (*Studies*) that "socialist North Vietnam is providing good support for the South Vietnamese revolution, and is serving as a strong base for the struggle for reunification." In May, President Kennedy dispatched Vice President Lyndon B. Johnson to Saigon to reassure Diem that withdrawal of American support from the Phoumists in Laos did not imply immediate American withdrawal of support from his own regime.

The following month, an American mission headed by Dr. Eugene Staley visited South Vietnam. Its members inspected the situation on the ground and gathered information for a report to the President. They discovered that the American MAAG detachments that had been training the South Vietnamese army since 1955 had rarely ventured outside the large towns where their training camps were located and knew virtually nothing of the extent of the insurgents' hold on the countryside.

In many cases, the Diem government had deliberately sought to keep the Americans ignorant of the deterioration of its authority. By the end of 1961, the insurgents were reported to have drawn up plans to set up a liberated area in the highlands near the Laos border, and to have created a shadow administration over all South Vietnam on the village level.

Finally, the crisis provoked in May, 1963, by the Diem regime's repressions against Buddhist priests revealed its isolation from the country at large. But the full extent to which the Americans had been deceived about the gravity of the situation did not become apparent until Diem was overthrown in a military *coup d'état* on November 1 of that year.

The situation had so deteriorated that the insurgents no longer depended upon the funneling of supplies from North Vietnam along the Ho Chi Minh Trail in Laos (although the use of this network of trails would again become essential in case of an escalation of the commitment of North Vietnamese men and material in South Vietnam). The estimate that the rebellion against the Saigon government had reached the "take-off point" explains North Vietnam's readiness to agree to negotiate for a neutralized Laos at Geneva in the spring of 1961.

At about the time of the Staley mission, Hanoi appears to have made a reappraisal of U.S. intentions and of its own prospects for "liberating" South Vietnam. June, 1961, saw the first (unsuccessful) U.S.-sponsored guerrilla raids from South Vietnam into the north. The new outburst of American activity in South Vietnam accorded with the North Vietnamese leaders' doctrine that the imperialists grow more desperate as the liberation struggle approaches its climax. American officers were now leading South Vietnamese troops into combat, and some were being killed. American pilots were flying combat missions in planes bearing the markings of the South Vietnamese air force. American helicopters piloted by American crews were ferrying troops into battle.

However, the use of massed formations of helicopters in South Vietnam threw the Viet Cong off balance and held them off balance during the first half of 1962 before they developed successful defensive tactics (unlike the Pathet Lao, the Viet Cong possessed no anti-aircraft guns). The American pressure on the Phoumists in Laos during these six months to agree to a coalition may have been regarded by Hanoi as a cover for a planned action against North Vietnam from both South Vietnam and the Meo-held areas of Laos. Taking into account the arrival of American troops in Thailand in May, 1962, in reaction to the Phoumist debacle at Nam Tha, Hanoi very probably concluded that North Vietnam was being threatened by hostile action, and possibly by full-scale invasion. Hanoi's nervousness at this prospect may well be imagined, given the state of tension between Peking and Moscow, which existed already, and Moscow's apparent reluctance to be drawn into an Asian adventure leading to a confrontation with the United States.

During the first week in August, 1962, photographic reconnaissance flights by RF-101 Voodoo jets, which had been making regular aerial surveillance of northern Laos in connection with contingency planning related to the deployment of American troops in Thailand, revealed a convoy of several hundred vehicles moving over the newly improved Route Nationale 7 from North Vietnam into Laos. Close inspection of the photographs (which were so sharp that the license plates on the trucks were legible) showed that the convoy, consisting of two main sections and a third smaller section, contained truckloads of North Vietnamese troops, tanks, armored cars, and a small number of towed artillery pieces. The force moved overland into Pathet Lao encampments on the Plain of Jars, where they constructed large camouflaged tank parks, seemingly indicating the arrival of further forces. (American aerial reconnaissance continued. On August 13, 1962, one of these RF-101 aircraft was hit by antiaircraft fire while over the Plain of Jars. Although badly damaged, the plane managed to return to its base at Bangkok. The existence of the aerial reconnaissance was made public by the State Department on May 21, 1964.)

These North Vietnamese combat troops were quite distinct from the technical experts and cadres that North Vietnam had maintained in Laos since the end of 1960, and by 1962 were fully integrated into Pathet Lao units as instructors and stiffeners. In the ensuing weeks, the new arrivals split up into battalion strength and moved southward to take up stationary positions along the entire length of the Laos-Vietnam border. Their presence there was screened by Pathet Lao control of the contiguous areas, and by the continued refusal of the Pathet Lao to permit officials on mission from Vientiane to enter these areas.

Just inside Laos, on the crests of the passes across the mountains, the North Vietnamese sat quietly. It is many times more difficult to defend a downward-sloping road than it is to hold the crown of a mountain pass. By the end of August, there were an estimated 10,000 North Vietnamese military personnel in Laos, including both the frontier-guard troops and the cadres integrated into the Pathet Lao units.

The stepping up of commitments in South Vietnam and Laos in 1961 and 1962 by the Americans and the North Vietnamese had complicated the working of the neutralization formula codified at Geneva in July, 1962. In very much the same way, the 1954 neutralization attempt had been corrupted by North Vietnam's increased commitment in South Vietnam after 1958. The link between Vietnam and Laos was clear.

The Vietnamese Who Weren't

The United States had set the tone for compliance with the Geneva Protocol provisions relating to withdrawal of foreign troops by starting as early as June 23 to pull out the White Star teams of military advisers who had been working with the Meo since 1961. Thereafter, the number of American military advisers in Laos, which had reached a peak of about 800 men, steadily decreased. The number of MAAG personnel processed at exit points by the ICC between the signing of the Protocol on July 23 and the October 7 deadline was 666. One of the last to leave, MAAG Commander Major General Reuben H. Tucker, referred to the situation in Laos as "a can of worms." Not a single American military man was left in Laos in uniform, except for the Embassy's military attaché and his small staff.

This strict compliance with the Geneva Protocol must have dumfounded the North Vietnamese. The American behavior was inexplicable, if not downright unimperialist.

Intelligence reports from the tightly sealed border areas during September indicated that here and there a few hundred troops had been pulled back into North Vietnam. As a *pro forma* gesture, Hanoi agreed to public withdrawal of a token number of North Vietnamese "advisers" and "technicians" whose presence in Laos had never before been officially admitted. The ICC was permitted to establish inspection teams at the Plain of Jars and at the village of Nom Ping in Khammouane Province, to check out the withdrawing personnel. Following an initial departure of five officers and twelve noncoms, another planeload of eight officers, five noncoms, and five "experts" left the Plain of Jars airfield for Hanoi on September 29 aboard an Ilyushin transport. On October 23, the ICC recorded the departure from Nom Ping of five men dressed in green fatigues without caps or insignia of rank. Their leader made a brief speech of farewell for the benefit of some 150 inhabitants of the surrounding region who had come to see them off. Officials of the Pathet Lao-appointed administration in the region thanked the five Vietnamese for their selfless services rendered to Laos during the past year. Then five village girls stepped forward and handed each of them a gift of pillows and bed sheets, whereupon the Vietnamese climbed aboard their single-engine Russian biplane and took off for Hanoi.

On October 7, the official North Vietnamese news agency carried this report: "The Vietnamese military personnel which were previously sent to Laos at the request of the Royal Lao Government have all been withdrawn from Laos." No such request had ever been made.

That same evening in Vientiane, Souvanna Phouma, puffing on his pipe and exuding optimism at a party in honor of his birthday, told his guests that he had reason to believe that the countries that had sent troops into Laos "will ensure with diligence that the last stragglers will leave with a minimum possible delay."[2]

The State Department estimated that "several thousand" Vietnamese troops had left Laos by the deadline, but this left several other thousands still within the country. U.S.S.R. Deputy Foreign Minister Georgi Pushkin, who had handled most of the Soviet negotiations at Geneva, had told State Department officials privately that the North Vietnamese troops would merely "fade into the jungle."[3]

This is, in effect, what happened. On November 10, when London released the text of the ICC's report on compliance with the troop-withdrawal provisions, a Foreign Office spokesman commented: "We know that at the time of the Laos cease-fire there were about 10,000 North Vietnamese troops in Laos. A number of those chose to withdraw secretly and only forty passed through the ICC check points. It is not at all clear what happened to the remainder and how many may have remained."

There was considerable debate in American diplomatic circles over whether to file a protest on the violation of the troop-withdrawal provision of the Geneva Protocol. Those who favored doing so argued that failure to act would set a dangerous precedent for violation of the provisions dealing with arms shipments and use of Lao territory for aggressive purposes. The opposing argument was that filing a protest would quite possibly dash any hopes of political unification of the country, which was far more important than checking out Vietnamese troops. Besides, the United States had the means of keeping track of these troops and thus determining whether they intended to follow up with any aggressive action against the Mekong Valley. Either the Communist signatories were

---

[2] Reuter dispatch, Vientiane, October 7, 1962.

[3] United Press International dispatch, Washington, October 4, 1962.

willing to support the tacit "no conquest" understanding among the Geneva signatories, in which case it was senseless to force a split over the first violation, or else they had no interest in such an understanding, in which case sending the ICC into the jungle to look for Vietnamese foot soldiers would prove nothing that was not already known, and the United States had better start thinking about an entirely different approach to the problem.

Despite ICC assurances that it was fully aware of the charges and countercharges about the presence of troops and that if and when it had reasonable evidence of a violation, it would "immediately take appropriate action about it as laid down in the Geneva Protocol," a combination of Pathet Lao secretiveness and Polish obstruction was to prevent the ICC from registering any formal violation of the provisions for troop withdrawals. The United States, while continuing to draw attention to the North Vietnamese presence and to pressure the ICC to undertake field investigations, did not make the issue a *casus belli*. The acceptance of the presence of these forces was part of the price to be paid for neutralizing Laos without committing American troops.

Aware of the extreme difficulties that confronted his government, Souvanna Phouma sought, and obtained, a vote of full powers from the National Assembly when it met in October, three and a half months after formation of the coalition. This allowed him to make decisions without recourse to votes of confidence. As the Assembly was strongly anti-Communist in composition (the deputies had been chosen in the rigged elections of 1960, and their mandate did not expire until 1965), the vote would seem at first glance to have been a matter of satisfaction to the Pathet Lao. However, they interpreted Souvanna Phouma's move to mean that he sought decision-making authority that would allow him to bypass consultations with the other two factions, as called for in the troika principle of the Plain of Jars agreement of June 11, 1962, a maneuver that they correctly judged would be a blow to their influence.

Souvanna Phouma, as later events were to show, did not believe he was invalidating the troika principle. He was firm in his refusal to be prevented from governing by Pathet Lao obstructionism. Nonetheless, he would take no action to provoke them.

(A Constitutional amendment had extended the deputies' term of office from four years to five years. On July 9, 1964, a government source in Vientiane reported that the Cabinet had decided to proceed with general elections in February, 1965.)

Treachery on the Plain of Jars

The North Vietnamese may well have begun asking themselves at this point what they had gained by the second conference at Geneva that they could not have gained by pushing the Pathet Lao forward in the nibbling process that had preceded the cease-fire. They had allowed themselves to be persuaded by Khrushchev to settle for something less than the complete exclusion of the Americans from Laos, much as in 1954 they had deferred to Molotov's desire to liquidate the Indochina question and had left the southern half of their country in the hands of the French-supported Bao Dai puppet government. Now, the Americans had been invited to join in support of the Souvanna Phouma government, and the neutralization that the North Vietnamese had hoped would work to their advantage was working against them. If these were the fruits of the second Geneva Conference, they were bitter indeed. Their efforts to place pressure on Kong Le's forces by pinching off his supplies had been frustrated by the Americans. And in the ICC, the Indian chairman was no longer favorably disposed toward the Pathet Lao, as he had been before 1958; that radical reversal could be chalked up to the Chinese attack in the Himalayas.

As a result of consolidation of positions by all factions during the second half of 1962, the military dispositions on the Plain looked like the interlocked pieces of a jigsaw puzzle. Kong Le estimated the size of the forces in confrontation as: for the centrists, 4,500 soldiers under his direct command; for the Pathet Lao, 6,000 men controlling irregular areas interspersed among the centrists and another 1,200 men controlling various high points on the Plain's perimeter. Outside the Plain, Kong Le had another 5,500 men, mostly scattered in small garrisons in central Laos and along the Royal Road. The Pathet Lao forces elsewhere in Laos, according to American estimates at the time, were 12,000 men, fairly evenly distributed all the way from Phong Saly and Sam Neua provinces to the Cambodian border. The 2,000-man army of General Khammouane Boupha in Phong Saly Province, nominally loyal to Souvanna Phouma, was regarded as strongly anti-Phoumist, due in part to the fact that the General found it advisable to remain on good terms with the Chinese, who had established a consulate in the capital of his province.

The largest military force in Laos was the Phoumist army, which had swelled to an estimated 48,000 men by the end of 1962. Most of them were in the Mekong Valley, but they included

THE SECOND COALITION • 243

detachments of Meo guerrillas scattered all over northern Laos. Thus, the jigsaw puzzle of centrist and Pathet Lao forces on the Plain of Jars was surrounded by areas occupied by tribal forces loyal to the Phoumists. Thus, a centrist company in a stream bottom might be overlooked by a Pathet Lao mortar position that was overlooked by a Meo mortar position farther away.

Control of the larger towns—Khang Khay, Xieng Khouang, Phong Savan, and Ban Ban—and the vital Plain of Jars airfield was shared by the centrists and the Pathet Lao. However, as Kong Le realized, in a showdown his limited forces could not hope to defend any of the town positions against the Pathet Lao. The airfield had virtually no value, since its use by either side could be interdicted by artillery and mortar fire.

Souvanna Phouma had never publicly announced his position on the airlifting of supplies to Kong Le's troops by Air America aircraft. On November 27, an Air America C-123 transport plane on such a mission was shot down as it landed at the Plain of Jars airfield, killing the two American crew members. The Pathet Lao charged that the United States was intervening in Laos in flagrant disregard of the Geneva Protocol. The clandestine Voice of the Lao Kingdom radio station crowed that the American plane had been "shot down by local air defense units of the Lao patriotic forces."[4]

The incident revealed in a flash the degree to which Pathet Lao agents had infiltrated the centrist forces. The antiaircraft unit that downed the plane was the Phetsarath Artillery Group (after Prince Phetsarath), commanded by Colonel Deuan Siphaseuth, the paratroop officer with whom Kong Le had quarreled in Vientiane. Of the group's 270 men, 60 were former members of the Pathet Lao who had been demobilized in 1957 and who had joined the centrist units on the Plain of Jars during 1961.

The destruction of an aircraft belonging to the strongest capitalist power in the world imbued the gunners with the *élan* of winning that is so vital to Communist revolutionary warfare. The Vietnamese political commissars who shepherded Colonel Deuan's dissidents celebrated the event in countless meetings. Kong Le's deputy commander on the Plain of Jars, Colonel Ketsana Vongsouvan, was outraged by the act. But his attempt to arrest Colonel Deuan's gunners was frustrated by the Pathet Lao.

In Vientiane, Souvanna Phouma dejectedly announced that the plane had been shot down by centrist, not Pathet Lao forces, and

[4] Quoted by New China News Agency, November 29, 1962.

weakly promised an investigation. The centrist delegate to the tripartite cease-fire commission, Colonel Somboun Vongphrachanh, threatened to order centrist forces to retaliate by shooting down any aircraft flying supplies to the Pathet Lao.

The Pathet Lao launched an attack on Air America, charging that they had never been consulted on its operations, which included liaison flights as well as cargo flights. Souvanna Phouma was in the middle: He had neither endorsed the Air America airlift (the contract was a carryover from the Boun Oum government, and had merely been initialed for the coalition by Keo Viphakone, Secretary of State for Social Welfare, a Phoumist) nor prohibited it.

In order to ease the problem, the American Embassy arranged that Air America turn a number of cargo planes over to Souvanna Phouma for exclusive use as supply transports to Kong Le's headquarters. These planes were marked with the Lao three-headed elephant, but had American crews because no Lao crews had been trained to fly them.

At this point, the Soviets stepped into the picture. On December 2, the first of a consignment of nine LI-2 twin-engine transports were delivered at the Vientiane airport. The Soviets, stressing their observance of the Geneva Protocol, stipulated that three of the planes were for the centrist faction, three for the Pathet Lao, and three for the Phoumists. It would be several weeks before Lao crews could be trained to operate the aircraft.

The Soviets, still seeking to cultivate their North Vietnamese comrades, turned over to Hanoi all the Ilyushin-14 aircraft that had been operated by Soviet crews on the airlift between Hanoi and Laos since December, 1960. In this way, the Soviets withdrew from the airlift picture in Laos, thereby forfeiting an important bargaining lever in the delicate balance of pressures. It was up to the North Vietnamese to keep the Pathet Lao in food and ammunition, a task made a great deal easier by the repair of the roads across the Annamite Mountains. Nonetheless, the Ilyushins, with Vietnamese crews, were almost immediately assigned to specialized missions, dropping military supplies and carrying personnel on liaison flights.

In January, a second incident showed how paper-thin was the peace prevailing in Laos under the troika government. An ICC helicopter, one of four painted white and used for liaison flights, made a forced landing between Vientiane and Luang Prabang, in an area under Pathet Lao control. For weeks, Souvanna Phouma was refused permission to send technicians to repair the helicopter.

After permission finally was granted, the repair team found the craft had been completely stripped by the Pathet Lao.

On February 11, Souvanna Phouma left Laos to accompany the King on a tour of signatory countries of the Geneva Protocol. The following evening, Colonel Ketsana was assassinated at his home in Phong Savan on the Plain of Jars. Ketsana had been one of the original seventeen officers who had joined Kong Le in planning and executing the August 9, 1960, *coup d'état,* and his loss by Pathet Lao treachery was deeply felt by the centrist military. Ketsana had resisted the growth of Communist sympathies among the centrists. Perhaps more immediately connected with his assassination were his statements urging the ICC to investigate reports of North Vietnamese troops in the border areas.

Kong Le issued orders that all Pathet Lao personnel and defectors to the ranks of Colonel Deuan were henceforth to be forbidden entry into zones controlled by his own troops. The tension between Kong Le and the Pathet Lao was increasing daily, despite efforts at mediation by Pheng Phongsavan, the Acting Prime Minister.

If the centrist soldiers were compelled to defend themselves, they would soon exhaust their ammunition. The intentions of the North Vietnamese among the Pathet Lao was another uncertain element in any engagement between the two factions. Several of Kong Le's officers and men reported recognizing their former Vietnamese instructors still in Laos in early 1963.

King Savang Vatthana and Souvanna Phouma concluded their tour abroad at the end of March. In Vientiane, on the evening of April 1, the King gave a reception for Cabinet ministers and foreign diplomats. One of those present was Foreign Minister Quinim Pholsena, who had busied himself ever since formation of the coalition with making sure that the Chinese Communist and North Vietnamese ambassadors felt at home in Vientiane. In December, he had unilaterally dispatched a message of felicitations to the National Liberation Front of South Vietnam on its second anniversary. He had then set about compiling regulations whereby foreign diplomats would have to obtain his ministry's authorization before requesting appointments with the Prime Minister.

After the reception, Quinim Pholsena and his wife returned to their home in his large black Mercedes-Benz convertible shortly after 9 P.M. As he descended from the car, a corporal on guard at the front entrance squeezed the trigger on his Russian submachine gun, instantly killing Quinim, one of the most complex and least loved Lao leaders.

The assassination of the avowedly anti-American Foreign Minister was the last straw for the Pathet Lao. In the last week in March, centrist positions in Khang Khay and Xieng Khouang came under fire from Colonel Deuan's dissidents. Simultaneously, the propaganda outlets of the Communist powers began a campaign charging the centrists with "provocations," a familiar gambit that usually signaled the start of a major Pathet Lao military effort to shift the balance of power in their favor.

On March 31, a series of shootings occurred, leading to full-scale fighting. The Pathet Lao may have underestimated Kong Le's willingness to resist the pressure put on him to withdraw from the positions his troops shared with theirs and with those of Colonel Deuan. Kong Le resisted bravely, and reported the situation back to Souvanna Phouma, who ordered him to defend himself but to take no action that could be interpreted as offensive.

Before April was many days old, Kong Le had suffered about thirty casualties and had been compelled to abandon the "hostage" positions his outnumbered garrisons held at Khang Khay, Xieng Khouang, and Ban Ban. Nevertheless, he was able to withdraw to safety in relatively good order, and deftly maneuvered to retrieve all his Russian armored cars from Xieng Khouang. He thereupon set about manning a more restricted defense perimeter. Establishing a new command post at Muong Phanh, three miles west of the Plain of Jars airfield, he deployed his troops so as to control the extreme western third of the Plain.

The three delegation heads of the ICC, in an effort to determine the facts of the fighting on the Plain of Jars, made a series of helicopter trips from Vientiane to Khang Khay, beginning on April 6. They returned from these trips with reports that cease-fire agreements were being negotiated, but each day their reports carried less conviction.

Souvanna Phouma convened an emergency Cabinet meeting in the capital on April 8, and, over his own signature, wrote a request to the ICC to dispatch an ICC team to the Plain of Jars for the purpose of controlling the cease-fire. Souphanouvong, aware that there was a split in the ICC over assigning responsibility for the fighting, opposed sending an ICC team to the Plain of Jars, claiming that the fighting was an internal dispute among the centrists, between the Kong Le forces and the forces loyal to Colonel Deuan;

in this contention, he was to be supported by Dr. Marek Thee, the chief Polish delegate.

Within hours of Souvanna Phouma's request to the ICC, Souphanouvong departed from Vientiane for Khang Khay, now controlled exclusively by the Pathet Lao. He said that security precautions in the capital had been inadequate since Quinim's assassination. He was followed on April 19 by Phoumi Vongvichit, whose Ilyushin-14 was struck en route to Sam Neua by ground fire, presumably by Meo guerrillas, an incident indicating that peace was precarious in other areas of Laos besides the Plain of Jars. The departure of the two Pathet Lao ministers left two junior Pathet Lao officials—Prince Souk Vongsak, Secretary of State for Public Works and Transport, and Kampheuane Tounalom, Secretary of State for Planning—to attend Cabinet meetings in Vientiane. Souphanouvong had learned from his experience during the break-up of the first coalition not to be caught off guard in Vientiane.

Failure of the ICC to Control the Conflict

The Indian Chairman of the ICC, Avtar Singh, had been under U.S. pressure to continue the on-the-spot investigations based on allegations of foreign troops in Laos. Two ICC investigations at the end of December had failed to substantiate these charges, although American intelligence had reported that large numbers of North Vietnamese troops were present in Laos. The ICC finally decided on trips to Tchepone (to check for North Vietnamese troops) and Phou Ka Te (to check for American troops), in the South, and to the Plain of Jars (to check for North Vietnamese and American troops in various sectors), after months of haggling over such details as how far from their landing point the ICC teams would be allowed to walk. The trips to Tchepone and Phou Ka Te were made on April 13; the trip to the Plain of Jars was delayed by the outbreak of fighting and the submergence of the troop-investigation issue by the more urgent need to police the cease-fire.

Avtar Singh's position became more difficult as the ICC delegates met to determine the content of their report to the Co-Chairmen on the Plain of Jars fighting. The Polish delegate, Dr. Thee, at first insisted that the Plain of Jars situation was less urgent than the Indian and Canadian delegates contended, since the opposing sides were reportedly negotiating a renewal of the cease-fire agreement, which had been broken barely hours after its conclusion. When pressed to submit a draft report, Dr. Thee produced an account of the fighting that fully supported the Pathet Lao position and sharply differed from the views of his two colleagues. Clearly, it would take days, if not weeks, of arguing for the ICC to get unanimity on the report, as required by the Protocol.

During this time, the three ICC delegates, accompanied by the British and Soviet ambassadors representing the Co-Chairmen, continued making their helicopter trips to Khang Khay, where they were hospitably received by Prince Souphanouvong, exuding good will and optimism. On one of these trips, when the Indian and Canadian delegates attempted to convey to the Prince the urgency with which they viewed the situation, Souphanouvong remarked that certainly the Pathet Lao were not attacking anyone, and all was calm around Khang Khay, as the distinguished foreign guests could see for themselves. British Ambassador Donald Hopson picked up this remark and declared that if this were the case, then Souphanouvong could have no objection to the dispatch to Khang Khay of an ICC inspection team. Souphanouvong expressed his agreement. Realizing that Souphanouvong had committed a most damaging *faux pas* in full hearing of the three ICC delegates and the British and Soviet ambassadors, Dr. Thee inserted himself in the conversation. Shortly after this incident, Souphanouvong communicated a radically different view to the ICC: On no condition, Souphanouvong now declared, would the Pathet Lao permit an ICC team at Khang Khay.

Meanwhile, the Pathet Lao and dissident centrists were steadily gaining ground against the Kong Le forces. Simultaneously, Communist propaganda adopted an ominous new slant on the fighting. On April 10, a New China News Agency dispatch accused the United States of sending agents to the Plain of Jars to provoke trouble between Colonel Deuan and Kong Le. The NCNA dispatch laid the groundwork for linking Kong Le's efforts to defend himself with American intervention, and for portraying Deuan as the true centrist commander. Deuan had remained with about 150 men at the Pathet Lao armed camp at Khang Khay, thus compounding his treachery to his former commander.

Two days later, the NCNA reported a statement from General Singkapo, the Pathet Lao commander, who took up the theme of U.S. intervention:

> They have dispatched large numbers of bandits disguised as neutral [centrist] troops to attack the Pathet Lao fighting units at Khang Khay, and to attack progressive-minded units of the neutral [centrist dissident] forces at both Khang Khay and Xieng Khouang. . . . U.S. imperialism and its lackeys have recklessly violated the Geneva

agreements and the cease-fire order and are pushing a wicked plan aimed at undermining the neutral [centrist] forces under Prince Souvanna Phouma, splitting the Lao national front, and whipping up greater confusion and tension in Laos.

The American Embassy in Vientiane soon disclosed that, for the first time since 1960, the U.S. was once again supplying arms and ammunition to Kong Le. Souvanna Phouma remained silent on this subject.

Souvanna Phouma was in despair over the failure of the international machinery established to deal with precisely such crises, and alarmed by a fresh Pathet Lao advance that had dislodged Kong Le's meager forces from the village of Phong Savan, thereby shattering the illusion that a cease-fire agreement was being negotiated. On April 19, he addressed a message directly to the Co-Chairmen asking them to "intervene with a view to ending the violations of the cease-fire." He also addressed an appeal to Souphanouvong to bring the Pathet Lao to heel. Privately, he denounced in exasperated tones the Pathet Lao for using Deuan's dissidents as a *"paravent"* ("screen") for their actions against Kong Le so they could claim that the fighting did not involve them but was a dispute within the centrist ranks.

The message from Souvanna Phouma forced the Russians' hand. On April 22, an editorial in *Pravda* confirmed the ominous turn in developments, echoing the Chinese line sounded twelve days previously; the Russians blamed the U.S. for the tension in Laos and virtually accused the U.S. of violating the 1962 Geneva agreements.

The ICC acted on Souvanna Phouma's request for a team on the Plain of Jars despite Polish objections that all factions of the coalition had not consented. Avtar Singh pointedly asked Dr. Thee whether he, who professed such concern for respecting the sovereignty of Laos, was proposing to challenge the Prime Minister's authority to make governmental decisions. Did the Polish representative mean to imply that Poland no longer regarded Souvanna Phouma as Prime Minister of the Royal Government of Laos? When confronted with this argument, Dr. Thee gave in.

However, the Polish delegation refused to permit participation of its members on the team, although Article 15 of the Protocol stipulated that only a majority vote was required to implement a Royal Government request. The team finally dispatched to the Plain of Jars, called a "temporary team on a continuing basis" in order to avoid the charge that it was a fixed team, comprised only Indian and Canadian personnel. As the British pointed out in a note to Moscow on May 7, the Polish delegate had directly violated Article 16, which stated:

> Each member-state of the Commission shall ensure the presence of its own representatives both on the Commission and on the inspection teams, and shall promptly replace them in the event of their being unable to perform their duties.

The ICC debate over the report to the Co-Chairmen on the fighting reached its climax at a stormy meeting in which Dr. Thee refused to modify his views, which were contrary to those drawn up in draft form by his colleagues. He finally declared that he intended to submit a minority report. This would go against Article 14 of the Protocol, which required unanimity on ICC decisions relating to cease-fire violations. Matters came to a head when Avtar Singh flatly rejected Dr. Thee's minority report. Dr. Thee rose from the table and walked out, a tactic he had employed, unsuccessfully, on at least one previous occasion. He sent his minority report directly to the Co-Chairmen.

Avtar Singh was resolved to have the ICC inspection functions reaffirmed; he felt that backing down on this provision of the Geneva Protocol would imply the Commission's abdication of any further responsibility for what transpired in Laos. The Indian and Canadian delegations debated, but did not act on, a suggestion to station teams to police the cease-fire not only on the Plain of Jars but also at other sensitive points such as Vang Vieng, where centrist, Pathet Lao, and Phoumist garrisons were in proximity, and Attopeu in the South.

North Vietnam's Unasked Aid

Kong Le's arsenal of Soviet-type weapons would soon be useless for lack of bullets. He had not received any matériel through Communist-bloc channels since the previous October, and he was still awaiting delivery of 6,000 tons of petroleum and other supplies that the Soviet Union had placed at his disposal but that were said to be blocked at Hanoi. In this situation, the American Embassy in Vientiane let it be known that the United States, acting at the request of the Royal Lao Government and within the limits allowed by Article 6 of the Geneva Protocol, had resumed shipments of American arms and ammunition to Kong Le. Again, as the previous November, Souvanna Phouma remained silent; it was not even known whether he had been consulted, or whether the request from the Royal Lao Government had been signed by a Phoumist minister. Souvanna Phouma, attempting to keep the coalition together, was reluctant to commit himself on such inflammatory matters. The Phoumist ministers could act in the name of the government *on matters to which Souvanna Phouma did not raise objections.* The Pathet Lao, for the moment, raised objections to decisions reached in this manner; they retained for the future their option to act also in the name of the Royal Lao Government.

The American arms and ammunition were parachuted from Air America aircraft onto the Plain of Jars. Also, Air America planes landed at Muong Phanh, where Kong Le had opened up a new dirt landing strip. For the time being, the Pathet Lao had failed in their attempt to expel him from the Plain of Jars.

By June, it had become so obvious that North Vietnam was providing the Pathet Lao with supplies and cadres that Souvanna Phouma no longer bothered with the politeness of avoiding reference to it. He openly decried the Pathet Lao dependence on foreign arms, but the denunciation had a hollow ring.

On the road between Khang Khay and Xieng Khouang, members of the French Military Mission had seen truckloads of Vietnamese soldiers wearing the uniforms and caps of the Pathet Lao. The French, unlike most Westerners, can easily tell a Lao from a Vietnamese. When they addressed these soldiers in Lao, the latter were unable to reply.

During the fighting on the Plain of Jars in the summer of 1963, Kong Le's radio officers almost daily monitored two-way conversations in Vietnamese, and heard firing orders given in Vietnamese. A detachment of Kong Le's forces reported the capture of eighteen Vietnamese soldiers on April 12 in fighting along the road to Xieng Khouang, but said their prisoners escaped two days later when the detachment was attacked. On April 21, documents taken from the bodies of three reportedly Vietnamese soldiers who were killed in an exchange of gunfire along the same road were sent to Vientiane by Kong Le's chief of intelligence, Colonel Soulivan Sihavara.

A significant incident revealed the extent of North Vietnamese duplicity concerning its personnel in Laos. The North Vietnamese Embassy claimed that between 300 and 350 Vietnamese "construction workers" had been in Laos making improvements in the town of Khang Khay under North Vietnam's aid program to Laos. After the Pathet Lao forced Kong Le to evacuate his troops from Khang Khay, Souvanna Phouma sought to effect the withdrawal of these "construction workers." He pointed out to North Vietnamese Ambassador Le Van Hien in Vientiane that the work called for under the aid program had long since been completed. The Ambassador protested that arrangements for evacuating the "construction workers" were proceeding with all possible speed. However, unaccountable and repeated delays seemed to befuddle the issue of whether, from the official point of view, there were any North Vietnamese in the Pathet Lao-held areas of Laos.

The issue, coupled with the fighting on the Plain, grew to such proportions that the official Vietnam News Agency announced that all Vietnamese personnel had left Khang Khay in accordance with the agreements between the Democratic Republic of Vietnam and the Royal Lao Government. But on June 6, Souvanna Phouma declared that he had received reports of a convoy of trucks moving behind the Pathet Lao lines on the Plain. On June 8, in an interview with a British correspondent, the North Vietnamese Ambassador stated that the "construction workers" were still at Khang Khay and that "more than fifty" trucks had arrived to transport them back to North Vietnam. Hours later, however, the North Vietnamese embassy distributed a mimeographed communiqué to Western correspondents in Vientiane claiming that the Ambassador had been misquoted and that he had actually said that all Vietnamese at Khang Khay had departed four days previously. It was clear that the borderline between legal aid to the coalition government and illegal aid to one faction thereof had grown murky.

Close liaison between London and Moscow, repeated trips by both British and Soviet ambassadors to Khang Khay, and another high-level mission by Harriman to Khrushchev all elicited Soviet expressions of cooperation in preserving the *status quo* in Laos. But they produced neither a less truculent attitude on the part of the Pathet Lao nor a noticeable moderation in the line followed by Radio Hanoi and Radio Peking. "I fear that Soviet influence on Hanoi is not totally effective," Souvanna Phouma said on December 16, 1963.[5] Clearly, the Russians were still caught between wanting no further entanglement in Laos, a motivation reflected in their support for Souvanna Phouma's government, and wanting the support of the men in Hanoi, a motivation reflected in their reluctance to exert restrictive pressure upon the Pathet Lao.

The machinery set up at Geneva proved unable to control the ground situation in Laos, which had no agreed cease-fire line and hundreds of miles of unpatrolled borders. This was well illustrated by the diplomatic interchanges made in the name of the Geneva Conference during that summer of 1963. The Soviet Government,

[5] *The New York Times,* December 17, 1963.

as one of the two Co-Chairmen of the Geneva Conference, based its messages to the Lao Government on minority reports by the Polish member of the ICC and on irregular communications from Souphanouvong at Khang Khay. The Soviets unilaterally published a number of these drafts, which placed the blame for violations of the Geneva Protocol on the United States and its Asian allies. The British Government, the other Co-Chairman, found these accusations objectionable and responded by publishing and circulating to signatory governments sets of documents presenting both sides of the question.

The Soviet behavior, coupled with the Poles' simultaneous obstruction of the ICC (which did not go so far as to break up that body), indicates that the Soviets were willing to go along with the North Vietnamese presence in Laos on condition that Hanoi did not provoke a showdown leading to the collapse of the coalition government in Vientiane. In other words, the Soviets were prepared to guarantee, within reasonable limits, that North Vietnamese infractions of the Geneva Protocol would not be censured by the ICC so long as the North Vietnamese themselves did not give their game away.

The insecurity resulting from the fighting on the Plain of Jars led to the reinforcement of the North Vietnamese border-patrol in the first half of May by two battalions, which moved into the area around Nong Het. This raised to eleven the number of battalions on the Laos side of the border. They were located as follows: two in Sam Neua Province; two near Nong Het in Xieng Khouang Province; three in Khammouane Province near the passes over the central spine of the Annamite Mountains; two in Savannakhet Province north and south of Route Nationale 9; and two in Attopeu Province, well south of the Seventeenth Parallel. The evenness with which they were distributed from north to south indicated that their mission was to guard the whole border, keeping cross-border trails open.

Each battalion numbered about 450 men, and rotated back and forth across the border to well-provisioned camps. In these camps, each battalion's support troops remained in readiness to march up to the crest line if its front-line troops engaged in action. In the North Vietnamese view, these troops were under a chain of command entirely separate from that of the cadres who had been integrated into Pathet Lao battalions. The ratio of encadrement was about forty per battalion for specific purposes (political teams, artillery teams, communications teams, and vehicle-maintenance teams).

A North Vietnamese villager, in an interview published in the West at about this time, reported that among the tasks assigned to the people of his village to fulfill their thirty days' *corvée* labor for the central government was the transport of provisions to North Vietnamese troops serving in Laos. This work was placed in the same category as building roads, strengthening dikes, and constructing bridges, houses, supply stations, and provision depots, so it may be judged what importance Hanoi attached to the maintenance of these border-patrol troops.[6]

The airfield at Tchepone was the second point in Laos at which the North Vietnamese set up antiaircraft installations. When the Soviet airlift stopped and the Ilyushins were turned over to the North Vietnamese, Tchepone became an important landing field. The members of an ICC inspection mission arriving at Tchepone on April 13, 1963, were politely but firmly detained on the field; the local Pathet Lao commander refused to let them investigate the installations in the vicinity.

Intelligence reports reaching Royal Army commanders testified to the seriousness of the Vietnamese foothold in southern Laos. During the dry season from September, 1962, to May, 1963, the Pathet Lao and their Vietnamese mentors completed work on two airstrips along the Vietnamese border south of Tchepone. A field at Chavane once used by the French and suitable for handling aircraft of the C-47 or Ilyushin-14 type, was rehabilitated, and a new field was constructed in a mountainous area of northern Saravane Province, near Ban Phaloung.

The Pathet Lao also made improvements in ground transportation in southern Laos by opening to truck traffic in the dry season a rough trail extending southward from Nhommarath to Muong Phine to Saravane. This strategic route through the mountains parallel to Route Nationale 13—envisaged but never completed by the Vichy administration—permitted the North Vietnamese to haul to South Vietnam loads too heavy to be carried by porters.

During April and May, 1963, Pathet Lao agents began appearing in villages on the left bank of the Kong River north of Attopeu to recruit coolie labor to carry supplies. Some 300 of them, interrogated by Phoumist agents upon their return to their home villages, revealed that they had carried wooden cases containing unknown

[6] P. J. Honey, "Village Life in North Vietnam," *China News Analysis* (Hong Kong), No. 486, September 20, 1963, p. 5.

goods from Chavane to a Pathet Lao supply depot at Sam Luang. Later, another 500 villagers were employed to carry similar cases from Sam Luang farther to the southeast, that is, toward the South Vietnamese border.

Installations used by the North Vietnamese in Attopeu Province were reported to include a rest camp at Vang Tat near the South Vietnam border for the use of Viet Cong insurgents, an infirmary at Pok Bay about six miles from the Cambodian border, a depot for food and arms at Phou Katom, a mountain also about six miles from the Cambodian border, and a small-plane airstrip at Hatha on the Cambodian border southeast of Attopeu town, on the Ho Chi Minh Trail.

During the spring of 1963, an unprecedented rice shortage developed in the southern reaches of the Mekong Valley around the island of Khong. This was attributed to Pathet Lao requisitioning of rice for transport eastward to supply the depots along the Vietnamese border. As a consequence, rice had to be flown in from Thailand by Air America aircraft to the populous Mekong Valley towns.

The privileged nature of this Vietnamese sanctuary in southern Laos was placed in question when, during a visit to South Vietnam in March, 1964, General Phoumi reached an agreement with Premier Nguyen Khanh allowing South Vietnamese forces to pursue insurgents across the border into Laos. In view of the consolidation of the North Vietnamese security network in the Pathet Lao-held border region of southern Laos, however, the agreement between the two governments was likely to be more theoretical than real.

By 1964, Communist broadcasts referred by name to Pathet Lao-appointed provincial governors in nine of Laos' sixteen provinces. (Ten governors were actually named at various times, but the Pathet Lao administration divided Attopeu Province in two, calling the portion contiguous with South Vietnam "Eastern Province." The Pathet Lao referred to the "governor of the liberated area of Savannakhet Province" only, since the town of Savannakhet, the provincial capital, was still in Phoumist hands.)

On April 19, 1964, the Phoumist commander of the Vientiane Military Region, Kouprasith Abhay, and the head of the paramilitary Department of National Coordination, Siho Lamphouthacoul, both now risen to the rank of general, took advantage of Ambassador Unger's absence from the capital and led troops under their command in an attempted putsch. Briefly, they held Souvanna

Phouma under house arrest. They made a series of charges against the coalition and against the ICC, which they claimed was unable to oversee the cease-fire. They declared that the purpose of their action was to strengthen the government by seeking a greater share of representation for the Phoumists. The name of General Phoumi, however, was not associated with their action.

The two officers may have been encouraged to act by the immediate support given by the United States to two military *coup d'état* groups in Saigon in a short space of time. But they failed to appreciate that the United States position in Laos was fundamentally different from its position in South Vietnam, a consequence of which was that in the latter place the United States had no alternative to supporting whoever held power in the name of an anti-Communist stand. In Laos, the anti-Communist stand had proved itself a disastrous failure because polarization benefited the Pathet Lao. Ambassador Unger hurried back to Vientiane, and in concert with other Western ambassadors, reaffirmed the West's support for Souvanna Phouma, pulling the rug out from under the feet of the generals, who were persuaded to give up their demands for greater Cabinet representation.

The Communist powers adopted a line condemning the putsch, but laced it heavily with warnings to Souvanna Phouma not to stray from the path of neutrality. On May 16, the dissident followers of Colonel Deuan Siphaseuth, with Pathet Lao and North Vietnamese support, compelled Kong Le to abandon a number of positions on the Plain and to evacuate his Muong Phanh command post. They subsequently claimed that certain units of the centrist forces on the Plain of Jars had mutinied against Kong Le. By the end of May, the Pathet Lao and the "true neutralists" occupied virtually all the ground that had been held jointly by themselves and Kong Le when the coalition was formed in June, 1962. Even repeated aerial attacks (by T-28 aircraft recently furnished the Royal Lao Air Force by the United States) on Pathet Lao positions and on North Vietnamese convoys coming up Route Nationale 7 were not sufficient to prevent loss of most of the Plain of Jars by Souvanna Phouma's commander.

The Soviets, consulted by the United States as soon as the fighting reached serious proportions, again revealed themselves either unable or unwilling to influence the Pathet Lao to cease their advance. At the most critical moment, the Polish chief delegate to the ICC, charging that he was being held practically under house arrest by Phoumist guards, left Vientiane for Warsaw and refused to allow his deputy to stand in for him at ICC meetings. This was another gain for the Pathet Lao over the previous summer, when they had had to contend at least with the ICC's threat to inquire into the situation.

Souvanna Phouma declared that he considered some form of international consultation on the situation desirable, provided that there was prior agreement on a cease-fire and that the Pathet Lao gave up their newly acquired ground. The French were reported to be studying means to strengthen the ICC, but lent their support to a Chinese proposal for reconvening the fourteen-nation Geneva Conference. The United States was reported to have made overtures to the Chinese seeking their cooperation in restraining the Pathet Lao. These were made through third nations having diplomatic representation in Peking. Peking publicly rejected a British overture.

Meanwhile, the South Vietnamese, partly as a result of General Phoumi's visit to South Vietnam earlier in the year, had re-established their embassy in Vientiane, giving that capital the distinction of having ambassadorial missions from both rival Vietnamese governments.

The experience of the centrists during their alliance with the Pathet Lao between December, 1960, and the final break in April, 1963—when the extent of North Vietnamese direction was revealed for the first time—had been one of shock and disillusionment. This disillusionment was expressed in many ways. Nowhere had it set in so deeply as among the loyal officers and noncoms around Kong Le. These men, many of whom had returned to Laos from studies abroad in the autumn of 1960 to offer their services to the paratrooper captain, had genuinely believed that the best chance of extricating their country from the eddies of the Cold War lay in declaring peace with the Pathet Lao, whom the Americans had encouraged them to look upon as enemies for six years.

A major in Kong Le's army told the author, and his sentiments were typical, that he had first understood what a foothold the North Vietnamese had when he had been dispatched to pick up a jeep at Sop Nao in northern Laos in the autumn of 1961. There he found that the jeep was being held in a large camp that the North Vietnamese had established near the village. His efforts to obtain the jeep were rebuffed by the Vietnamese, who treated him like a stranger in his own country.

Widespread disgust with the Pathet Lao who had opened the door to the Vietnamese was reflected by Kong Le's soldiers during the tricky withdrawal from Xieng Khouang and Khang Khay in

1963. Kong Le's soldiers called the Pathet Lao *"kap kap,"* the Lao expression for toads, apparently because of their propensity for digging trenchworks, a technique they had learned from the victors of Dien Bien Phu.

Souvanna Phouma himself was not immune to the feeling of disillusionment. He stayed on doggedly as Prime Minister through the discouraging events of 1963 and 1964, refuting recurrent reports that he might give up what appeared to be a thankless task and retire to the peace and comfort of life in France. What hurt the Prince most was the presence of the North Vietnamese on the side of the Pathet Lao. At a press conference, he exhibited identification cards and other documentary evidence of North Vietnamese involvement in the Plain of Jars fighting. When Souphanouvong cabled him from Khang Khay in May, 1964, requesting the dispatch of Prince Souk Vongsak, Kampheuane Tounalom, and the 100 Pathet Lao guards who had been in Vientiane since the summer of 1962, Souvanna Phouma replied that they would be sent, in the care of the ICC, to Hanoi, where Souphanouvong would no doubt arrange to contact them.

Souvanna Phouma's tenacity could not hide the fact that he became daily more of a figurehead in a situation over which he had little control. In response to the urgent need for a demonstration of firmness that would communicate to North Vietnam and China American unwillingness to tolerate constant changes in the *status quo* in favor of the Pathet Lao, the State Department publicly confirmed in May, 1964, that American jets were making reconnaissance flights over the Plain of Jars; there was no direct statement by Souvanna Phouma for almost three weeks. The State Department said that the reconnaissance flights had been authorized to assist the Royal Lao Government obtain information on the intentions and disposition of the attacking forces.

The Pathet Lao downed one of the American jets by antiaircraft fire and captured its pilot. The following day, a second jet was downed, and the State Department revealed that it was an armed escort for the reconnaissance flights, which originated aboard aircraft carriers off the Indochina coast. In retaliation, six F-100 jet fighter-bombers, flying from South Vietnam, rocketed Pathet Lao installations, including an antiaircraft position. Now Souvanna Phouma, alarmed by denunciations from Peking and Hanoi of the American action, broke his silence. He threatened to resign unless the U.S. ceased the attacks, about which he said he had not been informed in advance. He later announced to the press that all flights had been stopped. Two days later, however, following a conference with Unger, he said that the suspension of flights had been only temporary, to bring about a "calm in the operation zones." New information, Souvanna Phouma declared, "shows that important movements of Pathet Lao and Viet Minh [North Vietnamese] troops are taking place." The American reconnaissance flights were resumed.

Thus the man who had in previous years been considered by the United States as a weakling, blind to the Communist danger, was now recognized as the one hope for preserving the coalition, and the coalition was left as the sole means for avoiding the stationing of American troops on the Southeast Asia mainland, or worse yet, engaging them against an enemy on the enemy's terms.

Washington recognized that the need to render further advances by the Pathet Lao costly to the powers who supported them now outweighed the advantages of a carefully controlled escalation based on striking power rather than ground troops. The search was on for means to demonstrate forcibly to North Vietnam and Communist China their points of vulnerability.

Less than a week after the American air attack against the Pathet Lao positions, on June 11, an attack by Royal Lao Air Force T-28's on the Chinese cultural and economic mission at Khang Khay killed one Chinese, Kao Yun-peng, and wounded five others. The United States disclaimed responsibility for the attack, but *The New York Times* revealed that some of the T-28 pilots were nationals of Thailand, the first time that military personnel of Thailand had been publicly, and without an official denial, implicated in the Laos conflict.

The American *démarche* to Peking through the British chargé d'affaires had flattered the Chinese sense of self-importance in a sphere of influence they considered historically their own. With the North Vietnamese, who (despite a strong Chinese demand for the reconvening of the fourteen-nation Geneva Conference) retained predominant direction of the Pathet Lao movement, the American problem of communication was even more difficult.

Up to the round of fighting that broke out in the summer of 1964, the United States had not directly accused North Vietnam of violating the agreements concluded barely two years earlier. Since North Vietnam's violation of these agreements had been flagrant, there were obviously constraints of a very definite kind on any American step in this direction. These constraints resulted from American actions in Laos that might themselves be construed as violations of the Declaration on the Neutrality of Laos, especially the paragraph in which the signatories undertook to prohibit the introduction into that country of "military personnel in any form whatsoever." The ferrying of centrist soldiers in Air America helicopters (observed by an American journalist on the Plain of Jars in the spring of 1963 and acknowledged, upon presentation of photographic evidence, by a high embassy official in Vientiane), the participation of U.S. Air Force jets in actions over Laos in the summer of 1964, and the use of American "civilian" pilots from bases in northeast Thailand to fly T-28 fighter-bombers marked with the three-headed elephant of Laos all appeared to violate the Declaration signed by Secretary of State Dean Rusk at Geneva.

These actions were taken at critical moments and were intended to achieve specific objectives. Their nature was more defensive than offensive. The fact that they appeared to violate an international agreement might become, overnight, a matter of academic debate if—as seemed possible and as some sectors of American opinion urged—the confrontation between the United States and North Vietnam were expanded to the level of all-out war.

Largely because of the ambiguity surrounding its own position, the United States did not attempt to make an airtight case condemning North Vietnam for its illegal assistance to the Pathet Lao faction at the moment the first clash occurred in March, 1963, or in May, 1964. Nor did it make public photographs in American hands since August, 1962, of North Vietnamese truck convoys entering Laos. And having reacted to the North Vietnamese intervention with no more than verbal warnings, the United States joined the confrontation on disadvantageous terms. It was not until June 29, 1964, that the United States, in a joint communiqué issued in Vientiane by Unger, the ambassadors of Britain, Thailand, and South Vietnam, and the Canadian delegate to the ICC, accused North Vietnam directly of "a flagrant violation of the Geneva agreements." By then, the United States had already elected, by involving its own aircraft, to confront North Vietnam on other ground, in which international condemnation of North Vietnam as a violator of the Geneva agreements would play a role of secondary importance.

An exchange of gunfire between an American destroyer and three North Vietnamese torpedo boats off the Red River Delta on August 2, 1964, led to an announcement by the State Department that a formal protest would be directed to Hanoi. Thus came about the first communication between the United States and Ho's nineteen-year-old republic.

The action against the American destroyer in the Gulf of Tonkin was cited as a justification for retaliatory raids by aircraft from the Seventh Fleet on torpedo-boat bases at four locations along the coast of North Vietnam. The value of these raids, which occurred on August 5, as a forceful reminder of the disparity in armed strength between the United States and North Vietnam was somewhat offset by two considerations: (1) Overt armed action of this type threatened to expand the conflict in Indochina by further raising the commitments on either side, especially risking involvement of Chinese forces in defense of North Vietnam; (2) Also, and more serious, the attacks by American warplanes appeared to represent for the North Vietnamese visible confirmation of what their government had been telling them for a decade—that the American "imperialists" were, indeed, the implacable enemies of their country in the same sense that the French soldiers of the Expeditionary Corps had been.

The U.S. Congress voted a resolution granting President Johnson extraordinary powers to resist any Communist actions in Southeast Asia as he saw fit. North Vietnam, meanwhile, publicly rejected the U.S. protest transmitted to Hanoi through the ICC, and declined an invitation from the U.N. Security Council, adopted on a resolution by the Soviet Union, to provide that body with information regarding the events of early August. The North Vietnamese Foreign Ministry's reply stated that the Geneva Conference rather than the Security Council was the proper body to investigate charges of aggression in Indochina. The cautious tone of Soviet statements dealing with the crisis in the Gulf of Tonkin suggested that the Soviet Union was as anxious as ever to relinquish its embarrassing responsibilities in Indochina, if it could do so without completely surrendering its influence in the entire area to the Chinese.

Souvanna Phouma's efforts to hold the coalition together in the absence of firm Soviet backing and in the presence of American actions that tended increasingly to polarize the situation brought him into conflict with the Chinese. Marshal Chen Yi declared on May 26, 1964, that "the uprising of the neutralist centrist troops in the Plain of Jars on May 16 was the inevitable outcome of the military coup in Vientiane of April 19." He went on to warn:

> The Chinese Government believes that Prince Phouma fully understands that, by working for the cooperation of the three Lao groups as the leader of the neutralist [centrist] group, he is respected by the Lao people, and that otherwise, if he becomes the leader of the Rightist Phoumist group, which is alleged to have incorporated both the

neutralist [centrist] and Rightist [Phoumist] groups, he will completely forfeit his political standing. The neutralist [centrist] group represents a social force that objectively exists in Laos. People are bound to come forward to raise the banner of the neutralist [centrist] group.

It was an ominous warning. Never before had it been so clear that the continuing crisis in Laos had implications far beyond the immediate borders of the Kingdom and was unlikely to be solved by anything less than a confluence of big-power interests. Such a confluence would depend not only upon cooperation among the Western powers and between the United States and the Soviet Union, but also upon the state of relations among the various centers of attraction within the Communist bloc.

Disarray in the Communist Camp

While the machinery for preserving the neutralization of Laos had broken down by mid-1964, no workable new schemes appeared in the offing. The large powers were too much at odds with one another to forge new machinery, and the small nations, in whose interest it was to keep foreign intervention in Laos at a minimum, lacked the necessary authority to impose their views.

The French and the Chinese agreed that a full conference of the fourteen Geneva nations should be reconvened, and President de Gaulle favored a general discussion at such a conference of the issues in all the Indochina states. Premier Khrushchev, who was encountering serious difficulties in his relations with other Communist parties as a result of Chinese subversion efforts, at first gave support to a Polish proposal for a restricted conference on Laos grouping the ICC members and the three Lao factions. This proposal met with Chinese hostility, as a result of which the Russians withdrew their support from one week to the next. The Americans were determined to resist any move for a conference except on the triple condition that a cease-fire be in effect, that the Pathet Lao withdraw to positions they had held before the outbreak of the 1964 fighting, and that they make clear their recognition of Souvanna Phouma as the Prime Minister of the Royal Lao Government. Attempts to persuade Khrushchev to accede to these conditions, however, with the British once again playing the role of mediators for the Americans, failed, and Khrushchev, no doubt looking ahead to the general elections in both Britain and the United States in the autumn, threatened that the Soviet Union would withdraw from its responsibility as Co-Chairman unless a fourteen-nation conference was convened forthwith.

Unfortunately for the Western powers, the absence of any vital Soviet interest in faraway Laos was overbalanced by the fact that the Soviet Union's actions in that country were being watched as a weathervane in the internal round of arguments on peace and war going on in the Communist camp. In these arguments, the issue of support for national liberation movements was one of the most potent in the hands of the Chinese, who were engaged in a fierce competition with the Russians for the allegiance of Communist parties struggling for power in Asia, Africa, and Latin America.

The stepped-up fighting in Indochina resulting from the confrontation between the United States and North Vietnam produced a more categoric assurance of Soviet support to the North Vietnamese than previously. It is significant that this assurance coincided with hints in the official Soviet Communist Party newspaper *Pravda* suggesting that the bitter tone of the Chinese attacks on the Soviet leaders for their alleged "revisionism" implied that they expected no succor from Moscow if their actions landed them in hot water. Chinese statements, meanwhile, urged on the North Vietnamese leaders, as they had done for the past five years, a bold course of action in supporting the Pathet Lao and the Viet Cong.

The most disruptive effects of the divergences within the Communist camp were being felt within the Lao Dong Party itself, where the pressures of the confrontation with the United States had exacerbated the differences between the pro-Soviet and pro-Chinese factions. The former argued, in broad terms, that it was folly to jeopardize the gains of the socialist revolution in the north in order to speed up the national democratic revolution in the south. The latter argued that the cadres in Laos and South Vietnam required resolute backing for their militant action to liberate those territories from foreign oppression, and that it was unsocialist to hesitate and doubt at the most acute phase of the struggle when the imperialist powers had historically backed down in the face of extreme pressure.

It appeared that, in this schism among his faithful followers, Ho was in serious danger of losing his hitherto deciding say in the party's course. His economic realism and his appreciation of Southeast Asian history impelled him toward Moscow; on the other hand, the fear of affronting his giant neighbor, and the confidence that he could deal with the Americans in much the same way as he had dealt with the French, impelled him toward Peking. Watching the long and costly struggle in which his people were engaged, he certainly felt a bond of understanding with the Chinese when they said that, given sufficient firmness of nerve, the struggle would eventually be capped by victory and peace would be restored to an Indochina finally rid of American intervention.

12.

The Flawed Bastion

By making the struggle in Laos an extension of their own revolutionary war both in space and in time, the Viet Minh were able to overcome the stigma attached to them as foreigners and historic predators upon Laos.

Contrasted to the immense difficulties facing Ho Chi Minh's government in its devastated homeland, the Royal Lao Government started with a wealth of advantages. It was, first of all, a government on soil virtually untouched by the eight years of warfare that had ravaged Indochina. It faced in its first months after the Geneva cease-fire (and this should be remembered) *not* hostility from Communist China and the Soviet Union, but a guarded approach for friendship from these powers. Materially, it had at its beck and call the armed strength and practically limitless resources of the West, particularly the United States, which had made known its desire to assist Laos in making its independence a reality.

The Royal Lao Government was operating on its own soil. Its opposition was a disparate band of agents in the hands of the Vietnamese Communists. This difference alone should have given the Royal Government pre-eminence both at home and abroad.

There can be little doubt that if the Royal Government had been encouraged to make adroit use of the immense resources at its disposal, the Vietnamese could have been prevented from obtaining a stranglehold on Laos. To prevent them from doing so required an awareness of the threat, and the imagination to meet it. The Western powers spoke much about the former, but they failed to show the latter quality.

Instead of being used to counter the threat, the resources available to the Royal Government were squandered. In the interest of short-term gains, the over-all power balance between the powerful West, on the one hand, and the small and vulnerable North Vietnamese state, on the other, was lost sight of. In the end, the West's actions in Laos were so irrelevant to the situation that they were proving of more benefit to the Communists than to the West.

Britain and France, because their attention was engaged elsewhere after 1954, played a minor role in Laos. They disagreed with the line of action pursued by the Eisenhower Administration, but they clung to the not-very-glorious role of critical bystanders. In North Vietnam's growing intervention in Laos, they saw reason to treat Laos as a political rather than a military problem. Only the realization of the potential consequences of a Western forfeit of Laos to the Communist rulers of North Vietnam, and the Kennedy Administration's attempt to reverse the trend by courageously initiating a new policy, brought the British and French closer to the United States in a common last-ditch effort to obtain respect for Laos' independence.

The United States started out seeking no material acquisitions in Indochina and ended up being accused of neocolonialism. It started out by subordinating its principles of self-determination to what it judged to be the imperatives of a temporary situation, and sooner than anyone had expected, it found that the penalty of its involvement was the loss of its prestige. Because of its deepening involvement in Laos, the United States took on a special responsibility toward the peoples of that Kingdom and of the surrounding lands whose continued freedom from Communist amalgamation depended on the fulfillment of U.S. promises to protect them. A voluntary withdrawal became unthinkable. A protracted conflict, sometimes in the form of crisis, more often in a low key, became inevitable.

Many of the West's advantages in Laos were forfeited because of a faulty understanding of the problem—for example, the issue of nationalism, which was forfeited to the Communists. Others were forfeited as a result of omissions of action when the men on the ground knew action was vitally needed, as in the case of the tardy initiation of a civic-action program at the village level. Still others were lost simply because American involvement in Laos generated antagonism even among friends, leading to such political absurdities as the alienation of Prince Souvanna Phouma in the autumn of 1960.

Many explanations have been advanced for the U.S. failure to keep Laos and its people secure from the hands of the political commissar of Hanoi. Some say the United States was not firm enough, since it is a well-known fact that the Communists respect force. Others say the United States was too categoric in its opposition to any suggestion of a negotiated accommodation, that the bold phrases used by Administration spokesmen before Congressional committees were carried over into actual policy and torpedoed any chance of an accommodation short of outright military victory, which, of course, was out of the question.

An American who served in the Eisenhower Administration in negotiations with the Soviets in Europe has said, "Basically, we tried to solve a sociological problem by military means where we can't use our military." And there is some truth in that. The fact is that no single explanation totally accounts for the failure of the United States to achieve its goal in Laos—a viable state secure in its independence and livelihood. The outcome was determined by a number of mistakes committed (or simply permitted) by the United States and fully exploited by the Communists, plus a conjunction of unhappy circumstances. The American presidential election campaign of 1960 coincided with the most acute phase of the Laos crisis, marked by the establishment of a Soviet Embassy in Vientiane and the sending of Soviet aid to Souvanna Phouma. For the outgoing Administration, the penalties of sitting tight were less than those of shifting course. No fresh initiatives were forthcoming from Washington until the incoming Administration had its hands securely on the tiller.

By the summer of 1961, as we have seen, a very definite correlation had established itself between Pathet Lao aggressiveness and American unwillingness to escalate the conflict. The North Vietnamese, because they were in a position to adjust the pressure exerted by the Pathet Lao, could test their opponents' will to resist. The correlation that emerged, therefore, from the multiplicity of actions and words, input of arms, and threats from both sides, was precise almost to the single village or the length of roadway occupied by either side. Neither the pressure on the Communist side nor the resistance on the American side was constant; the former fluctuated with the estimation by the Hanoi leadership of risks involved, and the latter fluctuated in accordance with logistical obstacles, relations with the European allies, and was even affected by such factors as the changed mood of the President in the aftermath of the Bay of Pigs disaster. This neat correlation emerged, in any case, at a late stage of the conflict. It was an oversimplification, therefore, to argue that because Communist acquisition of new territory in Laos was proportionate to the "softness" of the American position, the solution to the predicament was a "hard" stand even at the expense of committing American forces.

In reality, the predicament was neither wholly circumstantial nor wholly a simple matter of an arithmetic equation. It is possible to identify a number of faults of omission or commission whose presence within the structure of American policy in Laos made inevitable its crumbling, regardless of the hardness of the material employed in its construction.

1. Nationalism was potentially the most powerful motivating force in the Indochina countries at the end of World War II. More than any other factor, the Viet Minh's monopoly of this appeal, coupled with the possession of a tightly organized machine to carry out orders, accounted for the Viet Minh success. Conversely, the United States failure to appreciate the significance of this force and to bend all its efforts toward making use of it contributed immensely to the governmental instability.

The evolution undergone by American thinking on the question of nationalism in Indochina can be summarized as follows: World War II saw frequent references to the fact that Americans attached supreme importance to the principle of self-determination of peoples. In the immediate postwar period, American actions subordinated this principle to other considerations. Finally, when the storm clouds gathered over Indochina and the United States found itself on the side of the colonial power, American statements tended to see in the vague and tardy concessions wrested from the French sufficient substance to satisfy the nationalist aspirations of the Indochinese peoples. Secretary of State Dean Acheson said American assistance to the French-sponsored governments in Indochina after 1950 was intended to help the Indochinese develop "genuine nationalism."[1] But who were the "genuine" nationalists? Members of the Lao Issara, who had formed their own government and proclaimed their own Constitution in 1945, were certainly genuine nationalists. The three princely brothers of Laos were genuine nationalists, and that is why the Viet Minh made efforts to win one of them to their ranks at the very time they were liquidating powerful Vietnamese nationalist rivals in Hanoi and Saigon. And it was to the French, rather than to these men, that American help went. Therefore, in the eyes of the Indochinese nationalist leaders, the Viet Minh victory at Dien Bien Phu was a defeat for the United States as well as for France.

[1] Department of State Bulletin, June 18, 1950, pp. 877–78.

Once the United States had forfeited the issue, it was never able to grasp it firmly again. American officials could not comprehend how peasants armed with homemade shotguns who came into a village at night to ask for a handful of rice could be welcomed as patriots. The Pathet Lao, recognizing the potential mobilizing force of nationalism, directly involved the people in what they called the struggle against the foreigner. In this effort, they even succeeded in overcoming the "foreignness" of their Vietnamese advisers, whom they portrayed as friends of the people of Laos. The vast American aid mission in Laos seemed to confirm the Pathet Lao contention that their country had come under the yoke of a new form of colonialism—a preposterous distortion of motivations, but nonetheless effective propaganda. There were more Americans in Laos in 1961 than there had been Frenchmen under the Protectorate at the outbreak of World War II.

2. The United States allowed American disapproval of the Communist regime of Ho Chi Minh to become confounded with American opposition to the expansion of Vietnamese Communist power into Laos and South Vietnam. This led to a rigidity of approach in policy-making that did not permit taking into account such factors as Ho's historic mistrust of the Chinese. Such considerations would have given American policy much more flexibility in dealing with Ho's expansionist aims. During the critical period when policy for Laos was being formulated, State Department thinking bore many resemblances to the 1947 dictum of French Admiral d'Argenlieu that there could be no negotiating with Communists. For example, Assistant Secretary of State for Far Eastern Affairs Walter S. Robertson declared on January 13, 1955: "The Chinese Communists and, for that matter, the other Asian Communists such as the Viet Minh, may have points of conspicuous physical difference from the Russians, but as Communists they are all identical."[2]

While infiltration of North Vietnamese cadres into and through Laos could not be prevented without a direct military effort, which the United States was not prepared to undertake, the U.S. voluntarily renounced all possibility of communicating with Ho through diplomatic channels, and of restraining him. North Vietnam was not treated as a state; it was ignored. Even its modest efforts to participate in Southeast Asian affairs on a nondiplomatic level—a recent example of which was its application to join the Economic Commission for Asia and the Far East (ECAFE) in March, 1962—were summarily rebuffed. The American attitude toward North Vietnam

[2] Department of State Press Release No. 23, January 13, 1955, p. 3.

from 1954 to 1964 was one that past experience had shown went against all prospect of reward.

The British took a more pragmatic approach in their Far Eastern policy. They fought the Communist terrorists in Malaya, most of whom were Chinese, while they maintained their diplomats in Peking. Likewise, they maintained a consul in Hanoi, as well as their embassy in Saigon. It was their experience, they explained, that dictators could best be handled by keeping lines of communication open rather than by ignoring their control of their countries (a stand the British have maintained in regard to trading with Cuba, despite U.S. protests). The rationale behind the U.S. isolation policy was that South Vietnam should be built up as an internationally recognized and sovereign state and that the Communist government of North Vietnam, weakened by a deteriorating economic situation, should be permitted to be overthrown in the course of an internal rebellion. Leaving aside the question of whether the population of a country is more united behind a government facing hostility abroad, the policy adopted gave the Saigon regime a restricting power over American diplomacy in Indochina. No official contacts could take place between Washington and Hanoi, since this would undermine the Saigon regime's contention to be the sole legitimate government of Vietnam. North Vietnam had no alternative but to remain in the Sino-Soviet camp, and lacking other sources of food, Ho had an even more urgent need to annex the rice-rich south.

3. On the ground in Laos, American effectiveness was hamstrung by an inability to visualize situations in terms meaningful to the local population. Ambassador Parsons' attributing opportunities for corruption in the aid program to loss of confidence in the kip sounded logical on Wall Street but hardly made sense in Laos. American methods were applied to the solution of problems in an underdeveloped country where the practices of fifteenth-century Europe would have been more appropriate. In contrast to the relatively ineffective aid program mounted by Americans who shut themselves up in air-conditioned cubicles, a small aid program with a large impact was carried on at the same time in Cambodia by the Chinese Communists, whose engineers and workmen lived in barracks on the construction sites of the factories they were building. A similar lack of rapport hampered American propaganda efforts. As General Heintges testified, "Do not forget . . . that 87 per cent of the population in Laos is illiterate. These people do not know what the word 'democracy' or 'communism' means."[3] The Pathet Lao,

[3] *Hearings*, III, p. 2375.

therefore, pitched their appeal on a level where it was meaningful—promising specific, visible benefits to the population and rejecting the sophistication of the Marxist-Leninist vocabulary in which their leaders conversed.

4. The United States, having taken an equivocal stand at the Geneva Conference in 1954 by unilaterally declaring that it would not impede the implementation of the accords, allowed itself to be bound by the most restrictive features of the Laos cease-fire agreement but made little or no effort to exploit the potential offered by that agreement's most favorable provisions. The United States abided by the Geneva prohibition against all foreign military missions in Laos except French, giving the French primary responsibility for training the American-financed Lao army, but benefited little from French experience in the field and proceeded on the basis of trial and error. (The French used their control over military training to reassure the Lao politicians who were nervous about American policy that they, the French, could restrain the Americans. The French maintained their military training mission at half strength, fulfilled their training responsibilities lackadaisically, and proclaimed on every side that they knew more about the situation in Laos than anyone else. This may well have been true, but with this dog-in-the-manger attitude on the part of the French and frustration on the part of the Americans, relations deteriorated steadily. When the best unit in the Lao army overthrew the "pro-American" government, its action was met with unconcealed French approval.)

5. The effect of the American aid program was bound to be disruptive. Nothing like it had ever been tried under the Protectorate. Its major effect was to exacerbate the disparities between the haves and the have-nots. Its results went against common sense. Chinese shops in Vientiane were well stocked with Scotch whisky, while a concrete floor for the capital's open-air market, a notable advance in sanitation benefiting some 60,000 people, was not provided until 1963. The Pathet Lao were able to make use of the visible difference between constructive aid and nonproductive aid in their propaganda. The aid program also exaggerated the isolation of a central government already one step removed from the countryside because its appointive authority stopped at the district level. The greater the accouterments of office in Vientiane, the less the government could understand the problems of the villages; the less it understood the villages, the less became its popular rapport; the less rapport, the more isolated it became; the more isolated, the more it had to be propped up by American aid; the more it depended on American

aid, the less popular it became and the more isolated from the villages.

6. The vicious circle resulting from the increasing Vientiane-centeredness of the government meant that the Americans could do nothing to help extend the government's authority to the country-side, at the very time when the newly installed Communist government in Hanoi was engaged in consolidating its own authority and creating autonomous regions for its ethnic minorities. As the loss of authority in the countryside became greater, the process of Cabinet-making in Vientiane retained less and less meaning, and political parties, aside from the Neo Lao Hak Sat, atrophied into little more than high-sounding names. The single serious attempt at party-building on a reformist platform by non-Communists was made by a group of army officers and failed miserably. The United States must take a large portion of the blame for neglecting to emphasize the crucial importance of the interaction between local democracy and central authority. The Royal Government gradually came to realize that it had forfeited the ability to communicate with its own people, that it was a stranger in its own land. The Pathet Lao, on the other hand, studied the system of local government in minute detail, since this was the key to success in winning the allegiance of the people in the Lao-inhabited areas of the Kingdom. Prince Sou-phanouvong, for instance, garnered the most votes of any candidate in Vientiane Province in the 1958 election; yet he also felt quite at home walking up and down the country from village to village.

7. The Royal Government's authority did not extend at all into the territories of the mountain tribes, because of their almost total lack of previous political organization and the age-old animosities between them and the lowlanders. This precluded any real possi-bility of creating a sense of national unity. Not until 1961, when U.S. Special Forces detachments arrived in Laos, was any effort made to recruit these tribesmen into the army. American support for a national army composed almost entirely of Lao prolonged the separation; when the army appeared in the upland villages, even outside the Pathet Lao-controlled provinces of Sam Neua and Phong Saly, it was feared as an army of foreigners rather than welcomed. For years, the tribesmen had been recruited into the Pathet Lao and given a cause to fight for. Their political indoctrination came from untiring Pathet Lao organizers like Sithone and Phay Dang, who traveled the jungle trails exploiting the fears and grievances of the Kha and the Meo. The French, whose military training mission had numerous contacts among the tribes, especially after 1959, made no

effort to get the Royal Government to give specific assurances to the tribesmen that it would not prevent them from having a representative voice in the government. Pathet Lao propaganda was, therefore, able to tell the tribes that they were victims of discrimination.

8. On a strategic plane, the United States overestimated the possibilities of military offensives open to Communist China and North Vietnam, with disastrous consequences for the programming of aid to Laos that began in 1955. The program was weighted heavily on the side of military defense, to the neglect of civic action, an imbalance rooted in Washington's reassessment of Communist intentions in the aftermath of the Korean invasion of June 25, 1950. There are indications that a grand strategy of offense against positions of Western influence on the rim of Asia may have been discussed by Stalin and Mao Tse-tung in Moscow during their prolonged talks in the winter of 1949–50.[4] Stalin may have been favorably impressed by a Chinese desire to exploit their own revolutionary momentum by a three-pronged attack against South Korea, Taiwan, and Indochina. After all, it was apparently the Chinese who convinced Stalin that Ho Chi Minh's appeal for recognition of January 14, 1950 (to which the Chinese acquiesced on January 18), should be favorably treated even though it went against Soviet preoccupation with European politics. The Chinese could not have failed to appreciate the fact that recognition would allow the French to portray what was essentially a colonial war as an anti-Communist crusade in order to win material assistance from the United States, and they could hardly have been unhappy about the prospect of being begged for help by their fraternal Vietnamese comrades. However, the swift and decisive American riposte to the invasion of South Korea warned Moscow and Peking that the United States would henceforth act to prevent the use of Red armies in outright attempts at territorial aggrandizement. After this warning, Moscow and Peking were compelled to re-examine the possibilities of offensive operations of the Korean type. After Stalin's death, in 1953, it is doubtful that the Soviets would have supported an effort by Chinese ground troops in Indochina on the side of the Viet Minh unless it had been provoked by direct American intervention on the side of the French. After 1954, North Vietnam, despite its army's success in fighting a su-

4 See, for example, Marshall D. Shulman, *Stalin's Foreign Policy Reappraised* (Cambridge, Mass.: Harvard University Press, 1963), p. 141. The likelihood that the Soviet Union was then poised to spread its control, by force of arms if necessary, in Europe, the Middle East, and Asia was discussed in a National Security Council paper called NSC-68 in early 1950 (*The New York Times*, April 13, 1964).

perior enemy, was hardly eager to risk the gains sealed by the Geneva settlement by mounting an invasion of Laos. Reports from observers who had contact with the Viet Minh delegation at Geneva indicate that the Viet Minh welcomed the settlement as a respite in which to consolidate their power at home; other accounts have sought to make it appear that the Viet Minh accepted the cease-fire unwillingly and only at Soviet Foreign Minister Molotov's insistence. The evidence seems irrefutable that the United States based its program of aid to Laos on premises that may have been valid in 1950 but were no longer valid in 1955.

9. In seeking to deter the military threat to Laos represented by its two stronger Communist neighbors, the United States based its planning on the protective "umbrella" provided by SEATO, apparently disregarding the fact that General Giap's guerrillas had prevailed over the 350,000-man French Expeditionary Corps in spite of the possibility of American intervention with nuclear weapons. The United States took over support of the Lao Territorials from the French on the supposition that the army was the only effective nation-building force in Laos. When this army found itself engaged in warfare against the Pathet Lao beginning in 1955, however, the U.S. proceeded to fashion it into a national army on the model of the French Army. Little or no attention was paid to defense against the village-by-village infiltration and subversion that had played such a predominant role in the Viet Minh success. Unfortunately, from the American point of view, the atypical battle of Dien Bien Phu served to reinforce the obsession with frontal attack. The Royal Lao Army inherited the barbed-wire and mud-fort mentality of the men responsible for that disaster. The Vietnamese Communists, on the other hand, retained their thousands of bicycles, whose mobility they had come to appreciate in the Tonkin highlands. The French repeatedly warned the American PEO that the tanks and artillery given the Royal Lao Army were well suited to fighting set-piece battles on the Korat Plateau or in the Mekong Delta, places where the Lao would probably not be called upon to fight, but were of little value in Sam Neua Province.

Dulles contemplated a conference of experienced leaders of Southeast Asia after ratification of the SEATO treaty to discuss how to meet the threat of "people's war"; however, the project was abandoned after the death of President Magsaysay of the Philippines. If it had taken place, the Royal Lao Army might have been in a better position to cope with the guerrilla tactics it later faced.

10. The creation of this army introduced an unstabilizing, rather

than a stabilizing factor. Not until January, 1960, was an effort made to draw the soldiers into civic action,[5] and so the Royal Lao Army was one of the least politicized in the world. Even the soldiers of the Foreign Legion had constructed kilns to bake bricks in the villages where its men were stationed in Laos; after 1954, the Royal Lao Army did none of this public-relations work, unlike the Pathet Lao. Rare was the officer, like Kong Le, who made his troops pay for food taken from local civilians. Most officers had little rapport with their own troops, and less with the people; the Phoumist officers at Nam Tha were in the forefront of the flight to the Mekong, leaving their men behind to fend for themselves. Defections were commonplace. But despite their lack of political sense, these officers had ambitions that could be translated into political action. First there was the attempted putsch in December, 1959, and eight months later the Kong Le *coup d'état,* brought off successfully by a small group of junior officers in protest against the politics of an allegedly corrupt government, whose leading Cabinet minister was a general officer. The Pentagon had originally advised the State Department that a Lao army of any size would have little military value in furthering the mutual-security policy of the United States in Southeast Asia. The Royal Lao Army, which had been supported by the United States primarily for political reasons, grew from a force level of 23,600 in 1955, to 30,000 four years later, and to 48,000 in another four years. At the same time, the territory it controlled shrank. The attempted putsch of April, 1964, one of whose leaders was a twenty-eight-year-old general, was evidence that the United States had allowed the army to develop along lines far from the initial intention of assisting Laos attain a stable nationhood.

11. The complexity of Communist motivations and the difficulty of predicting Communist actions are incontrovertible, but they constitute no explanation for the lack of foresight in so many American actions. The formal commitment of the United States toward Laos and South Vietnam, as well as toward Thailand, was clearly worded in the SEATO treaty. Nevertheless, this was a commitment with strictly limited ends. The United States, in the case of subversion in Laos, was legally obligated only to consultations. Therefore, in hard policy terms, the United States had no *obligation* to be led deeper and deeper into an involvement from which it derived no immediate gain (such as military bases) and raised the stakes more and more. The extent of U.S. control over

[5] *Hearings,* III, p. 2385.

the economy of Laos, for instance, led to the paradoxical situation that, if America threatened to cut off aid in order to pressure the Lao government, it could virtually bring about the downfall of the Vientiane government (at least, until the advent of economic aid from the Soviet bloc). The certain long-range effect of such an aid cut-off, however, was to halt the flow of hard goods into the country to soak up money paid out to the administration and army, and thus to produce a runaway inflation that might very well drive the country into the arms of the waiting Communists. The theory was that by exerting pressure on the Lao government, the United States could "polarize" the political situation to the point where there were only Communists and anti-Communists. This theory failed to consider that only the Communist side in this neat dichotomy possessed a widespread apparatus of obedience in the countryside. The United States was involved with all sectors but the one that counted most—the people. Again, the experience of the French in 1946 could have been instructive.

12. The American "country team" in Laos was a many-headed animal, analyzing the situation from many different viewpoints and producing as many interpretations. The military mission, for instance, had few illusions about the "bastion" concept of Laos, which found favor among the political experts of the State Department. Most of the military regarded the Royal Lao Army as a makeshift force that liked to ride at high speeds along the country's few paved roads and had a penchant for night-clubbing and new cars—all of whom might decide at a moment's notice not to fight when faced with a strong enemy, particularly a Vietnamese enemy. After it became evident that the invasion from China or North Vietnam would not, after all, take place, the American military viewed their role in Laos as a holding operation to give the "pro-Western" governments of Thailand and South Vietnam more time to solidify their own positions. What the military did not understand was that the greater the gains made by the Pathet Lao in the countryside, the less became the inclination of the Thais to bind themselves to the American alliance and the greater their inclination became to adopt "neutralism" themselves. The State Department understood the fears of the Bangkok government better than the military, which helps to explain why its spokesmen put a façade of boldness on an operation that the military knew to be much less than a do-or-die proposition. As for the CIA, its able agents in the field accumulated an encyclopedic knowledge of the country and its people that appears to have been carefully studied by

neither the Pentagon nor the State Department. The result was that while the men in Laos possessed accurate knowledge, in many cases those in Washington were talking to one another at cross-purposes, at least until President Kennedy began studying the details and reaching his own decisions on that basis. When the United States finally accepted the proposal in 1961 that Laos should be neutralized, if such neutralization was still possible, the contrast with the previous bold façade was so great that the impression gained widespread currency in the United States that Washington was "losing" Laos.

13. The "country team" system, accepted as the least unsatisfactory of the several possible organizational methods of implementing policy, in Laos reduced the Ambassador's authority to a point where it was no longer commensurate with the degree of American involvement. Theoretically, the Ambassador was advised by the mission heads of the various agencies operating in the field—the economic-aid mission, the military-aid mission, and the CIA. In practice, each of these missions functioned on its own initiative, maintained its own channels of communication to Washington, and had at its disposal a share of the American funds being expended in Laos. The Ambassador often had cause to wonder how much autonomy the members of his team enjoyed in dealing with the Lao. In 1959, the State Department protested a promise the PEO head gave to the Lao Defense Minister for more funds for army salaries, although this promise had been approved along the line of PEO's chain of communications to the Pentagon. The set-up was potentially dangerous because a skilled politician could play one agency off against another, or use the actions of one agency for his own internal political purposes against the wishes of another agency. The support given General Phoumi in the autumn of 1960 by the Defense Department and the CIA was used by the General as evidence that the United States was backing him in the contest for allegiance between himself and Souvanna Phouma, although the State Department had made distinct reservations on this score.

The adoption of General Phoumi by the Defense Department and the CIA led to a foreign-policy predicament not unlike that faced by the United States in China in the late 1940's. "The reactionaries in the Government have evidently counted on substantial American support, regardless of their actions," General George C. Marshall reported after the failure of his Chinese mediation mission. In the delicate negotiations for a coalition government in Laos in 1961 and 1962, President Kennedy attempted to make it clear that a political figure's standing in relation to the needs of his country—rather than his professions of anti-Communism—was the proper criterion for American backing. This reflected a nobility of purpose that had previously been sadly lacking in American actions in Indochina.

If the Ambassador could on occasion curb the agency representatives on his "team," the fact remained that his advice to Washington on the formulation of policy carried little weight there, and he was sometimes reduced to the role of titled messenger boy for the policy-makers in the State Department. At one point in October, 1960, Ambassador Brown was receiving telegrams from Washington informing him bluntly that aid to Laos was being cut off, or was being turned on again. It was Brown's task to acquaint the Prime Minister as best he could with the reasons for these sudden stops and starts. Frequently the Prime Minister had already got wind of Washington's action through news dispatches. The decisions were Washington's, and they were based on a broad view that attached greater importance to the effects of American actions on allies elsewhere in the Pacific than to their effect inside Laos.

The Ambassador's authority was further undermined at critical junctures by the flying trips· made by high-ranking State Department officials. The usefulness of such missions was limited by their brevity and by the inordinate amount of publicity they received. Both characteristics conflicted with an old Oriental notion that bargaining, if it is to be serious, should proceed quietly and only after several days of polite preliminaries. Such American visitors to Laos thus arrived with their bargaining position already undercut, and departed with little more understanding of the problem than they had possessed when they arrived. Their observations of Vientiane, Luang Prabang, and the countryside in between as seen from an airplane window left them still trying to come to grips with Laos. Souvanna Phouma managed to survive more than one "tough talk" process, which added to his prestige among the Lao.

14. The switch from a policy of consistency without victory to one of inconsistency without defeat caused bewilderment in Laos and in surrounding nations. Compelled to choose which among the princely politicians of Laos to support, just as the French had done sixty years before them, the Americans at first formed their closest relationships with those they viewed as anti-Communists, in the belief that these men had the best prospect of leading their country to nationhood and stability. American support was the *sine qua non* of political power in Laos, and in one case it allowed a general in

rebellion to prevail over a prince who had been three times Prime Minister. All-out support of this nature alienated those who felt that the wisest policy for their country was one of disentanglement and reconciliation rather than one of commitment and repression. However, the course of Washington's diplomacy soon shifted again, making possible a *rapprochement* with the protagonists of reconciliation. Of course, this stranded the men who had previously been hailed for their anti-Communism.

One man who had particular reason for wonderment at American actions was King Savang Vatthana. During the attempted putsch in January, 1960, he had been confronted with the ambassadors of all the Western powers, who, in a united voice, argued against the advisability of permitting a military dictatorship, even one that proclaimed itself reformist in platform, in favor of the preservation of parliamentary institutions. Three years later, he witnessed the U.S. failure to advance similar arguments when the Pathet Lao declared their intention to disregard the actions of this same parliament because it was known to have been packed by anti-Communists at the previous election.

The reactions of men like King Savang Vatthana went deeper than bitterness. They felt that Washington was treating their country like a political football. But they also wondered at the coherence of American policy in Southeast Asia. In surrounding countries as well, many leaders wondered whether the day might not come when they, too, might be left high and dry, their U.S. support suddenly withdrawn. In the long run, this is certain to be one of the most damaging effects of American actions in Laos. By contrast, the Chinese, the North Vietnamese, and the Pathet Lao gave an appearance of constancy to their actions, by cloaking their policy in the mantle of "support for the people of Laos," in 1964 as in 1954. There was nothing in the series of Communist statements on Laos to match the fluctuation in American statements, which at one time described Laos as a bastion of freedom and at another as a neutralist state. (This is not to say, of course, that the Communists have not shifted their affections frequently in dealing with the multiplicity of personalities offered by the Indochinese states. For instance, Peking once viewed Prince Sihanouk as the "puppet king of Cambodia." This characterization was dropped after Bandung and after Sihanouk abdicated the throne in 1955 to take an active part in Cambodian politics.)

15. The United States failed to make it clear to North Vietnam that it would prove against the interests of the men in Hanoi to

pursue a campaign of armed subversion in Laos in implementing the notorious Lao Dong Party platform of 1951. In other words, the United States' failure to translate the threat of military power into a valid check on these leaders left them free to act in Laos with impunity so long as they did not overstep the line of overt aggression. It may be assumed that they would have been loath to interfere in the internal affairs of Laos if they had been made to understand unmistakably that such interference would jeopardize their political power in Hanoi. A few guerrilla raids across the Laos border into North Vietnam would probably have sufficed to get the message across to these men. When both Hanoi and Washington knew that an accusation of formal aggression could not be proved, merely raising a hullabaloo about North Vietnam's actions in Laos, as in the summer of 1959, was not a sufficiently compelling action on Washington's part.

The roots of these mistakes and omissions were in the period of American monopoly on nuclear weapons, which gave the United States a short-lived illusion of security. Later, when both the United States and the Soviet Union had the capability to deliver a nuclear weapon on each other's homeland, threats of expanding brushfire wars into nuclear conflict mutually canceled each other; neither power had any desire for a nuclear war that would certainly be suicidal. In Laos, since the Royal Lao Army had no chance of putting down the North Vietnamese-backed rebellion of the Pathet Lao, and the United States was unwilling to risk suicide by escalating the fighting, there was little or no chance of the United States' defeating the enemy—anonymous commissars leading unseen troops behind the mountains and forests of the no man's land of Laos far from the towns and the capital. That they were fanatically loyal to Ho Chi Minh was virtually all that the Americans knew about their enemy as individuals.

Since the signing of the 1962 Geneva agreement, American policy has been aimed at minimizing the effects of these mistakes, while the North Vietnamese have been trying to maximize their effects.

13.

Conflict Without Victory

Just as the French had found they could not win within the limits of the frustrating war of attrition imposed upon them between 1946 and 1954, the United States found it could not win in 1962 in Laos without taking up the costly and risk-laden option of expanding the fighting. Eight years separated the two Geneva conferences that determined the future of Laos. Both conferences produced agreements that were devices to bring a temporary cease-fire to an inflammable situation in which none of the big powers desired to force a showdown. This type of situation placed a premium on the will to fight of the ragged, hungry men on the ground.

From their recent experience of war without front, the French were emphatic about avoiding another round of it in the guise of SEATO intervention in Laos. The American military, on the other hand, had had a few World War II experiences that were applicable, but essentially not since the Philippine insurrection of 1899 had they fought under conditions approximating those in Laos; moreover, the analogy was far from reassuring.

It is well, in this age of guided missiles and computerized war games, to recall once again what makes men fight—in the Philippines, or in Indochina. What makes youths in their teens, with sharpened bamboo spears and homemade revolvers, pit themselves against French tanks? What makes a squad of guerrillas who have lived for a week on a handful of rice a day brave machine-gun fire to assault a fortified outpost?

The State Department's characterization of Ho Chi Minh as "the mortal enemy of native independence in Indochina"[1] did not

[1] Department of State Bulletin, February 13, 1950, p. 244.

quite ring true with young men and women who at that moment were defending their villages against French flame-throwers and napalm bombs. It is not difficult to see why.

The popular support of the Viet Minh was amply documented by the reports of American observers on the scene early in the Indochina War. In 1951, for instance, correspondent Seymour Topping wrote:

> As nearly as the writer can determine, a majority of the politically conscious Vietnamese are in sympathy with the Ho Chi Minh regime. The political consciousness of the Vietnamese population has steadily broadened during the last four years under the influence of Viet Minh propaganda. Whatever the political character and intentions of the Communist leadership, the popular appeal of the Viet Minh is purely nationalistic. Unlike the Chinese revolution, which was generated essentially by social and economic factors, the insurgent movement in Vietnam is almost solely an expression of nationalism. It has, of course, social and economic roots; but the present-day political temper of the Vietnamese is a product of the experience of 90 years of French colonial domination, allowed to find expression in the past decade of world upheaval. The nationalist revolution in Vietnam is similar to the Chinese revolution in that the Communists are exploiting it as a useful vehicle upon which they can ride to power.[2]

To the effervescent forces of anticolonial nationalism, the Viet Minh brought the disciplined purposefulness of Communist organization and the methods of indoctrination, propaganda, and tactics. They steeled the anticolonial fighters for a long war, and taught them that the more cunning the enemy and the more terrifying his weapons, the harder the struggle becomes. But it goes on; there is no substitute for success in a "people's war" because the struggle must be carried ahead by its own momentum. These observations are true of Laos today, and it is the Pathet Lao who are being taught the basic application of the principles of "people's war" by the North Vietnamese.

The Tactics Behind the Conflict

The Pathet Lao action consisted of gradually drawing the villages away from the authority of the Royal Government in a first stage of subversion and guerrilla preparation, and then constantly exerting pressure in a second stage of armed force. Over-all, however,

[2] Seymour Topping, "Indo-China on the Razor's Edge," *Foreign Affairs,* April, 1951, pp. 471–72.

the North Vietnamese retained direct control of the movement, and used it to further their own goal—the reunification of Vietnam and the amalgamation of Laos and Cambodia into a "liberated" federation with Vietnam.

In the first stage in Laos, cadres returning from training in North Vietnam moved into the villages to organize cells and all the apparatus of family groups, peasant associations, and other fronts required to ensure the cooperation of the people in the villages. By having a Pathet Lao cadre in every village, the North Vietnamese were achieving their objective of excluding the Royal Government and its American friends from the countryside. The undermining by the Pathet Lao prepared the way for the cave-in. But the surface retained its aspect of solidity. Wherever possible, military engagements were avoided with the better-equipped but less mobile government armed forces.

The deterioration induced by this process prepared the way for the escalation of Pathet Lao military capability resulting from the Soviet airlift, which then permitted the North Vietnamese to move to the second phase—armed pressure against the Vientiane government, again without directly exposing themselves. Meanwhile, by a series of cleverly manipulated temporary alliances, the Pathet Lao progressively isolated their opponents. Originally, they had drawn into their movement all those elements of the population who had a record of resistance against the French, especially the tribal minorities, in order to wage a struggle against the Vientiane government. Then the Pathet Lao allied themselves with Kong Le, in order to wage a struggle against the Phoumists, and with Souvanna Phouma in order to be able to outvote the Phoumists at Ban Namone and Geneva when the Americans sought to win over the moderates. Then they brutally split with Kong Le, and built up the prestige of a defector from Kong Le's ranks in an effort to struggle against both the Phoumists and Kong Le. In this manner, they were able to use the moderates to build up their own strength and weaken their opponents.

The opponents of the Pathet Lao now find themselves a shrinking minority increasingly matching the description applied to them by the Communists of "puppets of the imperialists." Once a final effort has been made to win over the troops of the "puppet forces" from their misguided notions, their intractable leaders will go into a comfortable exile in Europe or the United States. It is a struggle in which there are no formal surrenders. Those who see the light are welcomed into the ranks of "the people."

When the "imperialists" have failed to defeat "the people" as they expected to, the Pathet Lao argument goes, they will agree to negotiations at the conference table. This will mark the start of a sequence of peace parleys and unenforced cease-fires, illustrated by the Ban Namone cease-fire talks of 1961, and of international pressure in which the solidarity of the fraternal socialist countries will count for more than the squabbling capitalist alliance. The Vietnamese were careful to point out to their Pathet Lao students that the "imperialists" invariably behave like ferocious beasts; they will not allow themselves to be subdued easily. Only when they have been boxed into a corner will the "imperialists" agree to discuss a political settlement.

"Imperialist" behavior follows a pattern, the Pathet Lao were told by their Vietnamese mentors, from intermittent repression against the people, to a sudden switch to total capitulation. This occurs at the climax of the protracted "people's war." The battle of Dien Bien Phu produced a mounting crescendo of U.S. threats to intervene in the conflict with air support or with ground troops. But the United States did not intervene. If the American "imperialists" did not intervene to save their allies the French in 1954, was it to be expected that they would intervene on behalf of General Phoumi in 1961?

In the North Vietnamese view (and this view is shared by the Communist Chinese), the "imperialists" do *not* intervene because in the final analysis they do not have any vital interest in a conflict far from home. They will use their lackeys to fight for them as long as these lackeys hold out any hope of keeping the "people's forces" at bay. But when the struggle calls for the sacrifice of the blood of the "imperialists" themselves, then they will avoid shedding it. The "people's forces," on the other hand, are directly involved in the struggle, which goes on around their ears and will determine their fate. Therefore, they fight valiantly against the "imperialists'" lackeys.

Unfortunately, the image of the United States as a "paper tiger" was heightened by the Eisenhower Administration's bold statements and half-measures, and by the Kennedy Administration's willingness to settle the crisis on the basis of something less than its predecessor had been talking about. This hesitancy in Laos had particularly widespread effects because of U.S. involvement with other Asian nations who had declared their readiness to rely on American support for their anti-Communist policies, which exposed them to certain risks. If either Thailand or South Vietnam, who were most directly threatened by Communist gains in Laos, had intervened in that country with covert American support of the type given the Pathet Lao by North Vietnam, even as late as 1960, it is doubtful that Hanoi would have taken the option of committing its forces to a conventional war in Laos. But without the certainty that the U.S. would back them up, neither country could take the plunge.

If the anti-Communist effort in Laos was jeopardized by the mutiny of 600 paratroopers in Vientiane on the morning of August 9, 1960, was there not every reason to suppose that Washington would react sharply? By dropping a few hundred Marines onto the Vientiane airfield that same evening, the United States could have put down the mutiny and restored the legal government to power so swiftly that few outside of Laos would ever have heard of Captain Kong Le.

It has been pointed out that Dean Acheson, in his now-famous speech of January 12, 1950, specifically omitted South Korea from a description of the United States "defense perimeter" in the Pacific; when the Communists invaded South Korea, however, Acheson met the challenge with force. With respect to Laos, the United States had no mutual defense obligation requiring unilateral American intervention to prevent Communist aggression; Acheson's successor, Dulles, gave the public impression, however, that the United States was determined to prevent aggression through the machinery for collective consultation embodied in the SEATO treaty. The aggression from North Vietnam came in such a veiled form, first in the border incursions of December, 1958, and then in the guerrilla campaign of 1959, that this treaty was not invoked. Although different in its overt manifestation, the end result—expansion of Communist control—was the same in Laos as it would have been in South Korea had the United States been fainthearted in 1950. By 1960, the balance of real strength in Laos had shifted to the disadvantage of the United States so that actions like American support for General Phoumi polarized the situation to the further benefit of the Communists.

Kennedy's Exploitation of the Sino-Soviet Dispute

The reluctance to intervene in Laos in 1960 in support of its policies meant that in 1961 the United States faced the choice between a much riskier intervention and a delicate tactical retreat. However, the new Kennedy Administration was spared the necessity of sending an expeditionary force to Laos to follow in the footsteps of the French Expeditionary Corps by a trend in world affairs that a few had predicted but that erupted with surprising rapidity: the growing divergence between Moscow and Peking.

The State Department was, up to the time of the split, in no position to analyze its significance for future American policy in Laos. In the summer of 1959, some sections of the American press were urging Eisenhower to call off the invitation to Khrushchev to visit the United States because of the guerrilla attacks then taking place in Sam Neua Province. Not until two years later did it become evident how little control Khrushchev had over the Pathet Lao and that he was sincere in indicating to Kennedy at Vienna that he had no wish to be dragged into a confrontation with the United States over an issue that he regarded as of secondary importance—the Laos civil war. To the Chinese, on the other hand, the Laos civil war was not an issue of secondary importance but a test case of Communist readiness to support revolutionary warfare in places where the United States was obviously on the defensive. Thus, Moscow and Washington were much closer than Moscow and Peking in their views on the situation in Laos.

Khrushchev realized that a negotiated accord with the United States would reinforce his contention that gains for the Communist cause can be won at the conference table as well as on the battlefield, and at considerably less risk. Thus, the Geneva Conference met in May, 1961, with at least an underlying understanding between the Americans and the Russians that neither wished to commit themselves to a showdown in Laos.

The North Vietnamese watched the growing divergence within the Communist bloc with grave misgivings. They had eked out a tenuous existence as a weak state on the rim of China by declaring their loyalty to both Peking and Moscow without aligning themselves completely with either. Now the Russians were telling them that the security of the Communist bloc demanded that they moderate their incontestably important gains in Laos, while the Chinese were urging them on with declarations of support for the "just war." On their behavior depended their continued aid and trade with both the Russians and the Chinese.

Nevertheless, within the limitations of the doctrinal formulas prescribed by the Russians or the Chinese, the North Vietnamese enjoyed the autonomy of decision-making in Laos that arose from the fact that their own men had predominant influence with the principal actors. There was every indication that they would seek to preserve Laos as their sphere of action. With the termination of the Soviet airlift in 1962, Soviet influence declined and North Vietnamese influence increased proportionately.

If the rupture of the Sino-Soviet alliance opened up new perspectives for American diplomacy in Southeast Asia, beginning in 1961, heralding the possibility that the convergence of Soviet and American interests might defuse not only Laos but also other hot spots of the region, it almost immediately became clear that the Soviets were not able automatically to brake the actions of the Asian Communists. The international agreement to neutralize Laos, with Britain and the Soviet Union as responsible Co-Chairmen, was, therefore, from the Western point of view, a calculated risk. At the time the Geneva Protocol was signed, it was obvious that Laos could remain neutralized only on condition that one of the two extreme factions within the country did not attain power (either by force or by parliamentary means), and on condition that none of the big powers opted for putting its troops into Laos.

The New Period of "People's War"

The period following the signing of the Geneva Protocol of 1962 was bound to be a difficult one for Laos. A decade of foreign meddling in the country's affairs—by the French, the Vietnamese, the Americans, the Russians, and finally the Chinese—had left its traditional patterns of culture shattered and the countryside in the grip of terror and disorder. King Savang Vatthana expressed his pessimism about the future of the monarchy that had extended in almost unbroken line since the fourteenth century in remarking to Prince Sihanouk of Cambodia in 1961: "Alas, I am doomed to be the last King of Laos."[3]

The *de facto* partition that had characterized the political situation in Laos virtually without interruption since 1954 continued after Geneva, and was likely to continue for the indefinite future. Neither the efforts of Prince Souvanna Phouma to hold the coalition together in Vientiane and to overcome the floating partition of Laos' territory, nor the attempts by Phoumist military officers to assert a greater measure of influence showed any signs of quenching what amounted to a state of civil war fed by outside fuel.

The Pathet Lao, while consolidating their hold on the countryside, with an eye on the National Assembly elections due in 1965, were showing caution about extending their control to the Mekong

[3] This observation, made at the funeral in Luang Prabang of King Sisavang Vong, was reported privately to the author.

Valley towns. Presumably they could argue that, not possessing the wherewithal to feed these towns, they preferred to let the Americans feed them temporarily.

Prince Souphanouvong began to reveal himself as the most assertive of the Lao leaders and the one most to be reckoned with by the big powers. He has preserved his ambitious plans for the economic development of Laos, plans for which so far the West has shown less interest than it did for those evolved by Sun Yat-sen in China. Souphanouvong appears to think of his political future in terms of a combination of leadership vested in his aristocratic standing and in his popularity in the countryside (he is one of the few Lao leaders who can appeal effectively to the ethnic minorities). Some observers claim that Souphanouvong dreams of becoming one day the Prince Sihanouk of Laos. In this, certainly, he is not impeded by any affection toward the royal house of Luang Prabang. He continues to feel that his half-brother Phetsarath was treated shabbily in the matter of his title of Viceroy, and he did not attend the funeral of the late King Sisavang Vong, manifesting the feelings of rivalry between the two families.

Ever since 1954, Souphanouvong has consistently sought to lend the Pathet Lao movement the attributes of a government administration on a par with the Royal Lao Government in Vientiane, a tactic that is in full accordance with the precepts of "people's war." Even when he has formed part of that government, he has not dismantled the administrative and military apparatus of the Pathet Lao and the NLHS. He has fought to keep this apparatus as free of Western domination as the Royal Lao Government has allowed itself to fall under that domination. In doing this, Souphanouvong has knowingly committed himself to an alliance with the North Vietnamese, a move he regards as a temporary necessity. The Prince told the Geneva Conference on June 14, 1961, that the Pathet Lao was not a Communist movement, and he outlined its political platform: respect for the throne and Constitution, recognition of democratic freedoms, and equality among ethnic groups. The Pathet Lao action program adopted in April, 1964, makes no mention of the Vietnamese-proposed federation of the Indochina states.

The extent of Souphanouvong's control of the Pathet Lao apparatus has been open to question at times, as shown by the May, 1959, integration *faux pas* and the reversal, four years later, of the Pathet Lao line on cooperating with Souvanna Phouma about ICC inspection teams. Souphanouvong's relations with the North Vietnamese and with the Pathet Lao faction led by Kaysone, which has had more intimate liaison with the Lao Dong Party than he has, are of crucial importance in assessing the future. If the Pathet Lao came to power, Souphanouvong would be engaged in a duel of the most deadly sort with the North Vietnamese. He would have to reveal himself either as a nationalist or as a Communist. In similar circumstances, Ho Chi Minh showed himself to be a Communist, although even today he is motivated by a desire to keep Vietnam free from excessive involvement with China. But Souphanouvong has had none of the Marxist-Leninist preparation that Ho had in his early years and in his work for the Comintern; it is therefore not inconceivable that one day Souphanouvong might decide to lead his movement against the Vietnamese Communists instead of with them.

The success with which the North Vietnamese have used the Pathet Lao, exploiting the sources of motivation leading men to fight for the Pathet Lao cause and giving these forces the cohesion of the matchless Communist organization, has given the men in Hanoi a very real interest in the future of a kingdom whose fate has historically been determined by its stronger neighbors. With the reunification of their own country an unfinished task, the North Vietnamese must continue to regard Laos as of vital strategic importance.

The North Vietnamese now have under their control good roads across the Annamite Mountains, a change of strategic balance in their favor. Although in the event of large-scale fighting in Laos, these roads could be rendered temporarily inoperable by aircraft from the U.S. Seventh Fleet, the disruption would probably be very short-lived; during the Indochina War, thousands of coolies laboring mainly at night kept the road network in Tonkin open to Viet Minh supply columns despite almost daily bombings by the French, who enjoyed complete control of the air.

Of perhaps more far-reaching strategic importance, however, is the construction of roads by the Chinese across Phong Saly and Nam Tha provinces, extending China's road network from Yünnan Province to the borders of Burma and Thailand. China thus has easy access to the rice bowl of Southeast Asia.

It is the Chinese, inheritors of an empire that traditionally exacted tribute from all the principalities of Southeast Asia and whose maps even today show the area as part of the historic sphere of Chinese suzerainty, who have emerged with the most substantial gains without committing so much as a single soldier in Laos or investing any large funds. The polarization process initiated by the

Eisenhower Administration virtually opened the doors to the Chinese in Laos by allowing them to come to the aid of Souvanna Phouma. Chinese statements have made the most of this, conveying the impression that the events in Laos prove beyond a shadow of a doubt that the American "imperialist" presence on the mainland of Asia is in its final stages. The Chinese now claim that they are the power that must be dealt with in the future. Their self-confident outlook is matched by their diplomatic patience. As Foreign Minister Marshal Chen Yi told a Western diplomat at Geneva in 1961, referring to China's satisfaction at seeing a neutral Laos, "Ten years later it will be Communist. We are patient. We can wait."[4]

The Chinese ability to convey the sense of power without an open commitment, increasing the prestige of a revolutionary government intent on seizing the leadership of the Communist parties in the underdeveloped areas of Asia, Africa, and Latin America, is extremely dangerous for the West. The Peking regime has now acquired a vested interest in disproving Khrushchev's contention that the way to the Communist society is a peaceful way through economic competition. Methods of Communist revolutionary warfare worked out by Mao and refined for Indochinese conditions by Giap have been successfully applied for the first time in a country belonging to the tier of Hinduized nation-states stretching from the crest of the Annamite Mountains all the way west to India. Moreover, they have been successfully applied in a country that has received large-scale aid from the West. In an age of rapid communications, the significance of this example has not been lost.

The biggest question mark in Laos, however, remains not the affinities of the Lao politicians, nor even the expansionist drive of the Vietnamese and the Chinese, but the conflicting loyalties of ethnic groups. These loyalties transcend all ideological groupings, and they are of a more permanent character. The basic question is still whether any government in Laos—Communist or non-Communist—can overcome the age-old animosities between lowlanders and mountain tribesmen. The Meo are split between a faction loyal to Phay Dang and the Pathet Lao and a faction loyal to Vang Pao and the Phoumists. The Kha of the southern plateaus are being stirred up by the Pathet Lao, on the one hand, and warned by the Phoumists, on the other, against giving help to the Pathet Lao.

The crosscurrents of ethnic affinities extend, like the habitat of the tribes on a map, across the political borders of the region. They extend to Yünnan, to Thailand, to Burma, to Vietnam, to Cam-

4 Quoted by C. L. Sulzberger in *The New York Times,* June 18, 1962.

bodia. What is more, they are constantly shifting. They therefore raise problems for governments outside Laos. Even the Communist Chinese Government, probably the most efficient apparatus for thought control that the world has ever seen, has not yet in fifteen years in power completely overcome the opposition to assimilation presented by the tribesmen who inhabit the southern Chinese provinces. Communist China, like North Vietnam, fully understands the strategic importance of ethnic relations. Its first ambassador in Laos, Liu Chun, was an expert on ethnic minorities. When the Chinese Communists established their embassy in Vientiane, they employed Han (majority) Chinese for key posts; on the Plain of Jars, many of their advisers with the Pathet Lao were cadres from the minority tribes.

Today, the Pathet Lao are stirring the currents among the sizable Lao population in northeast Thailand. There, the descendants of the Lao families who were resettled on the Korat Plateau by the victorious Siamese after the sacking of Vientiane in 1827 are being propagandized by Pathet Lao agents who infiltrate across the Mekong. They are being told that their obeisance is not properly to the Bangkok government, but to an autonomous Lao region that will be created after the Pathet Lao are victorious in Laos.

The propagandizing of the Lao population of northeast Thailand has been going on for years. After Kong Le's *coup d'état* in Vientiane, Thai Prime Minister Marshal Sarit Thanarat expressed concern about the security of his country if Communist members were taken into the government on the other side of the river. When the construction of the roads across Nam Tha Province by the Chinese Communists became known, Bangkok grew even more alarmed.

The threat of subversion and guerrilla warfare in the area of Thailand adjoining the Mekong Valley is principally a political one, and it can be met effectively only through counteraction by the Bangkok government on a civic-action level. Agents can slip across the river easily, since no government in Vientiane has succeeded in sealing this border. The Lao inhabitants represent for Bangkok a more immediate security threat than does the Chinese Communist standing army of 2.5 million men. The real danger has been, and continues to be, the erosion of the Bangkok government's authority within its own borders in the same manner as occurred in Laos and South Vietnam.

In a limited sense, therefore, the domino theory is a valid concept. But not in the popularly accepted oversimplification of large arrows spanning a map; we are not dealing here with Korea-type invasions and governments in flight, but with a formula for subversion that gains an additional measure of infallibility with each successful application. Leaders who rely on foreign backing rather than on earning popular support come to ignore the pressing need to deal effectively with the manifold grievances of their own populations and thereby play into the hands of their enemy. And it is not inconceivable that the Southeast Asian countries whose regimes have, through self-delusion, inertia, and corruption, forfeited the support of their own people may, one after another, come under the heel of Communist regimentation like falling dominoes.

Enforceable Neutralization

The survival of a Laos that is neither a colonial possession occupied by European or American garrisons nor a Vietnamese fief in a Communist-dominated Indochinese federation, nor a vassal of a powerful and expansionist China, depends on the effective neutralization of Laos by international consent. Souphanouvong has had to rely on the Vietnamese for support in his quest for victory, and Souvanna Phouma has found that "neutralism" alone is not enough to preserve Laos' independence. As I have said, neutralization, rather than neutralism, is the only possible way of extricating Laos from the currents of big-power politics.

The neutralization of Laos obviously presents greater problems than does, for instance, the neutralization of Finland, which has existed as a sovereign state on the border of the Soviet Union since World War II with a coalition government that includes Communists. In Finland, if a stranger asked a villager the way to a strategic installation in wartime, the Finn would immediately try to telephone the police. In Laos, however, a similar encounter would produce no call to the police. There are no police in most of the villages of Laos. Then, too, the villagers have little concept of modern statehood, and little contact with central authority; they tend to deal with strangers on a strictly local basis, and often this has meant evacuating their village and fleeing into the hills.

Soviet influence in Laos, the original basis for the neutralization attempt of 1962, had virtually disappeared two years later. The Russians lost their leverage over the Pathet Lao when they terminated their airlift, just as surely as the Americans lost their leverage over French actions in Indochina when the war there ended and American supplies and money for the French Expeditionary Corps were halted.

By 1964, the conflict in Laos revolved around the intentions and actions of the Americans and the North Vietnamese. There remained, however, certain fundamentals that could be lost sight of in the process of escalation as tragically as were the fundamental purposes for which France embarked on the "police action" in 1946. One of these fundamentals was that the United States had no vital interest in maintaining garrisons of its own troops in Laos and South Vietnam since it had no material possessions there and had no administrative responsibilities in the sense that a colonial power has. Another fundamental was that the United States could not afford to surrender these strategically important territories to Communist control without hastening the day when its influence on the mainland of Asia would count for nothing.

Neutralization provided a means of fulfilling both these objectives. However, in view of the breakdown of the mechanism of Soviet restraining power on Communist China, North Vietnam, and the Pathet Lao, it was evident that another dynamic would have to be found if the United States hoped to make neutralization work in Laos. There were a variety of possible elements for such an alternative dynamic, if the United States knew how to make use of them.

The period immediately following the formation of the Laos coalition demonstrated an important point: The combination of force wisely used and good diplomacy on the spot could to a large extent turn the tables against the exponents of "people's war" in Laos. The Communist takeover that had been so knowingly predicted in June, 1962, by those who had little understanding of the relative strengths and weaknesses inside the Communist bloc, and who unconsciously accepted the widely propagated image of Western rout, did not occur. Instead, less than one year after the formation of the troika in Vientiane, it was the Pathet Lao who were withdrawing in disgust; if they had concluded that developments in Laos favored them, they would hardly have relinquished a position that seemed to offer them so many advantages, only to saddle themselves with the onus of obstructing the functioning of the coalition.

The diplomacy of the Kennedy Administration, in withdrawing the "blank check" from General Phoumi, was skillful enough to restore the bridge of confidence with Prince Souvanna Phouma that had been broken in 1960. There is no guarantee that a similar effort could persuade Prince Souphanouvong that the United States is interested not in dominating Laos but in neutralizing it, and that part of the task lies in achieving a Laos free from domination by

North Vietnam or China. But it is a possibility that is worth exploring.

Until recently, the investigation of village life in Laos, its channels of authority and the allegiances of the villagers, was left almost entirely to the Pathet Lao and the North Vietnamese. Yet, since 1961, the Americans have learned that they could be just as effective propagandizers and recruiters among the mountain people as the North Vietnamese, and they managed to draw support away from the Pathet Lao in areas where the latter could be clearly identified with the Vietnamese foreigners. There is no fault of nature that prevents Americans, when they have the will, from becoming familiar with the customs and wants of the peoples of Laos. An Indiana farmer named Edgar Buell lived among the Meo of Xieng Khouang Province for four years, learned their language and customs, and won their affection so that when the Pathet Lao approached the Meo village where he was sleeping, its inhabitants came to warn him and guide him to safety—despite the terrible punishment that would have been meted out to them if they had been caught.

The American experience with the Meo proved that Communist claims of control are not irreversible, that no one actually controls vast areas of Laos. Light aircraft piloted by Americans were able to land in Sam Neua Province as easily as the Pathet Lao could send a squad of guerrillas through the forest. The only ones who have a substantial claim to control of the area are the people who live there.

In terms of Laos' neighbors, the vortex of forces surrounding the North Vietnamese leadership in Hanoi offers American diplomacy and strategy the most promising sources of leverage to obtain acceptance of lasting neutralization of Laos. If the United States could put these forces to work, the chances of enforcing a settlement without the actual commitment of American troops appear to be good.

Recent events have revealed that Ho's regime harbors certain clear, unsatisfied policy objectives, and that it is at the same time extremely vulnerable to external forces. Ho's apparently broad autonomy in Laos is hedged by a whole series of considerations of Communist-bloc policies. Ho cannot escape the fact that his is a small and relatively poor country heavily dependent on the Soviet Union for trade and aid, and bordering a giant neighbor with a long history of domination over Southeast Asia. And the sharper the confrontation with the "imperialists" in Laos, the more Ho risks reducing his country to the status of a satellite of China, which alone, by its geographical situation, offers the prospect of support for him in case of an escalation involving Vietnamese regular forces in fighting. No people in Southeast Asia have in the past suffered more at the hands of the Chinese than the Vietnamese, so it is likely that Ho wishes to avoid becoming a Peking satellite. Another possible wedge is offered by the threat that one day Ho may lose his hegemony of the Communist revolution in Laos to the Chinese through Peking's adoption of a more "activist" posture than his.

Ho must also keep in mind the realities of domestic power politics. If he allows his direction of the Party's affairs to slip to the point where they no longer produce success, he will find his faithful turning from him. A younger generation of Lao Dong Party cadres, better attuned to Peking than to Moscow, are rising to positions of prominence. These younger men may be less reluctant to engage North Vietnam in a mutual-defense alliance with Peking, and may agree to make Laos a combined Vietnamese and Chinese sphere of influence. In this sense, Ho is as much a prisoner of his constituents as is any American politician.

Conflict Without Victory

In both Laos and Vietnam, the protracted conflict of wills in which Washington and Hanoi had been engaged for a decade had become visibly sharper during 1964. Certain factors were identical in both Laos and Vietnam. Both were partitioned countries, with Communists in control of large portions of their territories. In Laos the partition was *de facto,* in Vietnam it was *de jure.* In both places, Washington enjoyed a clear over-all military superiority, but Hanoi had managed to use the tactics of infiltration and subversion that constitute the basis for "people's war" successfully to overcome this advantage.

In Laos, the United States attempted to promote a military victory by a conventionally equipped army over a local guerrilla army with North Vietnamese backing. The United States rejected the idea of coalition government in 1960, when, had it accepted such a coalition as offered by Souvanna Phouma, it might have given its support to a strong, anti-Communist government with a small minority of pro-Communist members and a minimum of Soviet and Chinese Communist intervention. This would have meant doing extensive work in the villages, something the United States did not embark on until *after* the Soviet and Chinese intervention.

When the United States did accept a coalition two years later, the Soviet airlift had enabled the pro-Communist minority to transform its guerrilla supporters into a regular armed force with relatively formidable equipment and encadrement. Since Laos was on the brink of being handed to North Vietnam by default, neutralization by international agreement froze the *status quo* at least temporarily, and avoided a most severe defeat for American foreign policy.

In South Vietnam, on the other hand, the United States was in 1964 still fighting on the terms the North Vietnamese had imposed in Laos prior to 1962. As a result, the United States was involved in a "people's war" far more vicious than the guerrilla fighting in Laos had ever been. Moreover, the United States had proclaimed that the war in South Vietnam was a test case to prove that Giap's formula was not infallible. Yet every development seemed to be proving precisely the opposite. By categorically ruling out the possibility of a negotiated settlement of the issues in dispute, American actions resembled more and more the actions of the French between 1946 and 1954, and thus threatened to fulfill almost to the letter Giap's theory that the "imperialists" go from total commitment to total capitulation overnight.

The insurgents employed the same political issues in South Vietnam as they did in Laos. They stimulated talk of neocolonialism and used the American aid program in village propaganda against the United States. They devoted untiring efforts to cultivating minority groups. The insurgents in South Vietnam also established the same structural organization of political and military power as in Laos. Behind the National Liberation Front of South Vietnam, they had created a hard-core Communist Party known as the Vietnam People's Revolutionary Party. These corresponded respectively to the Neo Lao Hak Sat and the Phak Khon Ngan, in Laos, and in an election the Front would undoubtedly play the role the NLHS played in Laos. The Vietnam People's Revolutionary Party was just as firmly tied to the Lao Dong Party as was the Phak Khon Ngan.

In belated recognition of the fact that a sympathetic local population within the borders of a country is an effective "human wall" to bar guerrilla infiltration, the United States began providing training for the mountain people of the South Vietnam highlands parallel to the training the Special Forces had provided with such good effect to the Meo in Laos after 1961. For the front line of defense of South Vietnam lies not in the highlands along the border between South Vietnam and Attopeu, Saravane and Savannakhet; it lies on the crests of the Annamite Mountains in Phong Saly and Sam Neua. The head of the PEO from 1957 to 1959, Brigadier General Rothwell H. Brown, appreciated the strategic significance to Thailand no less than to South Vietnam of the crest line of the Annamite Mountains. Here again, as in so many other instances in the American involvement in Indochina in the decade following Dien Bien Phu, a gap existed between the excellent knowledge of the Americans on the spot and the seeming inability of Washington to initiate action on the basis of this knowledge.

The neutralization agreement on Laos made it possible for the United States to influence events in that country by means other than a direct military presence. In fact, so long as the United States made clear its determination to oppose the moving of any foreign forces into Laos, it may well have enjoyed more influence after 1962 than it had enjoyed before; certainly Communist propaganda after the withdrawal of the large American military advisory mission showed more concern than ever about American actions in Vientiane.

Since the direct American intervention in Laos of the 1955–62 period proved to have such catastrophic consequences, since the American involvement in South Vietnam threatened to be a repetition of the Laos involvement, and since Cambodia had managed to retain its independence and sovereignty without an American alliance, there was much to be said in favor of adequately enforced neutralization in the Indochina states.

President de Gaulle, who had not participated in France's Indochina debacle, expressed the view that the option of a settlement based on neutralization in Laos, Cambodia, and also Vietnam was the only sensible one for the West to take, a view that certainly reflected the advice of men at the Quai d'Orsay who had long experience in Indochinese affairs. The option of neutralization, De Gaulle said, was the least costly of the ways by which the United States could extricate itself from what had all the makings of an unproductive war of defense that might drag on indefinitely.

That France could adopt the role of an adviser on military affairs to the U.S. and make itself the new champion of the self-determination of small states was a complete reversal of the situation a decade previously. It had then been the French who were fighting an interminable rebellion against an opponent with well-defined war aims. It had then been the United States who was the champion of the self-determination of peoples and the proponent of the elimination of foreign domination.

De Gaulle believed that in Vietnam the overthrow of the Diem regime in a *coup d'état* cleared the decks for a fresh approach to the problem of restoring a viable *status quo,* just as the Kong Le *coup d'état* in Vientiane had confirmed the French in their thesis that it was hopeless to pursue the war against the Pathet Lao as the Eisenhower Administration was doing it (that is to say, attempting to push the Pathet Lao *back* into the jungle away from the Mekong Valley to some ill-defined point at which the forested slopes and sawtooth ridges ceased to be Laos and became North Vietnam). De Gaulle felt that the inherent motive behind the 1954 Geneva accords, the attempt to remove Indochina from conflict, had been corrupted, that what was agreed to as a temporary partition of Vietnam had become ossified into a permanent one.

In De Gaulle's view, the advent of the Sino-Soviet dispute now made it worthwhile to deal with individual Communist states instead of with a monolithic bloc. The 1962 Geneva Protocol, based on a high-level American-Soviet understanding, showed the way to restoring the *status quo* of cease-fire in Indochina. If the 1962 neutralization agreement had proved to be something less than airtight, the fault lay not in the concept of neutralization, but rather in the fact that the conditions under which neutralization could be made to work had not been fulfilled. Therefore, De Gaulle reasoned, the West should update its diplomacy in accordance with the changed realities of the 1960's and see to it that these conditions were fulfilled. And many in the United States agreed with De Gaulle. The thesis that neutralization might be applied to Vietnam was recognized in a Central Intelligence Agency report dated June 9, 1964. The report, written by Willard Matthias, a member of the agency's Board of National Estimates, stated: "There is . . . a chance that political evolution within the country and developments upon the world scene could lead to some kind of negotiated settlement based upon neutralization."

Britain, on the other hand, gave its support to American Indochina policies. It may be Britain took this course because, while it possessed no direct interest in Indochina, it had a vital interest in the Federation of Malaysia, for which it needed American backing in the face of the threat from Indonesia.

A major reason that the 1962 neutralization attempt did not succeed in restoring peace to Laos was that the North Vietnamese kept pushing their agents forward, involving themselves to an increasing degree, even at the risk of breaking up the coalition. To this action, the United States reacted with military measures, and the gradual escalation that had been the rule before 1962 was resumed after only a short breathing spell. The United States had not succeeded in implicating the North Vietnamese in observance of the Protocol; after the 1962 Conference broke up, there was no more contact between the United States and North Vietnam than there had been before it met. In fact, there was even less, because the increased commitments on both sides in South Vietnam after 1961 gave rise to a state of unprecedented tension between Washington and Hanoi. This, coupled with the fact that by 1962 the Chinese had acquired a vested interest in maintaining an unstable situation in Laos (and here the French argument that China sought a period of peace to consolidate its economy appeared to be in error) meant that neutralization could not work, no matter how strong the United States. Nevertheless, by the summer of 1964, renewed North Vietnamese pressure on Laos, and a public debate in the United States over the reasons why the American effort in South Vietnam was no nearer victory, appeared to have resulted in an acceptance by American officials of the French view that the situation in the two places was part of the same kettle of fish.

The Uses of Power

In the sense that the "neutralist" seeks to extricate his country from the currents of big-power politics, Kong Le is probably the most genuine "neutralist" that twentieth-century Asia has produced. He has not only criticized foreign interference in his country's affairs; he has actually taken up arms and, with his small group of followers, fought in turn against the Americans and against the North Vietnamese. His observations on the use to which the United States has put its power are, therefore, born of conviction and experience.

"In Korea," Kong Le said early in 1964, "you Americans finally learned a lesson. It is that Communist force must be met with American force. More recently, you seem to have forgotten that lesson. No one doubts your great power, least of all the Communists. Yet you seem unsure. Compared to your strength, your policies seem weak in purpose. This is what makes it difficult for us Asians to understand you."[5]

Obtaining Communist acceptance of the neutralization of Laos would require the power of the United States, it was clear. But it would require that this power be as wisely used as was the power of

[5] Interview with Charles J. V. Murphy, in *Fortune,* May, 1964.

Britain in the nineteenth century in obtaining the creation of buffer states along the Himalayan border of its empire with imperial Russia and China.

The neutralization of Laos so as to provide for the security of the United States within the fundamentals outlined previously would be more complicated than merely drawing a line and threatening retaliation if the Communists overstep it. The static form of defense, best expressed in the cliché about the bastion of freedom, is outmoded.

It is time to stop talking about rolling back the Communists; the unpleasant reality is that if the Communists are to be rolled back, it will take more than General Phoumi's army in Laos to do the job.

In place of the vague hope that Communist regimes will be overthrown from within, Americans need a greater comprehension of means by which they acquire power and retain it—of power politics, in short. American diplomats must learn how best to employ power politics.

The wise use of power in the Laos situation would proceed from the recognition that the old, simple dichotomy of Communist versus anti-Communist is no longer a valid basis for policy. In the age of a Communist bloc that is polycentric rather than monolithic, the different motivations of each of its members must be reckoned with. In an age of rapidly evolving power balances, De Gaulle's France and Mao's China are more apt to see eye to eye with each other on some issues than they are to cling to viewpoints accepted without question through almost twenty years of Cold War. Too many small allies of the great powers have been let down in recent years—and too many "neutralists" have reaped the benefits of military and economic assistance when suddenly facing the threat of external attack —for the distinction between the two postures to have retained much meaning.

Under the umbrella of a nuclear stalemate, we now see fresh interest patterns emerging on a local level. The situation of the Indochina states involves these new power balances at their most delicate. The calculations involved in the idea of the United States' frontally attacking North Vietnam, for instance, can no longer stop at weighing the probable military riposte from a united Communist bloc. They must also consider that such an attack might lead to a healing of the rifts within the bloc, and thus cost the United States precious ground gained through shrewd exploitation of that rift.

On the other hand, a deft strike against a single sensitive North Vietnamese position might very well shake the conviction of those the Lao Dong Party has hypnotized with its apparently dazzling success against a superior enemy. This result could be achieved without producing the more widespread effects that would change the ground rules of the conflict now going on.

The sudden encirclement of one of the Vietnamese border patrol battalions in the Laos jungle of the Annamite Mountains and its noiseless liquidation by a determined and highly trained Special Forces unit working with the cooperation of local partisans would have a tremendous shock effect in Hanoi. The battalions are on the soil of Laos in violation of the provisions of the Geneva Protocol. Yet because of Communist obfuscation, there appears no legal recourse for securing their removal. Forcible removal of one of these battalions would convince Hanoi that the United States was serious about the neutralization of Laos.

It would soon become evident who was secure and who was insecure. Not many repetitions of this treatment would be required to produce a consensus in Hanoi that the Vietnamese should terminate a mutually unprofitable enterprise on the basis of a standoff.

However, such means to obtain neutralization must be carefully weighed so as not to destroy the leverage that can be obtained by leaving the Hanoi regime alternative routes, routes that can be made attractive through the proper use of the wealth of resources at the West's disposal. This implies, first of all, opening up contact with the Hanoi regime, which has remained virtually a closed book to us and about whose motivations we need to know more. Initial contacts might lead to trade, trade that could significantly lessen the regime's dependence on the Soviet bloc and reduce the pressure to reunify the country by force, and consequently reduce the pressure on Laos.

A council might have to be set up to deal with specific problems connected with the neutralization of Laos. Something more effective than ambassadorial consultations and less cumbersome than a reconvening of the Geneva Conference at foreign ministerial level is needed to restore respect for the Protocol's provisions in crises such as those in April and May of 1963 and May of 1964.

Such a council could also eliminate the objection that the United States, Britain, and the Soviet Union are trying to deal with the problem of neutralizing Laos without the participation of Communist China and North Vietnam, neither of whom is represented in Washington or at the United Nations. The United States now has contacts with these two countries through their embassies in Vientiane, and these contacts could easily be formalized in a council that could be called quickly into session upon notification of charges that the Geneva provisions were being violated.

Wise orchestration of American military power and diplomacy in this manner would necessitate scrapping many prejudices and pre-conceptions. The insistence on compartmentalizing the military, for one, stands in the way of effective action in Southeast Asia, where there is no neat distinction between military and political warfare. Americans would also have to scrap the belief that clandestine actions are undemocratic and immoral, even though the United States is dealing with countries that bear no resemblance to the democracies Americans know at home and in Europe. In Laos, the United States talked much about democracy, but when it was a question of preventing the Communists from sweeping the polls, as in 1960, Americans went out and bribed village headmen. The traditional American taboo against "interfering" in another country's affairs would also have to be re-examined; when the United States is providing three-quarters of a country's budget, it has responsibility, as well as honor, at stake in that country's actions.

The trials of dealing with countries just emerging from feudalism must not be allowed to estrange the United States from their peoples, with whom Americans share a common devotion to the goals of independence and liberty. The forward leap of technology—both in the United States and in the Soviet Union—has left the small, have-not countries of illiterate peasants and unstable governments far behind. The distance separating the haves from the have-nots today is the great gulf between the bamboo shack and the air-conditioned house. Yet Americans have a knack for dealing with foreign peoples on an individual basis that few other peoples have.

U.S. aid programs must be rethought and drastically overhauled. The State Department officers responsible for administering the aid program in Laos defended it as a success in 1959 on the ground that American aid, even if poorly administered, had "saved Laos from going Communist." The Congressional committee investigating administration of the program had the courage to reject this view categorically.[6] It is an extremely short-term view, and it reflects little credit on the Foreign Service officers in Laos who knew better than the aid administrators how the Communists operated.

However, the measure of success of American aid is more than

[6] "This assertion is purely speculative, and can be neither proved nor disproved. The subcommittee rejects the reasoning of ICA [International Cooperation Administration] officials, and, on the evidence, believes that a lesser sum of money more efficiently administered would have been far more effective in achieving economic and political stability in Laos, and in increasing its capacity to reject Communist military aggression or political subversion." (*Hearings*, II, p. 5.)

the determination of whether the recipient country has been invaded by a Vietnamese or a Chinese army, or whether a Communist government has been set up. The aid program in Laos cannot be considered a success in any sense unless it has given the Lao a reason to reject, and a means to resist, the offer of "liberation" by a "people's army." On balance, the United States is nearer today than in 1959 to bringing into focus its stake in countries such as Laos.

The crux of the matter is that the United States has never before been faced with a situation like that in Indochina, where protracted conflict over seemingly small prizes goes on without conclusive victory, and the means of avoiding defeat are primarily political and depend primarily on the active support of the people in many small ways. Unfamiliarity with the nature of the conflict was shown by a peculiar optical distortion: Responsible officials realized that a great deal was at stake. But since what was at stake was not a mine or the lives of American inhabitants, they were unable to define this stake clearly. These officials viewed politics as a means to winning a war, rather than viewing warfare as a means to political ends. Since it is generally agreed that politics are more permanent and pervasive than war, their view was a mirror image of what was needed to produce a sound policy.

The material resources of the Pathet Lao and North Vietnamese were so meager that it was plainly not these elements that posed a threat to the security of the United States. The threat of the Indochina Communists was different in nature. It was the threat to make the victory of Giap's "people's war" inevitable for all of Southeast Asia, to carry the revolution to a victorious conclusion against governments helpless to defend themselves against it, and by tearing the fabric of American protection to shreds, to destroy the belief in the American will to prevent the subjugation of the newly emerging nations of Asia, Africa, and Latin America.

Fifteen years have now been lost, fifteen years during which the United States has been engaged in the conflict almost without knowing it. It is time Americans understood the stake involved. Americans must learn to counter "people's war" by implicating the people in a conflict in which they have a most vital interest. The leaders of the American Revolution did as much in 1775.

APPENDIX I. THE LAO MONARCHY

(Based on Paul Le Boulanger, *Histoire du Laos Français* [Paris: Plon, 1931] and Katay Don Sasorith, *Le Laos* [Paris: Berger-Levrault, 1953].)

Kings of Lan Xang[1]	*Reign*
Fa Ngoun	1353–1373
Sam Sen Thai *or* Oun Hueun	1373–1416
Lan Kham Deng	1416–1427
Phommathat	1428–1429
Kham Tem *or* Pak Houei Luong	1429–1430
Sai *or* Mune Sai	1430
Khai or Fa Khai	1430–1433
Kon Kham or Kong Keo *or* Chieng Sa	1433–1434
Yukhon	1434–1435
Kham Keut	1435–1438
Sai Tiakaphat	1438–1479
Theng Kham *or* Souvanna Palang	1479–1486
La Sen Thai *or* La Nam Sen Thai	1486–1496
Som Phou	1496–1501
Lu Phe Sai *or* Visoun	1501–1520
Phothisarat	1520–1548
Sai Setthathirath	1548–1571
Sen Soulinthara (first reign)	1571–1575
Maha Oupahat	1575–1580
Sen Soulinthara (second reign)	1580–1582
Nakhone Noi	1582–1583
Interregnum	*1583–1591*
Nokeo Koumane	1591–1596
Thammikarath	1596–1622
Oupagnouvarath	1622–1623
Phothisarat	1623–1627
Mone Keo	1627
Oupagnouvarath	Dates unknown
Tone Kham	Dates unknown
Visai	Dates unknown
Souligna Vongsa	1637–1694

[1] Until the reign of Sai Setthathirath, the royal capital was Luang Prabang. Subsequently, it was moved to Vientiane.

Tian Thala	1694–1700
Nantharath	1700
Sai Ong Hue	1700–1707

In 1707, the Kingdom of Lan Xang split up into three separate kingdoms, the Kingdom of Vientiane, the Kingdom of Luang Prabang, and the Kingdom of Champassak.

Kings of Vientiane	*Reign*
Sai Ong Hue (nephew of Souligna Vongsa)	1707–1735
Ong Long	1735–1760
Ong Boun	1760–1778
Interregnum	*1778–1782*
Nan	1782–1792
In	1792–1805
Anourouth or Anou[2]	1805–1828

Kings of Luang Prabang	*Reign*
Kitsarat (grandson of Souligna Vongsa)	1707–1726
Khamone Noi	1726–1727
Inta Som	1727–1776
Sotika Koumane	1776–1781
Vong	1781–1787
Interregnum	*1787–1791*
Anourouth	1791–1817
Manta Tourat	1817–1836
Souka Seum	1836–1851
Tiantha	1851–1872
Oun Kham	1872–1887[3]
Zakarine	1894–1904
Sisavang Vong[4]	1904–1959
Savang Vatthana	1959–present

Kings of Champassak	*Reign*
Soi Sisamout (nephew of Souligna Vongsa)	1713–1737
Saya Koumane	1737–1791
Fay Na *or* Sairaja Khati Vongsa	1791–1811

[2] Anourouth died in Bangkok in 1835 after having attempted in vain to restore his throne in Vientiane, which had been sacked by the Siamese in 1827.

[3] An interregnum followed the sacking of Luang Prabang by Thai tribesmen from the Tonkin border region in 1887; Pavie confirmed the rights of the royal house of Luang Prabang after establishment of the French Protectorate in 1893.

[4] Under the terms of the Provisional Constitution of October 12, 1945, Sisavang Vong agreed, at the insistence of the Lao Issara provisional government, to exercise sovereignty over a unified Laos having virtually the same borders as the country has today; the exercise of this sovereignty was confirmed by the French in the *modus vivendi* of August 27, 1946.

Chao Nou   1811
  Interregnum   *1811–1813*
Phromma Noi   1813–1817
Chao Nho   1817–1826
Chao Houy   1826–1840[5]
Chao Nak   1841–1850
Chao Boua   1852
Chao Kham Nhai *or* Youtti Thammathone   1856–1858
Kham Souk *or* Youtti Thammathone II   1863–1900

[5] The Siamese court, which appointed the vassal rulers of Champassak, permitted the throne to remain vacant for varying periods of time after 1840.

APPENDIX II. PRIME MINISTERS OF LAOS

Prince Souvannarath   March 15, 1947–March 25, 1948
Prince Boun Oum na
  Champassak   March 25, 1948–February 24, 1950
Phoui Sananikone   February 24, 1950–October 15, 1951
Prince Souvanna Phouma   November 21, 1951–October 20, 1954
Katay Don Sasorith   November 25, 1954–February 13, 1956
Prince Souvanna Phouma   March 21, 1956–July 23, 1958
Prince Souvanna Phouma
  (Caretaker)   July 23, 1958–August 18, 1958
Phoui Sananikone   August 18, 1958–December 30, 1959
Kou Abhay (P)   January 6, 1960–June 3, 1960
Prince Somsanith   June 3, 1960–August 14, 1960
Prince Souvanna Phouma   August 16, 1960–December 11, 1960 (W)
Prince Souvanna Phouma   August 16, 1960–June 11, 1962 (C)
Prince Boun Oum na
  Champassak   December 15, 1960–June 11, 1962 (W)
Prince Souvanna
  Phouma (P)   June 11, 1962–present

NOTE: (P) = Provisional government
         (W) = Western recognition
         (C) = Communist recognition

Appendix III. Final Declaration of the Geneva Conference on the Problem of Restoring Peace in Indochina, July 21, 1954[1]

PARTICIPANTS: CAMBODIA, THE DEMOCRATIC REPUBLIC OF VIETNAM, FRANCE, LAOS, THE PEOPLE'S REPUBLIC OF CHINA, THE STATE OF VIETNAM, THE UNION OF SOVIET SOCIALIST REPUBLICS, THE UNITED KINGDOM AND THE UNITED STATES OF AMERICA.

1. The Conference takes note of the agreements ending hostilities in Cambodia, Laos and Vietnam and organizing international control and the supervision of the execution of the provisions of these agreements.

2. The Conference expresses satisfaction at the ending of hostilities in Cambodia, Laos and Vietnam; the Conference expresses its conviction that the execution of the provisions set out in the present declaration and in the agreements on the cessation of hostilities will permit Cambodia, Laos and Vietnam henceforth to play their part, in full independence and sovereignty, in the peaceful community of nations.

3. The Conference takes note of the declarations made by the Governments of Cambodia and of Laos of their intention to adopt measures permitting all citizens to take their place in the national community, in particular by participating in the next general elections, which, in conformity with the constitution of each of these countries, shall take place in the course of the year 1955, by secret ballot and in conditions of respect for fundamental freedoms.

4. The Conference takes note of the clauses in the agreement on the cessation of hostilities in Vietnam prohibiting the introduction into Vietnam of foreign troops and military personnel as well as of all kinds of arms and munitions. The Conference also takes note of the declarations made by the Governments of Cambodia and Laos of their resolution not to request foreign aid, whether in war material, in personnel or in instructors except for the purpose of the effective defense of their territory and, in the case of Laos, to the extent defined by the agreements on the cessation of hostilities in Laos.

5. The Conference takes note of the clauses of the agreement on the cessation of hostilities in Vietnam to the effect that no military base under the control of a foreign State may be established in the regrouping zones of the two parties, the latter having the obligation to see that the zones allotted to them shall not constitute part of any military alliance and shall not be utilized for the resumption of hostilities or in the service of any aggressive policy. The Conference also takes note of the

[1] Miscellaneous No. 20 (1954), *Further Documents Relating to the Discussion of Indo-China at the Geneva Conference, June 16–July 21, 1954,* Cmd. 9239 (London: HMSO, August, 1954).

declarations of the Governments of Cambodia and Laos to the effect that they will not join in any agreement with other States if this agreement includes the obligation to participate in a military alliance not in conformity with the principles of the Charter of the United Nations or, in the case of Laos, with the principles of the agreement on the cessation of hostilities in Laos or, so long as their security is not threatened, the obligation to establish bases on Cambodian or Lao territory for the military forces of foreign Powers.

6. The Conference recognizes that the essential purpose of the agreement relating to Vietnam is to settle military questions with a view to ending hostilities and that the military demarcation line is provisional and should not in any way be interpreted as constituting a political or territorial boundary. The Conference expresses its conviction that the execution of the provisions set out in the present declaration and in the agreement on the cessation of hostilities creates the necessary basis for the achievement in the near future of a political settlement in Vietnam.

7. The Conference declares that, so far as Vietnam is concerned, the settlement of political problems, effected on the basis of respect for the principles of independence, unity and territorial integrity, shall permit the Vietnamese people to enjoy the fundamental freedoms, guaranteed by democratic institutions established as a result of free general elections by secret ballot. In order to ensure that sufficient progress in the restoration of peace has been made, and that all the necessary conditions obtain for free expression of the national will, general elections shall be held in July 1956, under the supervision of an international commission composed of representatives of the Member States of the International Supervisory Commission, referred to in the agreement on the cessation of hostilities. Consultations will be held on this subject between the competent representative authorities of the two zones from July 20, 1955, onwards.

8. The provisions of the agreements on the cessation of hostilities intended to ensure the protection of individuals and of property must be most strictly applied and must, in particular, allow everyone in Vietnam to decide freely in which zone he wishes to live.

9. The competent representative authorities of the Northern and Southern zones of Vietnam, as well as the authorities of Laos and Cambodia, must not permit any individual or collective reprisals against persons who have collaborated in any way with one of the parties during the war, or against members of such persons' families.

10. The Conference takes note of the declaration of the Government of the French Republic to the effect that it is ready to withdraw its troops from the territory of Cambodia, Laos and Vietnam, at the request of the Governments concerned and within periods which shall be fixed by agreement between the parties except in the cases where, by agreement between the two parties, a certain number of French troops shall remain at specified points and for a specified time.

11. The Conference takes note of the declaration of the French Government to the effect that for the settlement of all the problems connected with the re-establishment and consolidation of peace in Cambodia, Laos and Vietnam, the French Government will proceed from the principle of respect for the independence and sovereignty, unity and territorial integrity of Cambodia, Laos and Vietnam.

12. In their relations with Cambodia, Laos and Vietnam, each member of the Geneva Conference undertakes to respect the sovereignty, the independence, the unity and the territorial integrity of the above-mentioned States, and to refrain from any interference in their internal affairs.

13. The members of the Conference agree to consult one another on any question which may be referred to them by the International Supervisory Commission, in order to study such measures as may prove necessary to ensure that the agreements on the cessation of hostilities in Cambodia, Laos and Vietnam are respected.

DECLARATION BY THE ROYAL GOVERNMENT OF LAOS, JULY 21, 1954

(Reference: Articles 4 and 5 of the Final Declaration)

The Royal Government of Laos is resolved never to pursue a policy of aggression and will never permit the territory of Laos to be used in furtherance of such a policy.

The Royal Government of Laos will never join in any agreement with other States if this agreement includes the obligation for the Royal Government of Laos to participate in a military alliance not in conformity with the principles of the Charter of the United Nations or with the principles of the agreement on the cessation of hostilities or, unless its security is threatened, the obligation to establish bases on the territory of Laos for military forces of foreign Powers.

The Royal Government of Laos is resolved to settle its international disputes by peaceful means so that international peace and security and justice are not endangered.

During the period between the cessation of hostilities in Vietnam and the final settlement of that country's political problems, the Royal Government of Laos will not request foreign aid, whether in war material, in personnel or in instructors, except for the purpose of its effective territorial defense and to the extent defined by the agreement on the cessation of hostilities.

DECLARATION BY THE ROYAL GOVERNMENT OF LAOS, JULY 21, 1954

(Reference: Article 3 of the Final Declaration)

The Royal Government of Laos,

In the desire to ensure harmony and agreement among the peoples of the Kingdom,

Declares itself resolved to take the necessary measures to integrate all citizens, without discrimination, into the national community and to guarantee them the enjoyment of the rights and freedoms for which the Constitution of the Kingdom provides;

Affirms that all citizens of Laos may freely participate as electors or candidates in general elections by secret ballot;

Announces, furthermore, that it will promulgate measures to provide for special representation in the Royal Administration of the provinces of Phong Saly and Sam Neua during the interval between the cessation of hostilities and the general elections of the interests of nationals of Laos who did not support the Royal forces during hostilities.

APPENDIX IV. COMMUNIQUÉS OF THE SECOND PARATROOP BATTALION[1]

Communiqué No. 1. All compatriots! The High Command of the Revolution informs the people that as of 0300 hours August 9 it has held in its hands all civil and military powers. The population is urged to remain calm and to continue work as usual and to respect the laws of the country.

CAPTAIN KONG LE

Communiqué No. 2. The High Command of the Revolution informs the people that the military *coup de force* is aimed at safeguarding and consolidating the Nation, the religion, the Throne, and the Constitution. The revolutionary group will apply justice and friendship to all those who remain quiet, continue their usual occupations, and observe all national laws and regulations. The revolutionary group will recognize all human rights. The revolutionary group will struggle against bribery, reorganize the parliamentary system and cleanse the administrative machinery. The revolutionary group will oppose foreign intervention in the country's military affairs and will expel all foreign bases. In the field of foreign policy, the revolutionary group recognizes the provisions of the Charter of the United Nations, and assumes the task of maintaining a neutral policy and entertaining friendly relations with neighboring countries. The revolutionary group intends to respect all agreements that have been signed by the Royal Government. In the field of economic affairs, the revolutionary group will encourage trade and industry in order to raise the people's living standards. The revolutionary group intends to accept aid from foreign countries, provided no strings are attached to this aid.

CAPTAIN KONG LE

[1] Broadcast by Radio Vientiane, August 9, 1960.

APPENDIX V. DECLARATION ON THE NEUTRALITY OF LAOS[1]

The Governments of the Union of Burma, the Kingdom of Cambodia, Canada, the People's Republic of China, the Democratic Republic of Vietnam, the Republic of France, the Republic of India, the Polish People's Republic, the Republic of Vietnam, the Kingdom of Thailand, the Union of Soviet Socialist Republics, the United Kingdom of Great Britain and Northern Ireland and the United States of America, whose representatives took part in the International Conference on the Settlement of the Laotian Question, 1961–1962;

Welcoming the presentation of the statement of neutrality by the Royal Government of Laos of July 9, 1962, and taking note of this statement, which is, with the concurrence of the Royal Government of Laos, incorporated in the present Declaration as an integral part thereof, and the text of which is as follows:

The Royal Government of Laos, being resolved to follow the path of peace and neutrality in conformity with the interests and aspirations of the Laotian people, as well as the principles of the Joint Communiqué of Zurich dated June 22, 1961, and of the Geneva Agreements of 1954, in order to build a peaceful, neutral, independent, democratic, unified and prosperous Laos, solemnly declares that:

(1) It will resolutely apply the five principles of peaceful coexistence in foreign relations, and will develop friendly relations and establish diplomatic relations with all countries, the neighboring countries first and foremost, on the basis of equality and of respect for the independence and sovereignty of Laos;

(2) It is the will of the Laotian people to protect and ensure respect for the sovereignty, independence, neutrality, unity, and territorial integrity of Laos;

(3) It will not resort to the use or threat of force in any way which might impair the peace of other countries, and will not interfere in the internal affairs of other countries;

(4) It will not enter into any military alliance or into any agreement, whether military or otherwise, which is inconsistent with the neutrality of the Kingdom of Laos; it will not allow the establishment of any foreign military base on Laotian territory, nor allow any country to use Laotian territory for military purposes of interference in the internal affairs of other countries, nor recognize the protection of any alliance or military coalition, including SEATO;

[1] Treaty Series No. 27 (1963), *Declaration and Protocol on the Neutrality of Laos, Geneva, July 23, 1962,* Cmnd. 2025 (London: HMSO, May, 1963).

(5) It will not allow any foreign interference in the internal affairs of the Kingdom of Laos in any form whatsoever;

(6) Subject to the provisions of Article 5 of the Protocol, it will require the withdrawal from Laos of all foreign troops and military personnel, and will not allow any foreign troops or military personnel to be introduced into Laos;

(7) It will accept direct and unconditional aid from all countries that wish to help the Kingdom of Laos build up an independent and autonomous national economy on the basis of respect for the sovereignty of Laos;

(8) It will respect the treaties and agreements signed in conformity with the interests of the Laotian people and of the policy of peace and neutrality of the Kingdom of Laos, in particular the Geneva Agreements of 1962, and will abrogate all treaties and agreements which are contrary to those principles.

This statement of neutrality by the Royal Government of Laos shall be promulgated constitutionally and shall have the force of law.

The Kingdom of Laos appeals to all the States participating in the International Conference on the Settlement of the Laotian Question, and to all other States, to recognize the sovereignty, independence, neutrality, unity and territorial integrity of Laos, to conform to these principles in all respects, and to refrain from any action inconsistent therewith.

Confirming the principles of respect for the sovereignty, independence, unity and territorial integrity of the Kingdom of Laos and non-interference in its internal affairs which are embodied in the Geneva Agreements of 1954;

Emphasizing the principle of respect for the neutrality of the Kingdom of Laos;

Agreeing that the above-mentioned principles constitute a basis for the peaceful settlement of the Laotian question;

Profoundly convinced that the independence and neutrality of the Kingdom of Laos will assist the peaceful democratic development of the Kingdom of Laos and the achievement of national accord and unity in that country, as well as the strengthening of peace and security in Southeast Asia;

1. Solemnly declare, in accordance with the will of the Government and people of the Kingdom of Laos, as expressed in the statement of neutrality by the Royal Government of Laos of July 9, 1962, that they recognize and will respect and observe in every way the sovereignty, independence, neutrality, unity and territorial integrity of the Kingdom of Laos.

2. Undertake, in particular, that

(a) they will not commit or participate in any way in any act which might directly or indirectly impair the sovereignty, independence, neutrality, unity or territorial integrity of the Kingdom of Laos;

(b) they will not resort to the use or threat of force or any other measures which might impair the peace of the Kingdom of Laos;

(c) they will refrain from all direct or indirect interference in the internal affairs of the Kingdom of Laos;

(d) they will not attach conditions of a political nature to any assistance which they may offer or which the Kingdom of Laos may seek;

(e) they will not bring the Kingdom of Laos in any way into any military alliance or any other agreement, whether military or otherwise, which is inconsistent with her neutrality, nor invite or encourage her to enter into any such alliance or to conclude any such agreement;

(f) they will respect the wish of the Kingdom of Laos not to recognize the protection of any alliance or military coalition, including SEATO;

(g) they will not introduce into the Kingdom of Laos foreign troops or military personnel in any form whatsoever, nor will they in any way facilitate or connive at the introduction of any foreign troops or military personnel;

(h) they will not establish nor will they in any way facilitate or connive at the establishment in the Kingdom of Laos of any foreign military base, foreign strong point or other foreign military installation of any kind;

(i) they will not use the territory of the Kingdom of Laos for interference in the internal affairs of other countries;

(j) they will not use the territory of any country, including their own, for interference in the internal affairs of the Kingdom of Laos.

3. Appeal to all other States to recognize, respect and observe in every way the sovereignty, independence and neutrality, and also the unity and territorial integrity, of the Kingdom of Laos and to refrain from any action inconsistent with these principles or with other provisions of the present Declaration.

4. Undertake, in the event of a violation or threat of violation of the sovereignty, independence, neutrality, unity or territorial integrity of the Kingdom of Laos, to consult jointly with the Royal Government of Laos and among themselves in order to consider measures which might prove to be necessary to ensure the observance of these principles and the other provisions of the present Declaration.

5. The present Declaration shall enter into force on signature and together with the statement of neutrality of the Royal Government of Laos of July 9, 1962, shall be regarded as constituting an international agreement. The present Declaration shall be deposited in the archives of the Governments of the United Kingdom and the Union of Soviet

Socialist Republics, which shall furnish certified copies thereof to the other signatory States and to all the other States of the world.

In witness whereof, the undersigned Plenipotentiaries have signed the present Declaration.

Done in two copies in Geneva this twenty-third day of July one thousand nine hundred and sixty-two in the English, Chinese, French, Lao and Russian languages, each text being equally authoritative.

U THI HAN (Burma), NHIEK TIOULONG (Cambodia), H. C. GREEN (Canada), CHEN YI (China), UNG VAN KHIEM (Democratic Republic of Vietnam), M. COUVE DE MURVILLE (France), V. K. KRISHNA MENON (India), A. RAPACKI (Poland), VU VAN MAU (Republic of Vietnam), DIRECK JAYANAMA (Thailand), A. GROMYKO (Union of Soviet Socialist Republics), HOME (United Kingdom), DEAN RUSK (United States)

PROTOCOL TO THE DECLARATION ON THE NEUTRALITY OF LAOS

The Governments of the Union of Burma, the Kingdom of Cambodia, Canada, the People's Republic of China, the Democratic Republic of Vietnam, the Republic of France, the Republic of India, the Kingdom of Laos, the Polish People's Republic, the Republic of Vietnam, the Kingdom of Thailand, the Union of Soviet Socialist Republics, the United Kingdom of Great Britain and Northern Ireland and the United States of America;

Having regard to the Declaration on the Neutrality of Laos of July 23, 1962;

Have agreed as follows:

Article 1. For the purposes of this Protocol

(a) the term "foreign military personnel" shall include members of foreign military missions, foreign military advisers, experts, instructors, consultants, technicians, observers and any other foreign military persons, including those serving in any armed forces in Laos, and foreign civilians connected with the supply, maintenance, storing and utilization of war materials;

(b) the term "the Commission" shall mean the International Commission for Supervision and Control in Laos set up by virtue of the Geneva Agreements of 1954 and composed of the representatives of Canada, India and Poland, with the representative of India as Chairman;

(c) the term "the Co-Chairmen" shall mean the Co-Chairmen of the International Conference for the Settlement of the Laotian Question, 1961–1962, and their successors in the offices of Her Britannic Majesty's Principal Secretary of State for Foreign Affairs and Minister for Foreign Affairs of the Union of Soviet Socialist Republics respectively;

(d) the term "the members of the Conference" shall mean the Governments of countries which took part in the International

Conference for the Settlement of the Laotian Question, 1961–1962.

Article 2.   All foreign regular and irregular troops, foreign paramilitary formations and foreign military personnel shall be withdrawn from Laos in the shortest time possible and in any case the withdrawal shall be completed not later than thirty days after the Commission has notified the Royal Government of Laos that in accordance with Articles 3 and 10 of this Protocol its inspection teams are present at all points of withdrawal from Laos. These points shall be determined by the Royal Government of Laos in accordance with Article 3 within thirty days after the entry into force of this Protocol. The inspection teams shall be present at these points and the Commission shall notify the Royal Government of Laos thereof within fifteen days after the points have been determined.

Article 3.   The withdrawal of foreign regular and irregular troops, foreign para-military formations and foreign military personnel shall take place only along such routes and through such points as shall be determined by the Royal Government of Laos in consultation with the Commission. The Commission shall be notified in advance of the point and time of all such withdrawals.

Article 4.   The introduction of foreign regular and irregular troops, foreign para-military formations and foreign military personnel into Laos is prohibited.

Article 5.   Note is taken that the French and Laotian Governments will conclude as soon as possible an arrangement to transfer the French military installations in Laos to the Royal Government of Laos.

If the Laotian Government considers it necessary, the French Government may as an exception leave in Laos for a limited period of time a precisely limited number of French military instructors for the purpose of training the armed forces of Laos.

The French and Laotian Governments shall inform the members of the Conference, through the Co-Chairmen, of their agreement on the question of transfer of the French military installations in Laos and of the employment of French military instructors by the Laotian Government.

Article 6.   The introduction into Laos of armaments, munitions and war material generally, except such quantities of conventional armaments as the Royal Government of Laos may consider necessary for the national defense of Laos, is prohibited.

Article 7.   All foreign military persons and civilians captured or interned during the course of hostilities in Laos shall be released within thirty days after the entry into force of this Protocol and handed over by the Royal Government of Laos to the representatives of the Governments of the countries of which they are nationals in order that they may proceed to the destination of their choice.

Article 8.   The Co-Chairmen shall periodically receive reports from the Commission. In addition the Commission shall immediately report to the Co-Chairmen any violations or threats of violations of this Protocol, all significant steps which it takes in pursuance of this Protocol, and also any other important information which may assist the Co-Chairmen in carrying out their functions. The Commission may at any time seek help from the Co-Chairmen in the performance of its duties, and the Co-Chairmen may at any time make recommendations to the Commission exercising general guidance.

The Co-Chairmen shall circulate the reports and any other important information from the Commission to the members of the Conference.

The Co-Chairmen shall exercise supervision over the observance of this Protocol and the Declaration of the Neutrality of Laos.

The Co-Chairmen will keep the members of the Conference constantly informed and when appropriate will consult with them.

Article 9. The Commission shall, with the concurrence of the Royal Government of Laos, supervise and control the cease-fire in Laos.

The Commission shall exercise these functions in full cooperation with the Royal Government of Laos and within the framework of the Cease-Fire Agreement or cease-fire arrangements made by the three political forces in Laos, or the Royal Government of Laos. It is understood that responsibility for the execution of the cease-fire shall rest with the three parties concerned and with the Royal Government of Laos after its formation.

Article 10. The Commission shall supervise and control the withdrawal of foreign regular and irregular troops, foreign para-military formations and foreign military personnel. Inspection teams sent by the Commission for these purposes shall be present for the period of the withdrawal at all points of withdrawal from Laos determined by the Royal Government of Laos in consultation with the Commission in accordance with Article 3 of this Protocol.

Article 11. The Commission shall investigate cases where there are reasonable grounds for considering that a violation of the provisions of Article 4 of this Protocol has occurred.

It is understood that in the exercise of this function the Commission is acting with the concurrence of the Royal Government of Laos. It shall carry out its investigations in full cooperation with the Royal Government of Laos and shall immediately inform the Co-Chairmen of any violations or threats of violations of Article 4, and also of all significant steps which it takes in pursuance of this Article in accordance with Article 8.

Article 12. The Commission shall assist the Royal Government of Laos in cases where the Royal Government of Laos considers that a violation of Article 6 of this Protocol may have taken place. This assistance will be rendered at the request of the Royal Government of Laos and in full cooperation with it.

Article 13. The Commission shall exercise its functions under this Protocol in close cooperation with the Royal Government of Laos. It is understood that the Royal Government of Laos at all levels will render the Commission all possible assistance in the performance by the Commission of these functions and also will take all necessary measures to ensure the security of the Commission and its inspection teams during their activities in Laos.

Article 14. The Commission functions as a single organ of the International Conference for the Settlement of the Laotian Question, 1961–1962. The members of the Commission will work harmoniously and in cooperation with each other with the aim of solving all questions within the terms of reference of the Commission.

Decisions of the Commission on questions relating to violations of Articles 2, 3, 4, and 6 of this Protocol or of the cease-fire referred to in Article 9, conclusions on major questions sent to the Co-Chairmen and all recommendations by the Commission shall be adopted unanimously. On other questions, including procedural questions, and also questions relating to the initiation and carrying out of investigations (Article 15), decisions of the Commission shall be adopted by majority vote.

Article 15. In the exercise of its specific functions which are laid down in the relevant articles of this Protocol the Commission shall conduct investigations (directly or by sending inspection teams), when there are reasonable grounds for considering that a violation has occurred. These investigations shall be carried out at the request of the Royal Government of Laos or on the initiative of the Commission, which is acting with the concurrence of the Royal Government of Laos.

In the latter case decisions on initiating and carrying out such investigations shall be taken in the Commission by majority vote.

The Commission shall submit agreed reports on investigations in which differences which may emerge between members of the Commission on particular questions may be expressed.

The conclusions and recommendations of the Commission resulting from investigations shall be adopted unanimously.

Article 16. For the exercise of its functions the Commission shall, as necessary, set up inspection teams, on which the three member-states of the Commission shall be equally represented. Each member-state of the Commission shall ensure the presence of its own representatives both on the Commission and on the inspection teams, and shall promptly replace them in the event of their being unable to perform their duties.

It is understood that the dispatch of inspection teams to carry out various specific tasks takes place with the concurrence of the Royal Government of Laos. The points to which the Commission and its inspection teams go for the purpose of investigation and their length of stay at those points shall be determined in relation to the requirements of the particular investigation.

Article 17. The Commission shall have at its disposal the means of communication and transport required for the performance of its duties. These as a rule will be provided to the Commission by the Royal Government of Laos for payment on mutually acceptable terms, and those which the Royal Government of Laos cannot provide will be acquired by the Commission from other sources. It is understood that the means of communication and transport will be under the administrative control of the Commission.

Article 18. The costs of the operations of the Commission shall be borne by the members of the Conference in accordance with the provisions of this article.

(a) The Governments of Canada, India and Poland shall pay the personal salaries and allowances of their nationals who are members of their delegations to the Commission and its subsidiary organs.

(b) The primary responsibility for the provision of accommodation for the Commission and its subsidiary organs shall rest with the Royal Government of Laos, which shall also provide such other local services as may be appropriate. The Commission shall charge to the Fund referred to in sub-paragraph (c) below any local expenses not borne by the Royal Government of Laos.

(c) All other capital or running expenses incurred by the Commission in the exercise of its functions shall be met from a Fund to which all the members of the Conference shall contribute in the following proportions:

The Governments of the People's Republic of China, France, the Union of Soviet Socialist Republics, the United Kingdom and the United States of America shall contribute 17.6 per cent each.

The Governments of Burma, Cambodia, the Democratic Republic of Vietnam, Laos, the Republic of Vietnam and Thailand shall contribute 1.5 per cent each.

The Governments of Canada, India and Poland as members of the Commission shall contribute 1 per cent each.

Article 19. The Co-Chairmen shall at any time, if the Royal Government of Laos so requests, and in any case not later than three years after the entry into force of this Protocol, present a report with appropriate recommendations on the question of the termination of the Commission to the members of the Conference for their consideration. Before making such a report the Co-Chairmen shall hold consultations with the Royal Government of Laos and with the Commission.

Article 20. This Protocol shall enter into force on signature.

It shall be deposited in the archives of the Governments of the

United Kingdom and the Union of Soviet Socialist Republics, which shall furnish certified copies thereof to the other signatory States and to all other States of the world.

In witness whereof, the undersigned Plenipotentiaries have signed this Protocol.

Done in two copies in Geneva this twenty-third day of July one thousand and nine hundred and sixty-two in the English, Chinese, French, Lao and Russian languages, each text being equally authoritative.

U THI HAN (Burma), NHIEK TIOULONG (Cambodia), H. C. GREEN (Canada), CHEN YI (China), UNG VAN KHIEM (Democratic Republic of Vietnam), M. COUVE DE MURVILLE (France), V. K. KRISHNA MENON (India), A. RAPACKI (Poland), VU VAN MAU (Republic of Vietnam), DIRECK JAYANAMA (Thailand), A. GROMYKO (Union of Soviet Socialist Republics), HOME (United Kingdom), DEAN RUSK (United States), Q. PHOLSENA (Laos)

APPENDIX VI. ACTION PROGRAM OF THE NEO LAO HAK SAT[1]

1. To unite all the people, unite various nationalities [tribal groups], strata, religious communities, political parties, patriotic personalities, and intellectuals, including individuals in the Royal Family and Buddhist monks and nuns who favor peace and neutrality, regardless of their political tendencies, beliefs and religion, also organizations and individuals who were formerly forced by the United States to follow it but now favor a policy of peace and neutrality; and to strive to consolidate and strengthen the alliance and mutual assistance between the Neo Lao Hak Sat and the patriotic Neutralist forces.

2. To struggle against the United States imperialists and their followers—the traitors—for a correct implementation of the 1962 Geneva agreements and the agreements reached among the three parties of Laos; to defend and consolidate the coalition government so as to fully carry out the political program aimed at restoring peace, building national concord, and consolidating the independence of the country; first of all to demand that the United States imperialists and their satellites withdraw all their troops from Laos, stop the introduction of weapons and war material into Laos and all acts of intervention in Lao affairs under whatever form and in whatever fields, and not set up military bases on Lao territory; to demand that the Phoumi Nosavan group put an end to aiding operations encroaching upon and terrorizing

---

[1] Adopted at the Second National Congress of the Neo Lao Hak Sat in Sam Neua Province, April 6–11, 1964, and reported by Vietnam News Agency (Hanoi), April 13, 1964.

the people and withdraw their troops to the positions existing when the 1962 Geneva agreements were signed; to demand that the Phoumi Nosavan group strictly implement the agreements concluded among the three parties: first of all to organize the mixed police and to neutralize Vientiane and Luang Prabang so as to restore the normal activities of the coalition government, and then to continue the tripartite negotiations in order to settle pending questions and other problems of the fatherland and people.

3. To correctly carry out the policy of peace and neutrality ensured by the Geneva agreements, implement the independent foreign policy on the basis of the Five Principles of Peaceful Coexistence, to establish diplomatic relations with all countries on an equal footing, receive aid without any conditions attached from all countries regardless of their political regimes, provided the latter respect the sovereignty and independence of Laos and sincerely help Laos' national construction; to actively support all movements for peace, democracy, and social progress, and the national liberation movement of all the Asian, African, and Latin American countries, and actively contribute to the safeguarding of peace in Southeast Asia and the world.

4. To heighten the spirit of self-reliance and at the same time make full use of assistance without any conditions attached from various countries to build an independent and self-supporting economy under the leadership and unified management of the coalition government; to wipe out the vestige of local despots and trade monopolies, and at the same time to help people develop production, tap forest products and natural resources, expand exchanges of goods, develop handicrafts, and build industry; to eliminate speculation and hoarding, oppose corruption and misuse of power to grab goods and economic monopolies; to help the peasants develop cultivation and livestock breeding; to encourage the improvement of cultivation and protection of crops, thus helping the peasants to raise their income; to help the workers to get jobs, to improve their living conditions, and create a regime of social insurance so as to enable them to restore and develop the national economy; to stimulate and help the traders and industrialists to invest in construction and commerce which benefit the national economy and the people's life; to create conditions for students and pupils to study and develop their abilities to serve the fatherland; to provide intellectuals, office employees, cultural workers, and artists with suitable jobs and security so that they may serve the people.

5. To organize and build a national army and police force to defend the independence of the fatherland and the security of the people; to help soldiers and policemen to come close to and help the people; to forbid all repression of the people by the army and the police; to ensure political rights and due pay for soldiers; to cancel the regime of ill treatment of soldiers and policemen; to work out a policy to improve the living conditions of wounded soldiers' and war martyrs' families.

6. To carry out all the democratic rights of the citizens as provided for by the 1947 Constitution, thus enabling them to devote all their abilities to serve national construction; first of all to release all political detainees and ensure the life and property of the people; to stop all acts of discrimination and reprisal against patriotic individuals and organizations in the areas temporarily controlled by the Phoumi Nosavan group, especially Vientiane.

7. To respect and defend the Throne, build and consolidate national solidarity, and realize national harmony and unification; to carry out the policy of national union, thus helping the various nationalities [tribal groups] to live on an equal footing and carry out mutual assistance, improving their living standards, helping each other in studying; to oppose all schemes of sowing discord among the nationalities [tribal groups] and ensure the legitimate rights of foreign residents in Laos.

8. To assure equality between men and women; help women in all fields so as to enable them to develop their ability to catch up with men; to help confined mothers and protect children.

9. To develop progressive national culture; to devote attention to education and develop both primary and secondary educational systems and other popular educational schools; to help all the people, especially the mountain people, to learn to read and write; to protect and develop good ethics; to strictly oppose the depraved and obscurantist culture of the United States and its henchmen; to eliminate gambling and other social vices; to respect freedom of belief, oppose all schemes to sabotage and split up religions; to protect pagodas and respect Buddhist priests.

10. While the United States imperialists have not yet given up their schemes to eliminate the Neo Lao Hak Sat and other patriotic forces, to turn Laos into a neocolony, a war-provocative base, and to turn the Lao people into their slaves, all the people of Laos have the task of defending and consolidating the liberated areas, strengthening the Neo Lao Hak Sat forces, helping to consolidate the other patriotic forces, resolutely smashing all schemes to encroach upon and occupy the liberated areas and to send bandits to disturb and sabotage these areas. The people of Laos must actively carry out all tasks which benefit the people and must bring them a happy life so as to help them build the liberated areas into a firm basis for the people's struggle for peace, neutrality, independence, democracy, unity, and prosperity.

Bibliography

Official Sources

Agreements and Decrees Prior to 1954

Terms of French Treaty of Protectorate over Laos, August 29, 1941: ADMIRAL DECOUX. *A la Barre de l'Indochine: Histoire de Mon Gouvernement General (1940–1945).* Paris: Plon, 1949. P. 297.

Text of statement to the Lao Issara by King Sisavang Vong: *The New Asia* (Bangkok), No. 8, March 10, 1946.

Text of royal decree proclaiming Provisional Constitution of October 12, 1945: *Tin-Vietnam (Vietnam News),* No. 4, July 14, 1946.

Text of Constitution of May 11, 1947: KINGDOM OF LAOS. *The Lao Constituent Assembly, March 15–May 10, 1947.* Saigon: Imprimerie Française d'Outre-Mer, 1948. Pp. 99–108.

Text of Franco-Lao General Convention of July, 1949: *Documentation Française* (Paris), No. 1241, December 7, 1949.

Text of decree dissolving the Lao Issara: KATAY DON SASORITH. *Le Laos.* Paris: Berger-Levrault, 1953. Pp. 131–35. Communiqué announcing dissolution: *Bangkok Post,* October 26, 1949.

Treaty of Amity and Association Between France and Laos: ALLAN B. COLE (ed.). *Conflict in Indo-China and International Repercussions; A Documentary History, 1945–1955.* Ithaca, N.Y.: Cornell University Press, 1956. Pp. 192–93.

1954 Geneva Conference

CMD. 9186. MISCELLANEOUS NO. 16 (1954). *Documents Relating to the Discussion of Korea and Indo-China at the Geneva Conference, April 27– June 15, 1954.* London: HMSO, June, 1954.

CMD. 9239. MISCELLANEOUS NO. 20 (1954). *Further Documents Relating to the Discussion of Indo-China at the Geneva Conference, June 16–July 21, 1954.* London: HMSO, August, 1954.

International Control Commission

CMD. 9445. LAOS NO. 1 (1955). *First Interim Report of the International Commission for Supervision and Control in Laos, August 11– December 31, 1954.* London: HMSO, May, 1955.

CMD. 9630. LAOS NO. 2 (1955). *Second Interim Report of the International Commission for Supervision and Control in Laos. January 1– June 30, 1955.* London: HMSO, November, 1955.

CMND. 314. LAOS NO. 1 (1957). *Third Interim Report of the International Commission for Supervision and Control in Laos, July 1, 1955–May 16, 1957.* London: HMSO, December, 1957.

CMND. 541. LAOS NO. 1 (1958). *Fourth Interim Report of the International Commission for Supervision and Control in Laos, May 17, 1957–May 31, 1958.* London: HMSO, October, 1958.

1961–62 Geneva Conference

CMND. 1828. LAOS NO. 1 (1962). *International Conference on the Settlement of the Laotian Question, May 12, 1961–July 23, 1962.* London: HMSO, October, 1962.

CMND. 2025. TREATY SERIES NO. 27 (1963). *Declaration and Protocol on the Neutrality of Laos, July 23, 1962.* London: HMSO, May, 1963.

U.S. Congress

COMMITTEE ON FOREIGN AFFAIRS, HOUSE OF REPRESENTATIVES. *Mutual Security Program in Laos: Hearings Before the Subcommittee on the Far East and Pacific, May 7 and 8, 1958.* (85th Cong., 2d sess.) Washington: Government Printing Office, 1958.

Hearings, I: COMMITTEE ON GOVERNMENT OPERATIONS, HOUSE OF REPRESENTATIVES. *United States Aid Operations in Laos: Hearings Before the Foreign Operations and Monetary Affairs Subcommittee, March 11–June 1, 1959.* (86th Cong., 1st sess.) Washington: Government Printing Office, 1959.

Hearings, II: COMMITTEE ON GOVERNMENT OPERATIONS, HOUSE OF REPRESENTATIVES. *United States Aid Operations in Laos: Seventh Report by the Committee, June 15, 1959.* (86th Cong., 1st sess.) Washington: Government Printing Office, 1959.

Hearings, III: COMMITTEE ON ARMED SERVICES, SENATE. *Military Cold War Education and Speech Review Policies: Hearings Before the Special Preparedness Subcommittee, Part 5, April 16, 17, 18, 19; May 11 and 14, 1962.* (87th Cong., 2d sess.) Washington: Government Printing Office, 1962.

Department of State

American Cooperation with Laos: A Vital Link in the Chain of Mutual Security. Report of the Director, U.S. International Cooperation Administration, U.S. Operations Mission to Laos, Vientiane, July, 1959.

A Threat to the Peace: North Viet-Nam's Effort to Conquer South Viet-Nam. U.S. Department of State Publication No. 7308 (in 2 parts). Washington: Government Printing Office, December, 1961.

Briefing Notes on the Royal Kingdom of Laos. Vientiane: USIS, May, 1959.

Comments by the Department of State and ICA on the Report of the House Committee on Government Operations. Washington: Government Printing Office, 1959.

Economic Cooperation Agreement and Notes between the United States of America and Laos. Treaties and Other International Acts Series, No. 2344. Washington: Government Printing Office, 1952.

Laos Fact Sheet: Mutual Security in Action. U.S. Department of State Publication No. 6842. Washington: Government Printing Office, 1959.

Mutual Defense Assistance in Indochina, Agreement between the United States of America and Cambodia, Laos and Vietnam. Treaties and Other International Acts Series, No. 2447. Washington: Government Printing Office, 1953.

The Situation in Laos. Washington: Department of State, September, 1959.

United Nations

Report of the Security Council Sub-Committee, under Resolution of 7 September 1959. New York: United Nations Security Council, November, 1959.

Report on Laos Recommends U.N. Development Aid. Bangkok: Economic Commission for Asia and the Far East (ECAFE), Press Release No. L/29, December, 1959.

Great Britain

Laos: Basic Facts and Figures. Reference Division, Central Office of Information. London: HMSO, 1958.

Laos: Political Developments, 1958–60. Reference Division, Central Office of Information. London: HMSO, 1960.

Laos. Reference Division, Central Office of Information. London: HMSO, 1961.

Laos: Political Developments, 1961. Reference Division, Central Office of Information. London, HMSO, 1961.

China

A Chronicle of Principal Events Relating to the Indo-China Question, 1940–1954. Peking: Shihchieh Chihshih (World Culture), 1954.

Concerning the Situation in Laos. Peking: Foreign Languages Press, 1959.

North Vietnam

The Problems Facing the Democratic Republic of Viet Nam in 1961. Hanoi: Foreign Languages Publishing House, n.d.

France

Annuaire Statistique de l'Indochine. Hanoi and Saigon: Direction des Affaires Economiques, Service de la Statistique Générale, 1927–49. *Indochine: Sud-Est Asiatique.* Paris. (Monthly from 1951.)

Laos

Annuaire Statistique du Laos. Vientiane: Ministère des Finances, de l'Economie et du Plan, Direction de la Statistique, yearly from 1950. *Lao Presse, Agence d'Information Télégraphique.* Vientiane. (Daily from 1953.)

GEOGRAPHY, HISTORY, ETHNOGRAPHY, AND GENERAL DESCRIPTION

ABHAY, NHOUY. *Aspects du Pays Lao.* Vientiane: Ministère de l'Education Nationale, Editions Comité Littéraire Lao, 1956.
AYABE, TSUNEO. *The Village of Ban Pha Khao, Vientiane Province: A Preliminary Report.* (Laos Project, Paper No. 14.) Los Angeles: Department of Anthropology and Sociology, University of California, 1961. (Mimeographed.)
AYME, G. *Monographie du Ve Térritoire Militaire.* Hanoi: Imprimerie d'Extrême-Orient, 1930.
AYMONIER, ETIENNE. *Voyage dans le Laos.* 2 vols. Paris: Leroux, 1895.
BERVAL, RENÉ DE. *Kingdom of Laos: The Land of the Million Elephants and of the White Parasol.* Saigon: France-Asie, 1959.
BRUK, S. I. *The Peoples of Indochina.* Translated from the Russian. (U.S. Joint Publications Research Service, Publication No. 6914.) Washington: March 14, 1961.
BUI QUANG TUNG. "Chao Anou, Roi de Vientiane: A Travers les Documents Vietnamiens," *Bulletin de la Société des Etudes Indochinoises,* XXXIII (1958), 401–6.
Bulletin de l'Ecole Française d'Extrême-Orient. (Hanoi, quarterly, 1901–57; Paris, from 1957.)
Bulletin Economique de l'Indochine. Saigon. (Monthly from 1898.)
Bulletin de la Société des Etudes Indochinoises. Saigon. (Quarterly from 1883.)
Bulletin Statistique du Laos. Vientiane: Ministère des Finances, de l'Economie et du Plan, Direction de la Statistique. (Quarterly from 1950.)
COEDÈS, GEORGE. *Les Etats Hindouisés d'Indochine et d'Indonésie.* Paris: E. de Boccard, 1964.
COOLIDGE, HAROLD J., and ROOSEVELT, THEODORE. *Three Kingdoms of Indochina.* New York: Crowell, 1933.

DEYDIER, HENRI. *Lokapâla: Génies, Totems et Sorciers du Nord Laos.* Paris: Plon, 1954.

DOBBY, E. H. G. *Southeast Asia.* 7th ed. London: University of London Press, 1960.

EMBREE, JOHN F., and THOMAS, WILLIAM L., JR. *Ethnic Groups of Northern Southeast Asia.* (Southeast Asia Studies.) New Haven, Conn.: Yale University Press, 1950.

FIASSON, JEANNINE. *Au Laos Avec Mes Hommes et Mes Eléphants.* Paris: Julliard, 1961.

France-Asie. Saigon and Tokyo. (Monthly and bimonthly from 1946.)

FRANCK, HARRY A. *East of Siam: Ramblings in the Five Divisions of French Indo-China.* New York: Century Press, 1926.

HALL, D. G. E. *A History of South-East Asia.* 2d ed. London: Macmillan, 1964.

HALPERN, JOEL M. *Government, Politics, and Social Structure in Laos: A Study of Tradition and Innovation.* (Southeast Asia Studies, Monograph Series, No. 4.) New Haven, Conn.: Yale University Press, 1964.

————. *The Lao Elite: A Study of Tradition and Innovation.* Santa Monica, Calif.: The RAND Corporation (RM-2636-RC), November 15, 1960.

————. (Laos Project.) Los Angeles: Department of Anthropology and Sociology, University of California, 1961: *The Role of the Chinese in Lao Society—1959* (No. 1); *Capital, Savings and Credit among Lao and Serb Peasants: A Contrast in Cultural Values* (No. 2); *Population Statistics and Associated Data* (No. 3); *American Policy in Laos* (No. 6); *Laotian Educational Statistics* (No. 7); *Government Statistics* (No. 8); *Laotian Agricultural Statistics* (No. 9); *Laotian Health Statistics* (No. 10); *Economic and Related Statistics Dealing with Laos* (No. 11); *The Natural Economy of Laos* (No. 17); *Laos Profiles* (No. 18); *The Rural and Urban Economies* (No. 19); *Laotian Health Problems* (No. 20); *Government, Politics and Social Structure of Laos: A Study in Tradition and Innovation* (No. 21). (Mimeographed.)

IWATA, KEIJI. "Boloban Kogen no Jinbun Chiri" ("Descriptive Geography of the Bolovens Plateau"), *Jinbun Kenkyū (Studies in Cultural Science)*, XI, No. 2 (1960), 46–70.

————. *Ethnic Groups in the Valley of the Nam Song and Nam Lik.* (Laos Project, Paper No. 15.) Los Angeles: Department of Anthropology and Sociology, University of California, 1961. (Mimeographed.)

————. *Minority Groups in Northern Laos—Especially the Yao.* (Laos Project, Paper No. 16.) Los Angeles: Department of Anthropology and Sociology, University of California, 1961. (Mimeographed.)

JANSE, OLOV R. T. *The Peoples of French Indochina.* (Smithsonian Institution War Background Studies, No. 14.) Washington: Government Printing Office, 1943.

KAHIN, GEORGE MCTURNAN (ed.). *Governments and Politics of Southeast Asia.* 2d ed. Ithaca, N.Y.: Cornell University Press, 1964.

LAFONT, PIERRE BERNARD. *Aperçus sur le Laos.* Vientiane: Comité de l'Alliance Française au Laos, 1959.

LANDON, KENNETH P. *Southeast Asia: Crossroads of Religions.* Chicago: University of Chicago Press, 1949.

———. "Thailand's Quarrel with France in Perspective," *Far Eastern Quarterly,* I, No. 1 (November, 1941), 25–42.

LE BAR, FRANK M., and SUDDARD, ADRIENNE (eds.). *Laos: Its People, Its Society, Its Culture.* New Haven, Conn.: Human Relations Area Files Press, 1960.

LE BOULANGER, PAUL. *Histoire du Laos Français.* Paris: Plon, 1931.

MOUHOT, HENRI. *Travels in the Central Parts of Indo-China (Siam), Cambodia, and Laos, during the Years 1858–1859, and 1860.* London: J. Murray, 1864.

PARMENTIER, HENRI. *L'Art du Laos.* 2 vols. Hanoi: Ecole Française d'Extrême-Orient, 1954.

PAVIE, AUGUSTE. *A la Conquête des Coeurs.* Paris: Presses Universitaires de France, 1947.

———. *Mission Pavie en Indochine, 1879–1895.* 10 vols. Paris: Leroux, 1898–1919.

PENSRI, SUVANICH. *Les Relations Entre la France et la Thaïlande (Siam) au XIXe Siècle d'Après les Archives des Affaires Etrangères.* Bangkok: Chalermnit, 1962.

REINACH, LUCIEN DE. *Le Laos.* 2 vols. Paris: A. Charles, 1901.

ROUX, COLONEL HENRI. "Quelques Minorités Ethniques du Nord Indochine," *France-Asie,* No. 92–93 (January–February, 1954), pp. 131–419.

SCHAAF, C. HART, and FIFIELD, RUSSELL H. *The Lower Mekong; Challenge to Cooperation in Southeast Asia.* Princeton, N.J.: Van Nostrand, 1963.

Thailand: How Thailand Lost Her Territories to France. Bangkok: Department of Publicity, 1940.

THOMPSON, VIRGINIA, and ADLOFF, RICHARD. *Minority Problems in Southeast Asia.* Stanford, Calif.: Stanford University Press, 1955.

VIRAVONG, MAHA SILA. *History of Laos.* (U.S. Joint Publications Research Service, Publication No. [N.Y.] 712.) Washington: October 1, 1958.

CONTEMPORARY POLITICS AND WARFARE

BOUN OUM NA CHAMPASSAK, PRINCE. "Allocution à l'Occasion de la Signature des Conventions Franco-Laotiennes," *France-Asie,* No. 46–47 (January–February, 1950), pp. 629–31.

BURCHETT, WILFRED G. *The Furtive War: The United States in Vietnam and Laos.* New York: International Publishers, 1963.

————. *Mekong Upstream*. Hanoi: Red River Publishing House, 1957.

CHASSIN, L.-M. *Aviation Indochine*. Paris: Amiot-Dumont, 1954.

China News Analysis. Hong Kong. (Weekly since 1953.)

COLE, ALLAN B. (ed.). *Conflict in Indo-China and International Repercussions; A Documentary History, 1945–1955*. Ithaca, N.Y.: Cornell University Press, 1956.

CROZIER, BRIAN. "Peking and the Laotian Crisis: An Interim Appraisal," *China Quarterly*, No. 7 (July–September, 1961), pp. 128–37.

————. "Peking and the Laotian Crisis: A Further Appraisal," *China Quarterly*, No. 11 (July–September, 1962), pp. 116–23.

"Der Kurs Moskaus und Pekings in der laotischen Krise." Unsigned article in *Neue Zürcher Zeitung*, January 3, 1961.

DEVILLERS, PHILIPPE. *Histoire du Viêt-nam de 1940 à 1952*. Paris: Editions du Seuil, 1952.

EDEN, ANTHONY. *The Memoirs of Anthony Eden: Full Circle*. Boston: Houghton Mifflin, 1960.

EPSTEIN, ISRAEL, and FAIRFAX-CHOLMELEY, ELSIE. *Laos in the Mirror of Geneva*. Peking: New World Press, 1961.

FALL, BERNARD B. "The International Relations of Laos," *Pacific Affairs*, XXX (March, 1957), 22–34.

————. *Le Viet-Minh, 1945–1960*. Paris: Armand Colin, 1960.

————. "Reappraisal in Laos," *Current History*, XLII (January, 1962), 8–14.

————. "The Pathet Lao—A 'Liberation' Party," in Robert A. Scalapino (ed.). *Communism in Asia*. New York and Englewood Cliffs, N.J.: Prentice-Hall, forthcoming.

————. "Problèmes des Etats Poly-Ethniques en Indochine," *France-Asie*, No. 172 (March–April, 1962), pp. 129–52.

HALPERN, A. M., and FREDMAN, H. B. *Communist Strategy in Laos*. Santa Monica, Calif.: The RAND Corporation (RM-2561), June 14, 1960.

————. "The Emergence of an Asian Communist Coalition," *The Annals of the American Academy of Political and Social Science*, CCCXLIX (September, 1963), 117–29.

HAMMER, ELLEN. *The Struggle for Indochina*. Stanford, Calif.: Stanford University Press, 1954.

HONEY, P. J. *Communism in North Vietnam*. Cambridge, Mass.: The M.I.T. Press, 1963.

JONAS, ANNE M., and TANHAM, GEORGE K. "Laos: A Phase in Cyclic Regional Revolution," *Orbis*, V (Spring, 1961), 64–73.

KARPIKHIN, A. "The U.S.A. Sabotages the Geneva Agreements on Indochina," *International Affairs* (Moscow), August, 1959, pp. 57–62.

KATAY, THAO. *Le Laos*. Bangkok: Editions Lao Issara, 1948.

LACOUTURE, JEAN, and DEVILLERS, PHILIPPE. *La Fin d'une Guerre: Indochine 1954*. Paris: Editions du Seuil, 1960.

LANCASTER, DONALD. *The Emancipation of French Indo-China*. London: Oxford University Press, 1961.

MARCHAND, JEAN. *Le Drame Indochinois.* Paris: Peyronnet, 1953.
MODELSKI, GEORGE A. *International Conference on the Settlement of the Laotian Question, 1961–62.* Canberra: Department of International Relations, Research School of Pacific Studies, Australian National University, 1962.
NAVARRE, HENRI. *Agonie de l'Indochine.* Paris: Plon, 1956 and 1958.
NAVILLE, PIERRE. *La Guerre du Viêt-nam.* Paris: Editions de la Revue Internationale, 1949.
ORGWALD. *Tactical and Organizational Questions of the Communist Parties of India and Indo-China.* The Pan-Pacific Worker, 1933.
PHAM VAN DONG. "The Foreign Policy of the Democratic Republic of Vietnam," *International Affairs* (Moscow), July, 1958, pp. 19–22.
QUANG MINH. *Au Pays du Million d'Eléphants et du Parasol Blanc.* Hanoi: Editions en Langue Etrangère, 1962.
ROY, JULES. *La Bataille de Dien Bien Phu.* Paris: Julliard, 1963.
SASORITH, KATAY DON. *Le Laos.* Paris: Berger-Levrault, 1953.
SISOUK NA CHAMPASSAK. *Storm Over Laos.* New York: Frederick A. Praeger, 1961.
SOUVANNA PHOUMA. "Le Laos, avant-garde du monde libre," *France-Asie,* No. 164 (November–December, 1960), pp. 1427–34.
———. "Le Laos: Le Fond du Problème," *France-Asie,* No. 166 (March–April, 1961), pp. 1824–26.
STAROBIN, JOSEPH R. *Eyewitness in Indochina.* New York: Cameron and Kahn, 1954.
TANHAM, GEORGE K. *Communist Revolutionary Warfare: The Vietminh in Indochina.* New York: Frederick A. Praeger, 1961.
TRAN NGOC HUNG. "The Role of the Indo-Chinese Communist Party in the Evolution of the Viet Minh: 1945–1951," *Australian Quarterly,* September, 1954, pp. 87–98.
VO NGUYEN GIAP. *Dien Bien Phu.* Hanoi: Foreign Languages Publishing House, 1962.
———. *People's War, People's Army.* Hanoi: Foreign Languages Publishing House, 1961; New York: Frederick A. Praeger, 1962 (facsimile edition).
ZAGORIA, DONALD S. *The Sino-Soviet Conflict, 1956–1961.* Princeton, N.J.: Princeton University Press, 1962.

EXTENDED BIBLIOGRAPHIES

CORDIER, G., *Bibliotheca Indosinica: Dictionnaire Bibliographique des Ouvrages Relatifs à la Peninsule Indochinoise.* Vol. I (1912), cols. 997–1084; vol. IV (1915), cols. 2789–2806. Paris: Imprimerie Nationale, 1912–15.
HALPERN, JOEL M. *Bibliography of Laos and Related Areas to 1961.* Edited by JOHN MCKINISTRY. Berkeley, Calif.: Center for Southeast Asian Studies, University of California, 1962. (Mimeographed.)

HAY, STEPHEN N., and CASE, MARGARET H. *Southeast Asian History: A Bibliographic Guide*. New York: Frederick A. Praeger, 1962.

HOBBS, CECIL. *Southeast Asia: An Annotated Bibliography of Selected Reference Sources*. Washington: U.S. Library of Congress, Orientalia Division, 1952.

KENE, THAO. *Bibliographie du Laos*. Vientiane: Ministère de l'Education Nationale, Editions Comité Littéraire Lao, 1958.

KEYES, JANE GODFREY. *A Bibliography of North Vietnamese Publications in the Cornell University Library*. (Southeast Asia Program, Data Paper No. 47.) Ithaca, N.Y.: Department of Asian Studies, Cornell University, September, 1962.

Index